THE COSMOS, THE PERSON, AND THE *SĀDHANA*

TRADITIONS AND TRANSFORMATIONS IN TIBETAN BUDDHISM
David Germano and Michael Sheehy, Editors

The Cosmos, the Person, and the *Sādhana*

A Treatise on Tibetan Tantric Meditation

With a translation of Master Tsongkhapa's Fulfilling the Bee's Hope

Yael Bentor

UNIVERSITY OF VIRGINIA PRESS
Charlottesville and London

The University of Virginia Press is situated on the traditional lands of the Monacan Nation, and the Commonwealth of Virginia was and is home to many other Indigenous people. We pay our respect to all of them, past and present. We also honor the enslaved African and African American people who built the University of Virginia, and we recognize their descendants. We commit to fostering voices from these communities through our publications and to deepening our collective understanding of their histories and contributions.

University of Virginia Press

Printed in the United States of America on acid-free paper

First published 2024

9 8 7 6 5 4 3 2 1

Library of Congress Cataloging-in-Publication Data

Names: Tsong-kha-pa Blo-bzang-grags-pa, author. | Bentor, Yael, translator.
Title: The cosmos, the person, and the Sādhana : a treatise on Tibetan tantric meditation : with a translation of Master Tsongkhapa's Fulfilling the Bee's Hope / Yael Bentor.
Other titles: Dpal gsang ba 'dus pa'i bskyed rim blo gsal bung ba'i re skong gnad dong sal ba. English.
Description: Charlottesville : University of Virginia Press, 2024. | Series: Traditions and transformation in Tibetan Buddhism | Includes bibliographical references and index.
Identifiers: LCCN 2023051398 (print) | LCCN 2023051399 (ebook) | ISBN 9780813951041 (hardcover) | ISBN 9780813951058 (paperback) | ISBN 9780813951065 (ebook)
Subjects: LCSH: Tripiṭaka. Sūtrapiṭaka. Tantra. Guhyasamājatantra—Criticism, interpretation, etc. | Tsong-kha-pa Blo-bzang-grags-pa, 1357–1419, Dpal gsang ba 'dus pa'i bskyed rim blo gsal bung ba'i re skong gnad dong sal ba. | Tantric Buddhism. | Dge-lugs-pa (Sect)—Rituals.
Classification: LCC BQ2157 .T7513 2024 (print) | LCC BQ2157 (ebook) | DDC 294.3/85—dc23/eng/20231122
LC record available at https://lccn.loc.gov/2023051398
LC ebook record available at https://lccn.loc.gov/2023051399

Cover art: istock.com/ookpiks
Cover design: Susan Zucker

CONTENTS

Introduction 1

1. The Cosmos and Cosmogony: Teaching Buddhism through Creation Stories 7

2. The Person: Death, the Intermediate State, and Rebirth 42

3. A General Explanation of the *Sādhana* 59

4. A Detailed Explanation of the *Sādhana* 99

Fulfilling the Bee's Hope; or, Clarifying the Essential Meaning of the Creation Stage of the Glorious Guhyasamāja—Fulfilling the Hope of the Clear-Minded Bee 141
Tsongkhapa Lozang Drakpa

Appendix 195
Notes 201
Bibliography 269
Index 287

THE COSMOS, THE PERSON, AND THE *SĀDHANA*

Introduction

Two key terms are at the core of this book: connections and continuity, *bandhu* and *prabandha* in Sanskrit.[1] The tension between them is a central theme in our discussion. The notion of connections between the cosmos, the person, and the ritual is often seen in early Indian literature. To quote Gavin Flood: "One of the fundamental vedic identifications or homologies, which becomes central in later esoteric traditions, is between the body, the universe and the sacrifice."[2] In our context, sacrifice is replaced by the practice of the *sādhana*—the tantric path of spiritual realization. In Sanskrit, the word "tantra" signifies a loom or a weave. It carries connotations of intertwining and braiding—and of continuity. We will see how the tantric path of the *sādhana* is interwoven with the fate of the cosmos and the person to create an intricate tapestry that explains how the *sādhana* practice works.

"Continuity" is one of the synonyms of the term "tantra." The *Subsequent Tantra,*[3] an important tantra of the Guhyasamāja cycle, explains that the word "tantra" means continuity[4] between three aspects: the cause, the fruit, and the method.[5] Tantra then is a continuous link between the point of departure and the goal of the practice preserved through the method. The method, explains Nāropā in his commentary on this tantra, is the *sādhana* practice;[6] hence, the continuity has a soteriological value. In Tibetan, "tantra" is translated as *gyü,*[7] meaning a string, a continuum, or a stream, especially a stream of being. This continuum connects the beginners in the practice to the awakened beings they can become at its end.

Yet both terms—connections and continuity in this context—are not easily explained in Buddhist lexicon. How is the microcosm (that is to say, a yogi meditating in isolation, whose life is subject to his or her individual karma) connected to the macrocosm formed by the shared karma of all people in the world? Or beyond connection, how can the microcosm even *affect* the macrocosm? What connects the dissolution of the meditator's ordinary environment to the destruction of the world? One of the foundations of Buddhist thought is a sequence of causation known as interdependent arising:[8] everything arises in dependence on interconnected causes and conditions. But what is the causal sequence that connects a person meditating on a *sādhana* and cosmological events? This question will be discussed at length below.

The notion of a continuity between a yogi who has just embarked on the *sādhana* practice and the awakened being this yogi will ultimately become is challenged by the Buddhist concepts of selflessness and impermanence, additional hallmarks of Buddhist thought. This contention, however, has been dealt with since early Buddhism; the concepts of selflessness and impermanence have always been accompanied by a notion of personal continuity—for example, one's karma that has begun in the past and continues forward into the future. Based on the various philosophical approaches, the continuity of a person can be explained as continuously changing from moment to moment or as a basis of designation[9] for sentient beings—to give only two examples.

The threads that connect the *sādhana* to the cosmos and the person in the context of *Guhyasamāja Sādhana,* our concern here, were explained by the famous Indian yogi and scholar of the *Guhyasamāja Tantra,* Nāgabuddhi, in his work entitled *Formulating the Guhyasamāja Sādhana*[10] in the late eighth to early ninth century CE.[11]

The commentary on this work, written by the Tibet's eminent scholar Tsongkhapa Lozang Drakpa (1357–1419), is the foundation of our discussion in this book.[12] As Thupten Jinpa writes, Tsongkhapa—"the founder" of the Geluk[13] school of Tibetan Buddhism—"earnestly sought to develop a truly integrated worldview"[14] on the basis of the numerous and diverse Indian scriptures and treatises. As we shall see, Tsongkhapa formulated a coherent system by integrating the tensions described above (or by finding the middle way between them) by using rational inquiry as his guideline. No doubt Tsongkhapa was inspired by the weblike, unified system suggested by Nāgabuddhi. He wrote his commentary, *Explanation of Formulating the Guhyasamāja Sādhana,* in 1404, even before composing his famous work on tantric practice entitled *The Great Treatise on the Stages of the Mantric Path.*[15] His reflections on *Formulating* likely impacted the *Great Treatise,* in which he refers to his earlier composition.

In his *Explanation,* Tsongkhapa stresses that not every similarity between the *sādhana* and the cosmos or the person has a soteriological value. Only certain homologies can serve to advance a yogi meditating on the *sādhana* toward their awakening. In following the *Subsequent Tantra* and Nāropā, mentioned above, Tsongkhapa emphasizes that only when there is a thread that continues without interruption from the ground to the goal can a yogi attain soteriological goals.

The goal of the *Guhyasamāja Sādhana,* according to Tsongkhapa, is the three bodies of a buddha:[16] the dharma, resources, and emanation bodies (*dharmakāya, saṃbhogakāya,* and *nirmāṇakāya*). To attain these three bodies of a buddha, certain homogenous causes[17] for them must exist from the point of onset and continue throughout the tantric practice. This means that at each of the three major stages of the practice (called the cause, the method, and the fruit in the *Subsequent Tantra*), there is a comparable feature.[18] These three major stages are often referred to in Tibetan literature as the "ground," the "path," and the "fruit."[19] The ground is the ordinary state in which a yogi embarks on the *sādhana* practice; the fruit or the goal of the practice is the awakened state of a buddha endowed with the three bodies; and the path that leads a yogi from the ground to the fruit is the tantric practice of the *sādhana.* Tsongkhapa maintains that the three bodies of a buddha cannot be attained without homogenous causes for each that have their roots in the ground and continue without interruption during every step of the tantric practice. (See the section "Purification" in chapter 3.) Moreover, an actual transformation is required in order to attain awakening, whether in a single life or in many lives.

As we shall see, the "very subtle body[20] made of winds and minds alone plays an important role in preserving the continuity from the ground state to enlightenment. This tantric approach stands in contrast to the "*nirvāṇa* without remainder"[21] attained by the historic Buddha at his death. *Nirvāṇa* without remainder put an end not only to the Buddha's mental faculties, and in particular afflictive emotions,[22] but also to all material aspects of his body.[23] The difference here is twofold. First, certain subtle elements of the person continue in the enlightened being, though in a modified form; and second, a certain corporeality must be present even after liberation from *saṃsāra* is attained. While in *nirvāṇa* without remainder all physical aspects of the Buddha's body discontinue, the Mahāyāna (the Great Vehicle) theory of the three bodies of a buddha assumes a certain corporeality in the state of enlightenment, and the tantric texts will develop this further.

The nature of the corporeal aspect present in enlightenment has been contested, especially in relation to the theory of Mind Only,[24] which is found in several important Indian Buddhis tantric treatises on the *Guhyasamāja Sādhana.*[25] Mind Only, however, is not widely accepted among Tibetan scholars as the highest philosophical theory. As we will see, Tsongkhapa cites

Indian scholars such as Āryadeva, who already in the early nineth century did not approve of the notion that the body attained at the culmination of the tantric practice is formed by the mind alone.[26]

Most Tibetan scholars regard the Prāsaṅgika Madhyamaka as the highest Buddhist philosophy, although their individual interpretation of this philosophy differs. Tsongkhapa, as a Prāsaṅgika Madhyamaka, saw the thread that carries a yogi from ordinary birth to enlightenment as continuous only to the extent that Prāsaṅgika philosophy allows it to be, or insofar as this thread acts as a basis of designation for sentient beings. (See the section "The Illusory Body" in chapter 3.) On the other hand, for Tibetan holders of the Buddha Nature in its strict sense,[27] all sentient beings possess an innate buddhahood since beginningless time.[28] But since Tsongkhapa does not accept such a view of Buddha Nature, his task of explaining "continuity" is more challenging.

The picture becomes even more complex when we explore the notion of connections. The idea of connections—homologies between the cosmos, the person, and practices—is the foundation of mysticism. They "might be said to be a principle of Indian religion."[29] This notion is pervasive in Indian treatises, including Nāgabuddhi's *Formulating the Guhyasamāja Sādhana,* on which Tsongkhapa comments. Moreover, numerous Tibetan scholars writing on the *Guhyasamāja Sādhana,* whether his predecessors or successors, took these homologies for granted. Tsongkhapa cannot simply reject the notion of homologies altogether. In addition, he favors coherent and comprehensive systems that weave together different worlds.

Here Tsongkhapa offers his integrative approach that finds the middle way between accepting and rejecting the notion of connections. We will see how Tsongkhapa accepts homologies between the cosmos, the person, and the *sādhana,* to a certain extent, and how he finds ways to explain his acceptance. However, Tsongkhapa finds a soteriological value only when there is unceasing continuance from ground to fruit. In taking this stance, he distanced himself from the method of other Tibetan scholars. Not only that, but his explanations are also more intricate in nature, as we shall see.

This book aims to clarify the working of the *sādhana* in relation to the cosmos and the person. Toward this end, the first chapter considers Buddhist notions of cosmogony and cosmology, while the second discusses the natural processes that human beings undergo—death, the intermediate state, and rebirth. The third chapter is dedicated to a general explanation of the *sādhana* in correspondence with macro- and microcosmic processes, and the fourth chapter provides a fuller explanation of the practice based on Tsongkhapa's *Fulfilling the Bee's Hope*. The final part consists of a complete English translation of that same work.

In this book I follow the Tibetan method of addressing three types of people: beginning, middling, and advanced practitioners. In writing the first two chapters, I had in mind mostly beginning students and nonexpert general readers who are interested in the topics of Buddhist cosmology and the three events during the lifecycle of a person—death, the intermediate state, and rebirth. Readers who continue to the third chapter will learn about the working of the *sādhana* in relation to the cosmos and the person in a general way. For middling and advanced readers, the first two chapters will serve to renew their acquaintance with Buddhist notions of the cosmos and the person. Those who are not intimidated by the complexity and details of the *sādhana* will benefit from reading the fourth chapter as well.

In the first chapter the reader will encounter two types of cosmological maps: vertical and spatial. These maps correspond to two different types of meditation. The vertical map corresponds to the notion of ascent through spiritual levels, while the spatial map is akin to circular representations and has bearing on the concepts of the center and its surroundings as well as on the configuration of the mandala.

1

The Cosmos and Cosmogony

Teaching Buddhism through Creation Stories

Creation stories are a nearly universal phenomenon. Such stories convey how cultures perceive human beings and the circumstances of their lives. For example, the two stories of creation that appear in the first two chapters of the book of Genesis reflect core ideas that the Judeo-Christian tradition holds about a creator-god and the world he created. Although the two stories express somewhat different ideas, their shared ideology informs us about the hierarchical relationship between the creator-god and humans as well as between humans and other creatures. Other important ideas, such as the source of suffering in the world, are presented in the descriptions of the original sin, the expulsion from paradise, the stories of Cain and Abel, and so on. Taken together, these biblical tales offer the reader an explanation of the world we live in.

Buddhist creation stories differ significantly from biblical ones. Yet they too present basic perceptions of the world and the human condition within it. Additionally, these stories convey central Buddhist teachings, including interdependent arising, the Four Noble's Truths, the path to awakening, karma, and more. These teachings are similar to those found in Buddhist scripture and philosophical treatises, but their presentation in story form gives them added potency. Furthermore, as a cosmogonical account (namely, as a narration about the origin of all things, from the physical universe to afflictions and suffering), such tales take on greater resonance.

Below, we will delve into Buddhist creation stories. First, however, I will draw on the work of the scholar of Tibetan Buddhism José Cabezón[1] to identify the main differences between the cosmogonies and cosmologies of the monotheistic and Buddhist traditions.[2] Table 1 points to four features that

TABLE 1. Creation in Buddhism versus Monotheism

	MONOTHEISM—UNIQUENESS	BUDDHISM—MULTIPLICITY
Time	Creation occurs once.	Creation is a cyclic event without a beginning.
Space	Our world alone exists in the universe.	There are numerous worlds in the universe.
Cause	Creation is the primary cause of our world.	A vast set of causes that work in a complex way create the world.
Creator	The world was created by a god who has unique status in the world.	There is no creator-god.

indicate how monotheistic traditions are characterized by uniqueness while Buddhism is characterized by multiplicity.

First, in monotheistic religions, creation is seen as a unique event, whereas Buddhism posits multiplicity and the simultaneous existence of things and ideas. In temporal terms, creation in the monotheistic tradition is a one-time event that took place in the distant past, while in the Indian conception, the world, which has existed since beginningless time, is periodically destroyed and recreated. The notion of beginningless existence is crucial to Buddhist thought. It implies that there was no moment when there was a state of total nonexistence. Furthermore, neither the creation nor the destruction of the world is total. For example, beings need not necessarily die when it is time for their world to be destroyed because they can migrate to other worlds in the universe.

This brings us to the second difference between the cosmologies of the monotheistic and Buddhist traditions. In spatial terms, Buddhists perceive our world as only one among many worlds in the universe that are accessible to us. Beings living in our world can reach the outer worlds, either in their next lives, by dying in this world and being reborn in one of these outer worlds, or in their present lives by means of meditation.

The third difference between the cosmogonies concerns causality: Buddhism does not assume a primary cause for the existence of the world. Accordingly, in Buddhism there is no creator or a figure of a God with a capital G. Is religion without a God possible? The answer is yes. Is Buddhism a religion? Yes. But there is no creator who holds a unique status in the world and exists beyond the suffering[3] that all beings are subject to. This is the fourth difference between the cosmogonies, which concerns personal uniqueness.

The periodic creation and destruction of world is the result of multiple causes that work interdependently, and these include the shared karma of the world's inhabitants.

Buddhist Creation Stories

The source for the Buddhist creation story presented here is the account by Tsongkhapa in *Fulfilling the Bee's Hope* (translated in full as the final section of this book). The version Tsongkhapa relates originated in India about two millennia ago and is known throughout the Buddhist world. Like any enduring tale, it is a shape-shifter, conforming to the context in which it is presented. Yet Tsongkhapa's version does not differ in essential points from the creation story found in Buddhist treatises composed during the first millennium CE, including the *Monastic Guidelines*,[4] the *Abhidharmakośa*,[5] the *Presentation on the World*,[6] and the *Yogācārabhūmi*.[7]

The cyclic process the world undergoes consists of four "seasons": creation, existence, destruction, and nonexistence.[8] The period of nonexistence is not simply a void. Rather, during this period the physical aspects of the world and its dwellers do not exist, while the higher realms of the world that are refined and devoid of coarse physical substances remain and subtle beings reside there. The period of creation begins with the recreation of the physical elements that comprise the lower realms of the world.

During the periodic creations of the world described in Buddhist texts, the physical world evolves first, after which the beings that dwell in the physical world are created. But since Buddhist cosmogonical accounts aim to describe human nature and how our minds bring about suffering, we will begin our discussion with the evolution of the first people in this world. Later, we will turn to narrations about the creation and destruction of the world itself.

How the First People Appear in the World

In *Fulfilling the Bee's Hope*[9] Tsongkhapa describes how during the re-creation of sentient beings, the first human beings evolve in the continent called Jambudvīpa, where we people live.[10] The first sentient beings that appear here are not humans but miraculous beings who before long devolve to become ordinary people. During the period of the nonexistence of the physical world, these beings abide in one of the highest realms, called Clear Light.[11] The name of this highest realm does not indicate the clear light that appears during death or meditation, though this similarity is not incidental. Following the re-creation of the physical world, the beings in Clear Light die there and are miraculously reborn in the continent of Jambudvīpa. Following various Indian scriptures,[12] Tsongkhapa describes how these beings appear on earth:

> Alone among all beings, those who reside in Jambudvīpa during the first eon are endowed with the following seven characteristics: (1) they are adorned with features similar to the major and minor marks of a buddha, (2) their lifespan may be infinite, (3) their faculties are complete, (4) they can travel in the sky by means of miraculous powers, (5) being free of dependence on physical food, they subsist solely on delight, (6) there being no distinction between day and night [no sun and moon], their bodies can illuminate with a light of their own, and (7) their birth is miraculous.[13]

We are told that the first beings residing in our world during the first eon are adorned with qualities similar to those of a buddha, such as the major and minor marks of a buddha. *Formulating the Guhyasamāja Sādhana,*[14] one of the texts on which Tsongkhapa relies, explains that these people are adorned with all the good qualities of the buddhas. But Tsongkhapa limits this in a significant way in stating that although the first beings are similar to the buddhas, they are not endowed with the buddhas' "true" qualities. Had they initially been equal to the buddhas in all ways and later forgone these qualities, their journey to enlightenment would be a return to their point of departure so that they can regain what they already once had. But Tsongkhapa perceives the path toward buddhahood as an advancement rather than as a return to a past stage. For him, the cessation of *saṃsāric* suffering is not a reversal of the creation process in order to return to the original state.

The first beings of the new eon are endowed with six additional good qualities that they soon lose. They are endowed with miraculous qualities such as long lifespans, and their features are related to light, delight, and lightness. They are radiant, endowed with the ability to fly, and are sustained by joy. They hover in space and glow with their own light, not needing the light of the sun and the moon. Likewise, they do not depend on physical food but are nourished by delight. Finally, they are born in a miraculous birth—that is to say, they are born instantaneously with all their limbs intact and all faculties sound and unimpaired. It is worth mentioning that miraculous birth is not unique to the beings of the first eon: gods, denizens of hell, and intermediate beings are born this way as well.[15]

The first beings in Jambudvīpa are also characterized by a lack of distinctions, including gender distinctions. Their environment, too, is without distinctions such as day and night. This is emphasized in the *Monastic Guidelines:*

"At that time, the sun, moon, and stars have not yet appeared in the world. Night and day do not exist, nor minutes, hours, fortnights, months, years, or seasons. There are no females nor males, and sentient beings are simply sentient beings."[16]

In the next paragraph in *Bee's Hope,* we see the beginning of the decline of these sentient beings or their "fall" from the Buddhist "paradise": "At that time, the surface of the great earth is covered with an earth nectar; its taste is like unrefined honey, and its color is like that of fresh butter. When an imprinted craving for physical food is awakened in one of the beings, s/he[17] dips a fingertip in it and tastes it. Upon seeing this, the others do the same."[18] Suddenly the earth becomes covered with a kind of "manna," a cream with wonderful color, smell, and taste, formed like the skin on boiled milk when it cools. One of the beings tastes the nectar, due to imprinted tendencies or habits remaining from former lives in which s/he was habituated to feeding on physical food. The point here is that craving for food is inherent in human beings; hence, the "original sin" in Buddhism is the thirst, longing, or desire inherent in all beings. The first beings need no other food but delight, but the yearning for physical food is embedded in them as part of their nature. Seeing one being who tastes the earth nectar, other beings do the same.

The text of the *Monastic Guidelines* elaborates on the way earthly desires are thus aroused, in its typical repetitive style: "Then, one being whose nature is greediness dips a fingertip in the earth nectar and tastes it. The more he has, the more he wants, enjoying it as one would enjoy physical food. . . . Seeing this, the other beings do the same. The more they taste it the more they desire it, and the more they desire it the more they eat, enjoying it as physical food."[19] We may note that it is not only in the Buddhist creation story that desire plays an important role. It is also found, for example, in one of the early Indian hymns from the *Ṛg Veda:* "Darkness was hidden by darkness in the beginning; with no distinguishing sign, all this was water. The life force that was covered with emptiness, that one arose through the power of heat. Desire came upon that one in the beginning; that was the first seed of mind."[20]

In *Bee's Hope* Tsongkhapa continues: "As a result of eating physical food, their bodies become coarse and heavy. No longer are they able to travel through space with their miraculous powers; the lights in their bodies vanish, and darkness prevails. Then they assemble and lament [the disappearance of the lights], and consequently the sun and moon appear through the karmic power of sentient beings. At that point, days, months, years, and seasons come into being."[21] Those who eat the earth nectar lose their miraculous qualities; their bodies become heavy, and they can no longer hover in the sky and shine. Therefore, the sun, moon, and stars appear to light their way—the celestial bodies are not created by a creator-god but through the karmic power of sentient beings. Karma, then, is central to the Buddhist creation. The tendencies embedded in these beings that brought them to taste the earth nectar are karmic conditioning as well. Though these beings now reside in a "paradise," their former tendencies remain within them. Imprinting, conditioning, and longing typify all beings in *saṃsāra,* the recurring cycle of life and death, and are the forces that create the world as we know it.

These forces are intertwined with all kinds of distinctions; they both create such distinctions and are reinforced by them. Notably, the Judeo-Christian creation story also depicts a process of increasing divergence. According to the first chapter in Genesis, on the first day God distinguished between light and darkness, on the second day between water and sky, on the third day between water and land, and on the fourth between day and night. Similarly, in the Buddhist story, when the first beings lose their own light and darkness prevails, the distinctions between day and night appear, and then all temporal divisions—days, months, years—evolve. Even prior to the appearance of the sun and moon, the appearance of earth nectar—the first event that took place after the rebirth of the first beings in the eon—creates a differentiation between the earth nectar and other phenomena. The earth nectar is distinguished by its pleasant color, smell, and taste. Hence, the first distinction arouses longing, and the longing creates further differentiation, as we are told subsequently: "While those who eat little of the earth nectar are beautiful, those who eat more of it develop ugly complexions. Therefore, the former say to the latter: 'I am beautiful, and you are ugly.' Due to their nonvirtuous spite, the earth nectar disappears. Again, they assemble and lament [the disappearance of the earth nectar]."[22] After the temporal divisions, further distinctions are made: those who, due to their karma, eat a small amount of the earth nectar are beautiful, but those who eat more of it become ugly. The *Monastic Guidelines* states this plainly: "Due to two amounts of food, two types of complexion manifest."[23] This creates a distinction between beautiful and ugly beings, which in turn causes the negative emotions of pride and arrogance. While the first emotion that has appeared in our world was craving or desire for physical food, now we encounter pride and arrogance—which produce torment and anguish.

Narrating Fundamental Notions of Buddhist Philosophy

The creation story described above expresses fundamental notions of Buddhist philosophy: specifically, how afflictive emotions create the *saṃsāric* world of suffering in which we live. Mental states such as unconditional love or compassion do not engender suffering and thus are not afflictive, while passion, jealousy, anger, pride, and delusions are poisonous and tormenting; hence, they are called afflictive emotions. In this creation story the beautiful and arrogant beings offend others, whom they regard as ugly, and thereby bring about significant consequences (such as the disappearance of the earth nectar) that catalyze their "fall from paradise."

Among the Buddhist teachings that the creation story narrates are the Four Noble's Truths.[24] According to the first truth, all beings are afflicted by existential suffering such as inherent dissatisfaction, discomfort, or distress. The second truth explains the reason for existential suffering: a persistent thirst that denotes longing and desire, and, in fact, all afflictive emotions. According to the third truth, suffering can be ended, and this is *nirvāṇa*. The fourth truth describes the path to *nirvāṇa*. The creation story explains how afflictive emotions that bring about suffering evolve and how, by avoiding them, *nirvāṇa* can be attained.

Regarding karma, the literal meaning of the word is "action," but in fact it refers to intentional acts committed by sentient beings and thus has mental dimensions as well. Karma is created by the mind and in turn leaves its imprints on the mind; these imprints can then cause sentient beings to act in certain ways in the future. Such actions affect not only sentient beings themselves but the entire community through the shared karma of its members.

According to the account regarding the first beings in the world, afflictive emotions, distinctions, and karma work together to create the world. Thus, the creation story narrates the theory of interdependent arising,[25] the principal Buddhist theory describing mutually reinforcing processes of cause and effect. While Buddhist scriptures and treatises explain interdependent arising by listing a series of twelve causal links, here this notion is presented through a story.[26]

Moreover, mental events—such as karma, afflictive emotions, distinctions, and interdependent causation—though not material in nature, have the power to achieve actual effect in the world. Not only do they create further mental states and distinctions; they also have the capacity to create the world. Hence, interdependent arising does not apply solely to individual beings. Its effects extend to societies and the physical world.

Back to the Creation Story

Facing the absence of the earth nectar, the beings assemble to mourn its disappearance. Before they had begun to eat the nectar, these beings were not social; they each happily travelled through air using their own individual lights and feeding on delight. But when their afflictive emotions redevelop, their misery makes them seek each other out to cry together over their misfortune. Next, Tsongkhapa describes:

> Once again, through the power of karma, the surface of the great earth is swathed with [a splendid] earth-cream, its taste similar to unrefined honey as before, and its color yellow like the *dong kha* flower. When the beings eat it, the events are repeated as before until once again they begin to despise each other, and due to their nonvirtuous actions, the earth-cream disappears, and they assemble and lament as before.
>
> Yet again, through the power of karma, the surface of the great earth is swathed in a splendid thicket of sprouts, which taste like unrefined honey and are orange like the *ka dam pu ka* flower. Again, they eat it, and events repeat as before.[27]

A new kind of earth-cream appears, delicious as before. Yet its color intensifies from white to yellow, and the previous events recur until the new earth-cream disappears. Then orange-colored sprouts appear and vanish. The *Monastic Guidelines*[28] recounts these events time and again, hammering home the point in classical Indian style, but Tsongkhapa abbreviates the story and moves on to describe the appearance of rice in the world: "Afterward, through the karmic power of the beings in the world, although no field has been plowed or planted anywhere, *salu*[29] rice appears on the surface of the great earth, devoid of husks and chaff, and with roots four fingers long. The rice they reap in the morning grows back that same morning, and the rice they reap in the evening grows back that same evening, with no sign that it was ever reaped."[30] At this stage, rice appears on its own without need of any human toil, free of husks and chaff.

Next: "Since this food is much coarser, when they eat the rice, its crude wastes turn into feces and urine, and the organs for their evacuation protrude differently for males and females."[31] The rice, less refined than the earth nectars and sprouts, cannot be digested in full; therefore, its crude waste turns into feces and urine that must be evacuated from the body. Through the power of karma, as the result of previous deeds, the male and female genitals develop. This distinction marks another important development: the difference between the genders is created; its immediate cause is the desire for food.

The text continues: "Then, in some beings, previous imprints for sexual intercourse are awakened, and they engage in sexual activity."[32] Again, distinctions bring about desire. The distinction between male and female beings creates attraction between the genders. Once again, the *Monastic Guidelines* emphasizes the way sexual desire is aroused: "[Being unclad] some of the beings with male organs and some of the beings with female organs look at each other, and the more they look at each other, the more they desire each other, and the more desire arises in them, the more they are overcome by fiery passion, and the more they are overcome by fiery passion they more they engage in sexual activity."[33]

Tsongkhapa continues: "Seeing this, others cast dirt at them and so forth, so to conceal themselves they build houses and so forth, and this is the origin of houses."[34] Tsongkhapa may have abbreviated this account because his audience was already familiar with the tale. Regarding the meaning of "others cast dirt at them and so forth," let us turn to the *Monastic Guidelines*: "When other beings see some men and women engaging in sexual activities, they cast dirt, clods of earth, pebbles, stones, and gravel at them, saying: 'O sinful people engaging in misdeeds! Why do you annoy other beings?' . . . Because of their unseemly deeds, these beings face great hostility. Then they build houses and walls in order to engage in their activities, and they say: 'Here we will engage in misdeeds.' In this way, houses came into being."[35] At this point, the account of the *Monastic Guidelines* comes to an end. Its message—the evils of sexual desire—has been delivered to its intended audience: monks and nuns. Other sources, such as the *Abhidharmakośa*[36] and *Yogācārabhūmi*,[37] however, continue the account, and Tsongkhapa follows them in his narration.

When these men and women engage in sexual activity, the others scold and shame them. Hence, once more, desire causes distinctions between "the bad," who engage in sexual activities, and "the good," who scold them. Moreover, being chastened and ashamed are also afflictive emotions; as a result, those who engage in sex seek to hide by building houses in which they can do what cannot be done in public. In other words, the first houses, too, were built on account of desire. This is another step in the social development of the first people. Each pair of beings is now partly isolated in their own homes. Furthermore, this development establishes the concepts of private property and ownership. The idea of owning property is further entrenched by the events that follow.

Tsongkhapa continues: "During that period, at dawn the beings gather the *salu* rice for their morning meal and at dusk for their evening meal. But some lazy beings gather rice for the morning and evening meals at the same time. Seeing this, others gather food for a week or more at a time. As a result, the harvested rice does not grow back; therefore it becomes necessary to sow seeds."[38] Now that they have their own quarters and a place to house their possessions, it occurs to one of them that s/he can store rice at home. There is no need to amass rice, as the field produces enough for everyone and the rice grows as soon as it has been reaped, but the beings who do so act out of the afflictive emotions of greed and laziness. As a result of these afflictive emotions, the harvested rice stalks no longer sprout on their own and develop husks and chaff. After that, it becomes necessary to cultivate the land by the sweat of one's brow, as in the Bible—to sow seeds and thresh grains. The *Abhidharmakośa*[39] and other parallel accounts tell us that due to these developments, people divide up the rice fields into plots marked by boundaries, and each family cultivates their own plot: they add divisions and increase the properties they own.

What follows: "Then, since in that land where the *salu* rice grows there are no treaties, the powerful snatch from the weak and others steal quietly. Consequently, one kills the other and so forth. This is the origin of the ten nonvirtuous ways of action."[40] After private property has been instituted, instead of growing the rice themselves in their individual plots, some people start stealing from the fields of others; thereby fights and murders begin. This is the origin of immoral behavior and violent crime. Because of this: "The elders consult and appoint as their leader a good-natured and wise person. They offer to him one-sixth of the harvest, and he administrates according to the proper law. His lineage is called the King Esteemed by Many,[41] and the Śākyas are also descended from him."[42] The first people realize that in order to become a society that functions properly, without falsehood, violence, and similar vices, they must be ruled and judged, so they elect a king who will reign over them in return for their taxes. The Śākya dynasty in which Buddha Śākyamuni was born descended from this first king.

To conclude, this account explains how the first beings in our world, who were endowed with miraculous qualities and knew no apparent suffering, became ordinary people in the span of a single lifetime. Their afflictive emotions and karma brought about various events in a chain of interdependent arising. When the first beings devolve into ordinary human beings, they become just like us, and the story of their decline is in fact the origin of our suffering.

Undoing Creation?

It is worth reiterating that *nirvāṇa* is not a return to the initial moment of creation of the first beings. This is because that initial moment took place within the world of *saṃsāra,* as these beings had not overcome their afflictive emotions in their previous lives. For a brief time, they were not yet afflicted by longing and desire—simply because they had not yet encountered objects that could arouse their afflictive emotions. Thus, although their initial happiness stands in contrast to *saṃsāric* suffering, it is not a liberation from *saṃsāra.* At the same time, in Buddhist literature one finds attempts to undo the process of creation and to return to the initial moment.

In one of his works on Buddhist tradition, the Tibetologist and Indologist Alex Wayman suggests that the Buddhist path can be interpreted as a series of steps that attempt to invert the creation story.[43] When monks and nuns join the Buddhist order, they renounce their properties and future inheritance, thus reversing the property ownership described as one of the last stages of the creation. They reverse the state of gender differentiation by minimizing the distinctness of their appearances through shaving their heads and wearing identical robes. By doing so, they also reverse obvious distinctions between beautiful and ugly beings. By adhering to celibacy, they strive to reverse the events that created sexual attractions. Monks and nuns are not supposed to grow their own food but eat only what is given to them as alms. In this way they return to the state of food growing "by itself." Their food is also simple and virtuous; thus, they reverse the state of eating coarser and coarser food and attempt to return their bodies to the state of purity. The hermits aim at returning to a state in which they are sustained by delight—namely, by the so-called Dharma food. They do this by dedicating their lives to practice and study, which are intended to gradually reduce their afflictive emotions and help them become free of *saṃsāra.* By doing so, they aspire to reach a state in which they will no longer be subject to the processes of creation.

Further Morals of the Story and the Discourse on the Origin of Things

Our creation story sets forth not only central Buddhist teachings but also the origin of Buddha Śākyamuni, the historical Buddha, who lived about two and a half millennia ago. We are told that he descended from the first king who was chosen to reign. To understand why the author of this story considered it important to explain this point, we need to turn to different contexts in which the Buddhist creation story is found.

One version, the *Discourse on the Origin of Things*[44] in the Pāli canon, is told in the context of a Buddhist-Brahmanic controversy. For the Tibetan author of our story, tensions between Buddhists and non-Buddhists in India were of little significance, but since the Pāli canon developed in the Indian subcontinent, it is not surprising to find the creation story situated within a frame-story that engages in dialogue with the Brahmanic tradition.

In the background of the *Discourse on the Origin of Things* is a Brahmanic-Vedic tradition about the origins of the four castes.[45] It tells us how the entire universe, animate and inanimate, was created from the body of the primordial cosmic person through a sacrificial act. The brahmans[46] were born from his mouth; the rulers and warriors[47] from his arms; the traders and ordinary people[48] from his thighs; and the servants[49] from his feet. While the purpose of this Brahmanic myth is to sanction the social order of caste, the Buddhist creation story has different messages.

In the *Discourse on the Origin of Things*, two Buddhist novices who were born into the brahman caste approach the Buddha. The Buddha expresses his hope that the novices, who had abandoned their families and traditions to join him, would not be condemned by the brahmans. The novices respond that the brahmans had indeed scolded them, stating that the brahmans, born from the mouth of the cosmic person, are the best of all classes, but the two had nevertheless resolved to give up their high status and join the lower class of the rulers, to which the Buddha was born.

The Buddha replies by telling the novices the creation story above, which not only reflects several central Buddhist theories about human nature but also concludes with a virtuous king who was the first of the ruling class to which the Buddha himself belongs. This is a common technique of debate, whereby the arguments of opponents are turned around on them. In the present case, the Buddhist tradition provides the brahmans who have joined its circles with an alternative narrative to justify their actions, while at the same time ascribing high social status to them. For this reason, the *Discourse on the Origin of Things* embeds the account of the origin of the four castes and the Buddhist order within the creation story. Other versions, such as the *Abhidharmakośa,* present the core story alone in order to convey the important Buddhist concepts it contains.

The British Buddhologist Richard Francis Gombrich has suggested that the creation story in the *Discourse on the Origin of Things* should not be understood at face value but rather as "satirical and parodistic in intent."[50] Other

Western scholars have followed Gombrich's approach.[51] Still, while the polemical technique of turning an argument on the opponent is always humorous, the creation story itself is not necessarily ironic.[52] The Indian treatises, Tsongkhapa, and other traditional Buddhist scholars who told this story certainly regarded it as a valuable technique of narrating Buddhist thought and even as a true account. Be that as it may, while the Pāli version of this fascinating creation story was translated into English in the early twentieth century,[53] its intended message was overlooked until the British scholar Rupert Gethin drew attention to it.[54]

Creation of the First Beings According to the "Brahmā's Net"

Another creation story appears in the discourse "The Sixty-Two Kinds of Wrong Views" found in the *Discourse on Brahmā's Net.*[55] As the title indicates, this story, too, is told in a polemical context, aiming to refute the Brahmanic notion of a creator-god. Echoing the creation story above, it begins with one being who, due to karma, passes away in the god-realm of Clear Light and is miraculously reborn endowed with the seven aforementioned good qualities. This being, however, is not born in the continent of Jambudvīpa, as in the previous creation stories, but in the heavenly palace of Brahmā. Then:

> As a result of dwelling there [in his palace] all alone for a long time there arises in him dissatisfaction and agitation, (and he yearns): "Oh, that other beings might come to this place!" Just at that moment, due to the exhaustion of their life span or the exhaustion of their merit, certain other beings pass away from the Realm of Clear Light and re-arise in the palace of Brahmā, in companionship with him. There they dwell, mind-made, feeding on rapture, self-luminous, moving through the air, abiding in glory. And they continue thus for a long, long time.[56]

The thought then occurs to the first being who was born in Brahmā palace: "I am Brahmā the Maker and Creator, and these beings were created by me. This is because as soon as I expressed my wish for companions, they appeared." Likewise, it occurred to the beings who appeared after him: "This is Brahmā; he made us, and he is eternal." This account echoes the Upaniṣadic creation story about the first person who, wishing for companions, created all the human beings and animals in the world, after which he thought: "I created all this."[57]

It is worth mentioning that the Buddhist tradition in India had no choice but to engage with beliefs in Brahmā, the quintessential Indian creator-god, who is well-regarded in Indian Buddhist literature. There is more to the Buddhist story, however, than an intrareligious debate. Like the previous creation story, the tale in *Discourse on Brahmā's Net* is no mere joke, as the philologist K. R. Norman explains.[58] While it is indeed amusing, it nevertheless communicates Buddhist notions similar to those we encountered in the first version of a Buddhist creation story.

This story is meant to illustrate how wrong views evolve. The descent of the first being and the descent of those who follow him are two distinct events that resulted from the same cause—the shared karma of the world. However the first being believes that he is the cause for the others; moreover, the others share this view. Since the others do not challenge the view of the first being, the mistaken notion is agreed upon by all. This story in the *Discourse on Brahmā's Net* demonstrates how the first mistake (or the first illusion) was created.

According to the Buddhist tradition that created this story, the first being had to leave the Realm of Clear Light and be born in a lower heaven because the karma for the recreation of the world had ripened, and his lifespan or merit had been exhausted. While for the Brahmanic tradition, Brahmā is eternal—he has always been here and always will be—the Buddhist tradition posits that everything in the world is impermanent and subject to the powers of karma and interdependent arising. Due to his good karma, Brahmā had been reborn in the highest heaven of Clear Light, but when the time came for the world to be created—or, in the terminology of the *Brahmā's Net,* to expand—Brahmā had to migrate to a different sphere: "But sooner or later, bhikkhus, after a long period has elapsed, this world begins to expand once again. While the world is expanding, an empty palace of Brahmā appears. Then a certain being, due to the exhaustion of his lifespan or the exhaustion of his merit, passes away from the Realm of Clear Light and re-arises in the empty palace of Brahmā."[59]

In this classic Buddhist view, when the designated time comes, the following events will inevitably take place. A certain being is reborn in the heavenly realm of Brahmā's palace, and likewise "due to the exhaustion of their lifespan or the exhaustion of their merit," other beings are reborn there as well. As already mentioned, the *Brahmā's Net* is a discourse about sixty-two wrong views, one of which is to perceive Brahmā as the eternal creator of the world.[60]

Let us recall that at the end of the first creation story we discussed, a king was enthroned, and his authority was accepted by common consent. In this case, a social convention facilitated the creation and maintenance of social order. We see, then, that not every convention in the creation stories is necessarily rejected. However, in the present story, while all the characters thought that Brahmā was the creator-god, this misconception was based, as the story shows, on an error that *saṃsāric* beings are prone to make: their ignorance prevents them from understanding what actually happens.

The point of this account is that Brahmā lives in *saṃsāra* and is subject to the shared karma of the world. To be freed of *saṃsāra,* he must reach awakening. We should not think that while Brahmā is not eternal, *saṃsāra* is eternal, because each and every being can be freed from *saṃsāra.* Therefore, for individual beings, *saṃsāra* is not eternal. Yet as long as they are in *saṃsāra,* they are subject to ignorance and obscurations that lead them to the sixty-two wrong views. Hence, just like the previous creation stories examined above, this narration in the *Brahmā's Net* conveys fundamental Buddhist theories, and it does so in a humorous way. Yet it cannot be taken as simply a joke.

The Inanimate World

Before beings can appear in the world, the physical world has to be created.[61] As Tsongkhapa details in *Fulfilling the Bee's Hope:* "The destruction of the world takes twenty eons, the empty period lasts twenty eons, its evolution takes twenty eons, and its abiding twenty. These eighty medium eons together are called one great eon."[62]

As noted in the section above, "Buddhist Creation Stories," in Buddhist thought the world goes through four cyclical stages: creation, existence, destruction, and material nonexistence. Each of these processes lasts twenty medium eons. Having been destroyed, the world remains in a state of material nonexistence for twenty medium eons. Yet it still exists, since its higher nonmaterial heavens do exist, and it contains the potential for material re-creation. When this potential is realized, the world is re-created during twenty medium eons and remains viable for another twenty medium eons. Such a complete cycle lasts eighty medium eons or one great eon; this is one year in the life of the world.

How long is a medium eon? According to one account,[63] there is a cubical enclosure of one *krośa* on each side and one *krośa* in height filled with sesame seeds.[64] Once every hundred years a single grain is removed. The time it takes to empty the cube is one medium eon. Another measure is based on a high mountain in the Himalaya; once every hundred years a bird who flies over it drizzles one drop of water on the mountain. The time it takes for the mountain to be worn down and disappear is an eon.

The heavenly Realm of Clear Light, which we encountered in the stories

TABLE 2. The Cosmic Realms and Meditative States

REALM	MEDITATIVE STATES AND COSMIC LEVELS
Immaterial Realm	Neither perception nor nonperception
	Absorptions on nothingness
	Infinite consciousness
	Infinite space
Realm of Subtle Materiality	Forth *dhyāna*
	Third *dhyāna*
	Second *dhyāna*
	Realm of Clear Light
	First *dhyāna*
	Brahmā's Palace
Desire Realm	Gods of the Desire Realm
	Human beings
	Animals
	Hungry ghosts[1]
	Hells

[1]Tib. *yi dwags*, Skt. *preta*.

on the creation of the beings dwelling in the world, is the lowest of the realms that remains during the period of the coarse material world's destruction. It is located in the Realm of Subtle Materiality or Form Realm,[65] the middle realm among the three realms[66] of *saṃsāra*. Above it is the Immaterial or Formless Realm,[67] and below it the Desire Realm (table 2). The Realm of Subtle Materiality consist of four levels called *dhyānas*. The Realm of Clear Light is the highest heaven in the second *dhyāna* in the Realm of Subtle Materiality, while the palace of Brahmā mentioned before is the top level of the first *dhyāna*.

The Deliberate Blurring of Cosmological Worlds and Meditative States

Lacking a coarse material basis, the *dhyānas* are not only cosmological levels but also mental states—and the blurring of these two is deliberate.[68] In other words, the distinction between the objective, macrocosmic outer world and the inner, microcosmic subjective mental states is intentionally ambiguous. In this regard, the Indian Buddhist monk Vasubandhu (fl. 5th c. CE) wrote in his *Abhidharmakośa:* "Each of the *dhyānas* is of two types: meditative absorption[69] and [a place of re]birth."[70] The Sanskrit word *dhyāna* means "concentration" and is equivalent to the Pāli *jhāna,* Chinese *chan,* and Japanese *zen.*

Since the *dhyānas* are heavens as well as mental states, they can be reached either through death in another world and rebirth in the Realm of Subtle Materiality or through meditation in another realm. Hence, a person meditating in the continent of Jambudvīpa may reach the realms of *dhyānas.* We cannot ask where that person really is—in Jambudvīpa or in an upper *dhyāna.* That person experiences being in a *dhyāna,* regardless of where s/he actually "is" and regardless of whether s/he took a mental journey or underwent death and rebirth. Notably, reaching the *dhyānas* either through rebirth or through meditation is the fruit of special types of meritorious activities and practices. The achievement of the level of a certain *dhyāna* through meditation in the preceding life can bear the fruit of rebirth in that *dhyāna.*

Some individuals prefer to take the cosmological map as symbolic or figurative descriptions of mental states, claiming that they do not exist even at a conventional level of truth. Yet both perspectives—the one that emphasizes the symbolic and psychological meaning and the one that posits all worlds as real (to the extent it posits reality)—are found within the Buddhist tradition. This tradition has its own ways of addressing contradictions and can easily assimilate the ambiguity between cosmological heavens and states of mind. Moreover, Buddhist traditions tend to ascribe great power to the mind and mental states, as the creation story of the first beings illustrates. The mental dimension attributed to the cosmological heavens grants them additional potency.

The Creation of the Inanimate World

The creation of the coarse material world begins from the second *dhyāna.*[71] As Tsongkhapa describes in *Fulfilling the Bee's Hope:* "A light wind from the second *dhyāna* flows downward, thereby forming the celestial mansions of the first *dhyāna.* Then a light wind coming from the first *dhyāna* flows downward, thereby forming in descending order the celestial mansions [of the higher gods of the Desire Realm]."[72] The first agent in this process is a light wind that forms the first *dhyāna* when it flows downward from the second *dhyāna* to the lower level. This wind is a harbinger of the evolution of world, as Tsongkhapa describes: "Then, through the shared karma of sentient beings, the early sign of the evolving world appears in space—the gentle wind that [at first] blows slowly and gradually increases."[73] Likewise, according to *Formulating the Guhyasamāja Sādhana:* "Through the power of the uninterrupted connection of interdependent arising, gentle winds are set in motion and gradually whirl faster."[74] Hence, during the creation of the inanimate world, as well, karma and interdependent arising are principal forces.

When the wind leaves the first *dhyāna*—the lower level in the Realm of Subtle Materiality—it reaches the Desire Realm, where it creates the heavens of the gods residing there.[75] Then the force of the wind increases, and the creation of the physical world begins. While the *dhyānas*, which lack coarse physicality, are formed from higher to lower, the lower material levels must rest one upon the other, as Tsongkhapa explains elsewhere: "The immaterial heavens evolve gradually from higher to lower, while the material ones evolve gradually from lower to higher."[76]

In *Bee's Hope* Tsongkhapa describes how the physical world evolves: "Thereupon a wind mandala evolves—one million six hundred thousand *yojanas* in height and innumerable *yojanas* in width—[a wind mandala] that even a great mighty *vajra* cannot destroy. Then a cloud in the nature of gold condenses in space, and a constant rain whose essence is gold—with drops the size of chariot wheels—falls from the cloud onto the wind mandala and accumulates over a long period. Thereby the water mandala is formed above the wind mandala."[77] Thus, the physical world rests on an immense cylinder of wind that itself floats in space. In case we might wonder about the safety of this cosmic structure, we are assured that the cylinder of wind is indestructible.

Then, a heavy rain with drops the size of chariot wheels falls, forming a cylinder of water upon the cylinder of wind. The *Abhidharmakośa* raises here another empirical query: What holds the cylinder of water in place and prevents it from flowing down? Two answers are supplied.[78] Thus the mythological account of creation is permeated with pragmatic concerns. Then: "A wind evolves through the shared karma of sentient beings and churns the water mandala from the four directions. Following that, the golden earth is formed, as a film is formed over boiling milk."[79] The wind that churns the water to create the layer of a golden earth recalls the Hindu creation myth of the churning of the cosmic ocean.[80] The height of the water cylinder is now reduced and upon it rests the golden earth.

The world thus rests on three cylinders of different heights, one atop the other.[81] The top layer is the earth, which rests upon water, and below the water is a cylinder of wind. Thus far in this description the world is made up of four elements: space above; wind, water, and earth below. The *Abhidharmakośa* does not include the element of fire among the constituents of the world, but the *Guhyasamāja Sādhana* instructs the yogis to visualize a mandala resting upon the four elements of wind, water, fire, and earth. Hence, Tsongkhapa must account for the presence of fire:[82] "Although a fire mandala is not specifically explained, the function of fire, its minute particles and so forth, is found [in latent form] within the other three mandalas. Hence, there is no flaw in the absence of a fire mandala as a corresponding object on the ground [during the world's ordinary existence]."[83]

Last, the mountains and the oceans are created upon the earth: "Through the shared karma of sentient beings, a cloud whose essence is various elements, condenses in space over the earth. A constant rain, whose essence is various elements, falls from this cloud over a long period and accumulates. In this way, the outer oceans are created. When the oceans are churned as before, Mt. Meru is formed from the finest elements; the seven ranges of golden mountains—from the medium elements; and the four continents and the eight subcontinents—from the inferior elements."[84] The rain contains various elements that eventually manifest into oceans and mountains.

Altogether, nine mountains rest on the golden earth. In the center is Mt. Meru,[85] surrounded by seven concentrical ranges,[86] depicted as either round or square. Though the seven ranges are called golden mountains, we are told here that they are made of the medium elements. The Outer Mountain Ring[87] made of iron defines the outer limit of the world. Between the seven ranges of mountains lie the inner seas, full of sweet water, endowed with the eight qualities.[88] Between the seventh range[89] and the Outer Mountain Ring is the outer Salty Ocean.

Meru, at the center of the world, rises above the water eighty thousand *yojanas* and is immersed in the water to a depth of eighty thousand *yojanas*, more than any other mountain.[90] With its head in the sky and its base at the depths of the ocean, it serves as the world's axis. Likewise, in the *sādhana*, yogis visualize themselves at the center of the mandala as the principal deity.

The four continents and the eight subcontinents rest on the outer ocean in the four main directions. Jambudvīpa, the location of the first creation story told above, is the major continent in the south. Mt. Meru, as noted earlier, is formed from the finest elements of four jewels: the eastern is made of silver, the southern of beryl, the western of (red) crystal,[91] and the northern of gold.[92] The color of each of these substances is reflected in the space that faces it. Here we learn why the color of our sky is blue. Because Jambudvīpa is south of Meru, we see the space above us in the color of the blue beryl. Moreover, Mt. Meru exhibits four of the five colors of the mandala—white, blue, red, and yellow.

Tsongkhapa describes the duration of the process of creation thus: "The formation of the world lasts for one medium eon, and the formation of its inhabitants—beginning from the formation of the first *dhyāna* up to the birth of one being in hell—lasts for nineteen medium eons."[93] Out of the twenty medium eons that encompass the creation of the world, nineteen are taken up by the creation of the beings who are to dwell in the world; its material aspects are formed in one medium eon. The emphasis, then, is on the living beings, and the physical world merely serves as their support. The physical world is created first and then it is slowly populated by beings who are born at different levels according to their karma, starting from the *dhyāna* level in the heavens above and gradually reaching down to the lowest hell.

The Beings of This World

According to the *Abhidharmakośa,* five main types of beings dwell in the world along a vertical axis;[94] the higher the karma, the higher a given being dwells. This contrasts with cyclic depictions, such as the wheel of life, although the wheel of life has a vertical dimension as well, with the gods situated above and the beings of hell below. The vertical and cyclic presentations reflect two different Buddhist worldviews. According to the former, the path to *nirvāṇa* ascends upward, while in the latter, existence is like a turning wheel and the location of the end of *saṃsāra* is unclear. In both depictions the karma that beings have accumulated in their previous lives determines on which level of the world they will be born. Hence, karma is a key factor not only in the evolution of the first beings in the world, but it also determines the next rebirth of all beings.

In the description of the *Abhidharmakośa,* the hells are located twenty thousand *yojanas* below the earth.[95] The principal dwelling of the hungry ghosts[96] is five hundred *yojanas* below Jambudvīpa, while the principal dwelling of the animals is the great ocean, though they also live on the land, in the fresh water, and in the air.[97] By locating the animals primarily in the ocean's water, the *Abhidharmakośa* maintains the vertical line, and by allowing animals to be found on the land and in the air, it embeds empirical knowledge. The humans live on the land, and the gods live in the sky. Other depictions of the world, such as the wheel of life, include also the *asuras*, or nongods, as a sixth category of beings somewhere between humans and gods.

Once again, the five or six realms of the world in their various physical locations are characterized by specific mental states. In each of these six states of existence, beings are afflicted by one of the dominant emotions that mar the *saṃsāric* world. The gods, being the highest, suffer from pride; the *asuras* are tormented by jealousy because a tree with wonderful fruits grows in their territory, but only the gods can enjoy the fruits. Human beings are afflicted by desire, animals by ignorance, and the hungry ghosts[98] by craving, because their tiny mouths cannot satiate their immense bellies. The inhabitants of hell, who are constantly tormented by heat, cold, and other agonies, experience hatred and anger. While these afflictive emotions are depicted as dominant in the six realms of existence, respectively, every being in the world suffers from every afflictive emotion.

Thus, the afflictive emotions play an important role not only in the creation of the world, as noted above, but also in its sustenance. In fact, if all the beings in one of the six realms were freed from their afflictive emotions, there would be no reason for that realm to exist. As such, the ambiguity between mental states and the realms of the world applies not only to the levels of the *dhyānas* in the higher Realm of Subtle Materiality but also to the lower levels in the Desire Realm. When a person in Jambudvīpa experiences hatred, in a sense, s/he experiences hell. One in Jambudvīpa who experiences a peaceful state of mind may have reached such a higher realm through meditation or by being born there.

Hence, not only are the distinctions between the worldly realms and the mental states blurred, but, in a sense, the spheres and realms described in Buddhist cosmologies portray all possible mental states and experiences. Likewise, the daily experiences of beings in the world are included in the cosmological map.

The Gods

In Buddhist thought, the term "god"[99] refers to many types of beings. All beings in the upper worlds, the Realm of Subtle Materiality, and the highest levels of the Desire Realm are called gods. However, these gods are part of the *saṃsāric* world and therefore are subject to karma. Awakened beings constitute another type of god, one whose status is fundamentally different from that of *saṃsāric* beings, since they are enlightened buddhas. To become an awakened being is the goal of the *sādhana* practice, as we will see in chapter 3.

The gods in the Desire Realm live above all other beings in this realm, spatially as well as in terms of their karma; thus, they live comfortably. However, due to their pleasureful existence, they do not develop an awareness of their *saṃsāric* condition or the possibility of attaining enlightenment. People who wish to be born as gods are classified by Tsongkhapa as being on the lowest of the three levels on the path to enlightenment.[100] For despite their relative karmic advantages, the gods in the Desire Realm are actually inferior to human beings because they are not motivated to free themselves from *saṃsāra.* Though their lifespan is immense, they are not eternal, and their happiness, too, is transient; eventually they will be reborn in one of the other *saṃsāric* realms.

To discourage people from wishing to be born as gods, in his *Letter to a Friend* Nāgārjuna describes how, while the lives of gods are enjoyable, they experience great suffering as their deaths approach. They know they are fated to be born in one of the lower realms when these five signs appear: their beautiful complexion fades; their thrones become uncomfortable; the garlands of flowers adorning them, which have previously remained fresh, wither; their elegant garments, which before were always fragrant, become malodorous; and sweat, which they never knew before, arises from their bodies.[101]

Human beings, by contrast, who experience both happiness and sorrow, do develop a proclivity to escape *saṃsāra* and attain awakening. In the following aphorism, we see how the Buddhist tradition encourages them to value their birth as humans.[102] A golden yoke floats on the surface of the vast ocean, carried here and there by the wind. A blind turtle lives in the depth of the ocean and surfaces to breath air once every hundred years. The chance the turtle will happen to put its head through the yoke is equivalent to the chance of being reborn as a human being.

The Brahmanic gods are integrated into the Buddhist cosmological map. Brahmā and his entourage, as already mentioned, abide in the first *dhyāna,* while the thirty-three gods,[103] including Śakra or Indra, the chief god, reside on the summit of Mt. Meru at the upper level of the Desire Realm. In this way, the Buddhist tradition accommodates the Brahmanic gods within the *saṃsāric* world—in contrast to the buddhas who freed themselves from *saṃsāra.*

Thus far, we have discussed the gods dwelling in the Desire Realm. Above the Desire Realm lie the Realm of Subtle Materiality and the Immaterial Realm. These two realms will be considered within the next section on the periodic destruction of the animate and inanimate world.

The Destruction of the World and Its Inhabitants

After the world has existed for twenty eons, the twenty-eon period of destruction begins. First, the world is emptied of all its inhabitants. When not a single being remains, the physical world is destroyed. The process of emptying the inhabitants begins from the lowest level and proceeds upward; in other words, the nethermost realm of the Hell of Ceaseless Torment[104] is emptied first. The moment no new beings are born in this hell marks the beginning of the destruction of the world.[105]

The section above titled "How the First People Appear in the World" describes the moment when the world is re-created and the inhabitants of the uppermost spheres—which were not destroyed—descend to the lower ones. Thus, the creation is, in a sense, a process of decline in the karmic status of the dwellers in the world, since those who had the good fortune to abide in the high Realm of Clear Light at the top of the second *dhyāna* become ordinary human beings only because the time for the world to be re-created arrives. Likewise, during the destruction of the world, when no new beings can be born in hell and those who dwell there must, after their deaths, be reborn elsewhere, they can only migrate to the higher realms of the world and thus improve their karmic status. Hence, during both the creation and the destruction of the world, beings are not reborn according to their individual karmas but according to the shared karma of all beings.

We find various attempts to account for the problematics in the operation of individual karma when the world is destroyed in various Indian Buddhist treatises. For example, in the chapter on meditative absorptions in his *Abhidharmakośabhāṣya*,[106] Vasubandhu explains that when the world is destroyed at the end of the eon, there is a unique force that enables beings in the lower spheres to be reborn in the higher spheres.[107] This force, called "the nature of things,"[108] arises due to a special increase of virtuous dharmas[109] during the periodic end of the world. According to the *Yogācārabhūmi*, a special karma operates during the creation and destruction of the world but not at any other time.[110] Likewise, in his *Path of Purification*,[111] Buddhaghosa explains that even beings who dwell in hell still have a latent good karma that enables them to be born in the highest spheres when the world is destroyed.

These treatises suggest unusual systems that are in effect only during this specific event of the re-creation of the world, calling them the "nature of things," "virtuous dharmas" or "latent good karma." The difficulty, however, is not resolved, because beings whose karma destined them to hell are still, at least theoretically, capable of being born in the *dhyānas* of the Realm of Subtle Materiality, where they will enjoy the good karma and high levels of meditation for a period of twenty eons—as long as the physical world is absent. It is perhaps for this reason that, in the context of cosmology in the same work, Vasubandhu presents a different position.[112] Taking into account that our world is not alone in the universe, Vasubandhu explains that when the hells in our world are emptied, beings whose karma still requires them to experience hell are sent to hells in other worlds' realms.

Tsongkhapa follows this interpretation: "Sentient beings in the Hell of Ceaseless Torment who have exhausted their karma and die are then born in fortunate realms, while those who have not exhausted their karma are born in the Hells of Ceaseless Torment that are found in other realms of the universe."[113] Since the worlds in the universe do not undergo creation and destruction simultaneously, beings who have not exhausted their karma in hell when this world comes to its periodic end are born into a corresponding sphere in another world. Only those who have exhausted their bad karma can be reborn in the higher spheres of this world.

Tsongkhapa continues: "In this way, the Hell of Ceaseless Torment of this world, characterized by the experience of suffering, is emptied of its beings. Then, through a similar method of emptying, the additional seven hot hells, the eight cold hells, the hungry ghosts who live in their principal habitats, and the animals who live in the ocean below are emptied in succession. The animals who live with the gods and humans are emptied together with the gods and humans."[114] In such manner the world is emptied from below upwards, and no hell-beings, hungry ghosts, or animals remain there. If their karma has been exhausted, the inhabitants of the three lower levels can be born in the higher realms of the Desire Realm, but not above it. Only people and gods can reach the *dhyānas* in the Realm of Subtle Materiality.

Tsongkhapa describes how human beings, who live in Jambudvīpa, are born in the first *dhyāna:* "How is the human world emptied? At that time the concentration of the first *dhyāna*[115]—attained through the nature of things—arises in the mental continuum of one person of Jambudvīpa. That person exclaims: 'Joy and bliss born of seclusion are bliss and peace.' When others hear this, the concentration of the first *dhyāna* arises in their mental continuum as well, and when they die, they are born as gods in the first *dhyāna.*"[116] Once again, a link is made between meditative states and cosmological spheres: if the first *dhyāna* arises in the mental continuum of the people in Jambudvīpa, they will actually be reborn there.

As stated earlier, the chapter on meditative absorptions in Vasubandhu's *Abhidharmakośabhāṣya*[117] explains that the nature of things arises in certain beings owing to virtuous dharmas that increase specifically at the end of the eon, regardless of their individual karma. But in the chapter on the cosmos, our present context, he glosses "through the nature of things" with "by himself, without a teacher."[118] This implies that the first person who ascends to the first *dhyāna* does it on his or her own without the guidance of others. Below we will examine accounts in which the Buddha describes how he found his own way to the first *dhyāna* without a teacher. According to Buddhist traditions, the Buddha attained enlightenment through his own spiritual powers and then led others to enlightenment. In the present narration on emptying the world of its inhabitants, the first person who attained the first *dhyāna* without a teacher announces his experience to the others.

When all human beings are born in the first *dhyāna*, Jambudvīpa is emptied of its people. Then: "Through a similar method of emptying, the concentration of the first *dhyāna* arises in the mental continuum of people of Pūrvavideha,[119] the continent in the east, and Godānīya,[120] the continent in the west. When they die, all of them are reborn in the first *dhyāna*. But the inhabitants of Uttarakuru,[121] the continent in the north, possess major obstructions to fruition,[122] and therefore are unable to free themselves of desire during that lifetime. When they die, they are born as gods in the Desire Realm."[123] Only people who dwell in the first three continents can be reborn in the first *dhyāna*. Those in Uttarakuru cannot rise to the Realm of Subtle Materiality because they cannot disengage from the pulls of desire and leave the Desire Realm. Instead, they are born as gods in the higher levels of the Desire Realm. In this way, the world is emptied of all human beings.

Then: "The concentration of the first *dhyāna* arises in the mental continuum of the gods of the six classes[124] of the Desire Realm. . . . When they die, they are reborn in the first *dhyāna*."[125] When all six types of gods are born in the first *dhyāna*, the Desire Realm is emptied. Then: "The concentration of the second *dhyāna*—attained through the nature of things—arises in the mental continuum of one god in the first *dhyāna*. He exclaims: 'Joy and bliss born from concentration are bliss and peace.' When others hear this, the concentration of the second *dhyāna* arises in their mental continuum as well, and when they die, they are born as gods in the second *dhyāna*. In this way, the sentient beings inhabiting the first *dhyāna* of existence are emptied."[126]

All beings dwelling in the *dhyāna*s of the Realm of Subtle Materiality are called gods. Therefore, our text says that the second *dhyāna* arises in the mental continuum of one god in the first *dhyāna*. While the human in Jambudvīpa above exclaims: "Joy and bliss born of seclusion are bliss and peace," the god in the first *dhyāna* calls out: "Joy born from concentration is bliss and peace." This is because those people in Jambudvīpa reached bliss and peace thanks to their separation from the Desire Realm, while the gods in the first *dhyāna* attained bliss and peace thanks to their concentration. Then: "In this way, not a single being remains in the various levels, from the hells to the first *dhyāna*. The process of emptying [the lower levels of] the world from its inhabitants lasts nineteen eons."[127]

Once there are no beings dwelling there, the physical world is destroyed.

Seven hot suns appear successively to dry out the plants, rivers, lakes, and the great ocean, and to burn the mountains and the four continents. The fire reaches up to the celestial palaces in the first *dhyāna,* and everything turns into a single nature of space.[128] The *Abhidharmakośa*[129] and *Yogācārabhūmi*[130] describe further destructions by water and wind, up to the third and the fourth *dhyānas* respectively, but Tsongkhapa does not discuss them here—possibly because these are not relevant to the practice of the *sādhana.* The destruction of the physical world lasts one eon; thus, after twenty eons in total, only the spheres of the second *dhyāna*—topped by the heaven of Clear Light—and the realms above it remain during the twenty eons during which the material world does not exist.

The Meditative States of the Realm of Subtle Materiality and the Immaterial Realm

Since the Immaterial (or Formless) Realm is devoid of matter or form, the *Abhidharmakośa* stresses that it is not a place and does not occupy a location.[131] Nonetheless, for the sake of convenience, it is depicted as if it were located above the Realm of Subtle Materiality. Just like the *dhyānas* in the Realm of Subtle Materiality, the names of the four levels in the Immaterial Realm denote meditative states. At the same time, the *Abhidharmakośa* asserts that the four levels of the Immaterial Realm as well are both realms of existence and meditative states.[132] Hence, the overlaying of cosmological and mental states is likewise preserved in this realm. Though these spheres cannot be located in space, beings can be born in the Immaterial Realm because unlike beings in the *dhyānas*, they possess only the four mental aggregates and no physical aggregates.[133]

The meditative states of the Realm of Subtle Materiality and the Immaterial Realm appear in certain episodes of the life of the Buddha told in Pāli and Sanskrit scriptures. Especially well known is the *Greater Discourse to Saccaka*[134] in the *Middle Length Discourses,* where the Buddha relates his own experience of going through each of the four *dhyānas* (Pāli, *jhāna*)[135] and finally reaching liberation.

> Then, quite secluded from sensual pleasures and unwholesome states, I entered upon and abided in the first *jhāna,* which is accompanied by applied and sustained thought, with the joy and bliss born of seclusion. But such pleasant feelings as arose in me did not settle in my mind and remain. With the stilling of applied and sustained thought, I entered upon

> and abided in the second *jhāna*. . . . With the fading away as well of joy . . . I entered upon and abided in the third *jhāna*. . . . With the abandoning of bliss and suffering . . . I entered upon and abided in the fourth *jhana*. . . . But such pleasant feelings as arose in me did not settle in my mind and remain.[136]

The experience described in the above passage is echoed in the description of emptying the world of human beings and gods in the Desire Realm, when a person in Jambudvīpa who has reached the first *dhyāna* exclaims, "Joy and bliss born of seclusion are bliss and peace," and later a god in the first *dhyāna* exclaims, "Joy born from concentration is bliss and peace." Hence, the separation of humans and gods from the Desire Realm and their ascent to the *dhyānas* in the Realm of Subtle Materiality bring them closer to enlightenment.

The Buddha describes here how the higher the *dhyāna* he achieved, the more traces of cognitive and emotional mental states were eliminated, until he reached a single-pointed concentration. Detaching himself from the Desire Realm and its sensual objects, the Buddha freed himself from the vast majority of afflictive emotions and reached the first *dhyāna*. When he eliminated the remaining cognitive faculties of investigation, he reached the second *dhyāna*. Then, when joy was forsaken, he reached the third *dhyāna;* with the relinquishing of both bliss and suffering, he reached the fourth *dhyāna*. In this way, the Buddha gradually reduced all the cognitive and emotional aspects of the mind and abided in a single-pointed concentration. With a pure concentrated mind, says the Buddha, he attained the three knowledges of his own past lives, the past lives of all beings, and the extinction of the taints. In so doing, he realized the Four Noble's Truths and was liberated.

Yet according to the *Discourse on the Simile of the Quail,*[137] after reaching the fourth *dhyāna,* the meditator continues to the four levels of the Immaterial Realm. The Buddha describes how after meditators abide in each of the *dhyānas*, it occurs to them: "That, I say, is not enough. Abandon it, I say; surmount it, I say. And what surmounts it?"[138] The higher *dhyāna* surmounts the one they abide in, so they proceed to the higher *dhyāna* only to find out that yet a higher *dhyāna* surmounts. When they abide in the fourth *dhyāna,* it occurs to them: "With the complete surmounting of perceptions of form, with the disappearance of perceptions of sensory impact, with nonattention to perceptions of diversity, aware that 'space is infinite,' a monk enters upon and abides in the base of infinite space. That surmounts it.[139] But that, too, I say, is not enough. Abandon it, I say; surmount it, I say. And what surmounts it?"[140]

In this way, the meditator reaches the first level of the Immaterial Realm and then ascends from infinite space to infinite consciousness, nothingness, and neither-perception-nor-nonperception (see table 2).[141] Finally: "By completely surmounting the base of neither-perception-nor-nonperception, a monk enters upon and abides in the cessation of perception and feeling. That surmounts it.[142] Thus, I speak of the abandoning even of the base of neither-perception-nor-nonperception. 'Do you see, Udāyin, any fetter, small or great, of whose abandoning I do not speak?' 'No, venerable sir.' That is what the Blessed One said. The venerable Udāyin was satisfied and delighted in the Blessed One's words."[143] The meditator transcends the fourth level of the Immaterial Realm to the cessation of perception and feeling,[144] reaching a peak state where no further attainment is possible. The fact that there is no cosmological equivalent to this level of meditative absorption may indicate that it is not part of the *saṃsāric* world. Nonetheless, there is no mention of *nirvāṇa* in this context.

The chapter on meditative absorptions in the *Abhidharmakośa*[145] describes a similar pattern of eight meditative levels, the four *dhyānas* successively leading to the four absorptions of the Immaterial Realm. Like the *Discourse on the Simile of the Quail,* the *Abhidharmakośa* specifically states that infinite space, the lower level in the Immaterial Realm, arises from the fourth *dhyāna,* the highest level in the Realm of Subtle Materiality.[146]

Yet the method described in the *Simile of the Quail* and the *Abhidharmakośa* is fundamentally different from that in the *Greater Discourse to Saccaka.* In the latter, the meditation concludes with the three knowledges, the realization of the Four Noble's Truths, and liberation from the cycle of rebirths, while in the *Simile of the Quail* and the *Abhidharmakośa,* the meditator's mind is gradually emptied of all cognitive and emotional states without gaining any new insight. In all three sources, the mental faculties are gradually reduced, but only in the *Greater Discourse to Saccaka* does the decrease in mental events make space for a new Buddhist realization. Yet only the meditation that combines the four *dhyānas* with the four absorptions of the Immaterial Realm and culminates in the state of neither-perception-nor-nonperception, as described in the *Simile of the Quail* and the *Abhidharmakośa,* corresponds to the cosmological map. This tension between meditative methods and cosmological maps is one among the various reasons for further developments of meditations and cosmologies.

New Meditations and New Cosmological Maps

We may never know whether the cosmological map preceded the meditations or the other way around. It is clear, however, that over time both the meditations and the cosmologies evolved and took new forms. Even so, the coupling of meditations with cosmology and cosmogony remained central in Buddhist thought.[147]

The meditative states of nothingness and neither-perception-nor-nonperception, as well as the state of cessation of perception and feeling, did not become synonymous with *nirvāṇa* or enlightenment. While the word "*nirvāṇa*" does mean "blowing out" or "extinction," the notion of complete cessation (*nirodha*) is difficult to reconcile in Buddhism. Annihilationism is one of the wrong views rejected in the *Brahmajāla Sutta.*[148] Moreover, meditation on eliminating all standpoints and stilling all formations threatens the meditators with their own annihilation.[149]

In particular, the meditations on the two highest levels in the Immaterial Realm—the absorptions on nothingness and neither-perception-nor-nonperception—lost their status as high attainments even before the crystallization of the *Nikāya Suttas*. These two meditations are found in early layers of these *Suttas*[150] but went out of favor and were attributed to the Buddha's early teachers.[151] Several Buddhist scriptures describe them as non-Buddhist practices or as practices that challenge Buddhist methods.[152] Nevertheless, various *Suttas* incorporated these two meditations within the stages of the path to awakening, mostly as lesser methods of subordinate status, at times as meditations that involve mindfulness in one way or another[153] or else as meditations meant only for the attainment of worldly goals.

Indeed, the Immaterial Realm does not play a role in the creation and destruction of the world. Hence, it is unsurprising that Tsongkhapa does not mention the meditative absorptions of the Immaterial Realm in *Bee's Hope.* But Tsongkhapa did devote a short work to the four *dhyānas* and the four absorptions of the Immaterial Realm.[154] The topic of the *dhyānas* and absorptions is still studied nowadays in the Geluk monastic system as part of the subject matter concerned with the path to awakening,[155] even though these meditations are not regarded as *the* Buddhist path. As Leah Zahler has noted: "The relationship between the actual meditative absorptions and the corresponding levels of rebirth is perhaps the most important reason for the continued study of the system in Buddhist cultures."[156] Indeed, in *Bee's Hope* the Immaterial Realm appears only in relation to levels of rebirth.[157] It is important to bear in mind, however, that while Tibetans hardly meditate on the four absorptions of the Immaterial Realm or even on the four *dhyānas*, "the map of cyclic existence continues to provide a mental cosmology."[158]

The path to enlightenment followed in most Buddhist traditions of the Mahāyāna (the Great Vehicle) does not include the notion that on their way to enlightenment meditators must ascend through the eight meditative-cosmological states, whereby their attachment to the *saṃsāric* world gradually diminishes while their experiences become subtler and approach cessation. Likewise, the view of a linear path leading directly up toward a state beyond all cognition and emotion has not been accepted. This applies not only to the meditative absorptions of the Immaterial Realm but also to the *dhyāna* levels of the Realm of Subtle Materiality. Buddhist traditions developed numerous methods of meditation, including that of the *Guhyasamāja Sādhana,* our topic below. Progressive practices in stages, such as the ten *bodhisattva* levels[159] or the five paths[160] are common, but the path to awakening is not necessarily a vertical one.

When the vertical map of meditative states, in which cognition and emotion are reduced, is no longer the principal Buddhist meditative method, the cosmology must be modified. This takes place especially within the Mahāyāna, which places an emphasis on spatial cosmologies[161] in which multiple buddhas in numerous worlds in the universe open new paths to enlightenment. The Vajrayāna (or the Vajra Vehicle) will further develop this soteriology by basing some of its practices on the circular array of the mandala. We will turn first to the move from vertical depictions of the cosmos to other spatial forms in the Great Vehicle.

Spatial Cosmologies

Earlier Buddhist scriptures refer to multiple buddhas in a linear manner, wherein one appears after the other; as, for example, the list of the seven buddhas culminating with Śākyamuni.[162] The Great Vehicle moves into a spatial depiction of buddhas who can appear concurrently, filling the cosmos in great numbers. We have already encountered a universe of multiple worlds, but, thus far, we have not encountered depictions of buddhas residing in a world other than our own.

Such buddhas appeared in Buddhist cosmologies of the Great Vehicle, which introduces several new worldviews. The ideal is not a buddha who has achieved *nirvāṇa* and is beyond the reach of *saṃsāric* beings but rather multiple enlightened buddhas who are able to act in the present for the sake of all sentient beings and instruct them on how to free themselves from *saṃsāra.*[163] However because of the objection to the idea of contemporaries buddhas found in early *Suttas,*[164] the creators of new Buddhist cosmologies of the Great Vehicle could not situate these completely enlightened buddhas in our world.

They were placed, therefore, in "buddha-fields"[165] or "pure lands" throughout the universe.[166]

Buddha-Fields

Buddha-fields are important to our discussion because they are a significant antecedent for the mandala. According to Mahāyāna Sūtras, such as the *Land of Bliss*,[167] these are separate worlds located in all directions of the universe, created and presided over by a buddha who teaches the Dharma and is immediately accessible not only to the inhabitants of his own world but also to the inhabitants of worlds like ours.[168] Similar to the higher heavens in the vertical cosmology, buddha-fields can be reached either through death and rebirth or through meditation, when certain conditions are met. In this way, the difference between meditation and rebirth remains blurred.

According to earlier Buddhist scriptures, the buddhas in our world are bound by a definite lifespan.[169] When they reach the end of their predetermined lifespans, they attain *parinirvāṇa* and become unapproachable. In contrast, the Mahāyāna buddhas are almost eternal.[170] These accessible buddhas, who have not passed into complete *nirvāṇa,* conform to the new notion of the buddha. The buddha-fields they create are called "fields" in the sense of a sphere of action or influence. They are also referred to as "pure lands," since their creation is a process of purification or transformation.

The notion of buddha-fields does have roots in earlier ideas about Maitreya, the future Buddha, and therefore it is not an entirely new innovation. When buddhas appear only in a linear succession, the possibility of meeting a buddha and hearing him teaching the Dharma is only in the future; when following the decline of the teachings of Śākyamuni, Maitreya will be born in this world. Hence, the wish to be born in the presence of Maitreya in our world gained popularity. Yet another way to meet Maitreya is to reach Tuṣita[171] or the Joyful Realm, the heaven where Maitreya dwells at present. This delightful heaven is the fourth godly realm among the six heavens of the Desire Realm,[172] which can be reached either through death and rebirth or through meditation. As a palace of a buddha, Tuṣita is endowed with supreme qualities.[173]

A number of similarities exist between buddha-fields and Tuṣita. In each resides a buddha who is teaching the Dharma continuously to his disciples. The disciples, in turn, spend their current prolonged lives in the immediate presence of a buddha, dedicating themselves to the study and practice of Buddhism under the guidance of that buddha. The best-known buddha-field is Sukhāvatī,[174] the Land of Bliss, created by the Buddha Amitābha in the western direction.[175] No doubt the magnificent displays (*vyūha*) and splendors of Buddha Amitābha's pure field described in the *Land of Bliss*, or in Sanskrit, *Sukhāvatīvyūha Sūtras*, and similar scriptures inspired the authors of tantric *sādhanas* and served as models for the visualized mandala.

The buddha-fields were created by the buddhas while they were still *bodhisattvas* on their way to awakening. These buddhas-to-be took vows to lead all sentient beings to enlightenment by creating purified "fields" where conditions facilitate the attainment of buddhahood. The spiritual quests of *bodhisattvas* such as these lie at the foundation of tantric visualizations.

Additional Buddhist Antecedents of Tantric Visualizations

Charles Orzech has recently discussed contemplations of the marks of a buddha as an example for a visionary practice in which practitioners see their own bodies bearing the marks of a buddha as an antecedent for meditations advocated in tantric texts.[176] Another clear antecedent of tantric visualization is the practice of *buddhānusmṛti*, recollecting or calling to mind a buddha. Modern scholars have pointed to the striking resemblance between recollections of buddhas or deities and tantric *sādhanas*.[177] But we should note the important distinctions between recollections of the buddha and deity yoga that were noted by Tsongkhapa.[178] Yogis do not simply visualize the deities residing in the mandala with their forms, colors, faces, and hands, but they must develop a total identification with these buddhas or maintain uncontrived divine pride[179] in being that buddha. While earlier scriptures are careful to avoid implying the complete transformation of a yogi into a buddha, tantric visualization readily takes this step.

Recollection regarding the body[180] is another antecedent of the *sādhana*. In this practice, meditators develop awareness of the body as a product of prior causes and conditions, as being empty of a self, impermanent, and so forth. In the Mahāyāna version of this meditation,[181] *bodhisattvas* vow to attain the imperishable and perfect body of the *tathāgata*, the *dharmakāya* or *vajrakāya*. They promise to turn their bodies made of the four physical elements into an agent that works for the sake of all sentient beings. When they realize the true nature of their bodies without falling into the two extremes, their bodies become free of afflictive emotions, pure and adorned with the buddha marks. Once more, through the recollection of the body, these meditators attain a stage just short of complete awakening, while the tantric practice will carry yogis to their actual enlightenment.

The practice of *buddhānusmṛti* is taken further in the *Samādhi of Direct Encounter with the Buddhas of the Present*, an early scripture translated into Chinese for the first time in 179 CE.[182] Paul Harrison points to certain elements in this *samādhi* that foreshadow the practice of deity yoga.[183] Through the power of *samādhi*, *bodhisattvas* directly encounter buddhas in other world systems, worship them, and hear the Dharma expounded.[184] Moreover, as Harrison has pointed out, this *sūtra* instructs the *bodhisattvas* to practice subjective identification with these buddhas: "I too shall in the same way become fully awakened to supreme and perfect awakening. And once I am fully awakened, I shall expound the Dharma to the four assemblies and the world with its *devas*!—thus should they train themselves."[185]

It is interesting to learn about Tsongkhapa's position regarding this *samādhi* from the viewpoint of the completion stage. According to the *Samādhi of Direct Encounter with the Buddhas of the Present*, the *bodhisattvas* actually see the buddhas in their buddha-fields and hear the Dharma while remaining in our world and without possessing any extraordinary faculties. In an explicit reference to the *Samādhi of Direct Encounter*, Tsongkhapa maintains that all visual experiences of pure fields, heavenly realms, gods, and other phenomena that arise during the waking state cannot be genuine but are mere appearances or illusions that resemble the real thing.[186] In the context of the completion stage, the subtle body alone, with its winds and channels, can bring true results. As is often the case, later practices deprive earlier ones of their powers, situating themselves at the top in terms of their ability to achieve the desired goals.

A famous prototype of the mandala is the multistoried palace[187] of Vairocana that is made to appear to Sudhana by the Bodhisattva Maitreya in the *Gaṇḍavyūha Sūtra*.[188] This palace is filled with reflections of hundreds of thousands of other similar but distinct multistoried palaces. Likewise in every single pore of the body of the Bodhisattva Samantabhadra, Sudhana saw quadrillions of buddha-fields entirely filled with buddhas.[189] Maitreya creates the palace in order to teach Sudhana about emptiness and illusion, while in practicing the *sādhana*, yogis themselves create the mandala palace for the sake of their own realization.

Western scholars have investigated forerunners of tantra in the *Gaṇḍavyūha Sūtra*, calling attention to striking parallels between the visionary episodes of the *Gaṇḍavyūha* and tantric visualization.[190] We should note that Tibetan scholars also recognized these similarities and incorporated the imagery of

Vairocana palace and the untold number of buddha-fields in each of the pores in Samantabhadra's body in their treatises on *sādhanas*. For example, the *Guhyasamāja Sādhanas* practiced by members of the Sakyapa,[191] Gelukpa,[192] and Jonangpa[193] schools depict a mandala of countless world realms in the three times and ten directions, reaching the limit of the space realm, arrayed like the clouds over the ocean, immeasurable like the reach of the sky. Each of these world realms dwells within the other without any hindrance. As we can see, Tibetan scholars were acutely aware of the affinity between the visions portrayed in Mahāyāna Sūtras, such as the *Gaṇḍavyūha* or the *Daśabhūmika*,[194] and tantric visualizations.

Circular Representations and Mandalas

A well-known circular representation of the world and its inhabitants is the wheel of life, which portrays the realms of sentient beings as a *saṃsāric* circle that revolves forever. Unlike the vertical depiction of the five realms in the *Abhidharmakośa*, the motion here is circular. The mandala is another type of circular representation in which the four main directions are essential.

According to the ninth-century *Commentary*[195] on a Tibetan-Sanskrit glossary,[196] the term "maṇḍala" consists of two parts. "Maṇḍa" means "heart/essence," "sphere/realm," or "center,"[197] and "la" means "taking" or "holding."[198] This is not necessarily a grammatical explanation of the word "mandala" but rather an attempt to convey its meaning. It stresses the center, core, or kernel of the mandala. The Tibetan translation of mandala is "*kingkhor*";[199] the first syllable means "center" and the second "circle" or "surrounding." For the Indian scholar Buddhaguhya, who interprets this word in his treatise on the mandala, the first part denotes the principal deity of the mandala at its center and the second part denotes the surrounding deities who emanate from the principal deity in all directions.[200]

Regarding the visualization of the mandala, in *Bee's Hope* Tsongkhapa explains: "Imagine all the deities as parts of the principal deity, and behold all the deities, the principal and surrounding deities, as indivisible bliss and emptiness."[201] Hence, the creation of the mandala is a spatial process from the center outward, while all its parts in the different directions are still contained within the deity at the center—although they appear as its emanations. We will come back to the visualization of the mandala in chapter 4.

To Conclude

According to the Mahāyāna (the Great Vehicle), multiple buddhas can appear at the same time in different buddha-fields of the cosmos, while according to the Vajra Vehicle a great number of buddhas can appear simultaneously in our world as well. The highest goal of the tantric practice is to become a buddha in the present life in this very world. Tantric yogis create their buddha-fields as mandalas with a design no doubt inspired by the descriptions of buddha-fields found in Mahāyāna Sūtras. In meditating on the *sādhana,* yogis are like *bodhisattvas* who vow to create their buddha-fields in which they will be enlightened for the sake of guiding others to enlightenment.

Taken together, the antecedents of tantric visualization as well as the antecedents of the mandala indicate that the *sādhana* is, at least as far as these elements are concerned, deeply rooted in the Buddhist tradition and a product of its own internal dynamics.

As noted in the section "Spatial Cosmologies," above, the Great Vehicle introduced more than a single worldview. According to one version, the goal of *bodhisattvas* is not a *nirvāṇa* beyond *saṃsāra,* but an "unlocated" *nirvāṇa,*[202] found neither in *saṃsāra* nor in *nirvāṇa.* The fruit of the *bodhisattva* path is not a liberation from *saṃsāra* by entering *nirvāṇa* but a state of not turning away from either *saṃsāra* or *nirvāṇa.*[203] In other words, *bodhisattvas* will be free of both *saṃsāra* and *nirvāṇa*[204] but will not leave *saṃsāra* behind. This goal does not correspond to any of the known cosmologies, since awakening will not entail a shift into another realm but will happen in this very world. As we shall see, the foremost tantric yogi who will attain enlightenment in a single lifetime does so in the Desire Realm, the lowest of the three worlds; moreover, only in Jambudvīpa, where we people live.[205]

2

The Person

Death, the Intermediate State, and Rebirth

Death and Meditations on Death

Meditations on death are meant not for the dead, of course, but for the living. They provide means to cope not only with death and the fear of death but also with the hardships of life. Indian and Tibetan Buddhism offers various descriptions of the death process and quite a few kinds of meditations on death. In the West there are innumerable accounts of people who have undergone a so-called near-death experience and have come back to life. Are the various descriptions culture-dependent, shaped by specific worldview, or are there universal aspects to death common to every human culture? Certainly, Buddhist meditations on death, the intermediate state, and rebirth offer some unique perspectives.

According to an early Buddhist theory, meditation on death is a powerful means for the realization of the three distinguishing marks of *saṃsāric* existence: impermanence, selflessness, and unsatisfaction.[1] *Saṃsāra* is described as an endless series of repeated deaths, while enlightenment brings release from the cycle and from subordination to karma. Death powerfully illustrates the impermanence of life and the limits of the self. A mindfulness meditation on impermanence and death reduces clinging to *saṃsāra* and encourages the meditator to engage in practices that will lead to enlightenment. Hence, in Tibet meditation on death became part of the practice that focuses on the stages of enlightenment.

Another well-known meditation on death is the meditation on the "foul,"[2] intended to counter the afflictive emotion of desire. Meditators on the foul develop mindfulness of more than thirty repulsive aspects of the body, such as the intestines, feces, fat, and mucus, or the stages of disintegration of corpses in charnel grounds. The meditation on decaying corpses provides insight into the body as transient and reinforces the recognition that there is no escape from such a fate. This meditation facilitates the development of a detached attitude to the body and an understanding of how the body serves as a source of the illusion of the notions of "self," "I," and "mine."

Since Buddha Śākyamuni attained final *nirvāṇa* at the moment of his death, Buddhism greatly emphasizes the soteriological importance of this moment. Certain practices designed to emulate the Buddha's life story focus on this very moment, which is seen as critical to achieving fundamental change. The moment of death is identified as a liminal step, or as a junction in which one path leads to a cycle of death and rebirth and the other allows change and transformation. Since this moment is not ruled by ordinary *saṃsāric* conditions, it provides the possibility for attaining enlightenment, and practitioners are encouraged to use this opportunity to transcend themselves.

However, it is assumed that ordinary people will undergo death while being unaware of their whereabouts and the soteriological opportunity at hand. Hence, they will likely find themselves reborn in one of the *saṃsāric* worlds. One purpose of practices that prepare for the moment of death is to maintain awareness throughout death and be able to direct the course of events.

Death according to Vajrayāna

The Vajrayāna developed detailed theories—based on yogic practices of the subtle body—to explain the ways in which the moment of death can facilitate the attainment of enlightenment. At the point of death, the coarse elements of the body dissolve, thereby enhancing the subtle elements that remain. The subtle mind that is capable of identifying the clear light[3] (here differentiated from the Realm of Clear Light described in chapter 1, though this resemblance is not arbitrary) and experiencing awakening is thought to unfold at the moment of death. Clear light appears in a number of crucial moments, including death, meditation, and deep sleep, yet the clear lights seen at these moments are fundamentally different from the clear light of enlightenment. If the clear light of death were identical to the clear light of enlightenment, all sentient beings would be awakened each time they die. Still, since these clear lights exemplify or illustrate the actual clear light, they can assist the yogi who is prepared for death in realizing the clear light of enlightenment.

As stated, the clear light of death appears naturally on its own, but ordinary people are unconscious during death and do not recognize it. Only highly qualified yogi can realize the clear light of enlightenment during that moment. Hence, the purpose of Vajrayāna meditations on death is to develop awareness during death itself and to eventually transform the clear light of death into awakening. The practice begins with becoming familiar with each stage in the death process and by simulating each stage in order to become intimate with it.[4]

The twenty-five coarse elements that dissolve at death are the five aggregates,[5] the four physical elements,[6] the six sense faculties,[7] the five inner objects of the senses,[8] and the five wisdoms at the ground time.[9] The term "ground time" refers to the beginning stage on the path to enlightenment, prior to any significant transformation; thus, these are the five ordinary wisdoms used in daily life. Hence, during the process of death, the aggregates and the senses that compose the self dissolve, as does the mental system that shapes our everyday view of the world. The twenty-five coarse elements dissolve in eight stages that resemble, to some extent, the cosmological map and the meditations of the four *dhyānas* and the four absorptions of the Immaterial Realm.[10]

The First Four Cycles of Dissolution

Tsongkhapa's *Fulfilling the Bee's Hope* describes the first stage of the dissolution: "When the people of the first eon in Jambudvīpa—who gradually become ordinary and come to be endowed with the six constituents—die: the form aggregate, the mirror-like wisdom at the ground time, the earth element, the eye faculty, and the forms within their continuums dissolve simultaneously."[11] In this passage Tsongkhapa links the death of human beings to the cosmogonic events associated with the first eon in Jambudvīpa. After the beings who descend from the higher realm become ordinary human beings,[12] their deaths are no different than those of other human beings in Jambudvīpa. By referring to them, however, Tsongkhapa reminds us of the cosmological connection. Only human beings in Jambudvīpa undergo these stages of dissolution upon death. No other beings in the six realms of the world, from the gods to the inhabitants of hell, do so. This is because human beings alone are "endowed with the six constituents," as Tsongkhapa points out.

The six constituents have been explained in various ways. Some Tibetan scholars state that they refer to the subtle body that only human beings possess; as such, they are seen as an important tantric means for awakening that other beings do not possess. Thus, according to Yangchen Gawé Lodrö (1740–1827),[13] the six constituents are earth, water, fire, air-wind, channels,[14] and drops.[15] The first four are the physical elements that build the coarse body. Earth refers to the hard elements, such as bones, nails, and hair; water to fluids in the body, such as blood and urine; fire to its warmth; and air-wind to breathing and moving.

The last three constituents, wind, channels, and drops, make up the subtle body (air-wind partakes in both the coarse and subtle bodies). The subtle winds, which serve as mounts for the subtle minds, move through the 72,000 channels. The white drop is located at the crown above and the red drop at the secret place below. During death, all the winds dissolve into the right and left channels and then into the central channel, while the two drops meet in the indestructible drop in the nave of the central channel at the heart.[16] Finally, only the very subtle life-sustaining wind[17] remains in the heart and serves as the mount of the very subtle mind, as described below.

Yangchen Gawé Lodrö[18] mentions another explanation for the six constituents that does not refer to the subtle body: the bones, marrow, and semen obtained from the father; and the skin, flesh, and blood obtained from the mother.[19]

Tsongkhapa follows the *Concise Sādhana*[20] in enumerating the five coarse elements that dissolve in each of the first four stages of death:

> (1) The form aggregate, the mirror-like wisdom at the ground time, the earth element, the eye faculty, and the forms within their continuums dissolve simultaneously.[21]
> (2) Following this, the aggregate of feeling, the wisdom of equanimity at the ground time, the water element, the ear faculty, and the sound within their continuums likewise dissolve simultaneously into clear light.[22]
> (3) Then the aggregate of perception, the wisdom of discernment at the ground time, the fire element, the nose faculty, and the scent within their continuums dissolve simultaneously.[23]
> (4) Next the aggregate of conditioning, the wisdom of purposive acts at the ground time, the air-wind element, the tongue faculty, the taste within their continuums, and tangible objects dissolve simultaneously.[24]

The coarser components of the body dissolve in stages, allowing the subtle body and mind to unfold, thus paving the way to the realization of the clear light of death. First the solid elements of the body dissolve (the form aggregate together with the earth element); this is followed by the fluidity, warmth, and motility of the body. The mental aggregates of feeling, perception, and conditioning dissolve together with the sense faculties of the eye, ear, nose, and tongue.

This process causes the ordinary mental system—which informs human beings about their world and exhorts them to act in response—to cease to exist. The ordinary mental system is what brings about attachment and clinging, and it is therefore the cause of suffering in *saṃsāra*. In other words, the network that prevents people from seeing things as they really are discontinues at death. Death, then, is a rare opportunity to rid oneself of the filters blocking our experience and to see things differently. The goal is not to sink into a state of unconsciousness but to maintain awareness so that one may benefit from this extraordinary moment. It is for this reason that practices simulating death are so important.

Together with the aggregates, the physical elements, and the sense faculties, the inner objects of the senses and the wisdoms at the ground time dissolve. What are the inner objects of the senses? Human beings cannot dissolve the external objects of the senses that have been created by the shared karma of all beings, but only the inner, subjective objects that are included within their mental continuums. Smells and tastes are always subjective; inner sounds include the humming sound inside the ear and inner forms are related to the colors and shapes of the body within.

The four wisdoms at the ground time are the mirror-like wisdom, the wisdom of equanimity, the wisdom of discernment, and the wisdom of purposive acts.[25] These are basic ordinary cognitive skills that are the *saṃsāric* counterparts to the five wisdoms of enlightenment. In fact, as we shall see, all the coarse elements that dissolve at death have equivalent enlightened aspects, but only the wisdoms share their names with elements of the mandala. To distinguish between the ordinary and the enlightened wisdoms, the dissolving wisdoms are called wisdoms at the ground time.

Tsongkhapa explains what the four wisdoms at the ground time are: The mirror-like wisdom is the instantaneous perception of entire objects, seen just as reflections appear in a mirror; it dissolves together with the eye faculty. The wisdom of equanimity is the ability to recognize categories and create generalization—for example, the understanding that beings with no legs, with two legs, and with many legs are of the same type. The wisdom of discernment is the opposite—it analyzes individual phenomena as parts of the whole. The wisdom of purposive acts brings to completion the activities of the body, speech, and mind for the sake of oneself and others.[26]

Next in *Bee's Hope*, Tsongkhapa describes the two types of signs, external and internal, that accompany these dissolutions.[27] For example, regarding the external signs during the first cycle of dissolution:

> The signs of the dissolution of the form aggregate are that the limbs of the body become thinner, the body becomes attenuated, loses its strength, and its capacity deteriorates. When the mirror-like wisdom at the ground time

> dissolves, sight becomes blurred and cloudy. The signs of the dissolution of the earth element are that the body becomes thin and loose. The signs of the dissolution of the eye faculty are that the dying persons are no longer able to open and close their eyes. The signs of the dissolution of the forms within their continuums are that the body's coloring fades.[28]

For the external signs that accompany the following cycles of dissolution, the reader may refer to the translation that follows these explicative chapters.

Next, Tsongkhapa describes the four inner signs: appearances that are mirage-like, smoke-like, firefly-like, and light like that of a butter lamp (the Tibetan equivalent of an oil lamp).[29] When ordinary visual perceptions crumble in the first cycle of dissolution, the phenomenal world appears differently. Instead of the ordinary sights, the mind perceives various apparitions and mirages that reflect other forms of awareness. In the second cycle, smoke appears, the classical sign for fire in Buddhist discourses on logic. Fire is not there yet, but the smoke is a sign that it will appear. In the third cycle, faint flickering light like that of fireflies appears. These are only gleams of light, but they signal a greater luminosity to come. Indeed, in the fourth cycle a light like that of a butter lamp appears. This is still a weak light, not like the sun, but the direction is clear. These signs progress toward the clear light of death. As long as most of the coarse elements of the aggregates, senses, and so forth have not dissolved, the glow is faint, but it gradually increases.

The Dissolutions of Consciousness

The significant leap occurs in the transition to the fifth cycle, when only subtle elements remain, such as the aggregate of consciousness. This shift is akin to the ascent from meditation on the Realm of Subtle Materiality to meditation on the Immaterial Realm. Recall how in the ascent from the Desire Realm to the first *dhyāna* in the Realm of Subtle Materiality (see "The Meditative States of the Realm of Subtle Materiality and the Immaterial Realm" in chapter 1), the Buddha overcame afflicted emotions, then he eliminated the cognitive faculties of investigation in the second *dhyāna,* the emotion of joy in the third *dhyāna,* and both bliss and suffering in the fourth *dhyāna;* thereby the Buddha attained a single-point concentration. Then, upon leaving the Realm of Subtle Materiality, the meditator reaches the level of infinite space (the first absorption in the Immaterial Realm) and then ascends to infinite consciousness, nothingness, and neither-perception-nor-nonperception.

Following the fourth dissolution at death, only the aggregate of consciousness remains. We may deduce that along with this aggregate of consciousness dissolve the space element, the mental faculty, and the wisdom of the *dharmadhātu* at the ground time. However, these are not mentioned in our text.[30] In *Bee's Hope*[31] Tsongkhapa describes the dissolution of the consciousness in four stages.[32] Before we consider this description, let us look at an important scriptural authority for these dissolutions in one of the explanatory tantras of the *Guhyasamāja Tantra*, the *Compendium of Vajra Wisdom Tantra:*

> The Blessed One said: The consciousnesses[33] that arise from clear light are mind, mentation, and consciousness.[34] These are the root of all phenomena, afflicted and purified, out of which conceptual duality of self and other arises. Consciousness is mounted on air-wind; from air-wind, fire arises; from fire, water; and from water, earth. From these arise the five aggregates, the five sense bases, and the five sense objects.[35] Each one of these consists of a wind and consciousness merged. From these [aggregates, sense bases, and sense objects] arise the experience of the clear manifestation of the intrinsic natures and the appearances[36] of the three consciousnesses.[37]

This tantra here describes how all phenomena arise from clear light in eight stages. Clear light gives rise to three types of awareness: mind, mentation, and consciousness, which are the source of all *saṃsāric* mental states. Consciousness rides on air-wind, which gives rise to the three other physical elements, out of which all psychophysical constituents of the body and mind are formed.

Likewise, in his *Stages of Self-Blessing*, the Indian Vajrayāna scholar Āryadeva explains the cause for the arising and cessation of sentient beings in eight stages:

> This is how sentient beings arise: From clear light arises the great empty; from the great empty, method; from method, wisdom; and from wisdom, air-wind. From air-wind arises fire; from fire, water; and from water, earth.
>
> That is how the triple world[38] ceases to be: The earth element dissolves into water; the water dissolves into fire; the fire dissolves into the subtle element; the wind dissolves into the mind;[39] the mind dissolves into mental events;[40] the mental events dissolve into ignorance;[41] and ignorance dissolves into clear light.[42]

On the whole, the process described in these two texts is similar, though the names for the three types of mind that arise from or dissolve into clear light are different. In his *Compendium of Practices*, Āryadeva interprets the multitude of terms in the following way:[43] "Mind, mentation, and consciousness" are the terms shared with the Great Vehicle, while in the Vajra Vehicle these are called "[white] appearance," "enhanced appearance," and "approaching attainment,"[44] or "the empty, the very empty, and the greatly empty states,"[45] or "mind, mental events, and ignorance."[46]

Āryadeva, then, explains the characteristics of the three kinds of mind that the Vajra Vehicle calls white appearance, enhanced appearance, and approaching attainment.[47] The nature of these three states is immaterial, free of body or speech. The nature of white appearance is clear, like the clear autumn sky suffused by the appearance of stainless moonbeams. Enhanced appearance is devoid of subject-object duality; its nature is extremely clear and pure, like the clear autumn sky suffused with sunbeams. Approaching attainment has characteristics of space, and its form is that of a non-thing, like the sky suffused with the darkness of the beginning of night; it is described as a great empty state that has the features of ignorance.

It might seem strange that the term "ignorance" is used to describe a state that, according to Āryadeva, occurs just before the final dissolution into clear light—on the verge of enlightenment. The *Compendium of Vajra Wisdom Tantra*[48] explains this state as a dark appearance that arises from the clear light and glosses it with the mind of approaching attainment.[49] This will be clarified below.

On the basis of these authorities, in *Bee's Hope* Tsongkhapa describes the three minds that dissolve into clear light:

> When the air-wind has dissolved into "[white] appearance," during [white] appearance itself, a radiant white appearance arises, like a clear autumn sky suffused by moonlight Then, once [white] appearance has dissolved into "enhanced appearance," during enhanced appearance itself, a radiant red appearance arises, like the clear autumn sky suffused with sunlight. Once enhanced appearance dissolves into "approaching attainment," during the approaching attainment itself, a radiant black appearance arises, like the clear autumn sky suffused with the dense darkness of the beginning of night. When approaching attainment has dissolved into clear light, during the "clear light" itself, there arises an appearance resembling the sky's own color—a clear autumn sky devoid of the three tainting conditions. This is the experience of the clear light of death.[50]

Tsongkhapa explains the meaning of the term "the former dissolving into the latter," as in the phrases "earth dissolving into water" or "one mind dissolving into another": when the capability of the former subsides and the capability of the latter becomes more apparent, it seems as if the former capability transfers into the latter.[51] Therefore, this process is called "dissolution." Importantly, however, this does not imply that one element in fact dissolves into another.

Consciousness now dissolves into the clear light of death in four stages. When the air-wind, the lightest physical element that still remains, dissolves together with its accompanying coarse elements, most mental activities inherent in the conceptual mind dissolve as well. This pacifies the majority of mental proliferations. Hence, there is a dramatic change in the level of the illumination experienced by the dying person—a light like that of a butter lamp turns into white appearance. This appearance is white since it resembles clear autumn sky illuminated by the white moonlight. Apart from the moonlight, nothing interrupts the perfect clarity of the sky.

In the second cycle of the dissolution of consciousness, subtle elements dissolve as well: namely, the consciousness is refined and freed of subtle conceptualization. Now dawns a radiant red appearance or experience called "enhanced appearance," since it is more intense that the previous one. Only the red sunlight breaches the total clarity of the sky.

In the third cycle, the clear light is nearly reached; hence, this stage is called "approaching attainment." It resembles the darkness of the clear autumn sky on a moonless night because no appearance arises in the mind. Toward the end of the third cycle, the awareness of darkness also subsides, and the dying person sinks into a state of unconsciousness. This is the state called "ignorance."

In the fourth cycle, the dying person awakens to a state of lucid clarity like that of the autumn sky, untainted by any dualistic appearances. In this period the moonlight has disappeared, while the sunlight has not yet appeared, and the sky's own color has not arisen. At this moment, the clear sky is free of the white, red, and black illuminations that impaired its perfection. This totally homogeneous and stainless awareness, which is very subtle, is the clear light of death. If the clear light of death is mixed with the actual clear light, the mind can attain enlightenment. Most people, however, are unaware of this state and continue on their *saṃsāric* journey. Therefore, the goal of the practice is to develop an awareness of the death process in order to reach realization of the clear light at the actual time of death or even before, during practice in this life.[52]

The minds are mounted on winds that carry them. As Nāgārjuna describes in the *Five Stages*, the minds, united with subtle winds, emerge through the sense organs to meet their objects.[53] They are borne wherever and whenever the winds travel; hence, without the winds, the minds cannot operate. To still the minds, the winds must dissolve. When the winds are withdrawn to the center of the heart, single-pointed concentration is achieved.

Therefore, for the mind of white appearance to arise in the first cycle of the dissolution of consciousness, the winds that carry the intrinsic activities of the conceptual mind[54] together with these minds must cease. Only when the coarser winds and minds dissolve can the clarity of radiant appearance arise. During death, all the winds in the 72,000 channels of the subtle body enter the right and left channels; they then dissolve into the central channel; and finally, the winds in the central channel dissolve into the center of the heart *cakra*. The minds riding on the winds dissolve along with the winds on which they ride, and only the very subtle wind-and-mind remains in the heart.

This process occurs in stages: During the first cycle of the dissolution of consciousness, all the winds in the right and left channels above the heart enter the central channel. During the second cycle, all the winds in the right and left channels below the heart enter the central channel. In the third cycle, the heart *cakra* loosens and the white drop (at the upper end of the central channel) and the red drop (at the lower end) meet at the center of the indestructible drops in the heart. Then, when these drops dissolve into the half-white, half-red indestructible drop at the heart, and all the winds within the central channel dissolve into the very subtle life-sustaining wind, the very subtle wind-and-mind is activated and the clear light of death dawns. If awareness is maintained, that mind can reach awakening.

As I have noted, in the *Compendium of Vajra Wisdom Tantra*[55] the four appearances are equated with four states of emptiness. White appearance is the empty state, enhanced appearance is the very empty state, approaching attainment is the great empty state, and the clear light is all empty.[56] Tsongkhapa explains that white appearance is an empty state because it is empty of the intrinsic activities of the conceptual mind and the winds that serve as their mount; enhanced appearance is empty of white appearance and its wind; approaching attainment is empty of enhanced appearance and its wind—therefore it is the great empty state.[57]

The term "empty" used here echoes the term "seclusion"[58] used in describing the ascent through the four *dhyānas* or *jhānas* in the *Simile of the Quail* and the *Abhidharmakośa*, mentioned above. When the Buddha secluded himself from sensual pleasures and unwholesome states, he entered the first *jhāna* and was filled with joy and bliss born of seclusion. Here we encounter another link between the death process and *jhāna* meditation: the cause for attaining the higher stage is the disappearance of the characteristics of the current stage.

As we have seen in the *Simile of the Quail* and the *Abhidharmakośa,* the mind is gradually emptied of all cognitive and emotional states and the meditator abides in the cessation of perception and feeling.[59] Conversely, in the *Greater Discourse to Saccaka,* when the mind is emptied of all cognitive and emotional states, the meditator realizes the three knowledges and the Four Noble's Truths and is thereby liberated from the cycle of rebirths. Likewise, during meditations on death, the goal is not to empty the mind of all its mental activities in order to realize the clear light of enlightenment. At the end of the death process on the ground of ordinary existence, the very subtle mental continuum with its wind is not terminated but rather continues to the intermediate state and rebirth.

In the *sādhana,* death is the ground of purification that eventually transforms into the *dharmakāya,* as we shall see. Yet the *dharmakāya* alone is not the goal of the *sādhana;* the *rūpakāya,* which consists of both the *saṃbhogakāya* and *nirmāṇakāya,* must be attained as well. Moreover, the meditations that lead to the *rūpakāya* during the creation stage require conceptual minds, as will be discussed in the following chapters. But now we turn to the intermediate state.

The Intermediate State

The intermediate state, or intermediate being,[60] takes place between death in one's previous life and rebirth in one's subsequent life, thus maintaining continuity between them.[61] Like death, the intermediate state is a liminal moment governed by conditions different than those of ordinary *saṃsāra;* hence, it offers an opportunity to attain release from *saṃsāra.* Furthermore, the intermediate state still precedes the next rebirth; therefore, a fundamental transformation during this state can bring an end to the cycle of rebirths.

The "Tibetan Book of the Dead" is part of a well-known Tibetan tradition about the intermediate state.[62] The original title of this work refers to liberation through hearing in the intermediate state, or "*bardo.*"[63] Notably, Tsongkhapa does not follow this tradition. His delineation of the intermediate state in *Fulfilling the Bee's Hope* is based on *sūtras,*[64] *śāstras,*[65] tantras,[66] and commentaries on tantras.[67] Tsongkhapa begins his description from a tantric point of view, in terms of the subtle body:

> How does the intermediate being evolve? The intermediate being who will be born as a human in Jambudvīpa has a body of wind that is conditional upon a substantial cause and a cooperative condition. The substantial cause is the wind endowed with light rays in the five colors [that serves as the mount of] the clear light of death, and the cooperative condition is the mind [of the clear light of death]. It is actually formed by way of its separation from the old body [and as it evolves], the signs from approaching attainment up to mirage-like arise in stages. The nature of the intermediate being is a subtle body that has left behind its coarse body endowed with physical elements.[68]

For the vast majority of people who remain in *saṃsāra,* in the moment following his or her death, an intermediate being evolves by separating itself from the old body and casting off coarse elements such as flesh and blood.[69] This being consists of mere-wind-and-mind that arises from the subtle wind-and-mind of the moment of death. Its mind rides on the wind that serves as its "body." Tsongkhapa stresses the importance of the corporeal aspect of the intermediate being when he refers to the wind as its substantial cause.[70] According to Tsongkhapa, the wind at the moment of death is endowed with light rays in the five colors, which during the *sādhana* will evolve into the mandala endowed with five colors—the aspect endowed with subtle shapes and figures. The cooperative condition[71] for the intermediate being is the mind of clear light of death—the aspect of emptiness.

The subtle body of the intermediate being (which consists of a wind as a support for the mind) has a great impact on the "physiology" of the being's buddhahood. Without it, according to Tsongkhapa, there is no accordant cause for the corporeal aspect of buddhahood, the *rūpakāya.* Hence the "body" of the intermediate being is of utmost importance in the tantric path to awakening. We shall return to this topic in the discussion of the *sādhana* below.

In the extract above, Tsongkhapa mentions that the evolution of the intermediate being is accompanied by signs that arise in stages, from approaching attainment up to mirage-like. This refers to the eight stages of arising from the clear light of death, which is the reverse of the process of death. First, the three minds of approaching attainment, enhanced appearance, and white appearance arise in this order. At the very moment the wind begins to waver slightly during the clear light of death, the experience of the clear light of death transforms into approaching attainment and the intermediate being begins to evolve.[72] Then the mind of enhanced appearance arises and thereupon the mind of white appearance, and finally the intrinsic activities of the conceptual mind are born, accompanied by the signs that are blazing light like that of a butter lamp, lesser light like fireflies, smoke-like, and mirage-like. In the excerpted passage, Tsongkhapa mentions only the last sign, the mirage-like. The description of the wind that begins to waver slightly echoes the beginning of the creation of the physical world, when a light wind flows down from the highest heaven in the second *dhyāna*—the Realm of Clear Light.[73]

Both tantric and nontantric sources depict the formation of the intermediate being as an instantaneous event. Tantric sources describe the arising of the intermediate being as simultaneous with the transformation of the clear light into approaching attainment. Nontantric sources delineate the cessation of the death state and the evolution of the intermediate state as being simultaneous, like the shifting balance of a weighted scale.[74] Since the intermediate being is born instantly, the *Abhidharmakośa*[75] lists that being among those who are born in a miraculous birth, which, as described previously, includes the first people in the eon as well.[76]

In *Bee's Hope* Tsongkhapa continues to describe the intermediate being on the basis of nontantric sources that are not informed by the yogic notion of the subtle body, but he does so without noting any difference between the tantric and nontantric sources.[77] Tsongkhapa mentions the synonyms used by the *Abhidharmakośa,* in relation to the intermediate being, that clarify its different aspects: "Its equivalent names are 'mind-engendered,' 'birth-seeker,' 'intermediate being,' 'scent-eater,' and 'verging-on-existence.'"[78] According to the *Abhidharmakośa,*[79] the intermediate being is called "mind-engendered"[80] because it arises from the mind without exterior elements such as semen and blood. Tantric sources, as has just been noted, explain that the intermediate being arises from the wind (and mind) of the subtle body. Still, both tantric and nontantric discourses agree that the intermediate being is free of any coarse element. The intermediate being is also called "scent-eater"[81] because, as its body is not coarse and it cannot eat solid food, it is nourished by scents. This portrayal of the intermediate being recalls the first beings of the eon, who did not eat coarse food and were nourished by delight; when they resorted to coarse food, they lost their miraculous qualities.

The names "birth-seeker"[82] and "verging-on-existence"[83] indicate that the mode of being in the intermediate state is that of one seeking a birthplace and, in fact, actually approaching rebirth. Therefore, while the intermediate state is a liminal moment that offers the possibility of a release from *saṃsāra,* achieving enlightenment as an intermediate being goes against its very nature.

In following the *Yogācārabhūmi,*[84] Tsongkhapa refers to the lifespan of the intermediate being.[85] It lives for seven days but is not assured rebirth within this period. Hence, if it does not find the conditions for rebirth by the seventh day, it dies as an intermediate being and is then reborn as an intermediate being. This is referred to as a "small death." It can die a small death in this way for up to seven weeks, but then the being is bound to be reborn. The notion of forty-nine days in the *bardo*, familiar from the "Tibetan Book of the Dead," is also found in Indian treatises such as the *Yogācārabhūmi* and the *Abhidharmakośa*.[86]

For more about the intermediate being according to Tsongkhapa, see the translation of *Fulfilling the Bee's Hope* below. In the *sādhana*, the intermediate being is the ground of purification that eventually will transform into the *saṃbhogakāya*.

Rebirth

In Buddhism, life begins at the moment of conception; thus, the birth phase includes both pregnancy and childbirth.[87] The earliest Indian treatises on pregnancy and childbirth date to the early centuries of the first millennium CE.[88] These texts are mainly concerned with medical issues (such as a successful pregnancy leading to a healthy and wise child, preferably a boy), yet they also incorporate Brahmanic and Buddhist notions. At the same time, Brahmanic and Buddhist scriptures adopted medical concepts for their soteriological goals.[89] An example is the *Sūtra on Entering the Womb*,[90] cited by Tsongkhapa, which is known since at least from the third century CE. Aiming to create an aversion to *saṃsāra*, this *sūtra* explains how the first truth of suffering is present at every stage of the process of rebirth.

In *Bee's Hope* Tsongkhapa begins his exposition on rebirth by describing the three conditions that must be present and the three flaws that must be absent for a woman to conceive.[91] These conditions, based on the *Sūtra on Entering the Womb*, include physiological elements as well as the role of karma. The parents must have accumulated karma that would result in their obtaining a child, and the child must have accumulated karma that would result in being born to them.

Tsongkhapa continues by describing the moment of conception, following the *Sūtra on Entering the Womb*,[92] the *Abhidharmakośa*[93] and the *Yogācārabhūmi*[94] in a way that Sigmund Freud would have found perfectly apt. Upon seeing its parents lying together: "If [the intermediate being] is to be born as a male, it is attracted to the mother and hates the father, and if it is to be reborn as a female, it feels desire for the father and hatred toward the mother."[95] When the intermediate being arrives at the place where its parents' organs are joined together, its mind is thus afflicted by desire and hatred, and consequently it develops false discernments with regard to its parents. In this state of mind, it dies and takes birth in the womb. Thus, rebirth is caused by afflictive emotions and mistaken minds. As Tsongkhapa describes: "Thus, [the intermediate being] creates conditions for its death, and its consciousness enters in the midst of the commingled semen and blood in the mother's womb."[96]

Since Tsongkhapa follows nontantric sources here, he refers to the intermediate being as consciousness alone and does not mention the wind. In fact, according to the *Yogācārabhūmi,*[97] it is the consciousness-base-of-all[98] endowed with all seeds[99] that enters the mingled semen and blood in the mother's genitals. In another work Tsongkhapa follows the *Yogācārabhūmi* and then adds: "Those who do not accept the consciousness-base-of-all say that it is the mental consciousness."[100] Thus Tsongkhapa circumvents Buddhist philosophical objections.

In following the tantric texts—the *Vajra Garland Tantra,*[101] *Saṃvarodaya Tantra,*[102] and *Formulating the Guhyasamāja Sādhana*[103]—Tsongkhapa describes how the intermediate being enters its future rebirth: "The *vajra* mind, the consciousness of the intermediate being, which is a passionate mind riding on a horse[104] [of wind], arrives posthaste and enters through the father's crown of the head and joins with the drop that descends through the 72,000 channels [of the parents]."[105] Here the intermediate being arrives "mounted on the wind as though riding a swift horse,"[106] or "riding on the mount of the wind, like a horse-rider,"[107] and enters the channels of the subtle body through the father's crown. The white and red subtle drops of the father and mother in their 72,000 channels are dissolved by the *tummo* fire[108] and descend to the mother's genitals. Semen and blood issue then from the father and mother, respectively, and the intermediate being enters into their midst.[109]

In following the *Yogācārabhūmi,*[110] Tsongkhapa states that the place where consciousness first enters into the mingled semen and blood will become the embryo's heart. Likewise, at death the consciousness departs from that very place.[111]

The *Sūtra on Entering the Womb,* in the version found in the *Monastic Guidelines,* discusses at length the relationship between the newly formed embryo on the one hand and the semen and blood of its parents on the other.[112] This scripture maintains that the embryo is neither identical to the semen and blood nor entirely different from them. The embryo evolves through a collection of causes and conditions, including the substances of the parents and its own karma. The main point here is that while the semen and blood initially belong to the parents, once the consciousness of the intermediate being combines with these physical elements, develops in the womb, and emerges into the world, this child is a separate individual. Whatever this person might do during his or her life is not a result of the actions or the karma of the parents but of their offspring.[113] This has important implications not only with regard to the personal responsibility of the child but also to the identity of the deities in the *sādhana* who are born in affinity with the child.

As the intermediate being enters the semen and blood and begins the process of rebirth, it experiences approaching attainment—the first of the three appearances—in the same order as it experienced them when it became an intermediate being: namely, in the reverse order of the process of death. In *Bee's Hope* Tsongkhapa describes how the experience of approaching attainment turns into enhanced appearance and that into white appearance.[114] Then the wind on which the mind of white appearance is mounted becomes coarser and capable of supporting consciousness. Likewise, the coarser winds that carry the fire, water, and earth arise in sequence, accompanied by the inner signs of that resemble butter lamp, fireflies, smoke, and mirage.

Tsongkhapa depicts the development of the fetus in the womb through five phases[115]—as described in Buddhist *sūtras*,[116] *vinayas*,[117] and *śāstras*.[118] After the intermediate being enters the womb, the white constituent develops gradually through the five phases:[119] (1) "the liquid-cream-like"[120] is like cream outside and highly liquefied inside; (2) "the viscous"[121] is thick like yogurt both inside and outside; (3) "the globular"[122] is fleshy, but cannot withstand pressure; (4) "the solidified"[123] can withstand pressure; and (5) "with the limbs slightly protruding"[124] bulges with the protrusions of the five limbs (the head, arms, and legs).

Tantric sources, including the *Saṃvarodaya Tantra*[125] and *Formulating the Guhyasamāja Sādhana*,[126] describe two sets of the five phases in the womb—one centered on the semen and the other on the blood—and apply each of them to the five *tathāgatas*. The phases outlined above refer to the semen or white constituent. Hence, in *Bee's Hope*, Tsongkhapa continues: "*Formulating the Guhyasamāja Sādhana*[127] applies these five phases to the five *tathāgatas*, beginning with Akṣobhya and concluding with Vairocana, respectively."[128] Tsongkhapa then lists the five phases of blood, or the red constituent, and how these are applied to the five *tathāgatas*: "The phases of development of the red constituent are also five: 'the fluid,' 'the red,' 'the glob,' 'the solidified,' and 'the commingled.' The *Saṃvarodaya Tantra*[129] applies these as well to the five *tathāgatas*. The first to Akṣobhya, the second to Amitābha, the third to Ratnasaṃbhava, the fourth to Amoghasiddhi, and the fifth to Vairocana."[130]

Next, Tsongkhapa describes how, while going through these five phases, the body, speech, and mind of the fetus develop:

> As the white and red constituents develop, the five aggregates, five physical elements, six sense faculties, six sense objects, and the limbs of the being in the womb evolve gradually. Subsequently the *body* of the being in the womb is completed, and breath—which circulates through the mouth and the eight bases of *speech,* including the tongue and the palate—as well as the awareness of *mental* consciousness that engages with objects, are completed. Likewise, the coarse and temporal as well as the subtle and innate aspects of the body evolve gradually.[131]

Thus, together with the coarser elements of the body, the subtle body evolves as well. Tsongkhapa ends this section by describing how the fetus abides in the womb and how it is born from the womb.[132]

In the *sādhana* practice, rebirth is the ground of purification that eventually transforms into the *nirmāṇakāya.* We turn now to the *sādhana* practice.

3

A General Explanation of the *Sādhana*

The introduction advanced the terms "connections" and "continuity," which are used to explain how the tantric practice works.[1] The connections are between the cosmos, the person, and the *sādhana*, while the continuity is between the ground, the path, and the fruit of the practice. Here we will see that many Indian and Tibetan scholars based their explanations about the working of the *sādhana* on both connections and continuity, whereas Tsongkhapa regards continuity alone to have a soteriological value. Concurrently, Tsongkhapa has been inspired by the connections between the cosmos, the person, and the *sādhana* that are at the foundation of Nāgabuddhi's *Formulating the Guhyasamāja Sādhana*, since he himself favors weblike systems that integrate diverse aspects.[2] Moreover, Tsongkhapa cannot dismiss the work of Nāgabuddhi, one of his main sources on this subject. Therefore, without recognizing the tension between connections and continuity in Tsongkhapa's writings, it is impossible to understand his view on the working of the *sādhana*. As we shall see, Tsongkhapa conceives a coherent system that bridges over these tensions.

The Working of the *Sādhana*

Purification

The concept of purification—central to understanding how the *sādhana* works—is clearly related to the notion of continuity. A process of purification or transformation takes the yogi from the ground of ordinary existence along the path to the fruit. As mentioned in the introduction, the ground is the original point, the ordinary state of the yogis before they began their practices. This state is transformed by following the path, or the tantric practice of the *sādhana,* step by step, in a prolonged process that may take numerous lifetimes. Eventually, the path can lead a yogi to the fruit or the goal, which is the awakened state of a buddha endowed with the three bodies. The ground in this transformative process is also called "the object to be purified,"[3] the path is called "the purifying practice,"[4] and the new state of the yogi upon completion of purification is the result or "the fruit of the purification."[5] The terminology of grounds of purification and their purifiers is found in an explanatory tantra of the *Guhyasamāja Tantra.*[6]

Nāgabuddhi's *Formulating the Guhyasamāja Sādhana,* on the other hand, elaborates on both connections and continuity. He points to correlations between the *sādhana* and stages of the evolution and destruction of the world—as well as the death, intermediate state, and rebirth of the inhabitants of the world. Nāgabuddhi describes the stages of the destruction and evolution of the world in relation to the dissolution of the meditator's ordinary environment and the creation of the celestial mansion of the mandala. Additionally, he describes the death, intermediate state, and rebirth of sentient beings living in the world in relation to the four yogas of the *sādhana.*

The eleventh-century Tibetan scholar and translator Gö Khukpa Lhetsé refined the system of *Formulating the Guhyasamāja Sādhana.*[7] Gö, who is said to have gone to India twelve times and studied with seventy teachers,[8] played an important role in the translation and revision of the *Guhyasamāja Tantra.*[9] In his treatise on central practices of the *Guhyasamāja* system[10]—one of the earliest such Tibetan works—Gö correlates individual cosmogonic and personal events with specific steps of the *sādhana* and refers to all of them as "grounds of purification and their purifiers." Gö's method was followed by other Tibetan scholars, including Rendawa Shönu Lodrö (1348–1412),[11] one of Tsongkhapa's most important teachers of the theory and practice of the *Guhyasamāja.*[12]

Tsongkhapa follows the tradition of drawing parallels in his *Explanation of Formulating the Guhyasamāja Sādhana.*[13] However, unlike his predecessors, he distinguishes between mere similarities and the correspondences that entail a continuity. For Tsongkhapa, only the latter can achieve purification of impure grounds by means of the *sādhana*—in other words, are of soteriological value. Thus, in his view, only in the case of continuity—and not of connections—can there be grounds of purification and their purifiers that are beneficial to yogis meditating on the *sādhana* in advance of their awakening. In the same *Commentary,* Tsongkhapa states: "Applying correspondences is not just a matter of collating similar phenomena in order to merely recognize that essentially there is a corresponding similarity between the meditation on the

Mantric path on the one hand, and the destruction and evolution of the habitat and the inhabitants of the world on the other."[14] Tsongkhapa uses the terms "Mantric path" and "Mantra Vehicle" as equivalent to Vajrayāna, the Vajra Vehicle.[15]

According to Tsongkhapa, since the fruit of the Mantric path is a buddha's three bodies—the *dharmakāya, saṃbhogakāya,* and *nirmāṇakāya*—it follows that only phenomena that correspond to them can be their grounds of purifications and purifiers. Moreover, for him, only a path that carries a thread—in other words, a continuity or tantra—from the ground to the three bodies of a buddha at the fruit can be a true purifier. Thus, Tsongkhapa points to a certain continuity from the ground to the fruit through the Mantric path that makes it possible for yogis to transform their future death, intermediate state, and rebirth into a buddha's bodies.

The three phenomena on the ground that correspond to a buddha's three bodies are, according to Tsongkhapa, the future death, the intermediate state, and the rebirth of the meditators on the *sādhana.* He refers to these phenomena as "ground *dharmakāya,*" "ground *saṃbhogakāya,*" and "ground *nirmāṇakāya,*" respectively.[16] Ground *dharmakāya* is the clear light of death that happens to ordinary human beings after their breathing stops, the inner winds dissolve, and the three experiences dawn.[17] Subsequently, the intermediate being, formed of mere-wind-and-mind, separates itself from the previous coarse body. This is the ground *saṃbhogakāya.* When the intermediate being "takes birth"[18] in the womb, it becomes the ground *nirmāṇakāya.* In correspondence with these three events, yogis begin their practice of the path by meditating on the *dharmakāya, saṃbhogakāya,* and *nirmāṇakāya* of the creation stage.

In his *Explanation of Formulating the Guhyasamāja Sādhana,* Tsongkhapa portrays the apparent similarities between the grounds and fruits of the *sādhana:*

> Because during death the aggregates and so forth dissolve and all the coarse mental proliferations subside, death corresponds to the *dharmakāya.* Because the intermediate being is formed of mere-wind-and-mind[19] and its body is extremely subtle, like a rainbow, it corresponds to the *saṃbhogakāya.* When the intermediate being takes birth, it turns into an object for the physical eye of ordinary beings and is capable of performing activities among them. Likewise, the *saṃbhogakāya* "takes birth" by displaying *nirmāṇakāyas* that are seen by ordinary beings on the path and acts for their sake.[20]

While ordinary people who have not engaged in the practice will undergo death, the intermediate state, and rebirth in the *saṃsāric* world, those endowed with the powerful methods of the Mantric path will be able to transform these three *saṃsāric* states into a buddha's three bodies. In a sense, these three bodies of a buddha are purified aspects of the continuum that begins with these *saṃsāric* states, as Tsongkhapa explains:

> Consequently, for yogis who completed their meditation on the three paths that are homogenous with the three bodies: instead of the death that takes place naturally for ordinary people, the *dharmakāya,* the actualization of ultimate truth, will arise; instead of the intermediate state that takes place naturally for ordinary people, the *saṃbhogakāya,* made of mere-wind-and-mind, will arise from clear light in the reverse order;[21] and instead of *saṃsāric* rebirth that takes place naturally for ordinary people, for the yogi there will be a *nirmāṇakāya* that takes birth at will for the sake of beings. These three bodies, unlike the three bodies explained in other treatises, are the supreme unique feature of this treatise.[22]

The tantric principle called "taking the fruit on the path" is well known. From the moment yogis embark on the *sādhana,* they connect the path (the *sādhana* practice) to its fruit (buddhahood), by meditating on themselves as buddhas. In other words, while practicing the path, they strive with minds that bring the fruit to the path. When they meditate on emptiness, they maintain the divine identity[23] of the *dharmakāya;* and when they arise as *saṃbhogakāya,* they develop divine identification with the deity—namely, genuinely seeing themselves as the deity.

The unique feature in the present context, however, is that all three phases—the ground, the path, and the fruit—are connected. Not only is the fruit "taken on the path," but the ground of purification, as well, is taken on the path that leads to the fruit. The yogas of the three bodies of a buddha take death, the intermediate state, and rebirth on the path that leads to the three bodies. The goal is to purify the future death, the intermediate state, and rebirth, and transform them into the three bodies. This would not be viable unless there is a special thread, or continuity, that links the ground to the fruit.

To conclude, the tantric path must consist of the three bodies of the path[24] that will link the grounds and the fruits of purification. The three yogas on the path of the creation stage are the yoga of taking death on the path that leads to the *dharmakāya,* the yoga of taking the intermediate state on the path that leads to the *saṃbhogakāya,* and the yoga of taking rebirth on the path that leads to the *nirmāṇakāya.* In the second part of this chapter, we will return to the workings of the *sādhana,* which consists of these three yogas. But first we need to clarify how purifications work in the context of the *sādhana.*

Methods of Purifications

Tsongkhapa[25] notes that the objects transformed through the Mantric path are different from those purified through the methods of the mundane and supramundane paths[26] that the Sūtric Way of the Mahāyāna offers.[27] The mundane path clears away afflictive emotions, conceptualizations, and so forth by eliminating their manifestation through remedies or antidotes. These remedies are virtuous mental states that counter nonvirtuous ones, as, for example, anger and hatred can be averted by cultivating loving-kindness, desire by contemplating "foulness."[28] According to Tsongkhapa, however, preventing death, the intermediate state, and rebirth from becoming temporarily manifest is not the goal of the three yogas. Moreover, no remedy can bring about a mental continuum of death, the intermediate state, and rebirth that is free of impurities even for a short time, because these three stages are inherently impure.

The supramundane path purifies by eradicating afflictive emotions, conceptualizations, and other impurities from their root. For example, the root of self-grasping, or grasping of the self as truly existing,[29] is eliminated through insight into selflessness. Again, for Tsongkhapa, the purpose of tantric yoga is not to eradicate death, the intermediate state, and rebirth from the root but to purify them without destroying the continuum of the yogi. The three yogas do not eradicate but rather transform death, the intermediate state, and rebirth into a buddha's three bodies.

But how can death, the intermediate state, and rebirth transform without bringing the person to a state of complete cessation? We may recall here the method described in the *Simile of the Quail* and the *Abhidharmakośa* that threatens the meditators with their own annihilation.[30] According to Tsongkhapa, in practicing the *sādhana,* a yogi creates the three bodies of the path that correspond to the grounds of purification as well as to the fruit. The three bodies of the path put an end to ordinary death, the intermediate state, and rebirth, while preserving their continuums. Through the three yogas, the grounds of purification are prevented from arising, and in their place the three bodies of the path and of the fruit that correspond to them are induced to arise. While this is impossible in the Sūtric Vehicle, the tantric "physiology" makes such a transformation viable because at death, the coarse elements of the person are abandoned but the subtle body, made of winds and minds, continues.

Nevertheless, the subtle body at the ground is impure. Hence, it is necessary to purify it through the practice of the *sādhana.* Unlike the coarse elements of the body, however, the subtle winds-and-minds can be purified by means of the completion stage. In this way the continuum is preserved, at least to the degree permitted by Prāsaṅgika Madhyamaka philosophy, while the yogi is eventually freed of ordinary death, the intermediate state, and rebirth.

In his *Explanation of Formulating the Guhyasamāja Sādhana,* Tsongkhapa explains: "The essential meaning of the purification is to render pure ordinary birth, death, and the intermediate state by means of meditation on a path which is similar to these three phenomena on the ground."[31] To "render pure" in this context means to transform ordinary birth, death, and the intermediate state into the three bodies of a buddha. Purification is equivalent to transformation into the divine state of a buddha, and the method of purification is meditation on phenomena that are similar to birth, death, and the intermediate state and preserve their continuity until the fruit.

The tantric path is twofold, consisting of the creation and completion stages. In both stages there are three meditations, which correspond to death, the intermediate state, and rebirth, as well as to a buddha's three bodies.[32] Put differently, there are two sets of three bodies on the path, the first set of three encountered during the creation stage and the second during the completion. The three bodies of the completion stage arise in place of the yogi's future death, intermediate state, and rebirth, while the three bodies of the creation stage serve to ripen the yogi's continuum for them.

One of Tsongkhapa's main disciples, Kedrup Jé Geleg Pelsangpo (1385–1438), specifies that a homogenous continuum[33] arising from habituation to the three bodies on the path of the completion stage, which transform into the actual three bodies of a buddha, is the unique feature of the *Guhyasamāja Sādhana.* In this regard, he writes: "These three bodies, unlike the bodies explained in other treatises, are the supreme special qualities of the system of the *Guhyasamāja.*"[34]

Special Affinities

Whereas this method of purification is specific to the Guhyasamāja cycle—though it found its way to other tantric cycles—there are certain principles of purification common to the Mantra Vehicle at large. One of these fundamental principles is the special relationships seen between the impure psychophysical elements of the human body and their purified aspects in the forms of the deities of the mandala. These affinities make it possible for an ordinary body of a yogi be transformed into a buddha's body. In the *Guhyasamāja*

Tantra this is expressed in the following lines: "Taken together the five aggregates are proclaimed the five buddhas; the *vajra* sense-bases [are called] the supreme mandala of *bodhisattva*[35] the earth is called Locanā; the water element, Māmakī; the fire, Pāṇḍarā; and the wind, Tārā."[36] Importantly, the five aggregates are not explicitly equated here with the five buddhas; rather, they are proclaimed[37] as buddhas. Hence, there is a certain ambiguity regarding the nature of these relations and the extent to which the aggregates and the buddhas may be regarded as identical. On the other hand, numerous Buddhist tantras understand the psychophysical elements of the human body and the deities of the mandala as completely identical.[38] The main point, however, is that in the tantric way, on the whole, these special affinities between *saṃsāric* and mandalic states allow the transformation of the impure psychophysical elements of the human body into the pure deities of the mandala.

Are the Grounds Shared by Their Two Purifiers— The Creation and Completion Stages?

According to Tsongkhapa, only death, the intermediate state, and rebirth are grounds of purification that can be purified through the creation and completion stages.[39] A related question is whether these two stages share the same grounds of purification or whether each stage purifies separate grounds. In *Compendium of Practices*, Āryadeva says: "If [yogis] fully realize that death is the ultimate truth and birth is the conventional truth and if they generate a firm resolution . . . and maintain it . . . , they will thereby become omniscient."[40] Shortly after this passage, we find the verse: "Birth is called 'conventional truth,' and the term for death is 'ultimate truth.' A yogi who finds these two stages through the grace of the guru becomes a buddha."[41]

On the basis of these statements, Tibetan lamas prior to Tsongkhapa tended to maintain that the creation stage purifies birth, while the completion stage purifies death.[42] Tsongkhapa does not endorse the idea that the grounds of purification of the creation and completion are different.[43] In order to avoid confrontation with the views of Āryadeva, Tsongkhapa offers an alternative reading of the Indian master's statement in the verse just cited: "A yogi who finds these two stages through the grace of the guru becomes a buddha." These two stages, he proposes,[44] cannot refer to ordinary birth and death because all sentient beings have already found ordinary birth and death without relying on the grace of the guru. Instead, he suggests, Āryadeva was here referring to merging death and clear light and then being born in the illusory body during the completion stage.[45]

According to Tsongkhapa, both creation and completion stages are necessary in order to purify death, the intermediate state, and rebirth. First, the three bodies of the creation stage ripen the yogi's mental continuum,[46] and then the three bodies of the completion stage can achieve an actual transformation: "This is because for purifying one ground of purification, lesser, middling, and profound realizations arise at the beginning, middle, and end of the path, like the stages of the rungs of a ladder."[47] The lesser realization arises during the creation stage, while the middling and profound realizations arise during the completion stage. For example, the lesser realization of the *dharmakāya* during the creation stages leads to the middling realization of the *dharmakāya* during the completion stage, and the middling realization leads to the profound realization at the completion of the Mantric path. Yet all three realizations on the path of the creation and completion stages are necessary.

All these realizations will be explained in due order in this and the following chapter. But before continuing with the meditation on the path, we need to clarify certain aspects of the ground. To do this, we turn now to the question: What kinds of births, deaths, and intermediate states are purified through the practice of the *sādhana?*

Which Birth Can Be Purified?

Buddhist texts, including the *Diamond Sūtra,*[48] mention four modes of birth: birth from an egg, birth from a womb, birth from heat and moisture, and miraculous birth.[49] In describing the evolution of the beings in the world in his *Formulating the Guhyasamāja Sādhana,* Nāgabuddhi, too, mentions these four modes of birth.[50] Basing themselves on this and similar scriptures,[51] a number of Tibetan lamas[52] prior to Tsongkhapa (as well as many Tibetan scholars who followed him) suggested four ways of visualizing the deity in correspondence with the four modes of birth.

For Tsongkhapa, yogis meditating on the creation stage should meditate on a human birth from a womb alone. They need not meditate in correspondence with various modes of birth and certainly need not purify these modes of birth. In his view, the explanations found in *Formulating the Guhyasamāja Sādhana* do not pertain to meditations on the Mantric path in general, but only to practices intended for the foremost disciples of the Unexcelled Mantra,[53] called "jewel-like persons."[54] Since these disciples will be awakened in one lifetime, they will not undergo birth from an egg, from heat and moisture, or a miraculous birth. Thus, for Tsongkhapa, the notion that there are four ways of visualizing the deity in correspondence with the four modes of birth has no ground.

Nonetheless, Tsongkhapa must explain why Nāgabuddhi mentions the four modes of birth in *Formulating the Guhyasamāja Sādhana*. In doing so, he suggests that the author uses the term "four modes of birth" to refer to all sentient beings that inhabit the world. As to why Nāgabuddhi would not refer to all dwellers in the world in the more usual term of the five *saṃsāric* realms,[55] Tsongkhapa writes that according to the *Abhidharmakośa*,[56] all sentient beings are included in the four modes of birth, but not all of them are included in the five realms.[57] The intermediate beings, for example, are not included in the five *saṃsāric* realms but are included among the four modes of birth as beings who are miraculously born.[58]

Tsongkhapa finds a support for his position in another passage in Nāgabuddhi's *Formulating the Guhyasamāja Sādhana*,[59] which cites the *Exceptional Secret Tantra*: "All the buddhas who appear in the past, present, and future are born as human beings, and as such, attain the *siddhi* of the omniscient stage."[60] Then Nāgabuddhi concludes: "This is the reason the stages of birth into human existence are taught here." Thus, *Formulating the Guhyasamāja Sādhana* maintains that since all the buddhas attained awakening in the physical form of a human body, the *sādhana* practice is meant exclusively for the purification of a birth from a womb.

But such an interpretation is not offered in the *Commentary on the Saṃvarodaya Tantra*, which likewise describes the four modes of birth in the context of the creation stage.[61] Therefore, Tsongkhapa asserts: "Even though these topics are explained differently in the *Commentary on the Saṃvarodaya* and here [*Formulating the Guhyasamāja Sādhana*], it seems that the interpretation of this master [Nāgabuddhi] is exactly as it should be. Therefore, also the meaning of the *Saṃvarodaya Tantra* should be [understood] in accordance with this [explanation]."[62] Tsongkhapa thus acknowledges the discrepancy between the two explanations, preferring Nāgabuddhi's view that while in general there are four modes of birth, for the creation stage, only birth into human existence is relevant. Moreover, Tsongkhapa suggests that such must be the meaning of the *Saṃvarodaya Tantra*, leaving no basis for the opinion that there are four ways of visualizing the deity in correspondence with the four modes of birth.

Additionally, Tsongkhapa queries why *Formulating the Guhyasamāja Sādhana* restricts the practice to those who are awakened in a human body, and therefore in the Desire Realm,[63] while some *bodhisattvas* are awakened in the No-Higher Heaven[64] and in other realms. According to Tsongkhapa,[65] in this context, *Formulating the Guhyasamāja Sādhana* is not referring to awakening in general but specifically to those who are awakened in a human body in the Desire Realm. These beings must be human beings residing in Jambudvīpa who are endowed with passionate bodies capable of practicing sexual yoga on the path, as we will see in the next section.

Why Do Our Texts Only Speak of Human Birth in Jambudvīpa and Not in the Other Continents?

In *Fulfilling the Bee's Hope* Tsongkhapa explains: "What is the reason that the foremost disciples of the Mantra Vehicle, the jewel-like persons, are human beings residing in Jambudvīpa? The foremost disciples of the Mantra Vehicle, the jewel-like persons, are able to take on the path the bliss arising when the male and female join their organs and the white and red constituents unite. From among all *saṃsāric* realms, such a person is found only in Jambudvīpa."[66] The jewel-like persons who are the foremost disciples of the Unexcelled Mantra are explained in the *Illuminating Lamp*[67] as the supreme among five types of disciples: disciples who are like an *utpala* blue lotus, a *puṇḍarīka* white lotus, a *padma* lotus, a sandalwood, and a jewel.[68] Those in the first four categories may participate in group teachings,[69] while the foremost jewel-like disciples may receive individual teachings as well.[70]

Tsongkhapa then clarifies why beings in all other *saṃsāric* realms are either unqualified to practice the tantric path or unable to do so.[71] Hell beings, hungry ghosts,[72] and animals in the three lower levels[73] of the Desire Realms are unqualified to meditate on any Buddhist teachings. Those who are unable to practice the *sādhana* are all the gods in the three *saṃsāric* realms: the Desire Realm, the Realm of Subtle Materiality, and the Immaterial Realm. The gods do not have the channels and wheels of the subtle body nor the white and red *bodhicittas* that are the basis for engendering great bliss and therefore cannot practice the completion stage.

Human beings in the other three continents[74] do experience bliss when the white and red constituents are united, but they do not abide on the ground of karma;[75] in other words, they share a common karma. By contrast, in Jambudvīpa the karma is individual: namely, the karma of each person ripens in accordance with his or her own deeds. Accordingly, people in Jambudvīpa who meditate on the path in this lifetime can attain its fruit in the same lifetime. Moreover, the fruit of previous karma creates significant differences in the sharpness of faculties among the people of Jambudvīpa; hence, the superior disciples on this continent are capable of achieving the fruit by practicing the Mantric path. For these reasons, according to Tsongkhapa, *Formulating the Guhyasamāja Sādhana*[76] explains that in their last life, the *bodhisattvas* are born only in Jambudvīpa and teach the Dharma there.

Consequently, those who are awakened in their present life in a passionate body through the Mantric path are human beings residing in Jambudvīpa. They practice not only in correspondence with the stages of birth into human existence, but also with death and the intermediate state of human beings in Jambudvīpa,[77] as we will see below.

Can Women in Jambudvīpa Reach Awakening in Their Present Lives?

Notably, both men and women can be awakened in their present life. In *Bee's Hope* Tsongkhapa writes: "Therefore, both male and female yogis take bliss on the path. Both must be able to cultivate a most stable deity yoga, to hold the *bodhicitta* without emitting it, and thereby unite bliss and emptiness. Likewise, both men and woman can belong to each of the five types of disciples: those who are like a blue lotus, white lotus, [*padma*] lotus, sandalwood, and jewel."[78] Hence, women are included among the foremost disciples of the Mantric path. Moreover, according to Tsongkhapa, both women and men may become fully enlightened in their lifetimes. His description of how women can achieve this reflects a striking sense of gender balance:

> How do women awaken in this very life? As for example, by relying on the mother, the father induces the four joys and the four empty states and generates the pure and impure illusory bodies from the [wind-and]-mind of clear light of the four empty states, and then attains the union of no more practice in that very life. Likewise, by relying on the father, the mother, too, induces the four joys and the four empty states and generates the pure and impure illusory bodies from the wind-and-mind of clear light of the four empty states, and then attains the union of no more practice in that very life. The way women are awakened is taught in chapter thirteen of the *Root Guhyasamāja Tantra* and its *Commentary*.[79]

Tsongkhapa refers here to Candrakīrti's commentary on the *Guhyasamāja Tantra*,[80] the *Illuminating Lamp*, which states: "It is not only men who achieve awakening born from passion, but women as well achieve this."[81] Hence, women too can awaken in this life through the unique path of Unexcelled

Mantra,[82] and they do so in exactly the same way as a male yogi. We will return below to examine the terms the four joys, the four empty states, pure and impure illusory bodies, and the union of no more practice.

The *Samādhi* of Great Bliss

The practices of the Unexcelled Mantra are meant for human beings with passionate bodies who are able to take desire on the path. In *Bee's Hope* Tsongkhapa cites one of the explanatory tantras of the *Guhyasamāja* cycle to support this view:

> The purpose of awakening by relying on sense pleasures of the consort, in the system of the Mantra Vehicle, is taught in the *Compendium of Vajra Wisdom Tantra:* "Unless [the male and female practitioners] activate their *vajra* and lotus by mantra and *mudrā,* and then join them, they will not be able to identify the three types of awareness.[83] Those unable to join their *bhagas* and *liṅgas* will not attain the *samādhi* of great bliss."[84] And: "Those who truly identify the intrinsic natures and appearances[85] through the bliss arising from conjoining the *vajra* and lotus, will abide at the stage of great bliss."[86]

Yet, here, Tsongkhapa does not explain how human beings, endowed with passionate bodies and capable of taking desire on the path, attain the goal of the practice. For this we must turn to his works on the completion stage of the Guhyasamāja, especially the *Lamp to Illuminate the Five Stages,*[87] where Tsongkhapa elaborates on the *samādhi* of great bliss. Great bliss is a unique feature of the Unexcelled Mantra and is referred to as "great bliss" or "actual innate bliss" to distinguish it from the bliss found in the Pāramitā Vehicle[88]—the nontantric path of the Mahāyāna[89] and the Lower Tantras.[90]

In the *Lamp to Illuminate the Five Stages,* Tsongkhapa describes how great bliss arises upon the penetration of the vital points in the body: "When the vital points of the *cakras* in the body are penetrated, the winds enter into the central channel and ignite the inner *tummo*[91] fire and as a result the *bodhicitta* melts."[92] There are two methods for penetrating the vital points in the body: the external method (yoga with a consort), and the internal method (meditation on the inner channels, winds, and drops).[93] Through either of these methods, the winds in the left and right channels are induced into the central channel, where they cause the inner fire to blaze; thereby, the *bodhicitta* melts and great bliss arises.

The mind experiencing great bliss is capable of uniting indivisibly with emptiness, like water mixed with milk. Tsongkhapa explains that as soon as great bliss evolves, it is already inseparable from emptiness.[94] In other words, the mind of great bliss (the subject) is nondual with its object (emptiness). This is the meaning of a direct realization of emptiness. If actual innate bliss has not arisen, however, the nature of phenomena is recognized indirectly, by way of applying the mind through conviction.[95] In these cases, the object and subject become a single taste through conviction alone. However: "When actual innate bliss arises, object and subject become a single taste like milk poured into water and even the subtlest dualistic appearance dissolves. . . . In this way [the mind of innate bliss] is united in a non-dual manner with the object of emptiness."[96]

Moreover, the mind that experiences actual innate bliss and the mind that realizes emptiness are not two separate minds: "The two minds are not of separate nature; they arise as a single segment."[97] According to Tsongkhapa, the object—namely, the emptiness that is realized in the Mantra Vehicle—is no different from the emptiness explained in the Pāramitā Vehicle. But the subject, the mind that sees emptiness, is innate bliss, which is unrivaled in its power to realize emptiness. Therefore: "Although there is no difference in the emptiness understood, the method of bliss is superior."[98]

According to Tsongkhapa, great bliss is also the key to the speed of the Mantric path.[99] In this regard, he cites the *Saṃpuṭa Tantra:* "The buddhahood attained over innumerable eons [in the Pāramitā Vehicle], you will attain in this life through sublime bliss."[100] He then reiterates: "With regard to the view of emptiness, there is no difference between the Unexcelled Mantra, the Pāramitā Vehicle, and the three Lower Tantras. However, the key for the swiftness of this path is the subject, the innate great bliss that meditates on the meaning of suchness."[101] Additionally, in *Bee's Hope*, Tsongkhapa cites the scriptural authority of the *Guhyasamāja Tantra* as well as its commentaries in advocating the practice of taking desire on the path:

> The seventh chapter of the *Guhyasamāja Tantra* teaches: "The passionate one who desires wisdom should rely constantly on the five sense pleasures,"[102] and the *Sādhana Incorporating the Scripture* teaches: "In order to demonstrate that the stage [of awakening] arises through passion, the Blessed One, in the first chapter of the *Guhyasamāja Tantra,* was absorbed in the *samādhi* called 'the method of great passion.'"[103] The *Illuminating Lamp* explains the meaning of this by asking: "For whose sake was this Tantra taught?"[104] And then replying:[105] "For the sake of passionate people."[106]

In his *Annotations to the Illuminating Lamp,* in the context of the *samādhi* called "the method of great passion," Tsongkhapa says:

> The chief disciples of the Mantra Vehicle are not found in the two higher realms (the Realm of Subtle Materiality and the Immaterial Realm),[107] but in the Desire Realm.[108] They are greatly attached to objects of the five attributes of passion[109] found in the Desire Realm, have very sharp faculties, and are intent on practicing the path of passion toward objects of desire. In order to teach them about liberation, which is the attainment of buddhahood in a single lifetime by enjoying the five attributes of passion of the consort, in the first chapter of the *Guhyasamāja Tantra,* the Blessed One was absorbed in the *samādhi* called "the method of great passion."[110]

We can see that the system of three cosmological realms arranged vertically is still pertinent. But in the context of his commentary on the *Guhyasamāja Tantra,* Tsongkhapa emphasizes that the main domain for the practice of the Mantra Vehicle is the lowest of the three worlds, the Desire Realm. According to *Bee's Hope,* as noted previously, the foremost disciples of the Unexcelled Mantra who will be awakened in their present life are only men and women residing in Jambudvīpa—in this world.

In the two extracts above, Tsongkhapa refers to the *samādhi* called "the method of great passion," found in the first chapter of the *Guhyasamāja Tantra,* in which the Blessed One was absorbed. Yogis of the *Guhyasamāja Sādhana* must enact this event in their practice. We will return below to the relations between the deeds Vajradhara or other tantric buddhas perform in the *Guhyasamāja Tantra* and the *sādhana* practice.[111] The terminology used in our text is the "past event"[112] (the precedent in the tantra), and "the practice that follows it."[113]

To conclude, the notion of purification by means of the Mantric path has been surveyed with an emphasis on the creation stage. We have inquired into questions such as the method and the goal of purification as well as what can be purified, mainly on the basis of Tsongkhapa's *Fulfilling the Bee's Hope.* Now we shall look more closely at the meditation itself, as well as its relation to the cosmos and the person.

Meditations in Correspondence with the Cosmos and the Person

The Meditation According to the *Sādhana*

Formulating the Guhyasamāja Sādhana begins with a synopsis of the practice that delineates the main steps taken during the core of the *sādhana*.[114] Its author, Nāgabuddhi, instructs the yogi:

> First, recite for a while the verse beginning with "in the absence of being," and bring everything animate and inanimate into emptiness. "Meditate on a wind mandala, abiding at the center of the space realm," and so forth, thereby, by visualizing the four mandalas [not to be confused with the greater mandala][115] successively, generate the ground. Upon it visualize the celestial mansion arising from *bhrūṃ*. In the celestial mansion, place the entire circle of deities [who reside in the mandala palace], beginning with Akṣobhya, "through special visualization."[116]
>
> Then, through the four yogas, namely: *yoga, anuyoga, atiyoga,* and *mahāyoga,*[117] generate yourself as great Vajradhara. Having united the male and female organs, emanate the deities of the mandala. Finally, meditate on and recite the mantras, request that the deities leave, and withdraw the visualization.

The synopsis begins with the dissolution of the ordinary world into emptiness in a ritual death that erases the ordinary reality of the yogis and their environment.[118] Then, out of emptiness a new reality, consisting of the special appearances of the celestial mansion of the mandala, is visualized. First, the four mandalas of the physical elements appear, one on top of the other, which then merge to create the crossed *vajra,* the ground upon which stands the celestial mansion of the mandala. Next the celestial mansion arises from the seed syllable *bhrūṃ*. The first part of the practice concludes with the placing of "the entire circle of deities": the first group of the thirty-two deities[119] who reside in the mandala, on their thrones in the celestial mansion.

In the second part of the practice, yogis visualize themselves as Vajradhara through the four yogas: *yoga, anuyoga, atiyoga,* and *mahāyoga.* This is the core of the *sādhana* regarded by Tsongkhapa as the yogas of a buddha's three bodies that are the purifiers of the grounds of purification. Neither in this synopsis nor in the main part of his work does Nāgabuddhi elaborate on these yogas, apparently assuming that his readers or listeners were familiar with them. The scarcity of detail, though, allowed much leeway in their interpretation by future generations of Buddhist scholars. Then, through the yoga with their consorts, yogis emanate the deities of the mandala. The practice concludes with the recitation of mantras, a request that the deities leave, after which the meditators dissolve the visualization.

Meditations in Correspondence with the Cosmos

In the detailed explanation of the *sādhana* that follows this synopsis, Nāgabuddhi explains that the first two steps, the dissolution into emptiness and the visualization of the celestial mansion, correspond to the destruction and evolution of the world—in other words, to the macrocosm.[120] It should be stressed, however, that the meditations in correspondence with the cosmos and with the person are two aspects of a single whole. When the cosmos is periodically recreated, first the physical world evolves, and soon after the people of the first eon appear there. Likewise, during the *sādhana* practice, after yogis visualize the celestial mansion of the mandala, they imagine that the first group of the thirty-two deities comes to reside there.

As I noted in the introduction, Tsongkhapa maintains that "continuity" (*prabandha*) has a soteriological value, while "connections" (*bandhu*) do not. At the same time, he finds an enormous significance in the connections between the macrocosm, the microcosm, and the *sādhana*. Tsongkhapa does not consider the macrocosm formed by shared karma as a possible ground of purification for the *sādhana* practiced by an individual yogi. For him, the grounds of purification are only the future death, the intermediate state, and rebirth of the yogi, which at the culmination of the practice transform into a buddha's three bodies.[121] This is because a continuity persists between these three life-cycle events and the three bodies in enlightenment.

Nonetheless, the affinity between the dissolution of the meditator's ordinary environment and the destruction of the world into an empty space is meaningful. It is part of the image of a perfect system of links between the cosmos, the person, and the *sādhana* that lies at the foundation of Tsongkhapa's *Bee's Hope*. Moreover, in this work,[122] Tsongkhapa regards Nāgabuddhi (who in *Formulating the Guhyasamāja Sādhana* explains the correspondence between the periodic destruction of the world and the first meditation on emptiness in the *sādhana*) as his authority.

Clearly, then, Tsongkhapa does not reject the links between the dissolution of the meditator's ordinary environment and the destruction of the world, links that assist Tsongkhapa in creating the web of affinities between the cosmos and the practice. At the same time, he does not regard the meditation as capable of purifying the outside world as its ground of purification.

Meditations in Correspondence with the Person— The Yogas of the Buddha's Three Bodies

In *Formulating the Guhyasamāja Sādhana,* Nāgabuddhi describes how the first beings in Jambudvīpa who have become ordinary people die, become intermediate beings, and are then reborn, and how a yogi should meditate on the *sādhana* accordingly.[123]

The heart of Tsongkhapa's *sādhana* is the meditation on the three bodies of the creation stage. This practice consists of visualizations of the deities residing in the mandala in correspondence with the person. This core of the *sādhana,* with its three yogas, will ultimately serve to transform the yogi's ordinary death, intermediate state, and rebirth into a buddha's three bodies. In the first step (within the core practices) on the *dharmakāya* of the creation stage, yogis dissolve their ordinary identity and attitudes into emptiness. From emptiness (the *dharmakāya*) they visualize themselves as the deities—first as the *saṃbhogakāya* and then as the *nirmāṇakāya.* While visualizing themselves as the deities, yogis also cultivate the deities' pride,[124] or their identification with the deities and their enlightened attitudes.

According to Tsongkhapa, this practice, referred to as "deity yoga,"[125] characterizes the Mantra Vehicle and is found in all four tantra classes, including the Lower Tantras, and in both the creation and completion stages of the Unexcelled Mantra. Moreover, for Tsongkhapa, it is deity yoga that makes the Mantra Vehicle superior to the Pāramitā Vehicle.[126]

As mentioned in the introduction, according to Tsongkhapa, to achieve a buddha's bodies, certain homogenous causes[127] for them must exist during the stages of the ground and path. In his *Great Treatise on the Stages of the Mantric Path,*[128] Tsongkhapa argues that the three bodies of the path are a unique feature of the Unexcelled Mantra and are not found in the Pāramitā Vehicle or the three Lower Tantras. According to Tsongkhapa, both the Unexcelled Mantra and the Pāramitā Vehicle offer causes that are homogenous with the *dharmakāya,* but only the Unexcelled Mantra offers causes that are homogenous with the *rūpakāya,* the corporeal body that consists of both the *saṃbhogakāya* and *nirmāṇakāya.* The homogenous cause for the *dharmakāya* is the meditation on emptiness, which, according to Tsongkhapa, leads to the *dharmakāya* because it accords with it in the sense that the nature of both is emptiness, suchness, and freedom from elaboration.[129]

However, the meditation on emptiness entails only wisdom and not method, whereas the *bodhisattva*'s practice must combine wisdom and method, or the realization of emptiness and compassion. Without the fruitional *rūpakāya,* the awakened being cannot act for the sake of all sentient beings by guiding them to enlightenment according to the *bodhisattva* vows. The fruitional *dharmakāya* is the embodiment of enlightenment for one's own sake, but this embodiment cannot be perceived by ordinary beings and thus is incapable of benefiting them. However, without achieving the aims of others, complete buddhahood cannot be attained.

The Pāramitā Vehicle offers as its method the practice of the first five *pāramitās*: giving, morality, endurance, forbearance, and concentration.[130] For Tsongkhapa, however, these are not homogenous causes for a buddha's bodies.[131] To support his position, Tsongkhapa cites the explanation of the *Vajra Canopy Tantra:* "Since the Teacher is endowed with the thirty-two major marks and eighty minor signs, the method through which He[132] can be attained is by taking on the Teacher's form."[133] Accordingly, in order to attain the state of the Teacher, the Buddha, a yogi must assume the Teacher's form with all his bodily marks and signs.

The *Vajra Canopy Tantra*[134] further explains that the method of the Mantra Vehicle is meditation on the mandala with the deities residing therein,[135] while maintaining the yoga of a buddha pride or identification with a buddha.[136] According to Tsongkhapa, this method is the principal way to attain the *rūpakāya* and is superior to that of the Pāramitā Vehicle.[137] A yogi who engages in this method and unites it with the wisdom that realizes emptiness can attain buddhahood swiftly, in contrast to the practice of the *pāramitās,* which requires three innumerable eons. This is because in this practice the yogi assumes the form of a buddha, which is a cause that is homogenous with the result. Tsongkhapa concludes thus: "The *Vajra Canopy Tantra* has been quoted here because it clearly teaches that a yogi must practice deity yoga as a cause of the *rūpakāya.* It is on the basis of this example that the explanation of other tantras should be understood."[138] Thus, appreciating the explanation about the *rūpakāya* found in the *Vajra Canopy Tantra,* Tsongkhapa employs it for his elucidations of the Mantra Vehicle at large.

Tsongkhapa stresses that since wisdom and method must be united, neither the *dharmakāya* nor the *rūpakāya* can be attained on its own, without the other.[139] Moreover, deity yoga, the special cause of the *rūpakāya,* is also a cooperative condition[140] for the *dharmakāya* and the wisdom realizing emptiness, while the special cause of the *dharmakāya* is also a cooperative condition for the *rūpakāya*.[141]

The Three Bodies of the Meditators on the Creation Stage

The *dharmakāya* of the creation stage is the clear light into which the first deities who reside in the mandala dissolve; the *saṃbhogakāya* of the creation stage is the First Lord,[142] and the *nirmāṇakāya* of the creation stage is Vajrasattva's *nirmāṇakāya*. These three bodies of the creation stage ripen the yogi's continuum for the three bodies of the completion stage: namely, the actual clear light, the pure illusory body formed of wind-and-mind, and the *nirmāṇakāya* of the path, who acts for the sake of others.

THE *DHARMAKĀYA* OF THE CREATION STAGE

The first body, the *dharmakāya* of the meditators on the creation stage that purifies their death, is the aforementioned clear light. According to Tsongkhapa, the visualization of the first circle of deities (see below) is just a preparatory step for their dissolution into clear light. These deities are visualized appearing instantly in their complete form upon their seats in the mandala and are then drawn one by one into various parts of the yogi's body, becoming indivisible with him or her. Only then, can the actual meditation on taking death on the path that leads to the *dharmakāya* commence. Tsongkhapa explains how to meditate on this in *Bee's Hope:*

> Visualize the respective places of your body [along with the deities indivisible with them] dissolving into clear light which is indivisible bliss and emptiness; and then visualize the principal deity, too, dissolving into clear light and meditate on the union of bliss and emptiness that arises from these dissolutions. Recite the mantra *śūnyatā* and cultivate divine identity[143] [of the *dharmakāya*] with the resolve: "The nature of wisdom, which is the indivisible objective emptiness and subjective wisdom, that am I."
>
> When yogis of the creation stage meditate in this way, they take their deaths on the path that leads to the *dharmakāya*.[144]

At the moment an ordinary person of Jambudvīpa dies, the clear light of death arises.[145] During the *sādhana*, a yogi meditates on the clear light of the path—which is a similitude of the actual clear light. The actual clear light itself may be realized only at the end of the entire tantric path, the fruitional level. The clear-light-emptiness meditated upon during the *sādhana* practice is the *dharmakāya* on the path of the creation stage. Into this clear light of the path the first deities dissolve, along with all the parts of the yogi's body that are indivisible with them.

A yogi meditates on clear-light-emptiness of the creation stage by reciting the mantra of emptiness: *oṃ śūnyatā jñāna vajra svabhāva ātmako 'haṃ.* This means "The indivisible nature of [objective] emptiness and [subjective] wisdom, that am I." For this reason, as in the extract above, Tsongkhapa instructs the yogi to meditate on the union of bliss and emptiness. As noted above (in the section "The *Samādhi* of Great Bliss"), for the sake of the realization of emptiness, the mind experiencing great bliss is significantly superior to the mind meditating on emptiness according to the Pāramitā Vehicle. Another difference between the meditations on emptiness in the Mantra and the Pāramitā Vehicles is the cultivation of divine identity or pride during the *sādhana*, as Tsongkhapa explains: "In the context of this [*Guhyasamāja*] *Tantra*, it is insufficient for yogis to merely apply their minds to the meaning of emptiness. '*Ahaṃ*' [that is, 'I'] means maintaining divine pride or identity. In the Mantra Vehicle yogis must maintain the identity of both the *dharmakāya* and *rūpakāya;* at this point, they maintain the identity of the *dharmakāya.*"[146] The mantras for maintaining divine identity end with *ahaṃ,* meaning "I." Hence, yogis focus not on the nature of things out in the world or on an object but rather on the subject, on themselves and on their new identities.

In *Bee's Hope* Tsongkhapa explains the yoga of taking death on the path that leads to the *dharmakāya:* "How does the *dharmakāya* of the meditators on the creation stage purify their death? In place of the death that would naturally occur to ordinary people, for a yogi, as the deities[147] dissolve into clear light, the *dharmakāya* will arise."[148] The *dharmakāya* of the creation stage will eventually ripen the yogi's continuum for the *dharmakāya* of the completion stage, the clear lights in the fourth and fifth steps.[149] These clear lights will bring about the attainment of the *dharmakāya* of a buddha, the fruit of the purification.[150]

Following the meditation on the yoga of taking death on the path that leads to the *dharmakāya,* the yogi proceeds to the yogas of taking the intermediate state and rebirth, respectively, on the path that leads to the *saṃbhogakāya* and *nirmāṇakāya,* the two aspects of the *rūpakāya.*

THE *SAṂBHOGAKĀYA* OF THE CREATION STAGE

The second body on the path, the *saṃbhogakāya* of the creation stage, is the deity called the First Lord,[151] the first deity that is visualized during the core practices of the *sādhana.* In *Bee's Hope* Tsongkhapa explains how the intermediate being is taken on the path to the First Lord: "How does the *saṃbhogakāya* of the meditator on the creation stage purify the intermediate being? In place of the intermediate being that occurs naturally for an ordinary person, for the yogi meditating on the creation stage, the First Lord will arise through the five manifest awakenings."[152] Tsongkhapa also instructs the yogi how to meditate on the First Lord: "Regard the First Lord . . . as a manifestation of indivisible bliss and emptiness, develop a clear appearance of the First Lord and maintain divine identification with him by cultivating the resolve: 'The pure wind-and-mind arising as the extremely subtle wisdom body, that am I.' This is the practice of taking the intermediate beings on the path to the *saṃbhogakāya*."[153] Like the intermediate being, the First Lord, the *saṃbhogakāya* of the meditator on the creation stage, is made of mere-wind-and-mind. During the completion stage, the illusory body, or the *saṃbhogakāya* of the meditator on the completion stage, is likewise formed of mere-wind-and-mind. This subtle aspect of the yogi's body will be purified and arise as the *saṃbhogakāya* of a buddha at the fruit.

THE *NIRMĀṆAKĀYA* OF THE CREATION STAGE

The *nirmāṇakāya* of the creation stage is Vajrasattva's *nirmāṇakāya*, the second set of deities visualized during the core practices of the *sādhana*. In *Bee's Hope* Tsongkhapa explains this yoga of taking rebirth on the path that leads to the *nirmāṇakāya*: "How does the *nirmāṇakāya* of the meditator on the creation stage purify rebirth? In place of rebirth that occurs naturally for an ordinary person, for yogis meditating on the creation stage, the *nirmāṇakāya* will arise through the transformation of the First Lord into Vajrasattva's *nirmāṇakāya*."[154] The way rebirth is taken on the path to the *nirmāṇakāya*, which consists of several steps, is described in chapter 4 in the section "Meditations that Correspond to Rebirth."

In conclusion, yogis attain the goal of the core practices when they have generated themselves as Vajradhara and cultivated the divine identity of Vajradhara's three bodies, the *dharmakāya*, *saṃbhogakāya*, and *nirmāṇakāya*. Maintaining divine identification with Vajradhara, in place of the yogi's ordinary identity, is the main purpose of this practice.

During the yogas of a buddha's three bodies, yogis engage in two aspects of this meditation. They maintain divine identification with deities and cultivate the clear appearance of the entire mandala with its deities. In his *Great Treatise on the Stages of the Mantric Path*, Tsongkhapa calls these two aspects of the meditation a "unique feature exclusive to the Mantra Vehicle."[155] The goal of the meditation on the special appearance is to avert the ordinary appearances of the yogis and of their environments. Divine pride or identity is cultivated to avert the clinging of the yogis to their own ordinary identification.

According to Tsongkhapa: "Meditating on the identity of being the mandala with its celestial mansion and the deities as an antidote to ordinary identity is of paramount importance, while meditating on the special appearance of the residence and its inhabitants, toward the goal of averting ordinary appearances, is secondary to it."[156] Tsongkhapa maintains that by means of the creation stage alone, yogis cannot become deities in actuality. But when a genuine identity of being a deity arises in them, the goal of the creation stage is attained. In *Fulfilling the Bee's Hope* Tsongkhapa notes that death, the intermediate state, and rebirth correspond to the three bodies of the meditator on the creation stage[157] by way of applying the mind to the wished-for goal through conviction.[158] By contrast, the three bodies of the meditator in the completion stage actually correspond to the three bodies of the fruit and therefore can achieve their goals.

The Three Bodies of the Meditators on the Completion Stage

Initially, the creation stage was probably regarded as an independent tantric practice that could bring a yogi to enlightenment.[159] Before the end of the first millennium in India, however, it had become subordinate to the completion stage that employs yogic exercises. As such, the creation stage is regarded as a meditation that only simulates the fruit of buddhahood and serves merely to ripen the roots of virtue for the arising of the completion stage.

It should be noted that when the creation stage is discussed on its own terms, we do find instances in which this practice is regarded as capable of carrying a yogi to the ultimate goal of enlightenment, with no reference to the completion stage. However, in descriptions of the tantric path that include both the creation and the completion stages, the first stage is considered as preparatory for the second. The discrepancy between these two approaches is often solved by taking the creation stage to be indispensable for the completion stage.[160]

Since a yogi must practice the completion stage in addition to the creation stage, it must be assumed that the second stage can achieve goals that the first stage cannot. Along these lines, Āryadeva, in his *Compendium of Practice* (a treatise dedicated to the completion stage), states that the actual body of the deity can be formed only during the completion stage. We may ask how the actual body of the deity arises when there was none before, and whether mind can create a body? And, if the creation stage is a meditation that only simulates the goal of the practice, how is the continuity—the thread that links the ground to the fruit, which begins with the ordinary death, intermediate state, and rebirth of the yogi on the ground of existence—preserved through the three bodies of the creation and the completion stages? Before we address these questions, we need to briefly describe the practice itself.

Five or six steps comprise the completion stage. The division into five steps is based on Nāgārjuna's famous work, *Five Stages*.[161] The names Tsongkhapa uses for these steps are "speech isolation," "mind isolation," "illusory body," "clear light," and "union."[162] When body isolation[163] is added to the list, it becomes the first among six steps, whereas in the system of five steps, body isolation is either included within speech isolation or is regarded as a preparatory step for the completion stage. Tsongkhapa compares body isolation to the meditation on the specially visualized deities during the creation stage that serves as a preparatory step for the yogas of the three bodies.[164] (See the section "The Meditation on the Specially Visualized Deities" in chapter 4.)

According to Tsongkhapa, neither body isolation nor speech isolation purifies a ground of purification;[165] only the last four steps of the completion stage purify grounds of purification. Mind isolation and clear light purify death, while the illusory body and union purify the intermediate being. In *Explanation of Formulating the Guhyasamāja Sādhana*, Tsongkhapa describes the steps during the creation and completion stages that are purifiers of the three grounds of purification:

> The meditations on the dissolution of the specially visualized deities into clear light [during the creation stage], mind isolation, and clear light [during the completion stage] correspond to death and purify it.
>
> The meditations on the First Lord, the illusory body, and union correspond to the intermediate being and purify it.
>
> The meditation on the transformation into the *nirmāṇakāya* in each of these three cases corresponds to rebirth and purifies it.[166]

In *Lamp to Illuminate the Five Stages*, Tsongkhapa explains how the final four steps of the completion stage are akin to death, the intermediate state, and rebirth at the ground of ordinary existence.[167] In correspondence with death or the clear light of the ground *dharmakāya*, yogis meditate on the clear light during mind isolation and during the fourth step, called clear light. In correspondence with the intermediate being or the ground *saṃbhogakāya*, yogis meditate on the impure and pure illusory body during the steps of illusory body and union, respectively. Finally, because the *saṃbhogakāya* cannot be seen by ordinary people, in correspondence with rebirth or the ground *nirmāṇakāya,* they emanate their *nirmāṇakāyas.*

To clarify the correspondence between the intermediate being and the illusory body, Tsongkhapa cites Āryadeva's *Compendium of Practices:* "For ordinary ignorant beings, the so-called intermediate being—the cause of *saṃsāra*—will take place. But for those who have obtained the transmitted instruction of all *tathāgatas* through the lineage of the gurus, the so-called self-blessing stage will take place. In the same way, [the yogis] whose essence is the *vajra* body . . . emanate in bodies endowed with all the excellent qualities of the buddhas."[168] Āryadeva explains here that when ordinary people die, they return once more to *saṃsāra* as intermediate beings who will be reborn in worldly realms. A yogi endowed with skillful teachings who engages in tantric practice, however, can attain the "self-blessing stage."[169] This is the third step of the completion stage in Nāgārjuna's *Five Stages,* called also the "step of the illusory body." Āryadeva is saying, then, that this yogi will attain the illusory body that will emanate the *vajra* body of the buddhas.

A similar, yet extended, explication of how the three buddha's bodies are attained is found in the *Oral Instruction of Mañjuśrī.*[170] This work is likewise dedicated to the completion stage of the Guhyasamāja cycle. Its author is Jñānapāda, "the founder" of the Guhyasamāja school named for him, who is dated to the late eighth to early ninth centuries CE.[171] In this treatise we find that "no doubt the yogi will attain the three *kāyas,*" when they undergo three experiences.[172] In his commentary, Vaidyapāda explains how these experiences relate to the attainment of the three buddha's bodies.[173] When yogis realize space-like clarity and supreme joy, they experience the *dharmakāya;* but this-worldly people who do not know the nature of the mind designate this experience "death." Then, when yogis experience an unparalleled perfect bliss,[174] they attain the *saṃbhogakāya;* but this-worldly people designate this experience "intermediate state." Finally, when yogis attain the *nirmāṇakāya,* this-worldly people designate this experience "rebirth." Therefore, the three stages seen by this-worldly people as death, intermediate state, and rebirth are for the yogi the three buddha's bodies.

Hence, while the *Compendium of Practices* mentions only how instead of the intermediate state that naturally occurs to ordinary beings, the capable yogi will arise in the self-blessing stage, the *Oral Instruction of Mañjuśrī* expands this notion to the three bodies of a buddha that will arise in place of the three ordinary cyclic events of a person. On this basis, Tsongkhapa presents his design that encompasses the three bodies of a buddha that will arise for a yogi in place of the ordinary death, intermediate state, and rebirth that take place for ordinary beings.[175]

We will look now in greater depth at the illusory body that arises for a qualified yogi (instead of the ordinary intermediate state) and examine its importance in the practice of the Guhyasamāja.

THE ILLUSORY BODY

According to Tsongkhapa, the way to attain the *body* of the deity is through the illusory body.[176] The illusory body first arises in the third step of the completion stage and is purified in the fifth, and final, step of the practice. At the fruit of buddhahood, it becomes the *saṃbhogakāya,* which in turn gives rise to *nirmāṇakāya* of the deity; these two *kāyas* are the corporeal aspects of the deity. But before considering the fruit, we need to ask: What is the material basis for the illusory body in the third step?

The Material Basis for the Illusory Body

According to the *Compendium of Practice,* throughout the creation stage and the isolations of body, speech, and mind, there is no deity body.[177] To paraphrase its author, Āryadeva: From the creation stage until the end of body isolation there is no deity body because the divine forms are merely visualized. During speech isolation, the yogi engages in *vajra* recitation alone; hence, there is no aspect of the deity there, either. Likewise, until the end of mind isolation, the yogi experiences only intrinsic natures and appearances;[178] hence, no actual deity body is found there. Tsongkhapa explains this: "Although your mind visualizes yourself in the deity's body, the material form that is the basis for cultivating divine pride in the form of the deity is none other than your old body made up of the physical elements in the form of a collection of particles."[179]

When yogis visualize themselves as deities, their minds need a referent for their visualizations—something that can be the basis of the visualization. Yogis do not visualize deities; they visualize *themselves* as deities. Yet we may ask: What is that entity called "himself" or "herself" who is visualized as a deity? In terminology of the Prāsaṅgika Madhyamaka that Tsongkhapa holds, this entity is called the "basis of designation"[180] for the deity's body. Tsongkhapa explains the statement in the *Compendium of Practice*—according to which, during the creation stage and the three isolations there is no deity body—by using the notion of a referent or basis of designation. According to Tsongkhapa, during the steps of the practice that precede the illusory body, the basis of designation for the deity is the yogi's old, coarse body, because there is nothing else that can be the referent for the visualization. There is only an appearance of the deity's body that the mind visualizes with reference to the yogi's ordinary body.[181]

The step of mind isolation is thus the last step devoid of a deity's body. How is the deity's body created during the transition from mind isolation to the illusory body? The deity's body cannot arise through mere conviction,[182] as is the case during the creation stage; nor can its basis of designation, the referent of the cultivation of divine identification, be the old, coarse body.[183] The ordinary, coarse body—the product of previous karma and afflictive emotion composed of impure aggregates—cannot transform into a buddha's body by means of mere visualization. Additionally, mind alone can produce an appearance of a body, but not the actual buddha's body.

A similar, yet not identical, question is raised by the disciple in the *Compendium of Practice* when he learns that until the end of mind isolation there is no deity's body:[184] "How, then, is the body of the deity—with all its features, such as arms and legs—formed by the mere mind alone?"[185] The *vajra* master replies: "What is the mount of the mind? The wind. The mind *vajra* travels wherever it wishes by riding on the wind as its horse. . . . From the mind bound by the wind, the illusory-like body of the deity, endowed with all qualities, will arise."[186]

The answer is provided here in terms of a very subtle body made of wind-and-mind alone. The wind—which serves as a mount for the mind, like a horse for its rider—is the key for the deity's body.[187] This wind-and-mind arises as the illusory body in the third step of the completion stage, following the isolations of body, speech, and mind.[188] Toward the end of mind isolation, all the winds that carry coarse conceptual mental states have already dissolved and the mind experiences the three appearances[189]—white appearance, enhanced appearance, and approaching attainment[190]—and finally reaches the clear light of mind isolation. The illusory body arises from the inseparable wind and mind of clear light.

The illusory body, then, is similar to the intermediate being, its ground of purification. When the clear light of death ceases, the intermediate being, formed of wind-and-mind alone, separates from the coarse elements of the old body. Likewise, at the end of the clear light of mind isolation, the illusory body formed of mere-wind-and-mind evolves.[191] Hence, through the same process that a new living-being-to-be arises from the dead body as an independent being endowed with a subtle body-and-mind, the body of the deity-to-be, together with its mind, separates itself from the ordinary body of the yogi.

Therefore, whereas the actual body of the deity cannot have as its basis the yogi's old body constituted of impure aggregates, the illusory body made of mere-wind-and-mind can withdraw from the old, coarse body and become a new, subtle body-and-mind free of the impurity of the coarse body. Yet, we may ask, how is the continuity—the thread or tantra—preserved from the ground of ordinary existence to the arising of the illusory body? To answer this question, we will turn to the innate body.[192]

The Innate Body and the Arising of the Illusory Body

According to Tsongkhapa,[193] on the ground of ordinary existence, human beings possess not only coarse, temporary bodies[194] made of the physical elements but also innate bodies made of subtle wind-and-mind. As its name indicates, this body is always innate, like the wetness of water, while the coarse body discarded at death is like the heat of water. The innate body is extremely subtle; its mind is not sensory consciousness[195] but only mental consciousness,[196] and its wind is only the subtle life-sustaining wind[197] and none of the other nine winds.[198]

The innate body can be within or without the coarse body; when the two bodies are together, they do not possess two separate mental continua. Instead, both the coarse and the innate bodies support the mind. The coarse body of ripened karma is the body of human beings—the support of that person—while the innate body made of wind-and-mind[199] is the foundation[200] of the illusory body. The latter evolves from the wind-and-mind of the innate body at the end of mind isolation and can separate itself from the coarse body and travel outside or inside the body. While the innate body has no form (such as arms, legs, and so forth), the illusory body, the intermediate beings, and the dream bodies, appear with forms and limbs.[201]

The substantial cause of the mind of the illusory body is the preceding mind of mind isolation, and its cooperative condition is the wind. Likewise, the substantial cause of the body of the illusory body is the wind of mind isolation, and its cooperative condition is the preceding mind at the end of mind isolation.[202] Hence, rather than being created through the mere imagination of the mind, the wind-and-mind of the innate body arises as the illusory body during the latter steps of the completion stage. This illusory body, then, differs from the body of the deity during the creation stage and the previous steps of the completion stage that were merely visualized by the mind.

The Name "Illusory Body"

The illusory body[203] is called so because, being made of mere-wind-and-mind without any coarse material substances, it is like a phantom or apparition. At the same time, the notions of "illusion" and "illusion-like" are fundamental to Buddhist thinking. Especially important is the term "illusion-like *samādhi*"[204] in both the Pāramitā and Mantra Vehicles. In his *Short Treatise on the Stage of the Path,*[205] a nontantric work, Tsongkhapa explains the meaning of the illusion-like *samādhi* for the Pāramitā Vehicle. When meditators arise into postmeditation after meditating on emptiness, all appearances arise as illusion-like—that is, while they are visible to the eye, they are devoid of intrinsic nature.[206] Likewise, in the *Five Stages,* a work on the completion stage, Nāgārjuna explains: "The entire world and its beings are said to be like an illusion. A yogi abiding in the illusion-like *samādhi* sees everything in this way."[207] In the same way, during the completion stage, the step of the illusory body follows the meditation on emptiness-clear-light during mind isolation; hence, when the illusory body is attained, the entire world and its beings are seen as an illusion.

However, during the completion stage, the meditations on emptiness and illusion are both unique. The meditation on emptiness is unique because it is induced by great bliss, and thus it is significantly more powerful than in the Pāramitā Vehicle. The illusion is unique because it is the innate body of sentient beings that is seen as mere-wind-and-mind.[208] Since the foundation of the illusory body is the very subtle body activated and purified during the completion stage, it is different from illusion in the Pāramitā Vehicle and the creation stage on the Mantra Vehicle.

Pure Illusory Bodies and Preserving the Continuity

As stated above, the first illusory body created during the third step of the completion stage is the "impure illusory body," which is transformed into the pure illusory body in the fourth and fifth steps—the meditations on the actual clear light and on unions.[209] The impure illusory body is purified by dissolving it into clear light through the successive four empty states,[210] in a process similar to the stages of dying and mind isolation.[211] Then, on the basis of the substantial causes and the cooperative conditions, the wind-and-mind of the pure illusory body arises in a process similar to the evolutions of the intermediate state and the impure illusory body.

In this way, while the coarse elements of the human body cannot be purified, the subtle winds-and-minds can be purified at the culmination of the completion stage. The subtle body that consists of subtle winds-and-minds is endowed with two properties: it preserves the continuity and can be purified. It is possible to purify some of the impure aspects of the subtle body, such as its winds, that have existed already at the ground of ordinary existence. These winds carry particular corporeal qualities from the ground of ordinary existence to the *rūpakāya* at the fruit and thus preserve the continuity. On the path, though, to be purified, these winds, as well as the mind, must be dissolved into the actual clear light.

Since this illusory body will eventually develop into the deity's body at the fruit, it provides an answer to the question of how the three bodies of the creation and completion stages preserve the continuity from the ground of ordinary death, the intermediate state, and rebirth to the fruit of being the deity. Moreover, since the illusory body arises from the innate body made of wind-and-mind that acts as a basis for the designation of "person," it preserves the continuity from birth to enlightenment, without violating the parameters of the Prāsaṅgika Madhyamaka.

Since the evolution of the pure illusory body consists of such a multiplicity of bodily transformations, Tsongkhapa maintains that human beings who are awakened in a single lifetime are not awakened in a single body.[212] They begin their practice in a human body, but before they can attain the fruit, their body must change. First, the illusory body separates itself from the old body, and then it is purified in the actual clear light. Hence the body does change without the yogi undergoing death and rebirth. For changing the body in this way, the illusory body is crucial. It enables the yogis to discard their coarse, ordinary bodies while retaining certain subtle corporeal elements of the wind upon which the subtle mind rides. This wind then gives rise to the corporeal aspect of buddhahood, but only after it is purified by the clear light, together with the mind. There are two implications here: first, as we have just seen, while it is possible to be awakened in one lifetime through the Mantric path, it will not be in a single body; second, since women, like men, can attain the illusory body, they can attain enlightenment through the Mantric path without first changing their female bodies into male ones.

Changing the body and maintaining continuity might seem like contradictory processes. Furthermore, continuity is a problematic notion in Buddhism. Nonetheless, the illusory body, as presented by Tsongkhapa in the context of Guhyasamāja practices, provides a bridging solution by maintaining a subtle continuity, a thread, a tantra, while purifying *saṃsāric* contaminations.

CONTINUITY ACCORDING TO BUDDHA NATURE

While this ingenious method offered by Tsongkhapa may appear overcomplicated, it remains within the boundaries of the theoretical views he holds. Had Tsongkhapa adhered to the theory of Buddha Nature, his explanation about the thread leading from the ordinary state of existence to buddhahood could have been more straightforward. Let us look once again at the nature of the point of onset of the tantric path, at the very beginning of the thread embedded within the ordinary state of existence. The *Subsequent Tantra* calls it the cause, which will eventually find its culmination, its fruit, through the practice of the *sādhana.*[213] In particular, we will examine which aspects of the cause are present in the fruit and are, thus, preserved by the thread, the tantra, or tantric method.

In his *Annotations to the Illuminating Lamp,* Tsongkhapa explains: "The causal tantra is the nature of the practitioner who is [of the supreme type] called 'jewel-like.'"[214] He adds: "Ratnākaraśānti[215] and Abhayākaragupta[216] explain that the causal tantra is the true nature of the mind."[217] Hence, in interpreting the meaning of the "cause," individual scholars vary in accordance with their philosophical view. For Tsongkhapa, the cause is the best tantric yogi. At a closer look, as already indicated (see "The Illusory Body" in this chapter), it is not the entire person of the yogi that serves as the actual cause, but rather the yogi's innate body made of wind-and-mind. Based on the Prāsaṅgika Madhyamaka thought Tsongkhapa holds, he explains that the innate body acts as a basis for that yogi's designation; there is no innate body beyond this.[218]

On the other hand, in following Indian scholars such as Ratnākaraśānti and Abhayākaragupta, other Tibetan authors, especially of the Kagyu and Nyingma schools, explain the tantric cause from the diametrically opposed position of Buddha Nature.[219] For example, after citing the aforementioned verses of the *Subsequent Tantra,* Dakpo Tashi Namgyal (1512–87) explains that the "cause" that initiates the continuity is buddha nature, the true nature,[220] suchness,[221] the cause of buddhahood, with which all beings in the six realms of existence are endowed.[222] Likewise, in his *Treasury of Knowledge,* Kongtrul Yönten Gyatso (1813–99) explains the same verses by saying that the causal tantra is "the natural condition of the mind that continues from the state of an [ordinary] sentient being up until buddhahood and, like the sky, abides without ever changing."[223] Kongtrul then adds that the natural condition of the mind—called by various names such as suchness, causal Vajradhara, and original buddha—is indivisibly united with forms or appearances. This union is the substantial cause of awakening.

Hence, holders of the Buddha Nature approach can provide a straightforward explanation for the everlasting continuity from the yogi's ordinary ground of existence up until awakening. Tsongkhapa—who does not accept the theory of Buddha Nature in such a way—offers an intricate and sophisticated resolution to the notion of continuity from ground to fruit.

The Stage of Union and the Buddha's Bodies of the Fruit

The pure illusory body is the main and unique cause of the *rūpakāya* (consisting of both the *saṃbhogakāya* and *nirmāṇakāya*), which replaces the limitless accumulation of merit found in the Pāramitā Vehicle.[224] Likewise, the wisdom of great bliss that directly realizes actual-clear-light-emptiness is the substantial cause[225] for the *dharmakāya.* These are the unique homogenous causes[226] for the two buddha's bodies on the fruit, the *rūpakāya* and *dharmakāya* indivisibly united.

The fifth, and final, step of the completion stage is the union of the pure illusory body and the actual-clear-light. The two aspects and their union continue throughout the Pāramitā and Mantra Vehicles. In the Pāramitā Vehicle, they are called "method" and "wisdom." In the creation stage, we may recall,[227] the wisdom and method are the meditations on clear-light-emptiness and deity yoga. During the yoga with the consort, we have encountered the indivisible union of the mind experiencing great bliss and emptiness. In the step of union, the pure illusory body and the actual-clear-light exist as a single inseparable entity. In terms of wisdom and method, the illusory body is the method, and the clear light is the wisdom.[228]

Both wings in the union of bliss and emptiness, however, are aspects of wisdom alone—the wisdom of great bliss that realizes emptiness-clear-light. In the fifth step of the completion stage, this wisdom that realizes the actual-clear-light is now united with the illusory body, made of very subtle wind-and-mind. In the step of union, mind and body are united: the mind of great bliss that realizes directly and the subtle body that will arise as the *rūpakāya.* We should remember, however, that these are not simply mind and body; the body itself is made not only of a subtle body but also of a subtle mind, and the two are a single entity.[229]

According to Tsongkhapa, the swiftness of the Mantric path, whereby enlightenment can be attained in one lifetime, is due to these two aspects: the indivisible bliss and emptiness on the one hand, and the illusory body on the other. Furthermore, he says, a clear description of the illusory body formed of wind-and-mind, the *saṃbhogakāya* of the meditator on the completion stage, is a unique feature of the Guhyasamāja cycle, which is not taught in other traditions, such as *yoginī* tantras.[230] Therefore, in his view, the explanation found in this supreme tradition should be made the basis of understanding other traditions as well.[231]

On the whole, yogic exercises of the subtle body did not find their way into the creation stage; hence, during the first stage, the subtle body is not considered to be activated, and there are no special references to the winds. During the creation stage, yogis meditate on the clear light of the creation stage,[232] from which they arise during the core of the *sādhana*, as the First Lord and Vajrasattva's *nirmāṇakāya*—deities created by mere visualization that correspond to the actual *dharmakāya, saṃbhogakāya,* and *nirmāṇakāya.*

Some Points Regarding Correspondences

Meditations in Correspondence with the First People in the Eon

In the section "Meditations in Correspondence with the Cosmos," above, we have seen that according to Nāgabuddhi's *Formulating the Guhyasamāja Sādhana,*[233] during the cosmological event, first the physical world is created and immediately thereupon the first beings descend there; likewise during the *sādhana,* after visualizing the celestial mansion, the yogi visualizes the first deities residing in it. This imparts a perfect harmony between the cosmos and the *sādhana.* Nāgabuddhi delineates in detail the cosmological events of the destructions and recreations of the world and then describes the extraordinary qualities of the first beings who appeared in Jambudvīpa and how they turned into ordinary people who transmigrate in *saṃsāra.*

Notably, the visualization of the first deities in the mandala corresponds to the appearance of the first inhabitants of Jambudvīpa soon after the world is created.[234] Furthermore, the death of the first beings in the world corresponds to the dissolution of the first deities in the mandala into clear light. It is not surprising, then, that many Tibetan scholars before Tsongkhapa, including Gö Khukpa Lhetsé and Rendawa,[235] drew correspondences between the evolution of the first beings in the world and the first deities visualized in the mandala. On the other hand, as noted in the section "The Three Bodies of the Meditators on the Creation Stage," Tsongkhapa does not agree. We will now examine his reasons.

CAN THE MEDITATION ON THE FIRST DEITIES IN THE MANDALA PURIFY THE FIRST PEOPLE IN THE EON?

As noted above, in the section "Meditations in Correspondence with the Cosmos," Tsongkhapa rejects the position that events that took place during the first eon can be purified by the meditation on the present path. On this matter Tsongkhapa cites the *Pramāṇavārttika,*[236] where Dharmakīrti states that it is possible to prevent wrongdoings that are about to arise and the negative karma that would arise from them, but it is not possible to destroy what has already been done. According to Tsongkhapa: "The position that the meditation on the present path can purify the birth, death, and intermediate state of beings who lived and died during the first eon, together with their environment, can be likened to the idea of using this year's fire to burn the firewood that was destroyed last year: it is pointless."[237]

While Tsongkhapa disagrees with the Tibetan scholars who maintain that the meditation on the *sādhana* can affect past events or other people, he cannot object to Nāgabuddhi, who is one of his main authorities. Therefore, Tsongkhapa accepts that the three bodies of the meditator on the creation stage correspond to—but do not purify—the death, intermediate state, and rebirth of the first people in the eon who reside in Jambudvīpa. In *Bee's Hope* Tsongkhapa explains:

> What is the reason the three bodies—the *dharmakāya, saṃbhogakāya,* and *nirmāṇakāya*—of the meditator on the creation stage are applied in correspondences with the death, intermediate state, and rebirth of people living in the first eon in Jambudvīpa and not with other people? As *Formulating the Guhyasamāja Sādhana* teaches, the formation of the celestial mansion, the residence of the specially visualized deities [the first deities in the mandala], corresponds to the evolution of the world, while the circle of deities residing therein, the specially visualized deities themselves, corresponds to the people of the first eon. The *dharmakāya* arising when the specially visualized deities enter into clear light corresponds to the death of the people in the first eon. Likewise, the *saṃbhogakāya* and *nirmāṇakāya* of the meditator on the creation stage correspond to the intermediate being and rebirth of the people in the first eon.[238]

The first group of the thirty-two deities who dwell in the celestial mansion of the Guhyasamāja mandala are called the "specially visualized deities."[239] This name is unique to the *Guhyasamāja Sādhana* according to the Ārya tradition of Nāgārjuna. In the above quotation Tsongkhapa begins his explanation as to why, according to *Formulating the Guhyasamāja Sādhana,* the yogas of a buddha's three bodies should correspond not only to the death, intermediate state, and rebirth of human beings residing in Jambudvīpa in general, but specifically to the death, intermediate state, and rebirth of human beings residing in Jambudvīpa in the first eon. We may recall that Tsongkhapa postulates that yogis meditate on the yogas of the three bodies of a buddha in order to ultimately purify their own future death, intermediate state, and rebirth. But here he justifies the position of Nāgabuddhi.

DOES THE MEDITATION ON THE *DHARMAKĀYA* OF THE CREATION STAGE CORRESPOND TO THE DEATH OF THE FIRST PEOPLE IN THE EON?

It is not difficult to explain the correspondence between the meditation on the *dharmakāya* and the yogi's future death. The yogi's future death is that of a human being residing in Jambudvīpa, endowed with the six constituents and a body of passion. The *dharmakāya* of the meditator on the creation stage is the clear-light-emptiness into which the specially visualized deities—the first deities residing in the mandala—dissolve. Notably, the death of the first people living in Jambudvīpa in the new eon is no different than the future death of the meditator on the creation stage. Although upon their birth, these beings were endowed with marvelous qualities, gradually they became ordinary people and died an ordinary human death, similar to the future death of the meditator on the creation stage.[240]

Therefore, Tsongkhapa can accept the correspondence between the meditation on the *dharmakāya* of the creation stage—meant to purify the yogi's future death—and the death of the people of the first eon. However, he does not regard the death of the people of the first eon as a ground of purification for a yogi who meditates at present.

WHY DO THE MEDITATIONS ON THE *SAṂBHOGAKĀYA* AND *NIRMĀṆAKĀYA* OF THE CREATION STAGE CORRESPOND TO THE INTERMEDIATE STATE AND REBIRTH OF THE FIRST PEOPLE IN THE EON?

According to Tsongkhapa, the grounds of purification of the meditations on the *saṃbhogakāya* and *nirmāṇakāya* of the creation stage are the yogi's future intermediate state and rebirth. However, these two future events are not necessarily similar to the future intermediate state and rebirth of a person who died during the first eon in Jambudvīpa. This is because after their death, the people dwelling in Jambudvīpa in the first eon may be reborn in any realm of the world in accordance with their individual karma, and their intermediate state will be that of a being destined to be born in that realm. Tsongkhapa explains this in *Bee's Hope,* saying that the correspondences with the intermediate being and rebirth of the people of the first eon dwelling in Jambudvīpa "are not appropriate, because it is not certain that a human being who dies in Jambudvīpa will be reborn only as a human being in Jambudvīpa."[241]

Tsongkhapa, then, broadens the issue: "The three bodies of the meditator on the two stages [the creation and completion stages of the Mantric path], the *dharmakāya, saṃbhogakāya,* and *nirmāṇakāya,* correspond not only to the death, intermediate state, and rebirth at the ground of ordinary existence, but also to the three bodies of the fruit; and the *nirmāṇakāya* that the *saṃbhogakāya* takes in order to display the twelve deeds can be born only in a passionate body."[242] Tsongkhapa argues here that the correspondences must be drawn not only with the ground—ordinary death, intermediate state, and rebirth—but also with the fruit of the path, the three bodies of a buddha. As noted in the discussion on the working of the *sādhana* (see the section "Purifications" at the beginning of this chapter), the meditation on the path of the Unexcelled Mantra "takes the fruit on the path." Hence, it is insufficient to apply the meditation in correspondence with the ground of ordinary existence alone.

We have also seen that only human beings born in Jambudvīpa, endowed with the six constituents and a passionate body, can display the fruit of buddhahood through the Mantric path.[243] Therefore, the meditations on the *saṃbhogakāya* and *nirmāṇakāya* during the creation stage must correspond to the intermediate state and rebirth of those who will be reborn as human beings in Jambudvīpa. These meditations do not correspond to all types of intermediate states and rebirths.

Only when these two conditions are fulfilled—namely, that the correspondences are applied to the fruit and that the grounds are the intermediate state and rebirth of future human beings in Jambudvīpa—can we speak about a thread or tantra that connects the following three elements: the *ground* of ordinary existence, the Mantric *path,* and the *fruit* of the three bodies of a buddha. As noted above (in the section "Purification"), the unique feature of the *Guhyasamāja Sādhana* is that it takes on the path both the fruit and the ground of purifications that lead to the fruit. Therefore, the grounds of ordinary existence must be that of beings capable of attaining the fruit through the Mantric path: namely, the intermediate state and rebirth of human beings in Jambudvīpa.

For these reasons, Tsongkhapa maintains that a yogi meditating on the *saṃbhogakāya* and *nirmāṇakāya* during the creation stage does so in correspondence with the intermediate state and rebirth of beings who will be reborn as human beings in Jambudvīpa. He does not accept that the grounds of purification of this meditation can be an intermediate state and rebirth of the people in the first eon. He explains this in *Bee's Hope:*

> The three bodies—the *dharmakāya, saṃbhogakāya,* and *nirmāṇakāya*—of the meditator on the creation stage are applied in correspondences with death, the intermediate stage, and rebirth of a human being dwelling in Jambudvīpa during the first eon, yet death, the intermediate stage, and rebirth are not taken as grounds of purification [of these three bodies on the path]. This is so because the yogi who meditates in this way cannot purify the death, the intermediate stage, and rebirth of a person who is already dead and who is of a different mental continuum. Even if the yogi could do so, it would be irrelevant. What do the yogis purify then? They purify their own death, intermediate state, and rebirth that will occur in the future.[244]

Therefore, for Tsongkhapa, the first people in the eon cannot be a ground of purification of any step of the *sādhana.* But he accepts that the first people in the eon, who appeared in Jambudvīpa soon after it was created, can be taken as analogous to the specially visualized deities, the first deities residing in the mandala after the celestial mansion is visualized.[245] This is not only because these groups of people and deities are the first to appear in their dwelling, but also because the mode of appearance of these two groups is similar. The first people in the eon are born instantaneously through a miraculous birth; likewise, the specially visualized deities are generated at once and not through stages, as Tsongkhapa explains in *Bee's Hope:* "The instantaneous generation of the specially visualized deities corresponds to the people of the first eon in Jambudvīpa who were miraculously born."[246]

Since Tsongkhapa objects to the position that the meditation on the specially visualized deities can purify the first people in the eon, he interprets *Formulating the Guhyasamāja Sādhana* in a way that departs from the method of earlier Tibetan scholars of the *Guhyasamāja Sādhana.* Tsongkhapa sees the meditation on the specially visualized deities as a preparatory step for the yogas of the three bodies and regards only the latter as capable of soteriological import. For Tsongkhapa, then, a yogi visualizes the specially visualized deities in order to create a "person" whose death, intermediate state, and rebirth can be taken on the path during the core of the *sādhana* without serving any soteriological goal.

It must be stressed that Tsongkhapa finds a basis for his position in Nāgabuddhi's *Formulating the Guhyasamāja Sādhana*. We have seen[247] that while Nāgabuddhi[248] describes four types of rebirth and the characteristics of human beings in the four continents, he concludes that all the buddhas of the three times (past, present, and future) "take" their last rebirth (into the life in which they are awakened) as human beings in Jambudvīpa alone. Hence, Nāgabuddhi indicates that yogis who will be awakened in their present life must meditate on the *saṃbhogakāya* and *nirmāṇakāya* of the creation stage only in correspondence with the intermediate state and rebirth of beings who will be reborn as human beings in Jambudvīpa.

With What Do the Subsequent Steps of the Sādhana *Correspond?*

For Tsongkhapa, as we have seen,[249] the steps of the *sādhana* that are endowed with a soteriological value and thus can serve to purify a ground of purification are only those that correspond to the three bodies of a buddha and lead to their attainment. Hence, other than death, the intermediate state, and rebirth, there are no additional grounds that require purification. According to Tsongkhapa, the practices that follow the yoga of the three buddha's bodies—including the yoga with a consort and the meditation on the Supreme Kings—are undertaken not for the sake of the yogis themselves but for the benefit of other sentient beings.

Although yogis of the creation stage do not necessarily attain buddhahood, for the sake of their disciples they act as if they have attained a buddha's three bodies and have created a pure buddha-field. Therefore, the steps of the *sādhana* beginning with the yoga with the consort correspond only to the fruit of the path, buddhahood; especially to "deeds" of Vajradhara and other tantric buddhas described in the *Guhyasamāja Tantra*. These deeds that were performed for instructing yogis of the Mantra Vehicle during the "exemplary life" of these buddhas are called "past events."[250]

In *Bee's Hope* Tsongkhapa explains how the events with which the yoga with a consort and the emanation of the mandala correspond:

> The Teacher performed three "past events" in which he taught three types of practice. (1) Having descended from Tuṣita Heaven,[251] the Teacher taught practices without passion for disciples who adhere to the lower [path] and made them deeply understand the four truths. (2) The Teacher taught the practice of the grounds and perfections for disciples who aspire to the great extensive [path] and made them deeply understand the subtle selflessness of phenomena. (3) By absorbing in union with the queen, the

> Teacher taught the practice of great passion for disciples who earnestly intent on the profound [path] and made them deeply understand the union of the indivisible two truths.
>
> In the present context, [the yoga with the consort and the emanation of the mandala] correspond to the deed of the Teacher, who having absorbed in union with the queen, emanated the mandala with its deities and conferred initiation on the disciples. These practices do not correspond to the ground.[252]

The *Illuminating Lamp* explains the "past events" of great passion: "Now, to instruct those sentient beings—who are attached to objects in the Desire Realm—about liberation through the five attributes of passion, the *Guhyasamāja Tantra* teaches: 'Then, the Blessed One, the *Tathāgata* Great Vairocanavajra was absorbed in union in the *samādhi* called "the method of great passion of all *tathāgatas*."'"[253] This is the tantric method of taking desire on the path in order to overcome desire, a notion expressed in a well-known verse of the *Hevajra Tantra:* "By passion sentient beings are bound and by that very passion they are released."[254] A yogi who is suitable for practicing the Mantric path emulates here the deed of passion the *Tathāgata* performed at the opening of the *Guhyasamāja Tantra,* which led to the engendering of its mandala.

Tsongkhapa objects to the position taken by some Tibetan scholars that the union with the consort and the emanation of the mandala can be applied in correspondence with the ground of other sentient beings and serve to purify their *saṃsāric* processes. Thus, he writes:

> Tibetan lamas say that (1) the practice with a consort corresponds to taking a wife from another clan; (2) blessing the *vajra* and lotus and developing passion corresponds to arousing the sexual organs of the father and mother and developing passion; (3) engaging in the act of passion and making offering [of *bodhicitta*] corresponds to the husband and wife coupling and thereby satisfying their three doors;[255] (4) engendering the Supreme King of Mandalas corresponds to begetting children; (5) meditating on the Supreme King of Mandalas through the steps of offerings and so forth corresponds to nourishing and protecting the children and grandchildren until gradually they are grown up; (6) the meditation on the subtle drop for the sake of purifying the mind and the *siddhis* that arise thereby corresponds to the sons and grandsons who in order to purify their minds and develop wisdom, learn topics of knowledge and attain their own purposes and those of others.[256]

Among the Tibetan lamas who espouse this view are Gö Khukpa Lhetsé[257] and Rendawa Shönu Lodrö,[258] who describe correspondences between the yoga with a consort and subsequent steps of the practice that can purify the yogi's wife and descendants throughout the generations to come, as described by Tsongkhapa in the above citation.

Butön Rinchen Drup (1290–1364), who lived before Tsongkhapa, had already expressed the same position as Tsongkhapa: namely that the latter part of the *sādhana* does not correspond with the ground, but only with the fruit.[259] The two never met, since Butön died in central Tibet only seven years after Tsongkhapa's birth in Amdo. However, Tsongkhapa attests[260] that he studied with Butön's disciple Khyungpo Lhépa Zhönu Sönam.[261] In any case, Tsongkhapa follows Butön on this point and objects to the position of Gö and Rendawa without mentioning their names. He explains that it is inappropriate to maintain that yoga with a consort corresponds with activities of a householder such as begetting offspring and acting for their sake, since having a family will create attachment to relatives and produce negative karma.[262] Moreover, there is no need to do so: "Because all grounds of purification are already covered, it is sufficient to apply the meditation in correspondence with birth, death, and the intermediate state as explained before; and because otherwise there would be no end to the process of applying the correspondences."[263] In his usual method of reducing the opponent's position to absurdity, Kedrup Jé elaborates on Tsongkhapa's explanation why a position such as that of Gö and Rendawa is unreasonable:

> These are merely the mental fabrications of those who do not understand the meaning of the creation stage. None of their positions was ever taught by Ārya Nāgārjuna and his disciples. For the aim of purifying the ground of purification through the creation stage is the awakening of the yogis themselves; to achieve this, it is sufficient that they purify the stages of their own *saṃsāric* existence by meditating in correspondence with them. If, in order to attain enlightenment the yogis must purify all their sons, grandsons and so forth by meditating in correspondence with the stages of their descendants' *saṃsāric* existence, the consequences will be utterly absurd: (1) they will be unable to awaken until all their future relations do; (2) their relations will awaken without having actually meditated on the path; (3) no matter how much they purify themselves, in order to attain the stage of the three bodies, their path will include many grounds of purification belonging to the mental continuum of other people rather than

> their own birth, death, and intermediate state; and (4) they will have to meditate in correspondence with the stages of the *saṃsāric* rebirth of their own sons, grandsons, great-grandsons and their sons, grandsons, great-grandsons, and so forth.[264]

Not only yoga with a consort but also the subsequent steps of the *sādhana*—the Supreme King of Mandalas and the Supreme King of Deeds—have no ground of purification. These steps, which are practiced not for the sake of the yogis themselves but for the benefit of other sentient beings, correspond to the deeds of the fruitional buddha, as will be clarified below.[265]

In the next chapter, we will review the practice of the creation stage in detail, as described in *Fulfilling the Bee's Hope.*

4

A Detailed Explanation of the *Sādhana*

Most of *Fulfilling the Bee's Hope* is dedicated to an explanation of the text of the *sādhana*.[1] The work begins with a discussion on the framework of the *sādhana*[2] and an explanation of its preliminaries, but here we will look only at the main part, which consists of: (1) meditations on the dissolution of the ordinary environment and the arising of the celestial mansion of the mandala in correspondence with the destruction of the former world and the evolution of the subsequent one; (2) meditations on the yoga of a buddha's three bodies in correspondence to the death, intermediate state, and rebirth of the person; and (3) meditations on the emanated mandalas of the Supreme Kings.

As already mentioned in the previous chapter, meditations that correspond to the destruction and evolution of the world have significant affinity with the macrocosm, but according to Tsongkhapa they cannot act as its purifiers.

Meditations That Correspond to the Destruction of the World

The meditation on the dissolution of the yogi's ordinary environment that corresponds to the destruction of the former world is a specific type of meditation on emptiness, referred to as "meditation on the ground of wisdom."[3] During this meditation, yogis recite a mantra-like verse found in the *Guhyasamāja Tantra:* "In the absence of being, there is no meditation and meditation cannot be meditated upon. Therefore, a state of being that is nonbeing leaves no object for meditation."[4] In his *Sādhana* Tsongkhapa explains the meaning of this verse: "Since all phenomena included in the animate and inanimate realms are devoid of essence in ultimate truth, their nature is emptiness, signlessness, and wishlessness, in which meditation, object of meditation, and meditator cannot be perceived."[5] In *Bee's Hope* Tsongkhapa then remarks: "The object to which this meditation corresponds is taught in *Formulating the Guhyasamāja Sādhana.*"[6]

This treatise, written by Nāgabuddhi, is the source of most of the correspondences between the meditation, the cosmos, and the person. The first chapter of *Formulating the Guhyasamāja Sādhana* begins thus: "When the time for this world to be destroyed has arrived and not a single being remains in the three realms—the physical world alone remains, rays of light from seven suns appearing successively burn up the three realms, and turn them into the nature of space. In accordance with this, the meditator on the creation stage should recite and meditate on the verse that begins with 'in the absence of being.'"[7] Thus, when the world has been emptied of all its beings[8] and only the physical support remains, seven suns incinerate it and reduce it to space alone. In correspondence with this extinction, the yogis meditate on "the absence of being" and dissolve their ordinary environment and reality.

In *Bee's Hope* Tsongkhapa explains that the correspondence between the meditation and the cosmological event operates on two levels.[9] The first is the *absence* of the world[10] to the meditator's subjective mind,[11] and the second is the *nonappearance* of the world[12] at the objective level of appearances.[13] These two levels correspond respectively to the *absence* of the physical world during the empty eon and to its *nonappearance* during that time.

This meditation on the ground of wisdom differs from the typical Geluk meditation on emptiness, which is concerned with the ultimate way of existence and defines the object of negation with great precision according to the philosophy of Prāsaṅgika Madhyamaka. In tantric meditation, while the subjective mind understands that in ultimate truth no phenomena exist, all appearances visible at the level of the conventional truth[14] cease as well.

The difference arises because of the specific context of the meditation on the ground of wisdom. Here, meditators must dissolve their ordinary environment so that it could be replaced with a special environment, visualized as the celestial mansion of the mandala. Therefore, they negate all objects—and not only the objects of negation—in correspondence with the empty period of the world. At the same time, yogis meditate on emptiness through the tantric method that gives rise to the wisdom of great bliss,[15] the subjective aspect that is indivisibly united with emptiness, the objective aspect.

Tsongkhapa goes on to explain why this form of meditation on emptiness is called "meditation on the ground of wisdom." The cessation of all appearances of the animate and inanimate realms to the mind of *wisdom* arising from great bliss indivisible from emptiness is the *ground* for evolution of the celestial mansion of the mandala. Likewise, the empty space that remains after the physical elements of the world are destroyed is the *ground* for the evolution of the subsequent world. In *Bee's Hope* Tsongkhapa says: "Why is the wisdom of great bliss referred to as *ground* [or foundation]? As the space formed when the previous world is emptied serves as the *foundation* [or ground] for the evolution of the subsequent world, the *wisdom* of great bliss serves as the *foundation* for the evolution of the celestial mansion, and therefore it is called the *ground of wisdom*."[16]

In the next sentence, Tsongkhapa reminds us that although this meditation corresponds to the empty space between the former and subsequent worlds, the emptiness meditated upon here is none other than the three doors to liberation, which accords with the view of the Madhyamaka school: "Furthermore, the emptiness on which the yogi should meditate in this context is the three doors to liberation:[17] (1) the absence of the world and its inhabitants in ultimate truth; (2) the imperceptibility of the meditation, the object to be meditated upon, and the meditator, as true; and (3) the absence of intrinsic nature of the essence, cause, and fruit of phenomena."[18] Before closing this chapter, Tsongkhapa delineates the goals of the meditation on emptiness at the onset of the main part of the *sādhana:*

> There are several purposes of meditating on emptiness here by way of recitation of the verse beginning with: "In the absence of being": (1) Meditators with dull faculties will newly realize the view of emptiness; (2) meditators with middling faculties will recollect their forgotten realization of emptiness; and (3) meditators with sharp faculties will stabilize their already-attained realization of emptiness. (4) They will gather the accumulation of wisdom, and (5) will shed conceptualization of ordinary attitudes and appearances of their body, speech, and mind. This is (6) in order that the mandala with its celestial mansion and deities—that will be explained later—will arise as a display of emptiness; (7) in order to block the conception of true existence—the root of *saṃsāra;* (8) to serve as an ultimate protection; (9) to purify death on the ground [of ordinary existence]; (10) to ripen the mental continuum for the clear light of the completion stage; (11) to attain the fruitional *dharmakāya,* and so forth.[19]

In summary, those who have not realized emptiness will newly realize it; those who have realized it already will restore their realization; and those who have maintained their realization of emptiness will stabilize their realization and complete the accumulation of wisdom. (They have already accumulated merit during the preliminary phases.)[20]

The fifth goal—namely, shedding the conceptualization of ordinary attitudes and appearances[21]—is a fundamental aim of the *sādhana.* To attain this goal, yogis must dissolve their ordinary reality—the way they perceive themselves and their environment and the way they themselves and their environment appear to them. To tamp down the ordinary cognition that engages with the conventional world, they are enjoined to let their minds focus on emptiness. Otherwise, ordinary appearances will not cease to arise to their cognition. During the period of the world's creation, as described previously, the first beings in the eon gradually became ordinary. The goal here is to shed this ordinary existence and let the extraordinary celestial mansion of the mandala arise through the extraordinary practice of the *sādhana.*

This brings us to the sixth goal of the meditation on emptiness, which is of prime consequence: that the celestial mansion and deities will arise as a display of emptiness. When experienced meditators arise from an extended meditative absorption on the true nature of things, due to the impact of their meditation on emptiness, all phenomena appear to their minds as a display of emptiness. The diversity of phenomena appears to their mind as illusion-like—namely, they appear yet are devoid of intrinsic nature.[22] When such meditators arise from their absorption on emptiness during the creation stage, the entire mandala with its deities arises to their minds as illusion-like, too.

Yogis who do not achieve this level will simply replace one mistaken conceptual appearance with another. In place of the world as it ordinarily appears to them, they will see the mandala as a concretized entity, while the goal is to abide in the more-than-real experience of the mandala. In his *Great Treatise on the Stages of the Mantric Path,*[23] Tsongkhapa discusses how a single mind can be absorbed in both the meditation on the absence of intrinsic nature and the visualization of the mandala. While the subjective aspect of the mind is absorbed in emptiness, the objective aspect of this mind arises as the appearance of the deities.

The seventh goal of the meditation on emptiness is to eradicate the conception of true existence[24] or the grasping of things as real, considered a main cause of *saṃsāra.* According to Kedrup Jé,[25] in terms of its efficacy as an antidote to grasping at true existence, the mind that takes the circle of deities for its focus and apprehends the absence of its intrinsic existence is a hundred times superior to a mind that takes a sprout for its focus and apprehends there an absence of intrinsic existence.[26]

The meditation on emptiness provides the yogi also with an ultimate protection. While the conventional protection from unfavorable conditions is practiced during the preliminaries by means of the visualization of the protection wheel and meditation on the *vajra* enclosure,[27] various treatises, including the *Vajrasattva Sādhana,*[28] explain that meditation on the verse beginning with "In the absence of being" is the ultimate protection.[29] We will return to the last three goals listed by Tsongkhapa in the next section.[30]

Arising from the Meditation on Emptiness

The meditation on arising from emptiness[31] begins with the reappearance of the *vajra* enclosure of protection that was dissolved during the meditation on the ground of wisdom. In the next step, yogis visualize the "source of phenomena"[32] in the form of a white triangular pyramid standing on its point with its wide side pointing upwards.[33] The source of phenomena is, as its name indicates, the ground of all things. It is shaped like the birth-giving place of the consort, evoking the womb of the mother of all. According to Tsongkhapa:

> The white color of the source of phenomena signifies natural purity;[34] its three corners signify the three doors of liberation and the three wisdoms that realize them; its shape is that of the *bhaga*[35] and therefore signifies great bliss. The meditation on the mandala with its celestial mansion and the specially visualized deities contained within the source of phenomena signifies that all the good qualities of the fruitional time will arise on the basis of the meditation on the path of indivisible bliss and emptiness.[36]

Thus, when in the opening of the *Guhyasamāja Tantra,*[37] the teacher of the tantra is dwelling in the *bhaga* of the Vajra Queen, he is dwelling in the source of phenomena that encompasses the celestial mansion—and so are the meditators on the *Guhyasamāja Sādhana.*

Meditations That Correspond to the Evolution of the World

The meditation on the mandala palace, which as yet has no deities residing in it, corresponds to the evolution of the inanimate world before its inhabitants appear during the first eon. According to the *Sādhana,*[38] within the "source of phenomena," meditated upon in the previous step, yogis create the four mandalas of the physical elements: wind, fire, water, and earth, each arising from its seed syllables: *yaṃ, raṃ, vaṃ,* and *laṃ,* respectively. It is important to distinguish between these mandalas of the physical elements and the greater mandala that rests upon them. The former are referred to as mandalas because the objects to which they correspond are round or cylindrical.[39]

This meditation corresponds to the evolution of the four mandalas of the elements during the evolution of the physical world. Recall that during the creation of the inanimate world, gentle winds are set in motion, and when they whorl faster a wind mandala is created. (See the section "The Creation of the Inanimate World" in chapter 1.) A constant rain falls on the wind mandala and forms a water mandala, and then a wind churns the water to create a golden mandala upon the water. Nāgabuddhi tell us that within these mandalas, fire also abides.[40] In *Bee's Hope* Tsongkhapa explains how the four mandalas of the physical elements on which the world rests and on which the mandala stands correspond: "The meditation on the wind mandala corresponds to the evolution of the wind mandala on the 'ground' of ordinary existence, and likewise are the three other mandalas [of fire, water and earth]."[41] The term "ground"[42] refers to events the cosmos and person undergo, which in turn correspond to various steps of the meditation, as explained in the introduction.

As noted at the end of the section "Methods of Purifications" in chapter 3, special links are found between the impure psychophysical elements of the human body and their purified aspects as the deities of the mandala that make the transformation from the impure to the pure possible. In the present context, in his *Guhyasamāja Sādhana* Tsongkhapa states: "The natures of the four mandalas of the physical elements are respectively those of the four female buddhas, Locanā, Māmakī, Pāṇḍarā, and Tārā."[43] This means that these ordinary aspects of the body—its impure solidity, fluidity, warmth, and motility, represented by the four physical elements, will ultimately transform into the four female buddhas of the mandala.[44] For this reason, meditators on the *sādhana* visualize the four mandalas "in the nature" (or as possessing the essence)[45] of the four female buddhas.

Tsongkhapa then elucidates the significance of the four mandalas in the context of the completion stage: "The meditation on the four mandalas of the physical elements—wind, fire, water, and earth—signifies respectively the winds of the yogi during the completion stage: the yellowish green wind-wind, the 'uniform wind';[46] the red fire-wind, the 'ascending wind';[47] the white water-wind, the 'life sustaining wind';[48] and the yellow earth-wind, the 'descending wind.'"[49] These four winds, along with the "pervasive wind,"[50] are the five main winds that serve as the mounts for the minds.[51] Briefly, during the completion stage, all of the winds are withdrawn into the central channel of the subtle body[52] and are dissolved into the indestructible drop at the heart,[53] while the melting drops unite;[54] this give rise to great bliss and realization of the actual clear light. There are two methods for achieving this: the external one, involving yoga with a consort; and the internal one, involving meditation on the winds and drops of the subtle body.[55]

In *Bee's Hope* Tsongkhapa explains that the four mandalas of the physical elements signify the four winds of the subtle body that are the internal contributing causes for the arising of great bliss.[56] The external contributing causes[57] are the four female buddhas, also referred to as the "four goddesses": "The meditation on the four mandalas in the nature of the four goddesses, Locanā, [Māmakī, Pāṇḍarā, and Tārā],[58] signifies the four consorts, Padminī, [Śaṅkhinī, Hastinī, and Citriṇī],[59] which are the external contributing causes [for the arising of great bliss and clear light during the completion stage]."[60]

In the following step of the *sādhana*,[61] the four mandalas of the physical elements merge to create the crossed *vajra*, the base upon which stands the celestial mansion of the mandala. Tsongkhapa explains the significance of this merging in the context of the completion stage:

> The meditation on the crossed *vajra* formed from the four mandalas [of the physical elements] that have merged signifies the actual clear light of the fourth step [of the completion stage] that arises from the union with the four consorts—the external contributing causes—and the *vajra* repetition[62] based on the four winds—the internal contributing causes. The five prongs of the *vajra* signify the five wisdoms of clear light. The meditation on the mandala with its celestial mansion and deities upon the nave of the crossed *vajra* signifies the arising of the mandala with its celestial mansion and deities during the [fifth] step of union [at the culmination of the completion stage] that arises from the actual clear light.[63]

Hence, in *Bee's Hope* Tsongkhapa explains how the meditations on emptiness, on the source of phenomena, and on the crossed *vajra* topped by the celestial mansion signify the destruction and evolution of the world. Likewise, he elucidates the significance of these meditations during the completion stage. However, regarding the visualization of the celestial mansion, the abode where the deities reside,[64] Tsongkhapa explains the correspondence only in a general way: "The meditation on the celestial mansion upon the crossed *vajra* corresponds to the formation of the mountains and the continents on the ground of ordinary existence [at the beginning of the eon]."[65] This is because Tsongkhapa does not see a soteriological value in the "connections" between the cosmos on the one hand and the person and the practice on the other. (See the section "Meditations in Correspondence with the Cosmos" in chapter 3.)

Kedrup Jé explains in more detail what the meditation on the celestial mansion can achieve and what it cannot: "What does it mean to purify the impure world by meditating on the celestial mansion? It is not that, through your meditation on the celestial mansion, you can transform this present impure world into a pure celestial mansion. Rather, you can purify your own capacity to partake in the impure world in the future [meaning that you yourself will not experience the impure world]. The purpose of this meditative purification is to ripen your mental continuum for the completion stage, in which you will develop the capacity to partake in the celestial mansion of wisdom."[66] Thus, according to Kedrup Jé, yogis meditating on the *sādhana* cannot bring about a true transformation in their outer world. They can affect only themselves by transforming their own abilities to partake in the impure world in the future.

This concludes the discussion of meditations that correspond to the destruction and evolution of the world. We turn now to meditations in correspondence with the stages of the cyclic existence of human beings.

Preliminaries to the Meditations That Correspond to the Person

Prior to the meditation on the yogas of the three bodies,[67] yogis meditate on the deities called "specially visualized deities."

The Meditation on the Specially Visualized Deities

Before yogis meditate on the yoga of taking death on the path to the *dharmakāya,* in order to purify their future death, they must create "beings" capable of dying a human death. These beings are the specially visualized deities,[68] the first deities residing in the mandala. As their name indicates,[69] these deities are visualized for a special purpose, one that is not part of the yogas on the three bodies of a buddha. In the next step of the *sādhana,* which is included in the yoga of the *dharmakāya,* these deities will dissolve into clear light in correspondence with death. However, their visualization, their deeds, and their emplacement on the body are not part of this yoga.

The specially visualized deities, like all groups of deities residing in the Guhyasamāja mandala according to the Ārya tradition, are thirty-two in number and have three faces and six arms. At their center is the yogi, visualized as Vajradhara, embraced by his consort, Vajra Lady of Tangibles.[70] While during the yogas of the three bodies of a buddha, Akṣobhya is the principal deity of the mandala abiding in the center, as is typical in the Ārya tradition—here, in the context of the specially visualized deities, the principal deity of the mandala is Vajradhara, sharing his seat with his consort.[71] In the four cardinal directions, beginning with the east, are the four *tathāgatas*: Vairocana, Ratnasaṃbhava, Amitābha, and Amoghasiddhi. In the four intermediate directions, beginning with the southeast, are the four female buddhas, Locanā, Māmakī, Pāṇḍarā, and Tārā. Beyond them in the same directions are the four remaining *vajra* ladies—of forms, sounds, scents, and tastes.[72] On the seats to the right and left of every gate of the mansion are the eight *bodhisattvas*.[73] These deities are surrounded by the ten fierce deities in the main and intermediate directions as well as at the zenith and nadir.

The deity who is visualized during the yoga of a buddha's three bodies in the subsequent steps of the *sādhana* is generated in stages. By contrast, the specially visualized deities appear instantaneously in accord with the miraculous birth of the first people of the eon in Jambudvīpa, as Tsongkhapa explains in *Bee's Hope*: "Generate the specially visualized deities instantaneously without meditating on their seed syllables, emblems, and so forth, and then meditate by developing the clarity of the visualization, step by step."[74] Although the specially visualized deities appear instantly, yogis should then refine their visualizations in stages until they achieve clarity.

The Deeds of the Specially Visualized Deities and Their Withdrawal into the Yogi's Body

The meditation on the specially visualized deities during the preliminaries to the yogas of the three buddha's bodies consists of three steps. First these deities are generated, then they perform their deeds, and finally they are placed in the yogi's body. According to Tsongkhapa, these three steps correspond to the path and the fruit but not to the ground, because, as already indicated,[75] Tsongkhapa does not accept the position of early Tibetan scholars that the meditation on the specially visualized deities can purify the first beings in the eon in Jambudvīpa. In *Bee's Hope* Tsongkhapa explains: "The meditation on the deeds of the specially visualized deities and the meditation on their emplacement in the body take the fruit on the path, according to the exemplary life of the Teacher in the 'past event,'[76] but they have no correspondence to the ground of purification."[77]

The deeds of the specially visualized deities are activities that fulfill the *bodhisattva*'s vow to lead all sentient beings to awakening through the Mantric path. In performing these deeds, the yogis, as the principal deities of the special visualized deities, draw all sentient beings into the mandala through the four gates and initiate them. As a result, these sentient beings become Vajrasattvas and proceed to enlighten other beings. Hence, these deeds are the activities of buddhas undertaken after they become enlightened. For this reason, Tsongkhapa notes that in this step of the *sādhana* yogis take the fruit on the path according to the deeds of the Teacher of the *Guhyasamāja Tantra.*

Having performed their deeds, the thirty-two special visualized deities are drawn into certain areas of the yogi's body and become inseparable from the yogi. The specific location on the body each deity is drawn to is determined by the special affinities between the impure psychophysical elements of the human body and their purified aspects in the forms of the deities of the mandala, as described previously.[78] The specially visualized deities are placed on the same parts of the body as in the meditation on the body mandala.[79]

While not purifying any ground of purification for the sake of the yogis themselves, these three steps of the meditation on the specially visualized deities—their arising, deeds, and withdrawal into the yogi's body—lay the ground for the next step of the dissolution of the specially visualized deities into clear light. Moreover, they affect the subsequent stage of the path—the completion stage and its fruit—as Tsongkhapa discusses in *Fulfilling the Bee's Hope:* "Behold all the deities, the principal and surrounding deities, as indivisible bliss and emptiness. By meditating in this way, you will be able to abide in the actual mandala with its celestial mansion and deities during the completion stage and the fruit."[80] Ultimately, yogis will become the deities residing in the real mandala at the culmination of the completion stage and at buddhahood.

At this point, the meditations in correspondence with the destruction and creation of the cosmos and the first beings in our continent are concluded. As already indicated, Tsongkhapa regards them as preparatory steps to the yogas of the three bodies of a buddha. Only the latter can purify their grounds of purification and bring about soteriological goals. We shall now turn to meditations that correspond to the person.

Meditations That Correspond to the Death, Intermediate State, and Rebirth of the Person

This section constitutes the core of the *sādhana* that consists of the yogas of the three bodies of a buddha that serve to purify the future death, intermediate being, and rebirth of the yogis as their grounds of purification. These three future events are taken on the path to the *dharmakāya, saṃbhogakāya,* and *nirmāṇakāya,* respectively. Upon the completion of this yoga in its entirety, the soteriological goal of practice will be attained. Instead of the ordinary death, intermediate state, and rebirth that occur to ordinary people, the yogis will attain the three bodies of a buddha.

Meditations That Correspond to Death

The first step is the yoga of taking death on the path that leads to the *dharmakāya,* also called the meditation on the *dharmakāya* of the creation stage. In this practice, yogis meditate on themselves—with the specially visualized deities placed on their bodies—gradually dissolving into clear light, in correspondence with the process of ordinary death at the ground. Both the yogis and the deities dissolve because in the previous step of the meditation, the specially visualized deities were drawn into the yogis' bodies and became inseparable from those parts.

However, the deities do not simply dissolve into the parts of the body on which they are placed. It seems that the two steps—the drawing of the deities into the body and their dissolution into clear light—are adapted from two different practices. The former is akin to the meditation on the body mandala (for this process, see below in this chapter), while the latter follows the sequence of dissolution of the twenty-five coarse elements during ordinary death of human beings, the ground of purification of this meditation. Since, in the present context, the meditation must correspond to death, the process of the dissolutions at death determines the sequence of the meditation, regardless of where the deities were placed in the previous step.

As discussed in chapter 2 (in the section "Death according to Vajrayāna"), the twenty-five coarse elements that dissolve during death are the five aggregates,[81] the four physical elements,[82] the six sense faculties,[83] the five inner objects of the senses,[84] and the five wisdoms at the ground time (ordinary existence).[85] These twenty-five elements dissolve in stages through eight cycles.[86] Here is the first cycle of dissolution as described by Tsongkhapa in *Bee's Hope:* "Then, visualize the deities of the body mandala: Vairocana, Locanā, Kṣitigarbha, Rūpavajrā, Maitreya, Yamāntaka, and Acala one after the other dissolving into clear light.[87] This meditation corresponds to the dissolution into clear light at the ground [ordinary human death] of the form aggregate, the mirror-like wisdom, the earth element, the eye faculty, and the forms within their continuums."[88] Thus, in *the first cycle,* the following deities dissolve along with the coarse elements indivisible from them, in accordance with the first cycle of dissolution during ordinary death: Vairocana, indivisible from the form aggregate; Locanā, indivisible from the earth element; Kṣitigarbha, indivisible from the eye faculty; Rūpavajrā, indivisible from forms; Yamāntaka, Acala, and Maitreya, indivisible from the mirror-like wisdom at the ground time (ordinary existence).

Then, in accordance with the three subsequent cycles of dissolution at death, the other deities of the mandala dissolve together with the corresponding element of the body. Regarding this, Tsongkhapa makes the following brief remark: "You should know how to apply this in the three parallel cases below."[89] According to his *Sādhana,*[90] in the second cycle the following deities and coarse elements dissolve: Ratnasaṃbhava, indivisible from the aggregate of feeling; Māmakī, indivisible from the water element; Vajrapāṇi, indivisible from the ear faculty; Śabdhavajrā, indivisible from sounds; Aparājita and Ṭakkirāja,[91] indivisible from the wisdom of equanimity at the ground time.

The third cycle is characterized by the dissolution of Amitābha, indivisible from the aggregate of perception; Pāṇḍarā, indivisible from the fire element; Khagarbha, indivisible from the nose faculty; Gandhavajrā, indivisible from scents; Hayagrīva and Nīladaṇḍa, indivisible from the wisdom of discernment at the ground time.

In the fourth cycle we find Amoghasiddhi, indivisible from the aggregate of conditioning; Tārā, indivisible from the air-wind element; Lokeśvara, indivisible from the tongue faculty; Rasavajrā, indivisible from taste; Sarvāvaraṇavikṣambhin, indivisible from the body faculty; Sparśavajrā, indivisible from tangible objects;[92] Samantabhadra, Vighnāntaka, and Mahābala, indivisible from the wisdom of purposive acts at the ground time.

Then, in correspondence with the fifth cycle at death, in which consciousness dissolves in three stages (see the section "The Dissolution of Consciousness" in chapter 2), three additional deities dissolve, as Tsongkhapa describes in *Bee's Hope:* "Then, visualize the deities Uṣṇīṣacakravartin, Sumbharāja, and Mañjuśrī dissolving into clear light in stages, in correspondence with the dissolution of the air-wind into [white] appearance, [white] appearance into enhanced appearance, and enhanced appearance into approaching attainment."[93] These three dissolutions also correspond to the first three empty states: the empty, the very empty, and the great empty.[94] The fierce deities, Uṣṇīṣacakravartin and Sumbharāja, signify the entire body since the former is unified with the crown of the head and the latter with the feet. The *Bodhisattva* Mañjuśrī is unified with the mind.

The Actual Dissolution into Clear Light

After visualizing the deities as unified with areas of their body, yogis visualize how these areas, along with the deities inseparable from them, dissolve into clear light of indivisible bliss and emptiness.[95] Kedrup Jé describes this meditation in his *Ocean of Attainments:*

> When the signs of the dissolution of the form aggregates, the eye faculty and so forth, explained earlier,[96] begin to arise, you will recognize them, reflecting: "This is a sign of dissolution." After your form aggregate, which is indivisible from Vairocana; your eye faculty, which is indivisible from Kṣitigarbha; and so forth, dissolve into the clear light of indivisible bliss and emptiness, you should cultivate a stable meditation on the successive dissolutions into the continuing state of the clear light realized by the wisdom of indivisible great bliss and emptiness—empty of intrinsic existence.[97]

Four of the *bodhisattvas* are paired with four of the *vajra* ladies[98] because these *bodhisattvas* dissolve together with the sense faculties and the *vajra* ladies with the inner sense objects. When these deities are drawn into the body, Kṣitigarbha is placed on the eyes, Rūpavajrā at the entrance to the eyes; Vajrapāṇi on the ears, Śabdavajrā at the entrance to the ears, and so forth. In each of these couples, a *bodhisattva* and a *vajra* lady embrace one another to indicate the union of the sense faculties and their inner objects. Below, Kedrup Jé clarifies how the dissolution of Kṣitigarbha and Rūpavajrā should be visualized according to his own system:

> Here then is an example for the dissolution of the specially visualized deities into clear light: visualizing yourself as Vajradhara, meditate on Kṣitigarbha embraced by Rūpavajrā at the centers of your two eyeballs, and then maintain the conviction that the two deities are the essence of your eye faculty and the entire sensory sphere of the forms in your body. Then, do not merely think: "Kṣitigarbha and his consort have dissolved into clear light," but rather observe how your eye faculty and your sensory sphere of forms, which arose in the appearance of Kṣitigarbha with his consort, enter into the *dharmakāya* of indivisible bliss and emptiness. In this way, too, you should understand the other dissolutions. Habituation in this way will become a special and smooth ripener for a swift entry of the winds—the wind that circulates through the eye and so forth—into the central channel of the subtle body, and for the arising of the clear light during the completion stage.[99]

In this way, thirty-one of the deities and the respective constituents of the body indivisible from them dissolve into clear light. The last to dissolve is Vajradhara, the principal of the specially visualized deities, who alone remains, as Tsongkhapa explains in *Bee's Hope:* "Then meditate on the principal deity dissolving into clear light, in correspondence with the dissolution of approaching attainment into clear light, resulting in the experience of the clear light of death."[100] And: "Finally, visualize the principal deity as well dissolving into clear light and meditate by uniting the bliss and emptiness that arise from these dissolutions."[101]

We find various similes used to depict the dissolution of the bodily constituents indivisible from the deities. In his *How to Practice on the Path of Achieving the Stage of Vajradhara,* Tsongkhapa states that "they disappear like a rainbow fading away in the sky."[102] Kedrup Jé, in his *Ocean of Attainments,* likens the dissolution of the principal deity into clear light to steam evaporating on a mirror: "Then, maintaining a stable divine identity as Vajradhara, visualize this deity's body turning into a sphere of light, and this light withdrawn from above and below into your heart—as steam evaporates on a mirror—and dissolved completely into the continuing state of wisdom of indivisible bliss and emptiness. Be mindful of this wisdom as long as you maintain your mindfulness."[103]

Recall that it is the yogi's "divinized" body that has dissolved together with the specially visualized deities and not the ordinary coarse body. Now, while maintaining the divine pride or identity of Vajradhara, the yogi-deity dissolves in correspondence with the future death of the yogi in order to purify this death.

Meditation on Emptiness

As noted in our discussion of the stages of death (see the section "Dissolutions of Consciousness" in chapter 2), during the experience of clear-light-emptiness, subject and object or bliss and emptiness are nondual, since the wisdom that arises from bliss is indivisible from its object—emptiness—as Tsongkhapa clarifies: "Recite the mantra *śūnyatā* and cultivate the divine identity [of the *dharmakāya*] with the resolve: 'The essence of wisdom, which is the indivisible objective emptiness and subjective wisdom, that am I.'"[104] While reciting the emptiness mantra *oṃ śūnyatā jñāna vajra svabhāva ātmako 'haṃ,* yogis should maintain the divine identity or pride of the *dharmakāya.* The purpose of the recitation and meditation on the emptiness mantra is to stabilize the divine identity of the yogis as the *dharmakāya* while they are dissolved into clear light.[105] In this way, they take their deaths on the path that leads to the *dharmakāya,* as explained by Tsongkhapa: "When yogis of the creation stage meditate in this way, they 'take their deaths on the path that leads to the *dharmakāya.*' This step is referred to, alternatively, as 'manifest awakening from suchness,' 'the essential point of merging the specially visualized deities into clear light,' and 'the ultimate truth mandala.'"[106]

In the above passage Tsongkhapa mentions a number of terms for the meditation on the dissolution into clear-light-emptiness. The first, "taking death on the path that leads to the *dharmakāya,*" is the first among the three yogas on the three bodies of a buddha that takes the future death, intermediate state, and rebirth of the yogis on the path to the *dharmakāya, saṃbhogakāya,* and *nirmāṇakāya,* respectively. The second term, "manifest awakening from suchness,"[107] refers to the first among the five manifest awakenings[108]—the five stages through which the deity called the First Lord[109] is visualized in the *sādhana.* In this first manifest awakening, yogis meditate on suchness or emptiness by dissolving their ordinary existence into emptiness or obliterating their everyday reality in order to create a new reality in which they abide as deities in the mandala. The third term is "the essential point of merging the specially visualized deities into clear light." Tsongkhapa divides the *sādhana* into forty-nine essential points,[110] out of which this is the twelfth point[111] and the first in the core yogas. The fourth term, "the ultimate truth mandala," refers to emptiness, which is the aspect of ultimate truth, while the appearance of the mandala with its deities in the following steps of the *sādhana* is the aspect of conventional truth.

How Does This Meditation Correspond to the Ground, Path, and Fruit?

The meditation on the dissolution into clear light, also called "taking death on the path that leads to the *dharmakāya,*" serves to purify the yogi's future death. (Chapter 3 describes this in the section "The Three Bodies of the Meditators on the Creation Stage.") In *Bee's Hope* Tsongkhapa explains this point: "How does the *dharmakāya* of the meditators on the creation stage purify their deaths? In place of the death that would occur naturally to ordinary people, for the yogis, the *dharmakāya* will arise, as the specially visualized deities dissolve into clear light. In this way, the *dharmakāya* of the meditators on the creation stage purifies their deaths."[112] The ground *dharmakāya* is the clear light of death that can be purified through the entire tantric path and brings forth the *dharmakāya* of a buddha—the fruit of this purification. However, during the creation stage, yogis can attain only the *dharmakāya* of the creation stage, which is the clear light into which the specially visualized deities dissolve.

Tsongkhapa ends this section by explaining how the meditation during the creation stage corresponds to the respective steps of the completion stage during the path and to the fruit:

> What does this meditation ripen in the mental continuum of the meditator on the completion stage? It ripens the mental continuum through the arising of [clear light during the five steps of the completion stage]: (1) the metaphoric clear light during body isolation and speech isolation, (2) the mind isolation that is a genuine purifier of death, (3) the metaphorical clear light during the illusory body, (4) [the actual clear light during] the fourth step, and (5) the actual clear light during the fifth step [the step of union]. This brings about the attainment of the *dharmakāya* of a buddha, the fruit of the purification.[113]

There are several clear lights on the path. The first is the clear light into which the specially visualized deities dissolve during the creation stage. This clear light ripens the yogi's mental continuum for a corresponding clear light during each of the steps of the completion stage: the "preliminary" body isolation and the five steps of the completion stage.[114] During the early steps of the completion stage, from body isolation to the illusory body, actual clear lights do not arise but rather metaphoric or illustrative clear lights. During mind isolation, the winds of the subtle body enter, dwell, and dissolve[115] in the heart, thereby purifying the stage of death. The actual clear light appears in the step called "clear light" (the fourth) and in the step of union (the fifth), in which the actual clear light is united with the illusory body. This union leads to buddhahood.

Bearing the above in mind, the last three aims of the meditation on emptiness become clear:

(9) to purify death on the ground of ordinary existence;
(10) to ripen the mental continuum for the clear light of the completion stage; and
(11) to attain the fruitional *dharmakāya*.

(These are listed above in the discussion of meditations that correspond to the destruction of the world.) The actual clear light at the culmination of the completion stage is the basis for the arising of the deities at the fruit of the practice. Conversely, the *dharmakāya* of the meditators on the creation stage—the clear light into which the specially visualized deities have dissolved—is the basis for the arising of the first deity visualized during the core of the creation stage, the First Lord. Let us now turn to the meditation on the First Lord.

Meditations That Correspond to the Intermediate State

The second among the yogas on a buddha's three bodies is the yoga of taking the intermediate state on the path that leads to the *saṃbhogakāya.* This yoga serves to purify the yogi's future ordinary intermediate state by ultimately transforming it to the *saṃbhogakāya* of a buddha.[116] In correspondence with the arising of the intermediate being from the clear light of death, the deity called the First Lord[117] arises from the clear light of the creation stage. Notably, this name does not derive from any kind of primordial nature on the part of the deity but rather from the fact that it is the first to arise during the core meditation on a buddha's three bodies. As we shall see, the nature of this deity is a divine aspect of the intermediate being formed of mere-wind-and-mind. In the third yoga on the three bodies—the yoga of taking rebirth on the path that leads to the *nirmāṇakāya*—the First Lord will transform into Vajrasattva's *nirmāṇakāya* in correspondence with the intermediate being who takes birth in the womb.

The visualization of the First Lord consists of a number of nonlinear steps that entail both expansion and contraction. In *Fulfilling the Bee's Hope* Tsongkhapa relates each step to the ground, the path of the completion stage, and the fruit. Hence, we shall begin with an outline of these steps:

(1) Upon the central seat appears a *hūṃ* that becomes a solar disk.
(2) At the center of the solar disk appears an *oṃ* that becomes a lunar disk.
(3) Upon the lunar disk appears an *āḥ* that becomes a red, eight-petaled lotus with the three syllables *oṃ āḥ hūṃ* stacked one upon the other at its navel.[118]

The specially visualized deities have dissolved into clear light during the previous step of meditation, but the celestial mansion itself and the seats of the deities remain. Thus, the visualization begins with the seed syllable *hūṃ* that appears on the central seat of the mandala, where the First Lord will dwell. This is followed by the visualization of solar and lunar disks along with a lotus and three seed syllables *oṃ āḥ hūṃ* upon the throne of the First Lord. Then:

(4) All these mingle and become a moon orb, completely perfect in all its aspects.[119]
(5) Light rays emanating from the moon orb draw the entire animate and inanimate realms and dissolve them into the moon orb.
(6) The root of all phenomena, animate and inanimate, mere-wind-and-mind, appearing as a moon, that am I.[120]

Instead of expanding, the visualization contracts here; everything visualized until now merges to become a single moon orb.[121] Moreover, the entire animate and inanimate realms also dissolve into the moon orb. Elsewhere, I have noted that this step seems to have been a meditation on Mind Only,[122] indicating that the entire visualization arises as a mental event. Yet, in an ingenious move, Tsongkhapa takes Mind Only or mere mind here as mere-wind-and-mind. This move is ingenious because it enables Tsongkhapa to harmonize not only his *sādhana* with Madhyamaka view but also to reconcile the relations between the ground, the path, and the fruit of the practice, as we shall see. Then:

(7) On the moon a white *oṃ*, a red *āḥ*, and a blue *hūṃ* appear from the moon, like bubbles popping up from water.
(8) Light rays emanating from these syllables invite the five *tathāgata* families together with their numerous circles of deities from the ten directions.
(9) All of them dissolve into these syllables, which then become a white, five-pronged *vajra*, marked at the center with *oṃ āḥ hūṃ*.[123]
(10) The essence of the *vajra*, that am I.

At this point, another circle of expansion and contraction begins: the transformation of the moon orb—the origin of everything—into a *vajra*. First, seed syllables arise from the moon orb, emanating light rays that invite the deities of the five *tathāgata* families. This assemblage of deities imbues the syllables, thereby transforming them into a *vajra*, with which the meditator maintains a divine identification. Then:

(11) The *vajra* with the three syllables transform into myself, white First Lord, with three faces, white, black, and red, and six arms, the right ones holding a *vajra*, wheel, and lotus, and the left ones a bell, jewel, and sword. I, the First Lord, am adorned with precious ornaments and wear variegated silk robes.[124]

Finally, the *vajra* transforms into the First Lord with three faces and six arms.

In *Bee's Hope* Tsongkhapa describes the correspondence between these steps of the meditation and the evolution of the intermediate being—the ground of purification (table 3).[125] Tsongkhapa then describes the correspondence between the steps of the meditation and the fruit of purification (table 4), using the term "five manifest awakenings."[126]

He next explains how to meditate on the *saṃbhogakāya* of the creation stage: "Regard your visualization of the First Lord—beginning with the solar

TABLE 3. Steps of the Meditation and Their Grounds

MEDITATION	CORRESPONDENCE ON THE GROUND
The meditation on the solar disk, the lunar disk, and the lotus upon the central seat	The approaching attainment, enhanced appearance, and [white] appearance arising from the clear light of death
The meditation on the three syllables[1] that are the cause of the solar disk, the lunar disk, and the lotus	The three winds that are the cause for the approaching attainment, enhanced appearance, and [white] appearance
The meditation on the three syllables stacked up upon the lotus[2]	The three winds[3] serving as the mounts of approaching attainment, enhanced appearance, and [white] appearance
The meditation on all of these mingling into a single moon orb	The wind-and-mind of the intermediate being abiding as a single entity
The meditation on the three syllables upon the moon, stacked up	The speech of the intermediate being
The five-pronged white *vajra*	The mind of the intermediate being
The meditation on the First Lord	The body of the intermediate being
The meditation on the light ray[4] emanating from the seed syllables	The deeds of the intermediate being

[1] These are the three syllables (*oṃ, āḥ, hūṃ*) from which the lunar disk, the solar disk, and the lotus are visualized.

[2] These are the three syllables stacked up on the lotus after the lunar disk, solar disk, and lotus have been visualized.

[3] Each of the three minds is carried by two kinds of winds—engendering winds and coexisting winds; thus there are two sets of winds here.

[4] These light rays emanating from the seed syllables, invite the five *tathāgata* families together with a circle of numerous deities, and then dissolve them back into the syllables.

disk and up to its completion—as a manifestation of indivisible bliss and emptiness; cultivate the divine identification of the First Lord and its clear appearance. The divine identification is maintained with the resolve: 'The pure wind-and-mind arising as the extremely subtle wisdom body, that am I.' Meditating in this way is 'taking the intermediate state on the path to the *saṃbhogakāya*'; also referred to as 'manifest awakening from the complete body,' the 'First Lord,' and the '*saṃbhogakāya* of the meditator on the creation stage.'"[127]

Next, Tsongkhapa clarifies how the *saṃbhogakāya* of the meditator on the creation stage purifies the intermediate state: "In place of the intermediate

TABLE 4. Steps of the Meditation and Their Fruit

MEDITATION	CORRESPONDING FRUIT
The meditation on the moon orb of the manifest awakening from the moon[1]	Wind serving as the mount of the clear light at the fruit
The meditation prior to that on the solar disk, lunar disk, and lotus together with the seed syllables	The approaching attainment, enhanced appearance, and [white] appearance serving as the cause for the actual-clear-light, together with the wind on which it rides and the three winds that are the cause for that
The manifest awakenings from the seed syllable[2] and from the complete body[3] and the light rays that emanate and dissolve	The actual-clear-light arising in the aspects of the speech, mind, body, and deeds of a buddha
The five prongs of the *vajra*[4]	The [mind with its] five wisdoms of the actual-clear-light
The meditation on the three seed syllables at the navel of the *vajra*	The invisibility of the three *vajras* of the body, speech, and mind

[1] Tib. *zla ba las byang chub pa*; here it is the meditation on the moon orb.

[2] Tib. *sa bon las byang chub pa*. This is the visualization of the syllables that arise from the moon and invite the *tathāgata* families.

[3] Tib. *sku rdzogs pa las byang chub pa*. The manifest awakening from the complete body is the visualization of the First Lord.

[4] The manifest awakening from the emblem (Tib. *phyag mtshan las byang chub pa*) is the meditation on the *vajra*.

being that occurs naturally for an ordinary person, the yogi meditating on the creation stage will arise as the First Lord through the five manifest awakenings."[128] Finally, how does this practice ripen the mental continuum of the meditator on the completion stage? "The meditation on the First Lord ripens the mental continuum to the similitude illusory bodies during the three isolations,[129] to the [impure] illusory body of the third step, which is a genuine purifier of the intermediate state, to the [pure] illusory body during the fifth step, and finally, brings about the attainment of the *saṃbhogakāya* of a buddha at the fruit of the purification."[130]

Meditations That Correspond to Rebirth

The third among the yogas on a buddha's three bodies is the yoga of taking rebirth on the path that leads to the *nirmāṇakāya.* This yoga serves to purify the yogi's future ordinary rebirth by ultimately transforming it to the *nirmāṇakāya* of a buddha. The ground of purification of this practice is "taking" a new birth in the womb[131] and the beginning of a new *saṃsāric* life. The fruit is the transformation of the *saṃbhogakāya,* who cannot be perceived by ordinary beings, into the *nirmāṇakāya,* who, by taking on coarse elements, can act for the sake of the disciples. The meditation that serves towards the purification of rebirth, according to Tsongkhapa, consists of four stages: the transformation of the First Lord into Vajrasattva's *nirmāṇakāya;* the meditation on the body mandala; the blessing of the body, speech, and mind; and the generation into the triple *sattvas.*[132] When these meditations are completed, the yogi will "take birth" as *nirmāṇakāya* upon the central seat in the celestial mansion.

The Transformation of the First Lord into Vajrasattva's Nirmāṇakāya

According to Tsongkhapa's *Sādhana:* "The Father-Mother *Tathāgatas* from their natural abode are absorbed in union for the sake of guiding sentient beings. Akṣobhya[s] formed from their *bodhicittas* pervade the space realm in its entirety, and bless all sentient beings, who then attain pure bliss and mental rapture. Then all the Akṣobhyas merge together inside the celestial mansion of the mandala, and I [the First Lord] enter [that], and become a blue Vajrasattva's *nirmāṇakāya* with three faces and six arms."[133] According to *Formulating the Guhyasamāja Sādhana,*[134] this meditation is taught by means of the *samādhi* called "*vajra* overpowering of all *tathāgatas.*"[135] In the *Guhyasamāja Tantra:* "Then, the Blessed One, the Tathāgata Bodhicittavajra, dwelt in absorption in the *samādhi* called '*vajra* overpowering of all *tathāgatas.*' As soon as the Blessed One, the Lord of all *tathāgatas,* dwelt in absorption, the space realm in its entirety abided in the *vajra* nature of all *tathāgatas.* Then, all the sentient beings residing in the entire realm of space, through the blessing of Vajrasattva, attained the bliss and mental rapture of all *tathāgatas.*"[136]

In his commentaries on the *Illuminating Lamp*[137] and *Formulating the Guhyasamāja Sādhana,*[138] Tsongkhapa explains how these passages of the *Tantra* and *Sādhana* are related and thereby shows that the transformation of the First Lord into Vajrasattva's *nirmāṇakāya* corresponds to conception. The moment the First Lord enters into Akṣobhya in Tsongkhapa's *Sādhana* corresponds to the intermediate being taking birth in the womb. According to the tantric works already mentioned,[139] when the parents join their organs, the fire of great desire dissolves the white and red *bodhicittas*. These melted constituents fill the empty space within the 72,000 channels of the subtle body and descend into the mother's lotus. When the intermediate being enters in their midst, rebirth takes place.

Tsongkhapa's explanation of the correspondences is illustrated in table 5. Here the yogi as the First Lord enters into Akṣobhya—formed through the merging of all the Akṣobhyas—who abides on the central seat at the center of

TABLE 5. Steps of the *Sādhana* and Their Correspondences in the Tantra and on the Ground

SĀDHANA	*GUHYASAMĀJA TANTRA*	THE GROUND OF PURIFICATION
The Father-Mother *tathāgatas* from their natural abode are absorbed in union for the sake of guiding sentient beings.	Then, the Blessed One, the Tathāgata Bodhicittavajra, dwelt in absorption in the *samādhi* called "*vajra* overpowering of all *tathāgatas*."	The parents lying together.
The *bodhicittas* of the Father-Mother evolve into Akṣobhyas who pervade the space realm in its entirety.	As soon as the Blessed One, the Lord of all *tathāgatas*, dwelt in absorption, the space realm in its entirety abided in the *vajra* nature of all *tathāgatas*.	The "space realm" corresponds to the empty interior of the 72,000 channels of the parents. The "*vajra* nature of all *tathāgatas*" is the *vajra tathāgata* family of Akṣobhya. The "Akṣobhyas who pervade this space" correspond to the melting constituents of *bodhicitta* that fill the channels.
These Akṣobhyas bless all sentient beings, who thereby attain pure bliss and mental rapture.	Then, all the sentient beings residing in the entire realm of space, through the blessing of Vajrasattva, attained the bliss and mental rapture of all *tathāgatas*.	The parents experience bliss when the two organs are united.
Then all the Akṣobhyas merge together inside the celestial mansion.		The semen and blood of the parents commingling in the secret lotus.
I [the First Lord] enter [that] and become a blue Vajrasattva's *nirmāṇakāya* with three faces and six arms.		The intermediate being enters in the midst of the semen and blood; thereby rebirth takes place.

the mandala. Thereby the First Lord—who corresponds to the intermediate being on the ground and to the *saṃbhogakāya* on the fruit—transforms into the *nirmāṇakāya* of the path in correspondence with conception during ordinary existence and the *nirmāṇakāya* of the fruit. Tsongkhapa emphasizes that the view of some lamas that it is Akṣobhya who enters into the First Lord cannot correspond to the process of rebirth, because it is the intermediate being who enters in the midst of the commingled coarse constituents of the semen and blood, and not the semen and blood that enter the intermediate being.[140]

In *Bee's Hope* Tsongkhapa stresses that the transformation of the First Lord into Vajrasattva's *nirmāṇakāya* is only the first step in the process that purifies the yogi's future ordinary rebirth through the creation stage.[141] This purification proceeds through the meditation on the body mandala and the blessing of the body, speech, and mind, up to the generation into the triple *sattvas* and the sealing with the lord of the *tathāgata* family. All these steps of the practice correspond to the entire process of rebirth until the child emerges outside the womb, as we will see below.

Meditation on the Body Mandala

This meditation features two stages. In the first, the yogis meditate on their bodies as the celestial mansion of the mandala. In the second stage, they visualize the thirty-two deities on individual parts of their bodies.

MEDITATION ON THE BODY AS THE CELESTIAL MANSION OF THE MANDALA

In his *Sādhana*[142] Tsongkhapa describes how yogis meditate on all the parts of their body becoming the individual parts of the celestial mansion. For example, the front, back, right, and left sides of the body become the four sides of the mandala; the four orifices—mouth, nose, and the urinary and excretion pathways—become the four doors. The mental components of the yogis transform as well; the eye consciousness becomes the mirrors, the nose consciousness the garlands of flowers, and so forth.

In *Bee's Hope* Tsongkhapa instructs how to meditate on the body as the celestial mansion: "Bring together the respective parts of the celestial mansion of the outer mandala, such as the four corners, and so on, and the parts of the your body, such as the front and back [right and left]. Taking the former as the substantial cause and the latter as the cooperative conditions, meditate on the arising of [the celestial mansion of the body mandala] that is homogenous[143] with the outer mandala."[144] Elsewhere, Tsongkhapa explains this brief instruction.[145] The outer mandala is the previously visualized celestial mansion.[146]

The yogi, as Vajrasattva's *nirmāṇakāya,* abides on the central throne within this celestial mansion. The basis or object that will be transformed into the celestial mansion of the body mandala is the body of Vajrasattva's *nirmāṇakāya.* Nonetheless, yogis need not visualize anew Vajrasattva's body as the celestial mansion of the body mandala. They create the body mandala based on their earlier visualization of the outer mandala—by joining each part of the outer celestial mansion with the respective part of Vajrasattva's body. For example, the four sides of the outer mandala are united with the four sides of the yogi visualized as Vajrasattva's *nirmāṇakāya.*

Tsongkhapa sees the substantial causes of the body mandala as the parts of the celestial mansion visualized earlier, while the parts of the yogi's body are cooperative conditions. Some later Geluk scholars, however, reverse the substantial causes and the cooperative conditions. When the substantial causes are the parts of the celestial mansion visualized earlier, the nature of the celestial mansion of the body mandala is mental, whereas when the substantial causes are the parts of the yogi's body, the result is more material in nature. Nevertheless, it is important to bear in mind that the "body" of the body mandala is the body of the yogi as Vajrasattva's *nirmāṇakāya* and not simply the yogi's material body. It is possible that the Geluk scholars who regarded the body as the substantial cause were motivated by the idea that in this way their visualizations could achieve significant bodily transformation.[147]

Elsewhere Tsongkhapa emphasizes that yogis do not merely visualize the individual parts of the body as parts of the celestial mansion, because that would be a mere visualization and not a meditation on the body in its divine aspect.[148] Put differently, the meditation on the body as the celestial mansion here achieves an actual transformation of the ordinary impure body into a pure divine mansion.

PLACING THE DEITIES ON THE BODY

Next, the thirty-two deities of the Guhyasamāja mandala are placed on corresponding parts of the yogi's/Vajrasattva's body as the celestial mansion. The same parts of the body that formerly have been visualized as parts of the celestial mansion are now visualized as deities residing in the celestial mansion. For example, the eyes first become the Dharma wheels on top of the portals and then transform into Kṣitigarbha. As Kedrup Jé explains, if this were not possible, then how could yogis, who meditate on themselves today as Vajradhara be able to meditate on themselves as Vairocana tomorrow?[149] In other words, here Kedrup Jé implies that the result of the visualizations of the body mandala is changeable.

In *Bee's Hope* Tsongkhapa describes how to meditate on various parts of the body as the deities dwelling in the celestial mansion: "The yogis should meditate by making the parts of their bodies at their different locations—beginning with the form aggregates at the crowns of their heads—into indivisible essence with the thirty-two seed syllables respectively—beginning with the syllable *oṃ*."[150] Thus, yogis begin by meditating on the area from the crown of their heads to the hairlines, which is the essence of the form aggregate, as indivisible from the syllable *oṃ*. The form aggregate that is the impure aspect of Vairocana, fused with the seed syllable of Vairocana (*oṃ*), then transforms into Vairocana. Likewise, they meditate on the navel, which is the essence of the entirety of the body's earth element as indivisible from the syllable *laṃ*. The earth element, or solidity, which is the impure aspect of Locanā, fused with the seed syllable of Locanā (*laṃ*), then transforms into Locanā.

In a similar manner, the yogi meditates on the remaining thirty deities. Thereby, the five aggregates, the four physical elements, the five sense faculties and their five objects, the mind-heart, the joints, the channels with the sinews, and the ten limbs[151] become respectively the five *tathāgatas*, the four female buddhas, the five *vajra* ladies, the eight *bodhisattvas*, and the ten fierce deities. Tsongkhapa continues: "Then they [the yogis] cultivate the clear appearance of the thirty-two deities of the mandala, Vairocana and so forth, maintain their divine identity, and regard all these appearances as a manifestation of indivisible bliss and emptiness."[152] Kedrup Jé offers a different method for the above meditation, a fact that did not go unnoticed by later Geluk scholars.[153]

As stated already, the meditation on the body mandala is included within the practices that take rebirth on the path to the *nirmāṇakāya*. According to *Bee's Hope*,[154] by meditating on the body as the celestial mansion of the mandala, as well as on the deities merged with the bodies, yogis will attain the celestial mansion of the third step of the completion stage, and the actual celestial mansion on the fruit together with the deities residing in them.[155]

Blessing the Body, Speech, and Mind

This meditation is another method designed to render the yogis divine or buddhaized, by transforming their bodies, speech, and minds into a buddha's body, speech, and mind. The three *tathāgatas* of the body, speech, and mind (Vairocana, Amitābha, and Akṣobhya), respectively, together with their consorts (the female buddhas Locanā, Pāṇḍarā, and Māmakī), enter the yogis' crowns, tongues, and hearts as white, red, and dark blue light rays, respectively. Thereby the yogis attain mastery of body, speech, and mind.

What do such masteries entail? Mastery of the body is the ability to display billions of emanation bodies. Mastery of speech is the ability to teach the Dharma and to answer the questions of all sentient beings, in each of their languages. Mastery of mind is a nondual realization of suchness and a direct realization of all objects of knowledge without any conceptualization.[156] The blessing of the body, speech, and mind corresponds to these masteries at the time of fruition.

The blessings conclude with the yogi maintaining divine identification with *vajra* body, speech, and mind, who are respectively Vairocana, Amitābha, and Akṣobhya, through the recitation of the mantras. Divine identification with the two remaining *tathāgatas*, Ratnasaṃbhava and Amoghasiddhi, will take place during the yoga with the consort, described below.

To what do the blessings correspond on the ground of purification? The blessing of the body corresponds to the completion of the development of the embryo's body, including its hair and nails; the blessing of the speech corresponds to the evolution of its tongue and palate; and the blessing of the mind corresponds to the completion of its mental consciousness that engages objects.[157]

To understand Tsongkhapa's explanation about this meditation we need to review the six steps of each blessing. When the body is blessed: (1) A multitude of Locanās emanate from the yogi's crown filling the space. (2) Locanās invite an assembly of the male *tathāgatas* of their family, Vairocanas or *vajra* bodies, who absorb in union with them. (3) The yogi abiding before them requests the deities to bless him or her with the *vajra* body. (4) The deities experiencing the bliss of supreme joy dissolve into light rays that enter the yogi's crown and thereby the yogi attains the mastery of the body. (5) The yogi's body becomes endowed with the nature of a buddha's body. (6) The yogi maintains divine identification with the bodies of all the *tathāgatas*.

In *Bee's Hope* Tsongkhapa discusses these steps in terms of the objects being blessed and the method, nature, and aspect of the blessing:[158]

> How are the body, speech, and mind blessed? The *objects* being blessed are the body, speech, and mind of the yogi. The *method* of blessing is by emanating the three emblems—the goddesses [Locanā, Pāṇḍarā, and Māmakī], from the three seed syllables [*oṃ, āḥ, hūṃ*] and inviting the multitude of deities of the three *vajras* [Vairocana, Amitābha, and Akṣobhya].
>
> On account of the request made by the yogi, the assemblies of the deities of the three *vajras*[159] absorb in union; hence, the *nature* of the blessings is

> great bliss. The *aspect[s]* in which [the deities] enter into the yogi's crown, tongue, and heart successively are the white, red, and dark-blue light rays. [When the lights enter, the yogi] attains wisdom-great-bliss. After visualizing this, while reciting the three mantras successively,[160] the yogi cultivates divine identification with the resolve: "The *vajra* body, speech, and mind of all *tathāgatas*, that am I."[161]

Thus, yogis attain mastery of the *vajra* body, *vajra* speech, and *vajra* mind separately. Then they cultivate divine identification of all three *vajras* indivisibly and become Vajradhara.

Generation into the Triple Sattvas

The principal deity at the center of the mandala, Vajradhara, is visualized as embodying the triple *sattvas*: *samayasattva, jñānasattva,* and *samādhisattva.*[162] The *samayasattva* is the yogi visualized as Vajradhara. In this context, the term "*samaya*" is explained[163] not as pledge or commitment but as meeting or coming together, which refers to the *jñānasattva* who joins and unites with the *samayasattva* in *sādhanas* other than the *Guhyasamāja Sādhana. Jñānasattva* means "wisdom being" and *samādhisattva,* "concentration being." The three *sattvas* are characterized by increasing levels of subtlety. While the *samayasattva* is an emanation body (*nirmāṇakāya*), the *jñānasattva,* whose nature is wisdom, abides at the heart of the *samayasattva,* and the *samādhisattva* is a blue syllable *hūṃ* at the heart of the *jñānasattva.*

In *Bee's Hope* Tsongkhapa states, regarding the triple *sattvas*: "By meditating on the triple *sattvas*, yogis will attain the triple *sattvas* of the completion stage and the fruit."[164] According to Kedrup Jé, the *samayasattva,* meditated upon as the body of Vajrasattva's *nirmāṇakāya,* corresponds to the temporal coarse body of the fetus, while the *jñānasattva* and the *samādhisattva* correspond to its innate subtle body.[165] Most Geluk lamas agree that the two subtler *sattvas* correspond to the subtle mind-and-wind, but later Geluk scholars argue whether the *jñānasattva* corresponds to the very subtle mind and the *samādhisattva* to the very subtle wind or the other way around.[166]

With the generation into the triple *sattvas*, the yoga of taking rebirth on the path that leads to the *nirmāṇakāya* and consists of four stages is concluded. It begins with the transformation of the First Lord into Vajrasattva's *nirmāṇakāya,* continues with the meditation on the body mandala as well as the blessing of the body, speech, and mind, and then closes with the generation into the triple *sattvas.*

Tsongkhapa details how this yoga during the creation stage ripens the mental continuum of the meditator for the completion stage: "[The meditation on the transformation into the *nirmāṇakāya*] ripens the mental continuum for the coarse *nirmāṇakāya* that arises when the similitude illusory bodies enter the old body during the three isolations; and for the coarse *nirmāṇakāya* that arises when the pure and impure illusory bodies enter the old body. This will bring about the attainment of a buddha's *nirmāṇakāya* at the fruit of purification."[167]

Sealing with the Lord of the Tathāgata *Family*

This step concludes the core practices of the *sādhana.* Yogis visualize the lord of the *tathāgata* family, great Vajradhara with his consort Vajradhātvīśvarī, on the crown of their heads. Vajradhara here is white in color with one face and two arms holding a *vajra* and bell. A stream of *bodhicitta* nectar, arising through the union of Vajradhara and his consort, drips down and satiates the yogis' bodies. In this way, yogis "seal" their visualization.

Now that the yogis are endowed with the three bodies of the creation stage, they have attained the goal of the practice for their own sake. In the following steps they will act for the sake of guiding all sentient beings to enlightenment. But first they must engage in the yoga with a consort.

The Yoga with a Consort

To act for the sake of other sentient beings, yogis must emanate the mandala of the Guhyasamāja, called the Supreme King of Mandalas.[168] Before they can emanate the mandala, they should engender it by absorbing in union with their consorts.

Tsongkhapa designates the section on yoga with a consort in *Bee's Hope*[169] as an explanation "how the innate great bliss arises—the method for swift attainment of the three bodies." This is because another important goal of yoga with a consort is to experience great bliss in order to attain enlightenment. The great bliss that arises during the yoga with a consort can lead to a single-pointed mind of wisdom. (See the section "The *Samādhi* of Great Bliss" in chapter 3.) This wisdom on the part of the yogi and the consort is the subject that realizes its object, emptiness, through a direct perception. In other words, the mind of bliss, the subject, fuses with its object, emptiness, and thus a nondual union of bliss and emptiness is attained. Bliss and emptiness become of a single taste, like milk and water. Further, the mind that realizes emptiness and the mind experiencing bliss are not two separate mental states, but a single entity.[170] It is the mind of great bliss that makes the Mantra Vehicle superior to the Pāramitā Vehicle. The object, emptiness, is identical in the two vehicles, but the mind of great bliss has greater power to realize emptiness.

Tsongkhapa elaborates on the significance of attaining great bliss at the end of his explanation of the yoga with the consort:

> All these steps of the yoga with the consort—taking on the path passion toward objects of desire generated through these practices, blocking the root of *saṃsāra,* which is grasping at the self [of person and phenomena], the arising of the mandala with the celestial mansion and the deities dwelling therein as display of indivisible bliss and emptiness; and ripening the yogi's mental continuum for the experience of the four joys in relying on a consort during the completion stage—are "the essence of the path" for meditators on the creation stage.[171]

The consort, too, takes passion on the path, while relying on the male yogi, as noted above.[172] In taking passion on the path, the yogi's mind that experiences great bliss gives rise to wisdom that realizes emptiness or selflessness. Therefore, the mandala engendered by such a mind will arise as a display of indivisible bliss and emptiness, whereby the appearance aspect of the mandala is nondual with the emptiness of the mandala. As a result, the mandala will appear as illusion-like, or, put differently, like the moon in water or a rainbow in the sky, appearing yet devoid of intrinsic existence.[173]

In *Bee's Hope* Tsongkhapa refers to two types of consorts: actual consorts[174] and wisdom consorts.[175] The actual (or karma) consort is a real human being who arises through karma. Regarding this consort, Tsongkhapa explains: "The *sādhaka* [the yogi who practices the *sādhana*] of each of the five *tathāgata* families should seek daughters of a low-caste person, of a dyer, of a dancer, of a garland maker, and of a craftsman, respectively."[176] Thus, the consorts belonging to each of the *tathāgata* families come from low-class families. Tsongkhapa continues: "The tantras and their commentaries teach what are the characteristics the consorts should possess: their mental continuums need to be purified by the shared path;[177] they need to have received a pure initiation to properly guard their vows and commitments; to be well trained in the *Kāmaśāstra*[178] and in the tantra; to cultivate deity yoga; and to be highly devoted to the *sādhaka.*"[179]

It is not a simple matter to find a consort who fulfills these requirements. Not only must she master the sixty-four arts of love specified in the *Kāmaśāstra* and be highly devoted to the yogi, she must also be endowed with Mantric qualities just like the yogi. She should practice the Pāramitā Vehicle as well as the Mantra Vehicle, and, in accordance with the latter, she should have received a proper initiation, kept the vows and commitments as she promised during her initiation, and be accomplished in deity yoga. The conditions Tsongkhapa specifies indicate the scarcity of qualified human consorts, and he recommends that yogis rely instead on wisdom consorts.[180] Indeed, in his *Sādhana* the consort is not a real woman; rather, "a consort belonging to my own *tathāgata* family emanates from my heart."[181] The remaining part of the discussion of the consort in *Bee's Hope* deals exclusively with the wisdom consort.

Since the wisdom consort is not a human being but a creation of the yogi's mind, in order to visualize her appearance as stable and clear, the yogi should have mastered the practice of visualization through deity yoga. Tsongkhapa explains how to visualize her: "If the *sādhaka* belongs to the *tathāgata* family of Akṣobhya, for example, he should draw from his heart a consort belonging to his *tathāgata* family,[182] in the appearance of an actual girl."[183] Hence, even when she is a wisdom consort visualized by the yogi, she first appears in the form of a human consort.

In the next step, the consort visualized as a human being is transformed into a deity.[184] As Tsongkhapa instructs, the yogi "should purify her into emptiness, and from emptiness[185] visualize, as appropriate, the Vajra Lady of Tangibles[186] or Māmakī,[187] and place the twenty-nine deities on her body."[188] Just as the yogi has visualized the deities of the body mandala on his body,[189] he places the deities on the consort's body.

Then, *Bee's Hope* instructs the yogi to bless or transform the secret spaces of himself and his consort briefly by saying: "'I visualize away my secret place' and up to 'meditate that its opening is blocked by [a yellow syllable] *phaṭ*.'"[190] In this sentence Tsongkhapa points to his *Sādhana,*[191] in which the yogi is instructed to visualize away the male and female sexual organs into emptiness and from emptiness to generate a five-pronged *vajra* for the yogi and an eight-petaled lotus for the consort; the openings of both are blocked by the syllable *phaṭ*. The *vajra* and lotus are permeated with light rays in the five colors, whose nature is that of the five *tathāgatas* of the mandala. Accordingly, it is not the ordinary sexual organs of the yogi and consort that engage in the union.

Following the blessing into the *vajra* and lotus, the yogis become Ratnasaṃbhava and abide in divine identification with him. Then, by reciting the mantra *Oṃ sarva tathāgata anurāgaṇa vajra svabhāva ātmako 'haṃ,* they cultivate divine identification with passion, through the resolution: "The indivisible nature of the passion of all *tathāgatas*, that am I." However, even though yogis become Ratnasaṃbhava and abide in his divine identification, they still remain in the bodily form of Vajradhara.

Next, Tsongkhapa instructs the yogis to transform once more to the divine identification with Vajradhara: "Then, transform into the divine identification with Vajradhara and sing the song of *hūṃ*. As you and your consort are absorbed in union, draw the four joys, and meditate by uniting bliss and emptiness during innate bliss."[192] Singing the song of *hūṃ* means to recite aloud the syllable *hūṃ* while drawing out the sound. The four joys arise when the melted *bodhicitta* descends first from the crown to throat, second to the heart, third to the navel, and finally to the tip of the secret place respectively. Unlike the case of the completion stage, the melting of the *bodhicitta* in the creation stage does not entail the dissolution of the winds into the central channel of the subtle body.[193] When the *bodhicitta* reaches the tip of the secret place, bliss of supreme joy[194] or innate bliss is attained. This subjective mind of bliss unites with emptiness as its object.

Next,[195] yogis become Amoghasiddhi and abide in his divine identification, once more in the bodily form of Vajradhara. Then, by reciting the mantra *Oṃ sarva tathāgata pūjā vajra svabhāva ātmako 'haṃ,* they cultivate divine identification with the offering, through the resolution: "The indivisible nature of the offering to all *tathāgatas*, that am I." While reciting the syllable *phaṭ*,[196] they mentally offer the melted drop of *bodhicitta* to the deities of the body mandala, who are thereby satiated. Then the drop descends into the lotus of the wisdom consort. According to *Bee's Hope,* this step of the meditation is not included in the First Yoga, but in the subsequent meditation on the Supreme King of Mandalas.[197] This melted drop in the lotus of the Mother is the source of the celestial mansion and the deities of the mandala emanated in the following step of the *sādhana.*

At this point of the meditation on the *sādhana,* the yogis have maintained divine identifications with all five *tathāgatas* of the mandala. During the blessing of the body, speech, and mind separately, the yogis cultivate divine identification with Vairocana, Amitābha, and Akṣobhya, respectively. Then, during the blessing of the body, speech, and mind jointly, they become Vajradhara. In the present context, during the yoga with the consort, they cultivate divine identification with the two remaining *tathāgatas*: Ratnasaṃbhava and Amoghasiddhi. Although in the *sādhana* they do so in separate steps of the practice, the mantras recited while maintaining divine identifications with each of the five *tathāgatas* are found side by side in the *Guhyasamāja Tantra.*[198] Hence, these steps are linked.

The main goal of the yoga with the consort in the creation stage is to emanate the mandala; hence, while reciting the syllable *phaṭ*, yogis visualize the melted drop of *bodhicitta* emitted into the consort's lotus. However, when the goal of the union with a consort is to experience great bliss and to unite it with emptiness nondually in order for all appearances to arise as a display of bliss and emptiness, the drops of *bodhicitta* should not be emitted into the consort's lotus. This is because if the drop is emitted, the basis for attaining bliss will be lost.[199] For this purpose, the yogi has visualized the syllables *phaṭ* blocking the openings of the *vajra* and lotus.

Concurrently, due the union of bliss and emptiness attained while engaging in union with the consort during the creation stage, the emanated mandala will arise as a display of indivisible bliss and emptiness and will serve to ripen the yogi's mental continuum for the experience of great bliss during the completion stage. For this reason, as previously mentioned, Tsongkhapa calls this experience "the essence of the path" for the meditators on the creation stage.[200]

The name of the mandala engendered when the yogi and his consort, visualized as deities, are absorbed in union is Supreme King of Mandalas, the topic of the next section.

The Supreme Kings

The main part of the *Sādhana*—which begins after the completion of the preliminaries—consists of three *samādhis*: the First Yoga,[201] the Supreme King of Mandalas,[202] and the Supreme King of Deeds.[203] The First Yoga involves practices aimed at attaining the yogi's own enlightenment, while the two Supreme Kings are for the sake of guiding other sentient beings to enlightenment. The yoga with a consort is a transitional step that connects the First Yoga to the Supreme King of Mandalas. The deities conceived during the union with the consort emanate to create the Supreme King of Mandalas, called also "the emanated mandala." As noted already, in *Fulfilling the Bee's Hope* Tsongkhapa explains that the First Yoga continues up to the offerings of the melted drop of *bodhicitta* during the yoga with the consort, and then the Supreme King of Mandalas begins.[204]

The meditation on the two Supreme Kings that corresponds to the deeds of a fruitional buddha is divided into three parts that accord with the deeds of a buddha's body, speech, and mind. The Supreme King of Mandalas corresponds to the deeds of the body, the meditation on subtle objects during the Supreme King of Deeds corresponds to the deeds of the mind, and the mantra recitation during the Supreme King of Deeds corresponds to the deed of speech.[205]

The Supreme King of Mandalas

We recall that according to Tsongkhapa's *Sādhana*,[206] after the melted drop of *bodhicitta* is offered to the deities, the drop descends into the lotus of the wisdom consort and becomes the source of the emanated mandala with its deities.[207] One part of the drop becomes a *bhrūṃ* syllable that transforms into the celestial mansion, including the deities' thrones, while the other part of the drop splits into thirty-two parts that take their places on the thrones and become the thirty-two seed syllables of the deities, respectively.

In *Bee's Hope*[208] Tsongkhapa specifies three methods for visualizing the deities: through the "three rituals,"[209] the "seven steps,"[210] and the "four seals."[211] These are not alternative methods but rather different ways to refer to the visualization of the deities residing in the Supreme King of Mandalas. In fact, these deities are visualized through the "seven steps," as I will explain below.

The three rituals[212] are parallel to the last three rituals of the five-manifest-awakening that were the basis for visualizing the First Lord:[213] the manifest awakening from the seed syllable, from the emblem, and from the complete body. The deities of the Supreme King of Mandalas are visualized from their respective seed syllables interspersed with the three fundamental seed syllables, *oṃ āḥ hūṃ*. For example, the seed syllable of Akṣobhya is *hūṃ*; thus, he is generated from *oṃ āḥ hūṃ hūṃ*. The thirty-two seed syllables then transform into the thirty-two emblems;[214] the emblems then transform into the deities themselves. Tsongkhapa relates the seed syllables to speech, the emblems to mind, and the deities to body.[215]

The visualization of the deities through the seven steps is the method found in Tsongkhapa's *Sādhana*.[216] The first step, called "the step of generation,"[217] is equivalent to the three rituals just described. In the second step, "the step of sending forth," the yogi draws each of the deities—who still abide in the lotus of the consort—through his *vajra* into his heart, and then while pronouncing their name-mantra, sends them forth from his heart and causes them to multiply into countless emanations and to spread out to the ten directions of space. In doing so, the yogi is motivated by his great compassion for all sentient beings, since the deities will then act to bring all sentient beings to the stage of buddhahood.

In the third step, "performing the deeds," the deities perform the shared and specific deeds of buddhas. The "shared deeds" are called so because they are shared by both the Pāramitā and Mantra Vehicles—for example, teaching Buddhist theories and practices. The special or unique deeds of the five *tathāgatas* are to purify the afflicted emotions that torment sentient beings: hatred, ignorance, pride, desire, and envy, respectively. The four female *tathāgatas*, Locanā, Māmakī, Pāṇḍarā, and Tārā purify various kinds of illness and malevolent influences that afflict sentient beings. The five *vajra* ladies purify clinging to forms, sounds, scents, tastes, and objects of touch that afflict sentient beings, and offer them the bliss that arises in buddhas when they experience objects of the senses. The eight *bodhisattvas* purify the five bases of the senses, the base of the mind and body, as well as the channels, ligaments, and joints of all sentient beings. The ten fierce deities overcome the guardians in the main and intermediate directions, as well as various harmful beings.

In the fourth step, the "step of withdrawing," the yogi visualizes the innumerable emanations of each of the thirty-two deities who have pervaded the world realms drawing back and becoming a single deity. In the fifth step, the "step of merging," the yogi merges each deity indivisibly with his or her own *jñānasattva*.[218] In the sixth step, the "step of conferring initiation," the *bodhicitta* of the respective lord of the *tathāgata* family abiding in union with his consort confers initiation on each deity. In the seventh step, the "step of abiding on the seat," the deities take their individual seats in the outer mandala.

At the end of the First Yoga, yogis have visualized themselves as Vajradhara abiding on a lunar seat at the center of the mandala. However, at the beginning of the meditation on the Supreme King of Mandalas, the principal deity of the mandala, visualized in the lotus of the consort, is a peaceful Akṣobhya. During the seven steps, this Akṣobhya emanates, performs the deeds, and so forth, as do all the deities. Then in the seventh step of abiding on his seat, Akṣobhya first abides in the space before the yogi—visualized as peaceful Vajradhara. Then Akṣobhya takes his own seat in the mandala by entering Vajradhara's heart and merging with him. Thereby, Vajradhara transforms into blue Dveṣavajra, the fierce form of Akṣobhya, and at that moment the lunar seat of peaceful Vajradhara transforms into a solar seat of the fierce Dveṣavajra.[219] When Akṣobhya's consort, Vajra Lady of Tangibles[220] takes her seat, she dissolves into the original consort. The rest of the deities abide on their respective seats in the celestial mansion of this outer mandala.

The five male *tathāgatas*, the four female *tathāgatas*, and Vajra Lady of Tangibles dwell in the innermost part of the mandala that is divided into nine quadrants and surrounded by a *vajra* garland. Akṣobhya and his consort, Vajra Lady of Tangibles, share the central seat;[221] the other four male *tathāgatas* are in the four main directions, and the four female *tathāgatas* are in the intermediate directions. The remaining four *vajra* ladies are in the corners of the next square, the second square within the inner palace. The eight *bodhisattvas* are in the third and outer square within the mansion to the right and left of each of the gates. The ten fierce deities who guard the perimeter are in the same square, four at the gates, four at the intermediate directions, and two above and below the principal deities of the mandala.[222]

The third method that Tsongkhapa mentions for the visualization of the deities residing in the Supreme King of Mandala is through the four seals:[223] the dharma seal, the *samaya* seal, the great seal, and the karma seal.[224] The term "seal" in this context does not refer to seals held in the hand or to the consorts and other seals, but to steps of the visualization.[225] In *Bee's Hope*[226] Tsongkhapa explains that the thirty-two seed syllables are the dharma seal of speech, the emblems that arise from them are the *samaya* seal of mind, the deities who arise from the emblems are the great seal of body, and the enlightened deeds of purifying the afflictive emotions are the seal of karma.

Regarding the number of faces the visualized deities have: in the lower tantras most deities have one face, while in the *Guhyasamāja Sādhana* they generally have three. In *Fulfilling the Bee's Hope* Tsongkhapa explains the signification of the three faces: "The right face signifies method, the wisdom of great bliss; the left face signifies perfect wisdom that realizes emptiness; and the central face uniting the two signifies the indivisible bliss and emptiness. Furthermore, the right face signifies the conventional truth—the pure illusory body; the left face signifies perfect wisdom, the ultimate truth, wisdom of great bliss; and the central face signifies the union of these two, the body and mind. Meditate on the three faces by recollecting this signified meaning."[227]

Tsongkhapa concludes this section by explaining how the meditation on the Supreme King of Mandalas is applied in correspondences with the path of completion stage and the fruit: "By generating the deities of the Supreme King of Mandalas through the 'seven steps,' cultivating clear appearance of the deities and divine identification with them, and further regarding the [mandala] as a display of indivisible bliss and emptiness, the mandala—including the celestial mansion and deities dwelling in it—will be actually attained during the completion stage and the fruit."[228]

The Supreme King of Deeds

While the meditation on the Supreme King of Mandalas corresponds to a buddha's deeds of the body that act for the sake of other sentient beings through various emanations, the Supreme King of Deeds corresponds to the deeds of the mind and speech. The first step of the Supreme King of Deeds is the meditation on subtle objects that corresponds to the deeds of the mind, abiding in perfect inner absorption.[229]

Meditation on Subtle Objects

The objects meditated upon here are subtle in relation to the previous steps of the *Sādhana* that are regarded as coarse. When yogis achieve signs of stability in their earlier meditations and are thus able to eliminate ordinary appearances and attitudes through coarse yoga, they should meditate on subtle objects[230] to further increase the stability of their minds. The meditation on subtle objects is not included in Tsongkhapa's *Sādhana* but is described in his explanatory works on the *Sādhana*, including *Bee's Hope*: "Visualize yourself as Akṣobhyavajra. At the tip of the nose on your face visualize a five-pronged blue *vajra*, the size of a white mustard seed upon a solar seat, and perceive it in the nature of Akṣobhya. Meditate in this way until stable signs of touching and seeing appear."[231]

The two ends of the central channel along the subtle body are the tip of the nose on the face and the tip of the "nose" at the gate of the *vajra* or lotus. In the first step, yogis meditate on an emblem on the upper nose, and later they will meditate on a drop on the lower nose. In this context of the Guhyasamāja, yogis visualize themselves as Akṣobhya, and they meditate on Akṣobhya's emblem, a five-pronged blue *vajra* the size of a tiny white mustard seed. Yogis should cultivate their perception of this *vajra* in the nature of Akṣobhya until they attain signs.

Signs of stable seeing are a very clear appearance—much clearer than seeing directly with the eyes—that arises in the yogi's mind and remain until the end of the meditative session, without scattering for a single instant and without changing the form of the object. Signs of touching are the sense that the object can be touched with the hands.[232] According to Tsongkhapa,[233] the arising of these signs indicates that the meditating yogi has obtained mental quiescence.[234] Kedrup Jé adds that for this reason, tantric treatises do not teach the practice of mental quiescence apart from deity yoga.[235]

When yogis attain stable signs of touching and seeing, Tsongkhapa instructs: "Once stability arises, emanate from that *vajra* a second *vajra*, then a third, and so on, in stages, to fill the entire sky. Then withdraw the emanated *vajras* back in stages into the original *vajra*. When you have perfected the emanation and withdrawing into the emblem, transform the original *vajra* into Akṣobhya, and emanate [a second Akṣobhya, then a third, and so forth], in stages, to fill the entire sky and withdraw him back into the emblems in stages."[236] Thus yogis emanate a second five-pronged blue *vajra* from the original one, and then a third one, until the entire sky is pervaded by *vajras*. Next, they are instructed to withdraw these *vajras* in reverse order. When they attain stability in this meditation, they transform the *vajras* into the deities themselves and emanate and withdraw them as before. Finally, to let the mind rest, they withdraw everything they have emanated into the original *vajra* visualized on the tip of the nose, withdraw the *vajra* into their bodies through one of the nostrils, and dissolve it into the heart of the *jñānasattva* on their own hearts. Through this practice, according to Tsongkhapa,[237] yogis will gain special insight[238] and eventually will gain a perfect *samādhi* on the union of mental quiescence and special insight.[239]

Once the yogis' minds have attained stability in the meditation on the subtle emblem situated on the upper nose, they meditate in a similar fashion on a subtle object in the form of a drop on the lower nose at their secret place. When stable signs of touching and seeing appear, the yogis mentally send the drop forth to the tip of the nose of the lotus of their consorts. Now they visualize another mandala, called "son-mandala," with its celestial mansion and deities within that drop. Akṣobhya, the principal deity of the mandala, abides with his consort at the center of this son-mandala, and at the tip of his *vajra* there is once again a subtle drop. When yogis attain stability, they can proceed to visualize within this drop a grandson-mandala and meditate until they attain the signs of stable minds.

We can see here how Indian and Tibetan scholars incorporated into their *sādhanas* the imagery of Vairocana's palace and the untold multitudes of buddha-fields in each of the pores in Samantabhadra's body found in the *Gaṇḍavyūha Sūtra, Vimalakīrtinirdeśa,* and *Daśabhūmika Sūtra.*[240]

Mantra Recitation

While the first step of the Supreme King of Deeds, the meditation on subtle objects, corresponds to the deeds of the mind, the second step of mantra recitation corresponds to the deeds of speech—turning the wheel of Dharma for the sake of the disciples.[241] *Fulfilling the Bee's Hope* explains: "There are two types of mantra recitation: outer and inner recitations. In the outer recitation recite *vajradhṛk* and so forth, and in the inner recitation recite the three syllables."[242] The inner recitation during the creation stage, also referred to as "*vajra* recitation," is soundless and mental, performed without moving the tongue and lips. The outer recitation, also referred to as "voiced recitation," is performed aloud. The mantra recited soundlessly, accompanied by visualization, during the *vajra* recitation is the three syllables *oṃ āḥ hūṃ,* called the "essence of suchness."[243] In voiced recitation, the heart mantras are recited.[244] These are composed of the name mantras and seed syllable of each deity, interspersed with the three syllables *oṃ āḥ hūṃ*. The name mantras have been already recited during the Supreme King of Mandalas, for example, when Akṣobhya was drawn from the lotus of the consort into the yogi's heart and then sent forth to the ten directions; the name mantra recited was *vajradhṛk*. In the heart mantras, the name mantra is followed by the respective seed syllable—which in the case of Akṣobhya is *hūṃ*—preceded by *oṃ āḥ* and followed by *hūṃ*. Hence, the heart mantra of Akṣobhya is *oṃ āḥ vajradhṛk hūṃ hūṃ*.

Dissolution of the Principal Deities into Clear Light

To conclude the meditation session, yogis dissolve the visualization of themselves as the principal deity of the mandala only to arise as emanation bodies. In *Bee's Hope* Tsongkhapa discusses how to envision this: "Visualize that while you, as the principal deity with your consort, are absorbed in union, the triple *sattvas* enter clear light one after the other, thereby wisdom and emptiness are united."[245] According to Tsongkhapa's *Sādhana,*[246] first the Mother dissolves into the Father: namely, the consort Vajra Lady of Tangibles[247] dissolves into the principal deity Akṣobhya-Dveṣavajra. Next, the Father, who is the *samayasattva,* dissolves into the *jñānasattva* and the *jñānasattva* into the *samādhisattva*—the syllable *hūṃ*. Now the syllable *hūṃ* dissolves in stages: first the vowel sign *ū*[248] below the consonant *ha* dissolves into the *ha;*[249] then the *ha* dissolves into the head of the syllable,[250] and the head into the crescent moon.[251] The crescent moon then dissolves into the drop,[252] the drop into the *nāda,*[253] and the *nāda* dissolves into clear light. The *nāda* is the primordial sound out of which all creations emanate, and now, during the dissolution, everything dissolves back into it. Finally, the primordial sound as well dissolves into clear-light-emptiness.

Like all other steps during the Supreme Kings, this dissolution corresponds to deeds of a buddha on the fruit of the practice. When a buddha completes his deeds of body, speech, and mind for the sake of his disciples in a certain buddha-field, and no disciples remain to be guided by him there, he displays the deed of passing into *nirvāṇa*. The dissolution of the principal deities into clear light corresponds to this deed.[254]

The steps of meditation during Supreme King of Deeds not only correspond to the deeds of a buddha at the fruit; they also affect the path. They serve to ripen the mental continuum of the meditator on the completion stage during the different stages of the practice.[255] The meditation on the subtle objects ripens the mental continuum of the meditator on the completion stage during body isolation; the recitation of mantras ripens the mental continuum during speech isolation; the dissolution of the principal deity into clear light ripens the mental continuum during clear light. Our next topic, the arising in an emanation body in response to the invocation of the four goddesses, serves to ripen the mental continuum of the meditator on the completion stage during the arising from clear light in the illusory body.

Arising in Response to the Invocation of the Four Goddesses

When the principal deity has dissolved, the four goddesses, or the four female buddhas (Locanā, Māmakī, Pāṇḍarā, and Tārā), unable to behold him, are in great anguish. Wishing to see him, with melodious love songs they request him to arise.[256] The four goddesses, who are the essence of the four qualities beyond measure[257]—loving-kindness, compassion, empathetic joy, and equanimity, respectively—invoke these four qualities in the principal deity. In response, the principal deity arises in a form consisting of the triple *sattvas*, and all the deities of the mandala vividly perceive him.[258]

Notably, in addition to the general Mahāyāna notion of the four qualities beyond measure, the requests of the four goddesses, found in the *Guhyasamāja Tantra*,[259] are erotic in nature, thus open to interpretation in terms of the Mantric Vehicle. The goddesses request the principal deity to impart amorous pleasure on them and to "take delight in me if you wish me to go on living." According to *Bee's Hope*,[260] the goal of these requests is to "generate the wisdom of great innate bliss," in the principal deity of the mandala. Upon hearing this request, the principal deity arises as a display of indivisible bliss and emptiness in the form of the triple *sattvas*.

This meditation corresponds to the deed of a buddha, who—when his mind is stirred by the four qualities beyond measure—arises from clear light in an emanation body in buddha-fields in which direct disciples of the buddha are found.[261] In emulating the former act of a buddha, yogis enact at this stage of the path the deed they will carry out in the future after reaching awakening as buddhas out of great compassion for sentient beings.

Praises and Offerings

When an emanation body of a buddha appears in other buddha-fields for the first time and displays the deed of awakening, all beings there praise him and worship him with manifold exquisite offerings. In accepting them, the buddha becomes the recipient of offerings from the beings in that world. In correspondence, the yogis as the principal deity of the mandala sing praises and make offerings to "themselves."[262]

In *Bee's Hope* Tsongkhapa instructs the yogis: "Praise by specifying the good qualities of the five *tathāgata* families, beginning with Akṣobhyavajra,"[263] referring to five verses of praise found in the *Guhyasamāja Tantra.*[264] As the yogis recite the praises to the five *tathāgatas*, they visualize all the deities dwelling in the mandala reciting them as well while addressing the yogis themselves. Put differently, the deities proclaim that the yogis have been endowed with all the qualities of the five *tathāgata* families.

The offerings made here are of three kinds: outer, inner, and secret. The outer and inner offerings that are now presented were prepared and blessed during the preliminaries to the *sādhana.* While presenting the offerings, yogis should meditate on three spheres: themselves (the makers of the offerings), the recipients of the offerings, and the offering substances, in conformity with the two vehicles of the Mahāyāna. In accordance with the Pāramitā Vehicle, meditators should absorb themselves in the realization that the three spheres are devoid of intrinsic existence. In agreement with the Mantra Vehicle, yogis must free themselves of ordinary appearances and attitudes toward the three spheres. Hence, they must eliminate their tendency to allow the three spheres to appear to them as ordinary and to regard them as ordinary appearances; rather, they must cultivate the insight into the three spheres arising as a display of bliss and emptiness.

In *Bee's Hope* Tsongkhapa explains the three spheres in the present context: "The *presenter* of the offerings is the yogi who has maintained divine identification with the principal deity and attained great bliss. The *recipients* of the offerings are the lama and the deities residing in the mandala of Akṣobhya. The offering *substances* are those held in the hands of the goddesses who have emanated from the yogi's heart."[265]

While offering the first substance, the water for welcoming,[266] the yogi recites the mantra *oṃ sarva tathāgata arghaṃ pūjā megha samudra spharaṇa samaya śriye āḥ hūṃ,* while visualizing in stages: "While reciting *oṃ* visualize the goddesses emanating from your heart and sending forth in the ten directions the water for welcoming and the other offerings—vast as ocean-like clouds—for the lama and the deities of the mandala. Then after reciting: 'Please accept, please accept as pledge,' while pronouncing *hūṃ*, visualize the goddesses withdrawing into the *hūṃ* in your heart."[267] The offering of the remaining substances follow this example.

With regard to the inner offerings, Tsongkhapa says: "Having been blessed as nectar, the inner offerings generate special untainted bliss for the lama and the deities of the mandala."[268] As for the secret offerings: "As the principal deity and his consort are absorbed in union, all the deities surrounding them in the mandala are satisfied with great bliss."[269] Additionally, offerings of suchness are made, not as a separate ritual act but as a *samādhi* that arises from the secret offerings. When the deities of the mandala experience great innate bliss, they enter into a single-pointed *samādhi* of indivisibly united great bliss and emptiness.[270]

Dissolution

The final step of the Supreme King of Deeds, according to Tsongkhapa's *Sādhana*,[271] is the dissolution of all the surrounding deities of the mandala together with the celestial mansion into the principal deity and his consort. When only the yogis as the Father-Mother deities remain, they empower all sentient beings, purify their obscurations, and transform them into *hūṃ* syllables, out of which they arise as Vajradharas. Then, light rays emanating from the *hūṃ*s on the yogis' hearts draw all these Vajradharas and dissolve them into the yogis as the principal deities. The yogis and their consorts, visualized as the principal deities, remain.

Having visualized how they bring all sentient beings to buddhahood, the yogis arise from their meditation on the *sādhana*. In this postmeditative state, they regard everything that appears to them in the world as the celestial mansion and all sentient beings as deities of the mandala. No ordinary appearances and attitudes arise in their minds; instead, everything appears to them as divine and is experienced accordingly.

Fulfilling the Bee's Hope; or, Clarifying the Essential Meaning of the Creation Stage of the Glorious Guhyasamāja—Fulfilling the Hope of the Clear-Minded Bee

TSONGKHAPA LOZANG DRAKPA

Author's note: *Fulfilling the Bee's Hope*[1] is an explanation of Tsongkhapa's *Guhyasamāja Sādhana*[2] written for disciples who have memorized it. To facilitate modern readers, English translations of selected portions of Tsongkhapa's *Sādhana* are interspersed below, indented and in sans serif font.[3]

Prostrations to the Blessed One Vajrasattva.

Here I shall explain the stages of the clear realizations of the *Glorious Guhyasamāja Sādhana.* There are three sections here: (1) Explaining the preliminaries to the *Sādhana,* (2) explaining the text of the *Sādhana,* and (3) explaining the framework of the *Sādhana.*

[In the English translation here, the explanation of the framework of the *Sādhana* will appear at the end, since after reading the explanation of the practice, its framework will become clearer to the reader.]

EXPLAINING THE PRELIMINARIES TO THE SĀDHANA

There are two sections here: (1) establishing favorable conditions—amassing the accumulations, and (2) averting unfavorable conditions—meditating on the protection wheel.

Establishing Favorable Conditions—Amassing the Accumulations

The Sevenfold Worship

Favorable conditions are established through the sevenfold worship: (1) offerings, (2) prostrations, (3) confession, (4) rejoicing and dedication, (5) taking refuge, (6) generating the mind for enlightenment and pledging reliance on the path, and (7) maintaining the [unshared] vows.

Invitation of the Merit Field

I visualize myself as Akṣobhyavajra.[4] Hook-like light rays emanate from the blue *hūṃ* abiding upon a variegated lotus and a solar disk in my heart. These light rays invite from their natural abode the mandala of Akṣobhya who is nondual with my lama [into the foreground]. The light rays then dissolve back into my heart.[5]

Making Offerings to the Merit Field

[The offerings made here are the outer offerings that include water for welcoming, water for refreshing the feet, flowers, incense, light, fragrance, food, music, forms, sounds, scents, tastes, and objects of touch. The yogis visualize each of the offering goddesses emanating from their heart and sending forth the respective offering in the ten directions for the lama and the deities of the mandala.]

The water for welcoming is offered with the mantra *oṃ sarva tathāgata arghaṃ pūjā megha samudra spharaṇa samaya śrīye āḥ hūṃ*. For the other offerings *arghaṃ* in the mantra is replaced respectively with: *pādyaṃ, puṣpe, dhūpe, āloke, gandhe, naivede, śabda, rūpa, śabda, gandhe, rasa,* and *sparśa*.[6]

1. Offerings

The presenter of the offerings is the yogi who abides in divine identification with Akṣobhya. The recipient of the offerings is the mandala of Akṣobhya who is nondual with the lama. The inviters are hook-like light rays [emanating from] the blue *hūṃ* at the heart. There are three methods for inviting the lama [together with the merit field]: (1) inviting the lama in the appearance of Vajradhara alone [unaccompanied], (2) inviting the lama as the lord of the family of the principal deity, and (3) inviting the lama as inseparable with the principal deity of the mandala. The method here is the last. The lama [with the merit field] can be invited from three locations: cremation grounds, the No-Higher Heaven,[7] and the natural abode. [5a][8] The method here is the last.

There are two methods for the invitation from the natural abode: (1) When the place where the *saṃbhogakāya* was first awakened is regarded as the natural abode, the invitation is from that [*saṃbhogakāya*] in the appearance of the *nirmāṇakāya.* (2) When the *dharmakāya* is regarded as the natural abode, the invitation is from that [*dharmakāya*] in the appearance of the *rūpakāya.*

The offering substances are flowers and so forth,[9] held by the goddesses emanated [from the yogi's heart]. The offering mantras are taught in the explanatory *Vajra Garland Tantra:*[10] *Oṃ sarva tathāgata arghaṃ* [*pūjā megha samudra spharaṇa samaya śrīye āḥ hūṃ*]. This means: Please accept as *samaya*[11] this water for welcoming vast as ocean-like clouds that are sent forth in the ten directions as offerings to all *tathāgatas*. While reciting *oṃ* [of each mantra], visualize the respective offering goddess emanating [from your heart] and making her offerings. Then while reciting *hūṃ* after making the offerings, draw the offering goddess into the *hūṃ* at [your] heart. As for the meaning of these offerings: by presenting the offering in this way, a special untainted bliss arises as object for the six senses of the lama and the deities residing in the mandala.[12]

2. Prostrations

> I prostrate to all the immense ones equal to the mind-for-enlightenment: forms, feelings, perceptions, the conditioned, and consciousnesses, the six sense bases, the six faculties, earth, water, fire, wind, and space.
>
> I prostrate to the immense ones equal to the mind-for-enlightenment endowed with qualities of ignorance, fault, desire, and *vajra,* born out of union with the consort, perpetually joined, who experience variety through joy.
>
> I prostrate to the immense ones equal to the mind-for-enlightenment, gathering, joy, appearance, unchanging, the nature of the cause and the fruit, phenomena that pertain to the mind, delusion, anger, desire, obscurations, and *vajra.*[13]

To whom are you prostrating?[14] *I prostrate to those who are equal* in their abandonment and realization to Bodhicitta[15]—Vajradhara, the wisdom of nondual profundity and manifestation that arises through the union with the consort in the form of the *immense* deities of the mandala. [5b]

Who are the deities of the mandala? The five *tathāgata* families, Vairocana and so forth [Akṣobhya, Ratnasaṃbhava, Amitābha, and Amoghasiddhi],[16] who are the purified aggregates of *forms* and so forth [*feelings, perceptions, the conditioned, and consciousnesses*]; the five Vajra Ladies, the Vajra Lady of Forms and so forth [of Sounds, Scents, Tastes, and Objects of Touch],[17] together with Samantabhadra,[18] who are the six purified *sense bases;* the six *bodhisattvas,* Kṣitigarbha and so forth [Vajrapāṇi, Khagarbha, Lokeśvara, Sarvāvaraṇa-vikṣambhin, and Maitreya],[19] who are the *six* purified *sense faculties,* the eye and so forth [ears, nose, tongue, body, and mind]; the four female deities, Locanā and so forth [Māmakī, Pāṇḍarā, and Tārā][20] together with the *bodhisattva* Mañjuśrī,[21] who are the five purified physical elements, *earth* and so forth [*water, fire, wind, and space*].

Yamāntaka,[22] the fierce deity of the *tathāgata* family of Vairocana, who is purified *ignorance.* Prajñāntaka,[23] the fierce deity of the *tathāgata* family of Ratnasaṃbhava, who is purified *fault,* that is to say, pride. Hayagrīva,[24] [the fierce deity] of the *tathāgata* family of Amitābha, who is purified *desire.* Vighnanataka,[25] [the fierce deity] of the *tathāgata* family of Vajra Amoghasiddhi. *Gathering* is Ṭakkirāja,[26] *joy* is Nīladaṇḍa, *appearance* is Mahābāla, *unchanging* is Acala, *the cause* is Sumbharāja, *the fruit* is Uṣṇīṣacakravartin.

To these thirty-two deities you prostrate.

3. Confession

All the turbidity I have accumulated through my conceptual thoughts
in this beginningless river of existence,
I confess in the presence of the Greatly Compassionate Ones,
in accordance with the ritual method.[27]

Confess the *turbidity*—the ten nonvirtues and so forth—whose NATURE[28] is wrongdoing, that you *have accumulated* by *your conceptualizations* of the three poisons in their entirety since *beginningless* TIME, in this *river of existence—in the presence of the* SPHERE *of the Greatly Compassionate Ones,* the lamas and the deities residing in the mandala, [6a] through the METHOD that *accords with the ritual* taught by the victorious one, complete with the four antidotal powers[29] and suffused with the perfect wisdom that realizes that the three spheres [of confession][30] are devoid of true existence.

4. Rejoicing and Dedication

I truly rejoice in all the virtuous deeds of the fully awakened buddhas,
the *bodhisattvas*, the sublime beings, and others,
I wholly dedicate them
for the attainment of enlightenment.[31]

I truly rejoice in all the virtuous deeds of the buddhas, the bodhisattvas, the sublime disciples, and solitary buddhas, and all *others* who are not *sublime beings,* but ordinary beings; and *dedicate* the virtuous deeds accumulated in the three times to *the attainment* of supreme *enlightenment.*

5. Taking Refuge

Refuge in the Buddha

At all times do I seek refuge in the *Sugatas*
in whose mind dwells [wisdom]
and the method of supreme and boundless compassion
attained through the play of the untainted moon-like mind.[32]

Taking refuge in the Buddha is the promise to *seek refuge in the Sugatas* who teach the Dharma and *in whose mind* the two excellent qualities of method and perfect wisdom *dwell.* The quality of perfect wisdom is *attained through* a continual increase—*like* the waxing *moon*—of wisdom *untainted* by dualistic appearances, *the play of mind,* or its display. The utmost quality of *method* is *supreme and boundless compassion.*

Refuge in the Dharma

At all times do I seek refuge in the excellent Dharma,
the foundation of opulence of the sublime beings,
wholly free of conceptualizations,
whose essence is the single taste of all phenomena.[33]

Taking refuge in the Dharma is the promise to attain in your mental continuum the two teachings: the truth of the path and the truth of cessation. The truth of the path[34] is the *foundation* for the *opulence* of excellent qualities of abandonment and realization of the *sublime beings,* the superior *bodhisattvas, free* in the ground itself *of* all *conceptualization* of dualistic appearances at each respective level. The truth of cessation[35] is the true nature of *all phenomena* and their subjects that in suchness share a *single taste.* [6b]

Refuge in the *Saṅgha*

At all times do I seek refuge in the assembly of masters of rigorous practice,
truly freed from bondage,
endowed with splendor born of supreme compassion,
abiding on the [*bodhisattva*] levels of Joy and higher still.[36]

Taking refuge in the *saṅgha* is the promise to take as friends for attaining the path the *assembly* of sublime *bodhisattvas* who *abide on the bodhisattva levels of Joy and higher still,* and are *endowed with the splendor* of the mind-for-enlightenment *born of* the mother *of supreme compassion, truly free* of every *bondage* at their respective levels and are thus *masters* or superior to ordinary *bodhisattvas* in their *rigorous practice* of the Mahāyāna.

6. Generating the Mind-for-Enlightenment and Pledging Reliance on the Path

Generating the Mind-for-Enlightenment

I shall generate the mind for sublime enlightenment,
adorned with earnest aspiration,
that totally eliminates the habitual tendencies of all obscurations,
by means of pure resolve and ripening.[37]

Generating the mind-for-enlightenment, the mind *adorned with earnest aspiration* for the sake of others, both the wishing *resolve* and the engaging minds-for-enlightenment that *totally eliminate the habitual tendencies of all obscurations* [that result from] *ripening* [of previous karma].

Pledging Reliance on the Path

I shall truly abide on the singular path of the *Sugata*s and their Spiritual Sons,
in the perfections of generosity and so forth,
and in the excellent qualities of the ten virtues,
with a mind whose essence is all the fully enlightened buddhas.[38]

Pledging reliance on the path of the mind-for-enlightenment is the promise to practice *the singular path* trodden by *the Sugatas and their Spiritual Sons,* the six *perfections, generosity and so forth,* and the ethical conduct of the wholesome activity of *the ten virtues.*

7. Maintaining the Unshared Vows

Generating the Mind for Enlightenment

May all buddhas and *bodhisattva*s
turn their thoughts to me!
May I, named so and so, from this moment,
until I sit on the throne of awakening,
generate the unexcelled and
sublime mind for enlightenment,
just as [when] the lords of the three times
have firmly resolved upon their enlightenment.[39]

The meaning of these lines is the resolution: "*Just as* formerly *when* the buddhas, *the lords of the three times,* abided on the path of learning, they *generated the mind for enlightenment* and then actualized the stage of complete awakening, in order to place beings on the stage of buddhahood, I, too, the practitioner who is likewise learning, *generate the mind for enlightenment,* consisting of both the wishing resolve and the engaging mind, for as long as all sentient beings are not placed on the level of buddhahood, [7a] thereby I shall place sentient beings at the stage of nonabiding *nirvāṇa.*"

Vairocana's Vow

I shall keep firmly each of the three ethical conducts:
training in morality,
accumulating virtues,
and acting for the sake of sentient beings.
From now on I shall keep
the vow born from buddha yoga,
in the three unexcelled Jewels,
the Buddha, Dharma, and *Saṅgha.*[40]

I shall train six times daily in the [three ethical conducts]: the ethical conduct of avoiding wrongdoing, the ethical conduct of *accumulating virtues,* and the ethical conduct of *acting for the sake of sentient beings.* Having promised to take refuge in the *three* [Jewels], I shall generate the mind for enlightenment. These are the yogi's pledges and *vows* that are *born from buddha yoga*—the *tathāgata* family of Vairocana.

Akṣobhya's Vow

For the eminent and supreme *tathāgata* family of *vajra,*
I shall genuinely keep the [commitments of]
the *vajra,* the bell and the consort,
I shall keep also the master's [commitment].[41]

The commitment of the *vajra* is holding the properly measured five-pronged symbolic *vajra* and so forth in order to recollect the secret *vajra*—the mind of the victorious one, the indivisible wisdom.

The commitment of the *bell* is holding and resounding the properly measured symbolic bell in order to recollect the signified meaning of the ultimate truth bell—emptiness and perfect wisdom: the emptiness of intrinsic nature of all phenomena and the perfect wisdom of the nondual gnosis of the yogi.

The commitment of the *consort* is to visualize yourself in the body of a deity, such as Vajrasattva, together with the great consort, and then meditate on the union of emptiness and bliss that arises from embracing and absorbing in union with the karma and wisdom consorts. [7b]

The commitment of the *master* is to hold as the supreme object of reverence the master who has taught the Mantra [path], for example, conferred the initiation.

The commitment of the yogi who belongs to *the supreme tathāgata family of vajra,* the family of Akṣobhya, is to promise to adhere to these four commitments during the six sessions every day.

Ratnasaṃbhava's Vow

For the eminent and supreme *tathāgata* family of jewel
whose commitment delights my mind,
I shall always offer the four kinds of gifts,
during the six sessions every day.[42]

The commitment and vows of the yogi who belongs to the *jewel family, the supreme family* of Ratnasaṃbhava, is the promise to *offer the four kinds of gifts* to sentient beings *during the six sessions every day:* (1) material gifts, (2) gifts of Dharma such as dedicating the roots of virtue to others, (3) gifts of loving-kindness, such as meditating on loving-kindness beyond measure, and (4) gifts of protection from fear, such as meditating on equanimity beyond measure.

Amitābha's Vow

For the eminent and pure *tathāgata* family of the lotus,
which arises from great awakening,
I shall keep the true Dharma
of the outer, the secret, and the three vehicles.[43]

The commitment of the yogi who belongs to *the lotus family,* the family of Amitābha, is the promise to hold during the six sessions every day wholly and *individually* the *true Dharma of the outer, the secret, and the three vehicles. The outer* comprises the Kriyā and Caryā Tantras; the *secret* the Yoga and Unexcelled Tantras; *the three vehicles* are the Śrāvaka, Prayetkabuddha, and Pāramitā Vehicles.

Amoghasiddhi's Vow

For the eminent and supreme *tathāgata* family of karma,
I shall genuinely keep all the vows[44]
and practice the ritual of offerings
to the utmost of my ability.[45]

The commitment of the yogi who belongs to the *supreme family of karma,* the family of Amoghasiddhi, is the promise to make the four kinds of *offerings*—outer, inner, secret, and suchness *offerings*—to the lama and the deities residing in the mandala during the six sessions every day.

Concluding Verses

Having generated the sublime and
unexcelled mind for enlightenment,
and kept all the vows,
for the sake of all sentient beings,
I shall liberate those not liberated,
I shall free those not freed,
I shall relieve those not relieved,
I shall place all sentient beings in *nirvāṅā*.[46]

By keeping the vows of the five *tathāgata* families in this way, I promise *to liberate sentient beings* who are *not liberated* from the fetters of the two obscurations and have not entered the path, such as Brahmā; [8a] *to free* Arhats of Śrāvakas and Prayetkabuddhas who *are not freed* from the fetters of obscuration to knowables; *to relieve* sentient beings in the three lower realms of existence who are *not relieved* of sufferings; *to place* these *sentient beings in* nonabiding *nirvāṇa*.

This completes the limb of keeping the vows.

In the present context, vows that were not taken in the past are not taken, nor is this an occasion to restore vows that have been broken. The purpose here is to reinforce vows that have already been taken, because this pleases the lama and the deities of the mandala. For this reason, this practice is included within the step of amassing the accumulations.[47]

Averting Unfavorable Conditions—Meditating on the Protection Wheel

[Meditation on Emptiness]

The essence, cause, and fruit of phenomena are empty of existing by way of their own characteristics.[48]

Prior to the meditation on the protection wheel, you should meditate on the three doors of liberation: the essence, cause, and result of phenomena are empty of existing by way of their own characteristics.[49] Thereby, the protection wheel with its deities will arise as a manifestation of emptiness.

[Meditation on the Wheel, the Residence of the Protecting Deities]

Meditate on the ten-spoked protection wheel spinning swiftly clockwise and radiating a series of cloud-like *vajra* flames in the ten directions. This follows the *Later Tantra:* "A wheel yellow all around . . . [While the wheel is spinning, (the deities)] do not seem to be in motion."[50]

[Meditation on the Protecting Deities]

Meditate on the principal deity of the protection wheel as white Vajradhara,[51] [8b] in accordance with the instruction of Ārya Nāgārjuna.[52] Vajradhara has three faces and six arms, as Abhayākaragupta teaches,[53] and he embraces Vajradhātvīśvarī[54] as his consort, as Muniśrībhadra teaches.[55] Visualize Vajradhara as the triple *sattvas,*[56] with the three syllables [*oṃ āḥ hūṃ*] placed on the three places [his head, throat, and heart], as the *Later Tantra* teaches.[57] Visualize the fierce deities arising from long *hūṃ*s, as the thirteenth chapter of the *Guhyasamāja Tantra* and its commentary teaches.[58]

[You visualize yourself as Vajradhara, but] as Akṣobhya enters [into you as] Vajradhara, [you as Vajradhara] transform into Dveṣavajra,[59] who abides in absorption at the center of blazing and sparkling red light and embodies the triple *sattvas,* as the fourteenth chapter of the *Guhyasamāja Tantra* and its commentary teach.[60] The Father [Vajradhara] transforms into Dveṣavajra in order to command the fierce deities, and in congruence the Mother transforms into Vajra Lady of Tangibles.[61] Then the fierce deities are drawn from the Mother's womb[62] and placed on solar seats with their left legs stretched forth, as both Nāgārjuna[63] and Candrakīrti[64] teach.

Commanding Sumbharāja

Sumbharāja emerges from my heart and is placed within the lower spoke. . . . As I look at Sumbharāja below, he emanates a second Sumbharāja, who comes and abides before me and asks for instructions, saying: "What should I do?" I call on Sumbharāja: *Oṃ Sumbha Nisumbha hūṃ gṛhṇa gṛhṇa hūṃ gṛhṇāpaya gṛhṇāpaya hūṃ ānaya ho bhagavan vidyā-rāja hūṃ phaṭ.*[65] Catch and fetch the obstructors. Thereupon the *vajra* in his first right hand turns into a *vajra*-hook. . . . He catches . . . and fetches the principal obstructors and hands them over to the ten fierce deities, who then encase them in pits.[66]

Explaining the Meaning of the Mantra for Commanding Sumbharāja

The syllable *oṃ* is composed of three letters *a, u,* and *m,* which signify the three *vajras* [of body, speech, and mind]. When the *a* is combined with the *u*, it becomes an *o*. Then when the *m* is added as a drop on top of the *o*,[67] the [single] syllable *oṃ* is formed and this signifies the indivisibility of the three *vajras*. When you recite the *oṃ* at the beginning of a mantra while recollecting the meaning it signifies, you accumulate merit.

Sumbha means[68] [addressing Sumbharāja, O] Great Subduer; [9a] *Nisumbha* means [calling him] Great Subduer of All; *gṛhṇa gṛhṇa* means catch, catch!; *gṛhṇāpaya* pronounced twice means exhort your retinue to catch them wherever they flee![69] With *ānaya ho bhagavan vidyārāja* call Sumbharāja: "Fetch them Oh Blessed One! King of Knowledge!"

The *vajra*—the emblem of Sumbharāja—turns into a *vajra* hook, as the fourteenth chapter of the *Guhyasamāja Tantra* and its commentary teach. "The chief of the obstructers . . . are encased in pits," as *Kṛṣṇasamayavajra teaches.[70]

Driving the Stakes

[The stakes are driven into the heads of the obstructors, while the following mantra is recited:] *Oṃ gha gha ghātaya ghātaya sarvaduṣṭāṃ phaṭ phaṭ kīlaya kīlaya sarvapāpāṃ phaṭ phaṭ hūṃ hūṃ hūṃ vajrakīla vajradhara ājñāpayati sarvavighnānāṃ kāyavākcittavajraṃ kīlaya hūṃ hūṃ hūṃ phaṭ phaṭ.*[71]

Explaining the Meaning of the Mantra for Driving the Stakes

Oṃ has been already explained. *Gha gha* is *ghātaka* calling out, "Killer! Killer!" *Ghātaya ghātaya sarvaduṣṭāṃ phaṭ* means vanquish! Vanquish all the malevolent ones! *Kīlaya kīlaya* means drive the stakes and make them immobile![72] *Sarvapāpāṃ* are all those who have evil intentions. *Hūṃ* recited three times urges the suchness of [Vajra Stake's] body, speech, and mind [to act].[73] *Vajrakīla*[74] is the invocation of Vajra Stake! *Vajradhara ājñāpayati* means obey the command of Vajradhara![75] *Sarvavighnānāṃ* means [of] all the obstructers; *kāya vāk citta vajraṃ* is [*vajra*] body, speech, and mind; *kīlaya*[76] is as before [drive the stakes]; *hūṃ phaṭ* is piercing them. [9b][77]

[Meditation on the *Vajra* Enclosure]

The Four Fences

Ṭakki hūṃ jaḥ visualize an iron *vajra* fence beyond the fierce deities.
Ṭakki hūṃ jaḥ a water fence beyond that.
Ṭakki hūṃ jaḥ a fire fence beyond that.
Ṭakki hūṃ jaḥ a wind fence beyond that.[78]

Visualize an iron *vajra* fence beyond the fierce deities. The spaces between the larger *vajras* are filled with smaller *vajras* down to the tiniest ones, leaving no space between them. Beyond the iron *vajra* fence, visualize a water fence spraying water droplets outwards; a fire fence beyond that, ablaze with the fire of wisdom emanating in five colors—the pernicious ones cannot bear looking at it; and a wind fence swirling vigorously with fierce howls beyond that. The shape of the four fences is round, their height[79] is from No-Higher Heaven[80] to the wind mandala,[81] or else from the abode of Brahmā to the golden earth,[82] and their width extends to the iron mountains[83] or as wide as the mind can emanate.[84]

Protecting Oneself

Visualize white *oṃ*s upon lunar seats on the crowns of the [fierce] deities,
red *āḥ*s upon lotuses on their throats,
and blue *hūṃ*s upon solar seats at their hearts.
[Recite three times] *oṃ āḥ hūṃ*.[85]

While the meditation on the enclosure is for protecting the area, placing the three syllables on the three places of the fierce deities is for protecting oneself.

EXPLAINING THE TEXT OF THE SĀDHANA

There are two sections here: (1) Explaining how to meditate on the *Samādhi* of the First Yoga in correspondence with the stages of the evolution and destruction during the world's ordinary existence [the ground];[86] and (2) explaining how to meditate on the *Samādhi* of the Supreme King of Mandalas [and the Supreme King of Deeds] in correspondence with the deeds of a fruitional buddha.

Explaining How to Meditate on the *Samādhi* of the First Yoga in Correspondence with the Stages of the Evolution and Destruction of the World during the World's Ordinary Existence

There are two sections here: (1) Explaining how to meditate on the celestial mansion, the residence [of the deities], in correspondence with the stages of the evolution and destruction during the world's ordinary existence; and (2) explaining how to meditate on the yoga of the three bodies in correspondence with the stages of the evolution and destruction during the beings' ordinary existence in the world.

Explaining How to Meditate on the Celestial Mansion, the Residence [of the Deities], in Correspondence with the Stages of the Evolution and Destruction during the World's Ordinary Existence

There are two sections here: (1) How to meditate on the ground of wisdom in correspondence with the stages of emptying the previous world; [10a] and (2) how to meditate on the four mandalas of the physical elements in correspondence with the stages of the evolution of the subsequent world.

How to Meditate on the Ground of Wisdom in Correspondence with the Stages of Emptying the Previous World

There are two sections here: (1) Explaining the corresponding object; and (2) explaining the meditation that is applied in correspondence with it.

EXPLAINING THE CORRESPONDING OBJECT—DISSOLUTION OF THE WORLD AND ITS INHABITANTS

Dissolution of the Inhabitants

Sentient beings in the Hell of Ceaseless Torment[87] who have exhausted their karma and die are then born in fortunate realms, while those who have not exhausted their karma are born in the Hells of Ceaseless Torment that are found in other realms of the universe. In this way the Hell of Ceaseless Torment of this world, characterized by the experience of suffering, is emptied of its beings. Then, through a similar method of emptying, the additional seven hot hells, the eight cold hells, the hungry ghosts[88] who live in their principal habitats, and the animals who live in the ocean below are emptied in succession. The animals who live with the gods and humans are emptied together with the gods and humans.[89]

How is the human world emptied? At that time[90] the concentration of the first *dhyāna*[91]—attained through the nature of things[92]—arises in the mental continuum of one person of Jambudvīpa.[93] That person exclaims: "Joy and bliss born of seclusion are bliss and peace." When others hear this, the concentration of the first *dhyāna* arises in their mental continuum as well, and when they die, they are born as gods in the first *dhyāna*.

Then, through a similar method of emptying, the concentration of the first *dhyāna* arises in the mental continuum of people of Pūrvavideha,[94] the continent in the east, and Godānīya,[95] the continent in the west. [10b] When they die, all of them are reborn in the first *dhyāna*. But the inhabitants of

Uttarakuru,[96] the continent in the north, possess major obstructions to fruition,[97] and therefore are unable to free themselves of desire during that lifetime. When they die, they are born as gods in the Desire Realm.

After that, the concentration of the first *dhyāna* arises in the mental continuum of the gods of the six classes of the Desire Realm: the Four Great Kings,[98] the gods of the Thirty-Three,[99] the Free from Conflict,[100] the Joyful,[101] the Delighting in Emanations,[102] and the Masters over Others' Emanations,[103] and when they die, they are reborn in the first *dhyāna.*

After that, the concentration of the second *dhyāna*—attained through the nature of things—arises in the mental continuum of one god in the first *dhyāna.* He exclaims: "Joy and bliss[104] born from concentration are bliss and peace." When others hear this, the concentration of the second *dhyāna* arises in their mental continuum as well, and when they die, they are born as gods in the second *dhyāna.* In this way, the sentient beings inhabiting the first *dhyāna* of existence are emptied.

Emptying the Physical World

Then, since there are no sentient beings, the gods do not cause a timely rain to fall, and therefore the plants, trees, and forests dry up and are burnt by the present sun.[105] Then a second, extremely hot sun rises, and the small and large lakes dry up. [11a] Then a third extremely hot sun rises and dries the small and large rivers. Then a fourth extremely hot sun rises, drying up Lake Anavatapta.[106] Then a fifth extremely hot sun begins to dry up the great ocean. A sixth extremely hot sun dries the great ocean and begins to burn the four continents, the Iron Rim Mountain,[107] and Mt. Meru. The seventh extremely hot sun burns completely the continents and the mountains, turning them to a single flame. Since the wind stirs the flames, the celestial palaces up to the first *dhyāna* are incinerated and everything becomes a single nature of space. In this way the physical world is emptied.

EXPLAINING THE MEDITATION THAT IS APPLIED IN CORRESPONDENCE WITH IT

Meditation on the Ground of Wisdom

In the absence of being, there is no meditation, and meditation cannot be meditated upon. Therefore, a state of being that is nonbeing leaves no object for meditation.

Since all phenomena included in the animate and inanimate realms are devoid of essence in ultimate truth, their nature is emptiness, signlessness, and wishlessness, in which meditation, object of meditation, and meditator cannot be perceived.[108]

[The lines:] "In the absence of being, there is no meditation,"[109] and so forth up until "cannot be perceived," are taught in the *Concise Sādhana.*[110] The object to which this meditation corresponds is taught in *Formulating the Guhyasamāja Sādhana.*[111]

There are [two kinds of] correspondences [here]: [A. The correspondence between two *absences* of the physical world:] (1) The *absence* of the physical world to the subjective mind[112] of great bliss on the *ground of wisdom,*[113] which apprehends that the physical world is lacking intrinsic nature; and (2) the *absence* of the physical world during the empty period during the world's ordinary existence. [B. The correspondence between two *nonappearances* of the physical world:] (1) the *nonappearing* of the physical world from the perceptual perspective [the objective aspect][114] to the great bliss on the *ground of wisdom,* which apprehends that the physical world is lacking intrinsic nature; and (2) the *nonappearing* of the physical world during the empty period of the world's ordinary existence.

Why is the *wisdom* of great bliss referred to as *ground* [or foundation]?[115] As the space formed when the previous world is emptied serves as the *foundation* [or ground] for the evolution of the subsequent world, [11b] the wisdom of great bliss serves as the *foundation* for the evolution of the celestial mansion, and therefore it is called the *ground of wisdom.*

Furthermore, the emptiness on which the yogi should meditate in this context is the three doors to liberation: (1) the absence of the world and its inhabitants in ultimate truth; (2) the imperceptibility of the meditation, the object to be meditated upon, and the meditator as true; and (3) the absence of intrinsic nature of the essence, cause, and fruit of phenomena.[116]

There are several purposes[117] of meditating on emptiness here by way of the recitation of the verse beginning with "In the absence of being": (1) meditators with dull faculties will newly realize the view of emptiness; (2) meditators with middling faculties will recollect their forgotten realization of emptiness; and (3) meditators with sharp faculties will stabilize their already-attained realization of emptiness. (4) They will gather the accumulation of wisdom, and (5) will shed conceptualization of ordinary attitudes and appearances with respect to their body, speech and mind. This is (6) in order that the mandala with its celestial mansion and deities—that will be explained later—will arise as a display of emptiness; (7) in order to block grasping at true existence, which is the root of *saṃsāra;* (8) to serve as an ultimate protection; (9) to purify death on the ground [of ordinary existence, consisting of death, intermediate state, and rebirth]; (10) to ripen the mental continuum for the clear lights of the completion stage; (11) to attain the fruitional *dharmakāya,* and so forth.

How to Meditate on the Four Mandalas of the Physical Elements in Correspondence with the Stages of the Evolution of the Subsequent World

There are two sections here: (1) explaining the corresponding object; and (2) explaining the meditation that is applied in correspondence with it.

EXPLAINING THE CORRESPONDING OBJECT—HOW THE PHYSICAL WORLD EVOLVES

A light wind from the second *dhyāna* flows downward, thereby forming the celestial mansions of the first *dhyāna.*[118] [12a] Then a light wind coming from the first *dhyāna* flows downward, thereby forming in descending order the celestial mansions [of the four higher gods of the desire realm] from the Masters over Others' Emanations to the Free from Conflict.[119]

Then, through the shared karma of sentient beings, the early sign of the evolving world appears in space—the gentle wind that [at first] blows slowly and gradually increases. Thereupon a wind mandala evolves—one million six hundred thousand *yojanas* in height, and innumerable *yojanas* in width—[a wind mandala] that even a great mighty *vajra* cannot destroy. Then a cloud in the nature of gold condenses in space, and a constant rain whose essence is gold—with drops the size of chariot wheels—falls from the cloud onto the wind mandala and accumulates over a long period. Thereby the water mandala is formed above the wind mandala. A wind evolves through the shared karma of sentient beings and churns this water mandala from the four directions. Following that, the golden earth is formed, as a film is formed over boiling milk.

Although a fire mandala is not specifically explained, the function of fire, its minute particles and so forth, is found [in latent form] within the other three mandalas. Hence, there is no flaw in the absence of a fire mandala as a corresponding object on the ground [during the world's ordinary existence].[120]

Through the shared karma of sentient beings, a cloud whose essence is various elements, condenses in space over the earth. [12b] A constant rain, whose essence is various elements, falls from this cloud over a long period and accumulates. In this way, the outer oceans are created. When the oceans are churned as before, Mt. Meru is formed from the finest elements; the seven ranges of golden mountains—from the medium elements; and the four continents and the eight subcontinents—from the inferior elements.[121]

EXPLAINING THE MEDITATION THAT IS APPLIED IN CORRESPONDENCE WITH IT

Visualizing the *Vajra* Ground

From within the continuum of emptiness, a *vajra* ground complete with fence, tent, canopy, and a fire mountain arises instantly. At the center appears a white triangular pyramid of the "source of phenomena," standing on a point with its wide side pointing upward.

Inside the source of phenomena appears a variegated lotus. At its navel there is a light blue *yaṃ* syllable flanked by two *hūṃ* syllables. The *yaṃ* syllable transforms into a blue, bow-shaped wind mandala, and the two *hūṃ* syllables transform into two *vajras* adorning the wind mandala at its two sides.

Upon the wind mandala appears a red *raṃ* syllable flanked by two *hūṃ* syllables. The *raṃ* syllable transforms into a red triangular fire mandala, and the two *hūṃ* syllables transform into two *vajras* adorning the wind mandala at its two sides.

Upon the wind mandala appears a white *baṃ* [*vaṃ*] syllable flanked by two *hūṃ* syllables. The *baṃ* syllable transforms into a white, round water mandala, and the two *hūṃ* syllables transform into two *vajras* adorning the wind mandala at its two sides.

Upon water mandala appears a yellow *laṃ* syllable flanked by two *hūṃ* syllables. The *laṃ* syllable transforms into a yellow, square earth mandala, and the two *hūṃ* syllables transform into two *vajras* adorning the wind mandala at its two sides.

The natures [of these four mandalas] are respectively those of the four female buddhas, Locanā and so forth [Māmakī, Pāṇḍarā, and Tārā]. The four mandalas merge and transform into a crossed *vajra*.[122]

Visualizing the Celestial Mansion

Upon the navel of the crossed *vajra* appears a white *bhrūṃ* syllable, emanating light-rays of clouds of buddhas. The *bhrūṃ* transforms into a square celestial mansion with four portals . . .[123] and thirty-one seats for the mandala's deities. The principal deity has a solar seat . . . and the [deities] in the north have crossed *vajra* seats.

The meditation on the celestial mansion of the mandala,[124] the abode of the specially visualized deities beginning with: "From within the continuum of emptiness a *vajra* ground arises instantly," and so forth, up until "the [deities] in the north have crossed *vajra* seats," is taught in the *Concise Sādhana*,[125] and the object to which this meditation corresponds, the formation of the physical world, is explained in *Formulating the Guhyasamāja Sādhana.*[126]

How does [the meditation here] correspond [to the evolution of the physical world]? The meditation on the wind mandala corresponds to the evolution of the wind mandala on the ground of ordinary existence [during the evolution of the physical world], and likewise do the three other mandalas [of fire, water, and earth]. The meditation on the celestial mansion upon the crossed *vajra* corresponds to the formation of the mountains and the continents on the ground of ordinary existence [at the beginning of the eon].

What does this meditation signify regarding the completion stage? The source of phenomena standing on a fine point signifies that during the beginner stage the good qualities are minute, while the wide side pointing upward signifies that when you are [ascending through the stages of the path], to "engaging through belief"[127] and upward, the good qualities increase progressively. The white color of the source of phenomena signifies natural purity;[128] its three corners signify the three doors of liberation and the three wisdoms that realize them; its shape is that of the *bhaga*[129] and therefore signifies great bliss. The meditation on the mandala with its celestial mansion and the specially visualized deities contained within the source of phenomena signifies that all the good qualities of the fruitional time will arise on the basis of the meditation on the path of indivisible bliss and emptiness. The meditation on the source of phenomena as a triangle is taught in the *Later Tantra:* [13a] [The *bodhisattvas* ask:] "How should we meditate on the 'source of phenomena'?"[130] [The *tathāgatas*] explain: "Meditate on a triangle, because of the division into body, speech, and mind."[131]

The meditation on the four mandalas of the physical elements—wind, [fire, water, and earth]—signifies respectively the winds of the yogi during the completion stage:[132] the yellowish green wind-wind, the "uniform wind";[133] (2) the red fire-wind, the "ascending wind";[134] the white water-wind, the "life-sustaining wind";[135] and the yellow earth-wind, the "descending wind."[136] The meditation on the four mandalas in the nature of the four goddesses, Locanā, [Māmakī, Pāṇḍarā, and Tārā][137] signifies the four consorts, Padminī, [Śaṅkhinī, Hastinī, and Cetriṇī],[138] which are the external contributing causes [for the arising of great bliss and clear light during the completion stage].[139]

The meditation on the crossed *vajra* formed from the four mandalas that have merged signifies the actual clear light of the fourth step [of the completion stage] that arises from the union with the four consorts—the external contributing causes—and the *vajra* repetition based on the four winds—the internal contributing causes. The five prongs of the *vajra* signify the five wisdoms of clear light. The meditation on the mandala with its celestial mansion and deities upon the nave of the crossed *vajra* signifies the arising of the mandala with its celestial mansion and deities during the [fifth] step of union that arises from the actual clear light.

Explaining How to Meditate on the Yoga of the Three Bodies in Correspondence with the Stages of the Evolution and Destruction during the Beings' Ordinary Existence in the World

There are three sections here: (1) explaining how to meditate on the wheel of the specially visualized deities—the base for actualizing the three bodies; (2) explaining how to meditate on the yoga of the three bodies; and (3) explaining how the innate great bliss arises—the method for the swift attainment of that [the three bodies through the practice with the consort].

Explaining How to Meditate on the Wheel of the Specially Visualized Deities—The Base for Actualizing the Three Bodies

There are two sections here: (1) explaining the corresponding object; and (2) explaining the meditation that is applied in correspondence with it. [13b]

EXPLAINING THE CORRESPONDING OBJECT—HOW THE BEINGS DWELLING IN THE WORLD EVOLVED

At that time a god in the second *dhyāna*,[140] whose lifespan, merit, and karma have been exhausted, passes away and is reborn in the first *dhyāna*. Then the six classes of the gods of the Desire Realm[141] beginning with the Masters over Others' Emanations up to the Four Groups of Great Kings[142] evolve successively from the higher to the lower level. Then the beings beginning from Kuru, the Northern Continent,[143] until the eight hot hells successively evolve.[144] The following three events occur simultaneously: one sentient being is born in the Hell of Ceaseless Torment;[145] the eon of evolution is completed; and the period of the world's abiding begins. The destruction of the world takes twenty eons, the empty period lasts twenty eons, its evolution takes twenty eons, and its abiding twenty. These eighty medium eons together are called one great eon.[146]

Alone among all beings, those who reside in Jambudvīpa during the first eon are endowed with the following seven characteristics: (1) they are adorned with features similar to the major and minor marks of a buddha, (2) their lifespan may be infinite, (3) their faculties are complete, (4) they can travel in the sky by means of miraculous powers, (5) being free of dependence on physical food, they subsist solely on delight, (6) there being no distinction between day and night [no sun and moon], their bodies can illuminate with a light of their own, and (7) their birth is miraculous.[147]

At that time, the surface of the great earth is covered with an earth nectar; its taste is like unrefined honey and its color is like that of fresh butter. [14a] When an imprinted craving for physical food is awakened in one of the beings, they[148] dip a fingertip in it and taste it. Upon seeing this, the others do the same. As a result of eating physical food, their bodies become coarse and heavy. No longer are they able to travel through space with their miraculous powers; the lights in their bodies vanish, and darkness prevails. Then they assemble and lament [the disappearance of the lights], and consequently the sun and moon appear through the karmic power of sentient beings. At that point, days, months, years, and seasons come into being.

Then, while those who eat little of the earth nectar are beautiful, those who eat more of it develop ugly complexions. Therefore, the former say to the latter: "I am beautiful, and you are ugly." Due to their nonvirtuous spite, the earth nectar disappears. Again, they assemble and lament [the disappearance of the earth nectar].

Once again, through the power of karma, the surface of the great earth is swathed with [a splendid] earth-cream, its taste similar to unrefined honey as before, and its color yellow like the *dong kha* flower. When they eat it, the events are repeated as before until once again they begin to despise each other, and due to their nonvirtuous actions, the earth-cream disappears, and they assemble and lament as before.

Yet again, through the power of karma, the surface of the great earth is swathed in a splendid thicket of sprouts, which taste like unrefined honey and are orange like the *ka dam pu ka* flower. Again, they eat it, and events repeat as before.

Afterward, through the karmic power of the beings in the world, although no field has been plowed or planted anywhere, *salu*[149] rice appears on the surface of the great earth, devoid of husks and chaff and with roots four fingers long. The rice they reap in the morning grows back that same morning, and the rice they reap in the evening grows back that same evening, with no sign that it was ever reaped. [14b] Since this food is much coarser, when they eat the rice, its crude wastes turn into feces and urine, and the organs for their evacuation protrude differently for males and females.

Then, in some beings, previous imprints for sexual intercourse are awakened, and they engage in sexual activity. Seeing this, others cast dirt at them and so forth, so to conceal themselves they build houses and so forth, and this is the origin of houses.

During that period, at dawn the beings gather the *salu* rice for their morning meal and at dusk for their evening meal. But some lazy beings gather rice for the morning and evening meals at the same time. Seeing this, others gather food for a week or more at a time. As a result, the harvested rice does not grow back; therefore, it becomes necessary to sow seeds. Then, since in that land where the *salu* rice grows there are no treaties, the powerful snatch from the weak and others steal quietly. Consequently, one kills the other and so forth. This is the origin of the ten nonvirtuous ways of action. At that time the *salu* rice develops husks and chaff.

Then the elders consult and appoint as their leader a good-natured and wise person. They offer to him one-sixth of the harvest, and he administrates according to the proper law. His lineage is called the King Esteemed by Many,[150] and the Śākyas are also descended from him.[151]

EXPLAINING THE MEDITATION THAT IS APPLIED IN CORRESPONDENCE WITH IT

[There are three sections here: (1) generating the specially visualized deities, (2) the deeds of the specially visualized deities, and (3) drawing of the specially visualized deities into the body.]

Generating the Specially Visualized Deities

> Instantly, by mere special aspiration/visualization, the thirty-two deities simultaneously appear entirely perfected upon these seats.
>
> [These thirty-two deities of the Guhyasamāja mandala generated by mere special aspiration/visualization are therefore called the specially visualized deities. They appear on the seats of the celestial mansion visualized in the previous step. At the center of this mandala is the yogi visualized as Vajradhara:]
>
> On the central seat, myself blue Vajradhara with three faces blue, white, and red, and six arms . . .
>
> [He is embraced by his consort Vajra Lady of Tangibles,[152] and both are surrounded by the four remaining *tathāgatas*, the four mothers, the four *vajra* ladies, the eight *bodhisattvas*, and the ten fierce deities; the latter are] standing in the manner of annihilating the pernicious ones.[153]

The meditation on the specially visualized deities—from "Instantly [by mere] special/visualization" and so forth until [the fierce deities] "standing in the manner of annihilating [the pernicious ones]" [15a]—is taught in the *Concise Sādhana*,[154] and the object to which this meditation corresponds, the evolution of the beings in the world, is explained in *Formulating the Guhyasamāja Sādhana*.[155]

The Deeds of the Specially Visualized Deities

> Light rays emanate from the *hūṃ* on my heart and draw all sentient beings near me. They enter the mandala from the four directions without hindrance in the entry-mode of Vajrasattva. As I, the principal deity, and my consort are absorbed in union, light-rays of our *bodhicitta*s initiate them, causing them to attain the bliss and mental rapture of all *tathāgata*s and become Vajrasattvas. Then, they proceed to their own buddha-fields.[156]

The meditation on the deeds of the specially visualized deities begins with: "[Light rays emanating] from the *hūṃ* on my heart" and continues until "proceed to their own buddha-field."

Drawing the Specially Visualized Deities into the Body

> Hook-like light rays, emanating from the blue *hūṃ* in my heart, draw the [thirty] deities starting from Vairocana to Sumbharāja [from the mandala to me] and place them at points of my body, beginning with my head. They become inseparable in nature from [the respective constituents of my body] beginning with the form aggregate. Vairocana in my head . . . and Sumbharāja in the soles of my feet.[157]

The meditation on drawing the specially visualized deities into the body begins from: "[Hook-like light rays emanate from the blue *hūṃ* in my heart"] and continues until "and Sumbharāja[158] in the soles of my feet."

[Explaining the Meditation on the Specially Visualized Deities]

How [does the generation of the specially visualized deities] correspond [to the evolution of the first people in Jambudvīpa]? The instantaneous generation of the specially visualized deities corresponds to the people of the first eon in Jambudvīpa who were miraculously born. The meditation on the deities appearing as males and females corresponds to the people of the first eon who gradually took the form of men and women.

How to meditate [on the specially visualized deities]? Generate the specially visualized deities instantaneously without [meditating on] their seed syllables, emblems, and so forth, and then meditate by developing the clarity of the visualization step by step. Imagine all the deities as parts of the principal deity and behold all the deities—the principal and surrounding deities—as indivisible bliss and emptiness. By meditating in this way, you will be able to abide in the actual mandala with its celestial mansion and deities during the completion stage and the fruit.

The meditation on the deeds of the specially visualized deities and the meditation on their drawing into the body take the fruit on the path, according to the exemplary life of the Teacher in the "past event,"[159] but they have no correspondence to the ground of purification.

How is the mandala entered? [15b] There are four modes of entering into a mandala: disciples enter the mandala through the eastern gate; entering through the power of the *vajra* is by way of visualizing that the mandala is raised and you slide in from below; the entry of the *jñānasattva* into the *samayasattva* is entering directly from above; Vajrasattva enters through the four direction of the mandala without hindrance. In the present case, sentient beings enter through the latter mode of entry.

Explaining How to Meditate on the Yoga of the Three Bodies

There are three sections here: (1) explaining how the specially visualized deities dissolve into clear light—the cause for purifying death and attaining the *dharmakāya;* (2) explaining how to generate the First Lord through the five manifest awakenings—the principal method for purifying the intermediate being and attaining the *saṃbhogakāya;* and (3) explaining how the First Lord transforms into Vajrasattva's *nirmāṇakāya*—the principal method for purifying birth and attaining the *nirmāṇakāya.*

EXPLAINING HOW THE SPECIALLY VISUALIZED DEITIES DISSOLVE INTO CLEAR LIGHT—THE CAUSE FOR PURIFYING DEATH AND ATTAINING THE *DHARMAKĀYA*

There are two sections here: (1) explaining the corresponding object, and (2) explaining the meditation that is applied in correspondence with it.

Explaining the Corresponding Object—The Stages of Death

When the people of the first eon in Jambudvīpa—who gradually become ordinary and come to be endowed with the six constituents[160]—die:[161]

(1) The form aggregate, the mirror-like wisdom at the ground time,[162] the earth element, the eye faculty, and the forms within their continuums dissolve simultaneously. Two types of signs, external and internal, accompany these dissolutions. As for the external signs: The signs of the dissolution of the form aggregate are that the limbs of the body become thinner, the body becomes

attenuated, loses its strength, and its capacity deteriorates. When the mirror-like wisdom at the ground time dissolves, sight becomes blurred and cloudy. The signs of the dissolution of the earth element are that the body becomes thin and loose. The signs of the dissolution of the eye faculty are that the dying persons are no longer able to open and close their eyes. [16a] The signs of the dissolution of the forms within their continuums are that the body's coloring fades. As an inner sign of those dissolutions, a mirage-like experience arises.

(2) Following this, the aggregate of feeling, the wisdom of equanimity at the ground time,[163] the water element, the ear faculty, and the sound within their continuums likewise dissolve simultaneously into clear light.[164] These dissolutions as well are accompanied by both external and internal signs. As for the external signs: As a sign of the dissolution of the aggregate of feeling during ordinary death, the feelings of happiness and sorrow that are the principal among the sensory consciousnesses become indistinct. As a sign of the dissolution of the wisdom of equanimity at the ground time, the feelings of happiness and sorrow that are among the mental consciousnesses become indistinct. As a sign of the dissolution of the water element, the saliva and blood dry up. As a sign of the dissolution of the ear faculty, the outer and inner sounds are no longer heard. As a sign of the dissolution of the sound within their continuums, the humming sound inside the ear no longer arises. As an inner sign of these dissolutions, a smoke-like experience arises.

(3) Then the aggregate of perception, the wisdom of discernment at the ground time,[165] the fire element, the nose faculty, and the scent within their continuums dissolve simultaneously. Here also two types of signs appear.[166] As for the external signs: As a sign of the dissolution of the aggregate of perception, the dying person can no longer recognize their relatives and so on. As a sign of the dissolution of the wisdom of discernment, the dying person no longer remembers the names of their relatives and so forth. As a sign of the dissolution of the fire element, the ability to digest food and drink diminishes. [16b] As a sign of the dissolution of the nose faculty, the dying persons' exhalations are forceful and elongated, while they are unable to inhale, and their breathing becomes feeble. As a sign of the dissolution of scent within their continuums the dying persons are no longer able to sense any of the three types of smell. The inner sign of these dissolutions is the arising of an appearance resembling fireflies.

(4) Next the aggregate of conditioning, the wisdom of purposive acts at the ground time,[167] the air-wind element, the tongue faculty, the taste within their continuums, and tangible objects simultaneously dissolve.[168] Here again

external and internal signs appear. As for the external signs: As a sign of the dissolution of the aggregate of conditioning, the body is no longer able to perform its activities or move. As a sign of the dissolution of the wisdom of purposive acts at the ground time, the dying person is no longer mindful of external activities and purposes. As a sign of the dissolution of the air-wind element, the ten winds[169] shift from their respective places into the heart. As a sign of the dissolution of the tongue faculty, the tongue becomes short and swollen and its root turns blue. The sign of the dissolution of the taste within their continuums is that the tongue no longer experiences any of the six tastes.[170] As a sign of the dissolution of feeling of touch, the dying person no longer senses any of the bodily feelings of touch. The inner sign of these dissolutions is the arising of an appearance like a blazing butter lamp.

(5) When the air-wind has dissolved into "[white] appearance,"[171] during [white] appearance itself, a radiant white appearance arises, like a clear autumn sky suffused by moonlight. Then, once [white] appearance has dissolved into "enhanced appearance,"[172] during enhanced appearance itself, a radiant red appearance arises, like a clear autumn sky suffused with sunlight. Once enhanced appearance dissolves into "approaching attainment,"[173] during approaching attainment itself, a radiant black appearance arises, like the clear autumn sky suffused with the dense darkness of the beginning of night. [17a] When approaching attainment has dissolved into clear light, during "clear light" itself, there arises an appearance resembling the sky's own color—a clear autumn sky devoid of the three tainting conditions. This is the experience of the clear light of death.

Explaining the Meditation That Is Applied in Correspondence with It

Then, visualize the deities of the body mandala: Vairocana, Locanā, Kṣitigarbha, Rūpavajrā, Maitreya, Yamāntaka, and Acala one after the other dissolving into clear light.[174] This meditation corresponds to the dissolution into clear light during ordinary death of the form aggregate, the mirror-like wisdom, the earth element, the eye faculty, and the forms within their continuums. You should know how to apply this in the three parallel cases below.

[These are the three parallel meditations that correspond to the second, third and fourth dissolutions:[175]

Then visualize the deities Ratnasaṃbhava, Māmakī, Vajrapāṇi, Śabdhavajrā, Prajñāntaka/Aparājita, and Ṭakkirāja dissolving one after the other into clear light.[176] This meditation corresponds to the dissolution into clear light during ordinary death of the aggregate of feeling, the wisdom of equanimity, the water element, the ear faculty, and the sound within their continuums.

Then visualize the deities Amitābha, Pāṇḍarā, Khagarbha, Gandhavajrā, Hayagrīva, and Nīladaṇḍa dissolving one after the other into clear light.[177] This meditation corresponds to the dissolution into clear light during ordinary death of the aggregate of perception, the wisdom of discernment, the fire element, the nose faculty, and the scents within their continuums.

Then visualize the deities Amoghasiddhi, Tārā, Lokeśvara, Rasavajrā, Sarvanīvaraṇavikṣambhin, Sparśavajrā, Samantabhadra, Vighnāntaka, and Mahābala dissolving one after the other into clear light.[178] This meditation corresponds to the dissolution into clear light during ordinary death of the aggregate of conditioning, the wisdom of purposive acts, the air-wind element, the tongue faculty, the taste within their continuums and tangible objects.]

Then [during the fifth dissolution] visualize the deities Uṣṇīṣacakravartin, Sumbharāja, and Mañjuśrī dissolving one after the other into clear light,[179] in correspondence with the dissolution of the air-wind into [white] appearance, [white] appearance into enhanced appearance, and enhanced appearance into approaching attainment. Then meditate on the principal deity dissolving as well into clear light, in correspondence with the dissolution of approaching attainment into clear light resulting in the experience of the clear light of death.

As the *Vajra Garland Explanatory Tantra* teaches:

(1) Included[180] in the form aggregate are the mirror-like wisdom, the earth element, the eye faculty, and form as the fifth aspect together with the two fierce deities;[181]

(2) the aggregate of feeling, the wisdom of equanimity, the water element, the ear faculty, and sound as the fifth aspect together with the two fierce deities; [17b]

(3) the aggregate of perceptions, the wisdom of discernment, the element of fire, the nose faculty, and scent as the fifth aspect, together with the two fierce deities;

(4) the aggregate of conditioning, the wisdom of purposive acts, the air-wind element, the tongue faculty, and taste as the fifth aspect, together with the two fierce deities;

(5) the intrinsic natures and appearances[182] together with[183] the fierce deities above and below enter the aggregate of consciousness, and consciousness too enters into clear light. This is explained as "accompanied by *nirvāṇa*," all-empty and *dharmakāya*. In order to stabilize your

> meditation, you should recite the mantra *oṃ śūnyatā jñāna vajra svabhāva ātmako 'haṃ.*[184]

Meditate on the constituents of your body on the respective places of your body—beginning with the form aggregate on the crown—as indivisible in nature with the respective deities of the mandala beginning with Vairocana. Then visualize the respective places of your body dissolving into clear light of indivisible bliss and emptiness; and then visualize the principal deity, too, dissolving into clear light and meditate on the union of bliss and emptiness that arises from these dissolutions. Recite the mantra *śūnyatā* and cultivate the divine identity [of the *dharmakāya*] with the resolve: "The nature of wisdom, which is the indivisible objective emptiness and subjective wisdom, that am I."

When yogis of the creation stage meditate in this way, they "take their deaths on the path that leads to the *dharmakāya*." This step is also referred to as "taking death on the path that leads to the *dharmakāya*," "manifest awakening from suchness," "the essential point of merging the specially visualized deities into clear light," and the "ultimate truth mandala."

How does the *dharmakāya* of the meditators on the creation stage purify their death? [18a] In place of the ordinary death that would occur naturally to ordinary people, for the yogis the *dharmakāya* will arise as the specially visualized deities dissolve into clear light. In this way the *dharmakāya* of the meditators on the creation stage purifies their death.

What does this meditation ripen in the mental continuum of the meditator on the completion stage? It ripens the mental continuum through the arising of [clear light during the five steps of the completion stage]: (1) the metaphoric clear light during body isolation and speech isolation, (2) the mind isolation that is a genuine purifier of death, (3) the metaphorical clear light during the illusory body, (4) [the actual clear light during] the fourth step, and (5) the actual clear light during the fifth step [the step of union]. This brings about the attainment of the *dharmakāya* of a buddha, the fruit of the purification.

EXPLAINING HOW TO GENERATE THE FIRST LORD THROUGH THE FIVE MANIFEST AWAKENINGS—THE PRINCIPAL METHOD FOR PURIFYING THE INTERMEDIATE BEING AND ATTAINING THE *SAṂBHOGAKĀYA*

There are two sections here: (1) explaining the corresponding object—how the intermediate being evolves; and (2) explaining the meditation that is applied in correspondence with it.

Explaining the Corresponding Object—How the Intermediate Being Evolves

How does the intermediate being evolve? The intermediate being who will be born as a human in Jambudvīpa has a body of wind that is conditional upon a substantial cause and a cooperative condition. The substantial cause is the wind endowed with light rays in the five colors [that serves as the mount of] the clear light of death, and the cooperative condition is the mind [of the clear light of death]. The intermediate being is actually formed by way of its separation from the old body, [and as it evolves], the signs from approaching attainment up to mirage-like arise in stages. The nature of the intermediate being is a subtle body that has left behind its coarse body endowed with physical elements.

All its faculties are complete, it moves without hindrance through mountains and so forth, and even a buddha cannot block its karmic miracles.[185] [18b] Its equivalent names are "mind-engendered," "birth-seeker," "intermediate being," "scent-eater," and "verging-on-existence."[186] The body size of the intermediate being destined to be born in the human realm is "as a five- or six-year-old child."[187] Its life span is seven days, yet if it cannot find the conditions for rebirth by the seventh day, it dies a "small death." [It can die a small death in this way] for up to seven weeks and then certainly it will find conditions for rebirth.[188]

[Characteristics of Intermediate Beings According to Their Destination]

As for distinctions in their appearance, an intermediate being destined for the lower realms resembles the night suffused with darkness or a black mat unfurled, and an intermediate being destined for the fortunate realms resembles the night suffused with moonlight or a white woolen cloth unfurled.[189] This is taught in the *Primary Ground.*[190] Further, the color of an intermediate being destined for hell resembles a log burnt by fire, that of an intermediate being destined for the animals resembles water, that of an intermediate being destined for the hungry ghosts resembles smoke.[191] Intermediate beings destined to be gods of the Desire Realm are gold-like in color, and intermediate beings who will be born in the Realm of Subtle Materiality are white. This is taught in the *Longer Sūtra on Entering the Womb.*[192] There are no intermediate beings destined for birth in the Immaterial Realm.[193]

What do the intermediate beings see? They see intermediate beings of their own type and their future places of birth.[194] How do they move? Intermediate beings destined for the lower realms proceed upside down, those who will be born as humans move straight ahead, and those who will be born as gods proceed upward.[195] Can they change their destiny? The *Abhidharmakośa* teaches that an intermediate being destined for a certain realm cannot avoid this and proceed to another realm,[196] while Asaṅga's *Compendium of Abhidharma* explains that [its future birth can still] change."[197]

Explaining the Meditation That Is Applied in Correspondence with It

Generation of the First Lord

1. Arising of the Solar Disk and So Forth [from Emptiness-Clear-Light]
Upon the central seat [in the celestial mansion of the mandala] appears a *hūṃ* that becomes a solar disk. At the center of the solar disk appears an *oṃ* that becomes a lunar disk. Upon the lunar disk appears an *āḥ* that becomes a red eight-petaled lotus with the three syllables *oṃ āḥ hūṃ* stacked up one upon the other at its navel.

2. Focusing on the Moon
All these mingle and become a single moon orb, completely perfect in all its aspects.

3. Abiding in Absorption in Wisdom Alone
Light rays emanating from the moon orb draw the entire animate and inanimate realms and dissolve them into the moon orb. *Oṃ dharma dhātu svabhāva ātmako 'haṃ.* The root of all the phenomena, animate and inanimate, mere-wind-and-mind, appearing as a moon, that am I.

4. Manifest Awakening from the Seed Syllable
Upon the moon a white *oṃ*, a red *āḥ*, and a blue *hūṃ* appear from the moon, in the way that bubbles pop up from water [on its surface].

5. Manifest Awakening from the Emblem
Light rays emanating from these syllables invite the five *tathāgata* families together with their numerous circles of deities from the ten directions. They dissolve into the [three syllables], which then become a white five-pronged *vajra,* marked at the center with *oṃ āḥ hūṃ. Vajra ātmako 'haṃ.* The essence of the *vajra,* that am I.

6. Manifest Awakening from the Complete Body
The *vajra* with the three syllables transforms into myself, white First Lord, with three faces, white, black, and red, and six arms, the rights holding a *vajra,* wheel, and lotus, and the lefts a bell, jewel, and sword. I, the First Lord, am adorned with precious ornaments and wear multicolored silk robes.[198]

[The lines:] "Upon the central seat," and so forth, up until [the yogi appearing as] the First Lord, are taught in the *Concise Sādhana.*[199] The way the corresponding object—the intermediate being—evolves is taught in *Formulating the Guhyasamāja Sādhana.*[200] [19a]

Here are the correspondences to the evolution of the intermediate being on the ground: The meditations on the solar disk, the lunar disk, and the lotus upon the central seat correspond to the experiences—arising from the clear light of death—of approaching attainment,[201] enhanced appearance,[202] and [white] appearance.[203] The meditations on the three syllables[204] that are the cause of the solar disk, the lunar disk, and the lotus correspond to the three winds[205] that are the cause for the approaching attainment, enhanced appearance, and [white] appearance. The meditation on the three syllables upon the lotus, stacked up[206] corresponds to the three winds[207] serving as the mounts of approaching attainment, enhanced appearance, and [white] appearance.

The meditation on all of these mingling into a single moon orb corresponds to the wind-and-mind of the intermediate being abiding as a single entity. The meditation on the three syllables stacked upon the moon corresponds to the speech of the intermediate being. The white, five-pronged *vajra*[208] corresponds to the mind of the intermediate being. The meditation on the First Lord corresponds to the body of the intermediate being. The meditation on the light rays[209] emanating from the seed syllables corresponds to the deeds of the intermediate being.

How are these meditations applied to the fruit? The meditation on the moon orb of the manifest awakening from the moon corresponds to the wind serving as the mount of the clear light at the fruit. The meditation prior to that on the solar disk, lunar disk, and lotus together with the seed syllables corresponds to the approaching attainment, enhanced appearance, and [white] appearance serving as the cause for the actual clear light together with the winds on which they ride and to the three winds that are the cause for them. The manifest awakenings from the seed syllable and [19b] from the complete body and the light rays that emanate and dissolve, correspond respectively to the actual clear light arising in the aspects of the speech, mind, body, and deeds of a buddha. The five prongs of the *vajra* signify the [mind with its] five wisdoms of the actual clear light. The meditation on the three seed syllables at the navel of the *vajra* signifies the indivisibility of the three *vajras* of the body, speech, and mind.

How to meditate [on the *saṃbhogakāya* of the creation stage]? Regard your visualization of the First Lord—beginning with the solar disk and up to its completion—as a manifestation of indivisible bliss and emptiness; cultivate the divine identification of the First Lord and its clear appearance. The divine identification is maintained with the resolve: "The pure wind-and-mind arising as the extremely subtle wisdom body, that am I." Meditating in this way is "taking the intermediate state on the path to the *saṃbhogakāya*"; also referred to as "manifest awakening from the complete body," "the First Lord," and "the *saṃbhogakāya* of the meditator on the creation stage."

How does the *saṃbhogakāya* of the meditator on the creation stage purify the intermediate being? In place of the intermediate being that occurs naturally for an ordinary person, for the yogi meditating on the creation stage, the First Lord will arise through the five manifest awakenings.

How does the meditation on the First Lord ripen the mental continuum of the meditator on the completion stage?[210] This meditation ripens the mental continuum to the similitude illusory bodies during the three isolations,[211] to the [impure] illusory body of the third step, which is a genuine purifier of intermediate state, to the [pure] illusory body during the fifth step, and finally brings about the attainment of the *saṃbhogakāya* of a buddha at the fruit of the purification. [20a]

EXPLAINING HOW THE FIRST LORD TRANSFORMS INTO VAJRASATTVA'S *NIRMĀṆAKĀYA*—THE PRINCIPAL METHOD FOR PURIFYING BIRTH AND ATTAINING THE *NIRMĀṆAKĀYA*

There are two sections here: (1) explaining the corresponding object—taking birth in the womb; and (2) explaining the meditation that is applied in correspondence with it.

Explaining the Corresponding Object—Taking Birth in the Womb

[Conditions for Pregnancy]

(1) The mother is healthy and still fertile, (2) the scent-eater [intermediate being] hovers nearby, and (3) the male and female desire each other and join together.[212]

The three flaws that should be absent for a woman to conceive: The three flaws in the mother's womb: (a) obstructions of wind, bile, and phlegm, or (b) an ant-waisted-like womb, or (c) a barley-grain-like womb. Flaws in the seeds [pregnancy fluids]: when the semen [and blood] of the father and mother do not descend at the same time, but one after the other; or else, when they do descend simultaneously but in a decayed state. Flaws of karma: the scent-eater has not accumulated karma that would result in the male and female becoming its parents, or the parents have not accumulated karma that could result in the scent-eater becoming their child. These are taught in the *Sūtra on Entering the Womb.*[213]

How Does the Intermediate Being Take Birth in the Womb?

The *vajra* mind, the consciousness of the intermediate being—which is a passionate mind riding on a horse[214] [of wind]—arrives posthaste and enters through the father's crown of the head and joins with the drop that descends through the 72,000 channels [of the parents]. If it is to be born as a male, it is attracted to the mother and hates the father, and if it is to be reborn as a female, it feels desire for the father and hatred toward the mother. Thus, [the intermediate being] creates conditions for its death, and its consciousness enters in the midst of the commingled semen and blood in the mother's womb.

It is then reborn while experiencing approaching attainment. From the mind of approaching attainment arises enhanced appearance, and from enhanced appearance, [white] appearance arises. [20b] From the wind [on which] [white] appearance [is mounted] arises the wind-wind that becomes coarser than the wind of [white] appearance capable of supporting consciousness. From that arises a fire-wind that becomes coarser than the wind of wind capable of supporting consciousness. From that arises a water-wind that becomes coarser than the wind of fire capable of supporting consciousness. From that arises an earth-wind that becomes coarser than the wind of water capable of supporting consciousness. The signs that accompany the arising of these winds are respectively appearances resembling a butter lamp, fireflies, smoke, and mirage.

[Development in the Womb]

After the intermediate being enters the womb, the white constituent develops gradually, through the five phases: "the liquid-cream-like," "the viscous," "the globular," "the solidified," and "with the limbs slightly protruding."[215] The first is like cream outside and highly liquified inside; the second is thick like yogurt both inside and outside; the third is fleshy, but cannot withstand pressure; the fourth is [fleshy and] can withstand pressure; while the fifth bulges with the protrusions of the five limbs. *Formulating the Guhyasamāja Sādhana*[216] applies these five phases to the five *tathāgatas*, beginning with Akṣobhya and concluding with Vairocana, respectively.

The phases of development of the red constituent are also five: "the fluid," "the red," "the glob," "the solidified," and "the commingled." The *Saṃvarodaya Tantra*[217] applies these as well to the five *tathāgatas*. The first to Akṣobhya, the second to Amitābha, the third to Ratnasaṃbhava, the fourth to Amoghasiddhi, and the fifth to Vairocana. [21a]

Then as the white and red constituents develop, the five aggregates, five physical elements, six sense faculties, six sense objects, and the limbs of the being in the womb evolve gradually. Subsequently the *body* of the being in the womb is completed, and breath—which circulates through the mouth and the eight bases of *speech*, including the tongue and the palate[218]—as well as the awareness of *mental* consciousness that engages with objects, is completed. Likewise, the coarse and temporal as well as the subtle and innate aspects of the body evolve gradually.

How does the fetus abide in the womb? If it is to be born as a male, it will dwell in the right side of the womb facing the back of the mother; and if it is to be born as a female, she will stay at left side facing forward.

It remains in the womb for nine whole months and the beginning of the tenth, and in terms of weeks thirty-eight weeks. In the thirty-sixth week the fetus has the notion that the womb is filthy and malodorous. In the thirty-seventh, it no longer wishes to remain in the womb and wants to leave it. By the thirty-eighth week, a wind born of prior karma, called "limbs,"[219] propels it toward the door of the source of phenomena. Then a wind called "facing downward"[220] turns the fetus around, pushes it into the door of the source of phenomena, and it emerges outside. Then the stages of childhood, youth, adulthood, middle age, and old age take place.

Explaining the Meditation That Is Applied in Correspondence with It

Transforming the First Lord into Vajrasattva's *Nirmāṇakāya*

> The Father-Mother *Tathāgatas* from their natural abode are absorbed in union for the sake of guiding sentient beings. Akṣobhya[s] formed from their *bodhicittas* pervade the space realm in its entirety and bless all sentient beings, who then attain pure bliss and mental rapture. Then all the Akṣobhyas merge inside the celestial mansion of the mandala, and I [the First Lord] enter [that], and become a blue Vajrasattva's *nirmāṇakāya* with three faces (blue, white, and red), six arms (the rights holding a *vajra*, wheel, and lotus; and the lefts a bell, jewel, and sword), I as Vajrasattva's *nirmāṇakāya* am adorned with precious ornaments and multicolored silk robes.[221]

[The lines:] "The Father-Mother *Tathāgatas* from their natural abode," and so forth up until "sealing with the Lord of the *tathāgata* family"[222] are taught in the *Concise Sādhana*,[223] while *Formulating the Guhyasamāja Sādhana*[224] teaches the corresponding object. [21b]

How does the meditation correspond to rebirth? The lines of the *Sādhana*: "The Father-Mother *Tathāgatas* from their natural abode are absorbed in union"[225] correspond to the father and mother who are absorbed in union at the ground [conception during ordinary existence]. [The lines:] "All the

Akṣobhyas," up until "the triple *sattvas*,"[226] are applied respectively to the intermediate being entering in the midst of the white and red constituents in the mother's womb, its rebirth up until the development of its subtle innate body. Meditating on the deity endowed with three faces and sealed with the lord of the *tathāgata* family corresponds to the newly born emerging from the womb.

Explaining how to Meditate on the Body as the Celestial Mansion

> The front, back, right, and left sides of my body become the four sides of the mandala. The four orifices—mouth, nose, and the urinary and excretion pathways become the four doors. . . . In this way all the parts of my body become individual parts of the celestial mansion.[227]

How to meditate on the body as the celestial mansion, the deities' residence? Bring together the respective parts of the celestial mansion of the outer mandala, such as the four corners and so on, and the parts of your body, such as the front and back [right and left]. Taking the former as the substantial cause and the latter as the cooperative conditions, meditate on the arising of [the celestial mansion of the body mandala] that is homogenous[228] with the outer mandala. By meditating in this way, the celestial mansion of the third step of the completion stage and the actual celestial mansion of the fruition time will be attained.

Explaining how to Meditate on the Deities of the Body Mandala

> The area from the crown of my head to my hairline, the essence of the form aggregate, white *oṃ*, transforms into white Vairocana. . . . At each of my soles appears a *hūṃ* syllable, the essence of my soles. These transform into blue Sumbharāja.[229]

The yogis should meditate by making the respective parts of their bodies at their different locations—beginning with the form aggregates at the crowns of their heads—into indivisible essence with the respective seed syllable from among the thirty-two seed syllables—beginning with the syllable *oṃ*. Then they should cultivate the clear appearance of the thirty-two deities of the mandala, Vairocana and so forth, maintain their divine identity, and regard all these appearances as a manifestation of indivisible bliss and emptiness. [22a] By meditating in this way they will actually attain the thirty-two deities residing in the mandala during the third step [of the completion stage] and during the fruition time.

What are the purposes of these meditations individually? By meditating on the four Mothers and five *tathāgatas*, the yogis will actually attain these individual deities during the completion stage and the fruit. By meditating on the [the essence of the five sense faculties transforming into] the five *bodhisattvas*, Kṣitigarbha and so forth, they will attain the five kinds of clairvoyance. By meditating on the body faculty as Sarvāvaraṇavikṣambhin,[230] they will attain the *vajra* body, and by meditating on the limbs of the body as the fierce deities, no obstruction will arise for the yogis. By meditating on all these deities jointly, they will ripen their mental continuum through the great bliss that arises from absorbing in union with the consort during the completion stage and the fruit.

Blessing the Body, Speech, and Mind

Blessing the Body

From the *oṃ* on the crown of my head appears a perfectly rounded lunar disk; at its center there is a white *oṃ* emanating light rays of five colors and radiating a multitude of Locanās filling the space. Instantly the Locanās invite a multitude of deities of Vairocanas, Body *Vajras*, who [also] fill the space, with the principal Vairocana and Locanā at their center abiding in union. I sit before them.[231]

> May the holder of a buddha body, endowed with glory, on whom I meditate as indivisible from the three *vajras*, bless me now with *vajra* body.
> May the buddhas who reside in the ten directions, on whom I meditate as indivisible with the three *vajras*, bless me today with *vajra* body.

Having made this request to Vairocana and the deities who surround him, the two assemblies of deities, the Locanās who were emanated and the Vairocanas who were invited, develop desire toward one another, absorb in union, and experience the bliss of supreme ecstasy. They enter into me in the nature of white light rays through the gate of Vairocana, in the manner of *jñānasattvas*. I attain the ground of wisdom; my entire body is filled, and I am satisfied, and thereby I attain the mastery of body.

> Like the body of all buddhas complete with the five aggregates, may my body too be endowed with the nature of a buddha body.

Oṃ sarva tathāgata kāya vajra svabhāva ātmako 'haṃ.
The indivisible nature of the body of all *tathāgatas*, that am I.

Blessing the Body, Speech, and Mind Together

I am great Vajradhara, the indivisible triple *vajra* body, *vajra* speech, and *vajra* mind of all *tathāgatas*.

> *Oṃ sarva-tathāgata-kāya-vāk-citta-vajra-svabhāva-ātmako-'haṃ.*
> The indivisible nature of the body, speech, and mind of all *tathāgatas*, that am I.[232]

How are the body, speech, and mind blessed? The *objects* being blessed are the body, speech, and mind of the yogi. The *method* of blessing is by emanating the three emblems—the goddesses [Locanā, Pāṇḍarā, and Māmakī], from the three seed syllables [*oṃ āḥ hūṃ*] and inviting the multitude of deities of the three *vajras* [Vairocana, Amitābha, and Akṣobhya].

On account of the request made by the yogi with the verse "[May the holder of] a buddha [body,] endowed with glory," and so forth,[233] the assemblies of the deities of the three *vajras*[234] absorb in union; hence, the *nature* of the blessing is great bliss. The *aspect[s]* in which [the deities] enter into the yogi's crown, tongue, and heart successively are the white, red, and dark-blue light rays. [When the lights enter, the yogi] attains wisdom-great-bliss. After visualizing this, while reciting the three mantras successively,[235] the yogi cultivates divine identification with the resolve: "The *vajra* body, speech, and mind of all *tathāgatas*, that am I." Finally, the yogi cultivates divine identification with the resolve: "The nondual three *vajras*, that am I." [22b] By means of [these meditations] the yogi will attain the separate three *vajras* and the indivisible three *vajras* during the completion stages and during the fruition time.

Generation into the Triple *Sattvas*

> I appear as the *samayasattva* blue Vajradhara. . . . In my heart is the red *jñānasattva*. . . . On the *jñānasattva*'s heart is the *samādhisattva*, a blue syllable *hūṃ*.[236]

By meditating on the triple *sattvas*, yogis will attain the triple *sattvas* of the completion stage and the fruit.

> **Sealing with the Lord of the *Tathāgata* Family**
>
> On the head-crown of the *samayasattva* is great Vajradhara, white in color with one face and two arms holding a *vajra* and bell. Through his absorption in union with Vajradhātvīśvarī, a stream of *bodhicitta* nectar drips down satisfying my entire body.[237]

[Concluding the Discussion on Purifying Rebirth and Attaining the *Nirmāṇakāya*]

How does the *nirmāṇakāya* of the meditator on the creation stage purify rebirth? In place of rebirth that occurs naturally for an ordinary person, for the yogis meditating on the creation stage, the *nirmāṇakāya* will arise through the transformation of the First Lord into Vajrasattva's *nirmāṇakāya.*

How does this meditation [during the creation stage] ripen the mental continuum of the meditator for the completion stage? [The meditation on the transformation into the *nirmāṇakāya*] ripens the mental continuum for the coarse *nirmāṇakāya* that arises when the similitude illusory bodies enter the old body during the three isolations [of body, speech, and mind during the completion stage]; and for the coarse *nirmāṇakāya* that arises when the pure and impure illusory bodies enter the old body. This will bring about the attainment of a buddha's *nirmāṇakāya* at the fruit of purification.

[Some General Considerations]

Some say that the yoga of the three bodies of meditators on the creation stage should be carried out by way of correspondences with death, intermediate stage, and rebirth of a person of Jambudvīpa and no other sentient beings. [We will discuss this matter in the following paragraphs.]

[How Do the Three Bodies of Meditators Correspond to Death, Intermediate Stage, and Rebirth?]

Death at the ground of ordinary existence and the *dharmakāya* of the meditator on the creation stage correspond by way of applying the mind to the wished-for goal through conviction,[238] while the *dharmakāyas* of the meditator on the completion stage and on the fruit actually correspond [to death at the ground of ordinary existence]. Likewise, the intermediate being at the ground of ordinary existence and *saṃbhogakāya* of the meditator on the creation stage correspond by way of applying the mind to the wished-for goal through conviction. Rebirth at the ground and *nirmāṇakāya* of the meditator on the creation stage also correspond by way of applying the mind to the wished-for goal through conviction. [23a]

[Why a Person of Jambudvīpa?]

What is the reason that the foremost disciples of the [Mantra] Vehicle, the jewel-like persons, are human beings residing in Jambudvīpa? The foremost disciples of the Mantra Vehicle, the jewel-like persons, are able to take on the path the bliss arising when the male and female join their organs and the white and red constituents unite. From among all *saṃsāric* realms, such a person is found only in Jambudvīpa, for the following reasons: the gods in the

Immaterial or Formless Realm lack aspects such as faces and limbs; the gods in the Realm of Subtle Materiality and in the upper levels of the Desire Realm do have forms but lack male and female organs; the gods in the two lower levels of the Desire Realm do have male and female organs, but when their organs are joined, there are no white and red constituents for them to unite—they merely emit a tiny amount of air; beings in the three lower realms experience bliss when the white and red constituents are united, but do not qualify to practice the Dharma; beings of the other three continents as well experience bliss when the white and red constituents are untied, but they abide on the ground of resources and thus in this life experience the fruit of karma they have accumulated in previous lives, but they do not abide on the ground of karma where they can attain in this life the fruit of meditating on the path in the present life.[239] For *Formulating the Guhyasamāja Sādhana* teaches:

> All the buddhas who appear in the past, present, and future [23b] are born as human beings, and as such, attain the *siddhi* of the omniscient stage. This is the reason the stages of birth into human existence are taught here.[240]

Can Women in Jambudvīpa Reach Awakening in Their Present Lives?

Therefore, both male and female yogis take bliss on the path. Both must be able to cultivate a most stable deity yoga, to hold the *bodhicitta* without emitting it, and thereby unite bliss and emptiness. Likewise, both men and woman can belong to each of the five types of disciples: those who are like a blue lotus, white lotus, lotus, sandalwood, and jewel.[241]

How do women awaken in this very life? As, for example, by relying on the mother, the father induces the four joys and the four empty states and generates the pure and impure illusory bodies from the [wind-and]-mind of clear light of the four empty states, and then attains the union of no more practice in that very life. Likewise, by relying on the father, the mother, too, induces the four joys and the four empty states and generates the pure and impure illusory bodies from the wind-and-mind of clear light of the four empty states, and then attains the union of no more practice in that very life. The way women are awakened is taught in chapter thirteen of the *Root Guhyasamāja Tantra*[242] and its *Commentary.*[243]

[Great Bliss]

The purpose of awakening by relying on sense pleasures of the consort, in the system of the Mantra Vehicle, is taught in the *Compendium of Vajra Wisdom Tantra:* [24a] "Unless [the male and female practitioners] activate their *vajra* and lotus by mantra and *mudrā*, and then join them, they will be unable to identify the three types of awareness.[244] Those unable to join their *bhagas* and *liṅgas* will not attain the *samādhi* of great bliss."[245] And: "Those who truly identify the intrinsic natures and appearances through the bliss arising from conjoining the *vajra* and lotus, will abide at the stage of great bliss."[246]

The seventh chapter of the *Guhyasamāja Tantra* teaches: "The passionate one who desires wisdom should rely constantly on the five sense pleasures";[247] and the *Sādhana Incorporating the Scripture* teaches: "In order to demonstrate that the stage [of awakening] arises through passion, the Blessed One, in the first chapter of the *Guhyasamāja Tantra,* was absorbed in the *samādhi* called 'the method of great passion.'"[248] The *Illuminating Lamp* explains the meaning of this by asking: "For whose sake was this *Tantra* taught?"[249] And then replying: "For the sake of passionate people."[250]

[Why Are the Correspondences Applied to People Living in the First Eon and What Does the Sādhana *Purify?]*

What is the reason the three bodies—the *dharmakāya, saṃbhogakāya,* and *nirmāṇakāya*—of the meditator on the creation stage are applied in correspondences with the death, intermediate state, and rebirth of people living in the first eon in Jambudvīpa and not with other people? As *Formulating the Guhyasamāja Sādhana* teaches, the formation of the celestial mansion, the residence of the specially visualized deities, corresponds to the evolution of the world, while the circle of deities residing therein, the specially visualized deities, corresponds to the people of the first eon. The *dharmakāya* arising when the specially visualized deities enter into clear light corresponds to the death of the people of the first eon. [24b] Likewise, the *saṃbhogakāya* and *nirmāṇakāya* of the meditator on the creation stage correspond to the intermediate being and rebirth of the people of the first eon.

[Query:] Some say in this regard that the first set of correspondences [between the *dharmakāya* and death] is fine, but the latter sets [the correspondences of the *saṃbhogakāya* and *nirmāṇakāya* with the intermediate being and rebirth of people of the first eon in Jambudvīpa] are not appropriate, because it is not certain that a human being who dies in Jambudvīpa will be reborn only as a human being in Jambudvīpa.

[Reply:] The three bodies—the *dharmakāya, saṃbhogakāya,* and *nirmāṇakāya*—of the meditator on the two stages correspond not only to the death, intermediate stage, and rebirth at the ground of ordinary existence but to the three bodies of the fruit as well; and the *nirmāṇakāya* that the *saṃbhogakāya* takes in order to display the twelve deeds can be born only in a passionate body. The three bodies of the meditator on the creation stage are applied in correspondences with death, intermediate stage, and rebirth of a human being dwelling in Jambudvīpa during the first eon, yet the death, intermediate stage, and rebirth are not taken as grounds of purification [of these three bodies]. This is so because the yogis who meditate in this way cannot purify the death, intermediate stage, and rebirth of a person who is already dead and who is of a different mental continuum. Even if the yogis could do so, it would be irrelevant. Then what do the yogis purify? They purify their own death, intermediate state, and rebirth that will occur in the future.

The Yoga with a Consort—Explaining How the Innate Great Bliss Arises—The Method for Swift Attainment of the Three Bodies

The Yoga with a Consort

A consort belonging to my own *tathāgata* family emanates from my heart. *Oṃ śūnyatā jñāna vajra svabhāva ātmako 'haṃ.* The consort dissolves into emptiness. Within the state of emptiness arises a *khaṃ* that turns into a *vajra* marked with *khaṃ.* The [*vajra*] transforms into a blue Vajra Lady of Tangibles,[251] crowned by Akṣobhya. She has three faces, blue, white, and red, and six arms. . . .

[The consort's body mandala is created.]

I visualize my secret place away. Within this state [of emptiness] arises a syllable *hūṃ,* that becomes a blue five-pronged *vajra;* the jewel that is its central prong is marked with the syllable *oṃ,* and its opening is blocked by a yellow syllable *phaṭ.*

I visualize the secret place of the consort away. Within this state [of emptiness] arises a syllable *āḥ,* that becomes a red, eight-petaled lotus, and its opening is blocked by a yellow syllable *phaṭ.*

Light rays endowed with five colors permeate within the *vajra* and the lotus.

I become Ratnasaṃbhava. *Oṃ sarva tathāgata anurāgaṇa vajra svabhāva ātmako 'haṃ.*

I become Vajradhara. *Hūṃ* by engaging in the act of absorbing in union, I attain bliss of supreme ecstasy.

I become Amoghasiddhi. *Oṃ sarva tathāgata pūjā vajra svabhāva ātmako 'haṃ.*[252]

The *sādhaka* of each of the five *tathāgata* families should unite respectively with daughters of a low-caste person, of a dyer, of a dancer, of a garland maker, and of a craftsman, respectively. [25a] The tantras and their commentaries teach what characteristics the consorts should possess: their mental continuums need to be purified by the shared path;[253] they need to have received a pure initiation; to properly guard their vows and commitments; to be well trained in the *Kāmaśāstra*[254] and in the tantra; to cultivate deity yoga; and to be extremely devoted to the *sādhaka.*

Regarding the wisdom consort, while there are nine [female] deities, Locanā and so on,[255] how should she be visualized? If the *sādhaka* belongs to the *tathāgata* family of Akṣobhya, for example, he should draw from his heart a consort belonging to his *tathāgata* family, in the appearance of an external girl. Then he should purify her into emptiness, and from emptiness visualize, as appropriate, Vajra Lady of Tangibles[256] or Māmakī and place the twenty-nine deities on her body. He should prepare the consort and bless the secret spaces while reciting: "I visualize my secret place away" and up to "meditate that its opening is blocked by [a yellow syllable] *phaṭ*."[257]

Reciting "I become Ratnasaṃbhava,"[258] abide in the divine identification of Ratnasaṃbhava and while pronouncing the mantra: *Oṃ sarva tathāgata anurāgaṇa vajra svabhāva ātmako 'haṃ,*[259] cultivate the divine identification of passion with the resolve: "The indivisible nature of the passion of all *tathāgatas*, that am I." Then, transform into the divine identification with Vajradhara and sing the song of *hūṃ*. As you and your consort are absorbed in union, draw the four joys, and meditate by uniting bliss and emptiness during innate bliss.

Then, while abiding in the divine identification with Amoghasiddhi, recite *oṃ sarva tathāgata pūjā vajra svabhāva ātmako 'haṃ*. [25b] In this way maintain divine identification with offering through the resolve: "The indivisible nature of the offerings to all *tathāgatas*, that am I."

All these steps of the yoga with the consort—taking on the path passion toward objects of desire generated through these practices; blocking the root of *saṃsāra,* which is grasping at the self; the arising of the mandala with the celestial mansion and the deities dwelling therein as display of indivisible bliss and emptiness; and ripening the yogi's mental continuum for the experience of the four joys in relying on a consort during the completion stage—are "the essence of the path" for the meditators on the creation stage.

Explaining How to Meditate on the *Samādhi* of the Supreme King of Mandalas [and the Supreme King of Deeds] in Correspondence with the Deeds of the Fruitional Buddha

There are two sections here: (1) explaining how to meditate on the *Samādhi* of the Supreme King of Mandalas, in correspondence with the deeds of the body; and (2) explaining how to meditate on the *Samādhi* of the Supreme King of Deeds, in correspondence with the deeds of the mind and speech.

Explaining How to Meditate on the Samādhi *of the Supreme King of Mandalas, in Correspondence with the Deeds of the Body*

Visualizing the Supreme King of Mandalas

The melted *bodhicitta* drop that descends into the Mother's lotus is the source of all the deities [of the Supreme King of Mandalas], the five *tathāgatas* and so forth. One part of the drop becomes a *bhrūṃ* syllable that transforms into the celestial mansion, perfect with all its characteristics, such as having four sides and four gates, and so forth, including the deities' thrones. The other part of the drop splits into thirty-two parts that take their place upon the thrones and become . . . [the thirty-two seed syllables of the deities, respectively, interspersed with *oṃ āḥ hūṃ*]. The seed syllables transform into the emblems. . . . The emblems transform in stages into the thirty-two deities. . . .[260]

EXPLAINING HOW TO MEDITATE ON THE CELESTIAL MANSION OF THE SUPREME KING OF MANDALAS

The meditation on the celestial mansion mentally emanated while reciting "the [melted] drop [descends] into the lotus of the Mother"[261] is taught in *Formulating the Guhyasamāja Sādhana.*[262]

EXPLAINING HOW TO MEDITATE ON THE DEITIES RESIDING IN THIS MANDALA

There are four sections here: (1) generation through the "three rituals," (2) generation through the "seven steps," (3) generation by means of the sealing with the four seals, and (4) explaining the meaning signified by teaching that all the deities have three faces.

Explaining How to Meditate on the Deities Residing in the Mandala through the "Three Rituals"

The three rituals are: (1) generating from the thirty-two seed syllables, interspersed with the three syllables *oṃ āḥ hūṃ*, is manifest awakening from the seed syllable, speech; (2) generating from the thirty-two emblems, *vajra* and so forth, is manifest awakening from the emblem, mind; [26a] and (3) generating the thirty-two deities, Akṣobhya and so forth, is the manifest awakening from the complete body.

Sending Out the Deities and So Forth

Akṣobhya is drawn into my heart. *Vajradhṛk!* He emerges out of my heart, [multiplies], and emanates in the ten directions, performing the enlightened deeds of a buddha, turning the wheel of Dharma, and so forth. In particular, they purify the hatred of sentient beings afflicted by hatred and place them on the stage of Akṣobhya. All the emanations of Akṣobhya combine into a single body of Akṣobhya, who then merges indivisibly with his *jñānasattva.* He receives initiation by the *bodhicitta* of the lord of the *tathāgata* family abiding in union with his consort. He returns and abides before me; and then enters my heart and merges with me. Thereby I as peaceful Vajradhara transform into blue Dveṣavajra, while my former lunar seat dissolves into a solar seat. I have three faces and six arms.[263]

Explaining How to Meditate on the Deities Residing in the Mandala through the "Seven Steps"

Each of the deities is generated through these "seven steps": (1) the "step of generation" is generating through the three rituals; (2) the "step of emanation" is drawing into the heart and sending forth in the ten directions; (3) the "step of deeds" is the enlightened deeds, turning the wheel of Dharma, and so forth; (4) the "step of withdrawing" is drawing back the emanations into one; (5) the "step of merging" is the merging of the deities indivisibly with their *jñānasattva;* (6) the "step of conferring initiation" is the conferral of initiation by the *bodhicitta* of the lord of the respective *tathāgata* family abiding in union with his consort; (7) the "step of abiding" is appearing once more and taking their individual seats.

Explaining How to Meditate on the Deities Residing in the Mandala by Means of the Sealing with the Four Seals

The following steps are included in [or sealed within] the visualization of all the deities through the generation rituals; hence their purpose is to seal with the four seals: (1) the dharma seal of speech is the thirty-two seed syllables interspersed with the three syllables; (2) the *samaya* seal of mind is the thirty-two emblems, *vajra* and so forth; (3) the great seal of body is the thirty-two deities, Akṣobhya and so forth; (4) the [karma] seal of enlightened deeds is the enlightened deeds of purifying hatred and so forth.

Explaining the Meaning Signified by Teaching that All the Deities Have Three Faces

[Query:] The majority of deities have one face. This is the case in the *Ubhaya Tantras,*[264] the *Compendium of Truth,*[265] *Caryā Tantras,*[266] the *Perfect Awakening of Vairocana,*[267] as well as in the *Unexcelled Tantras* such as *Cakrasaṃvara Tantra* and so forth. [26b] So what is the meaning signified here [in the *Guhyasamāja Tantra*] when it is taught that all the deities have three faces?

[Reply:] The right face signifies method, the wisdom of great bliss; the left face signifies perfect wisdom that realizes emptiness; and the central face uniting the two signifies the indivisible bliss and emptiness. Furthermore, the right face signifies the conventional truth and the pure illusory body; the left face signifies perfect wisdom, the ultimate truth, and wisdom of great bliss; while the central face signifies the union of these two, the body and mind united. Meditate on the three faces by recollecting this signified meaning.

HOW ARE THE CORRESPONDENCES APPLIED TO THE PRACTICE WITH THE CONSORT AND THE SUPREME KING OF MANDALAS?

The Teacher performed three "past events"[268] in which he taught three types of practice. (1) Having descended from Tuṣita Heaven,[269] the Teacher taught practices without passion for disciples who adhere to the lower [path] and made them deeply understand the four truths. (2) The Teacher taught the practice of the grounds and perfections for disciples who aspire to the great extensive [path] and made them deeply understand the subtle selflessness of phenomena. (3) By absorbing in union with the queen, the Teacher taught the practice of great passion for disciples earnestly intent on the profound [path] and made them deeply understand the union of the indivisible two truths.

In the present context, [the yoga with the consort and the emanation of the mandala] correspond to the deeds of the Teacher,[270] who having absorbed in union with the queen, emanated the mandala with its deities and conferred initiation on the disciples. These practices do not correspond to the ground; [they do not purify *saṃsāric* processes]. [27a]

By generating the deities of the Supreme King of Mandalas through the "seven steps," cultivating clear appearance of the deities and divine identification with them, and further regarding the [mandala] as a display of indivisible bliss and emptiness, the mandala—including the celestial mansion and deities dwelling in it—will be actually attained during the completion stage and the fruit.

Explaining How to Meditate on the Samādhi *of the Supreme King of Deeds—In Correspondence with the Deeds of the Mind and Speech*

[MEDITATION ON A SUBTLE EMBLEM]

Visualize yourself as Akṣobhyavajra. At the tip of the nose on your face,[271] visualize a five-pronged blue *vajra* the size of a white mustard seed upon a solar seat and perceive it in the nature of Akṣobhya. Meditate in this way until stable signs of touching and seeing appear. Once stability arises, emanate from that *vajra* a second *vajra*, then a third,[272] and so on, in stages, to fill the entire sky. Then withdraw the emanated *vajras* back in stages into the original *vajra*. When you have perfected the emanation and withdrawing into the emblem, transform the original *vajra* into Akṣobhya, and emanate [a second Akṣobhya, then a third, and so forth] in stages to fill the entire sky and then withdraw the Akṣobhyas back into the emblems in stages.[273]

[MEDITATION ON A SUBTLE DROP]

When you have perfected the meditation on the subtle emblems at the upper gate, visualize yourself as Akṣobhya, your secret place as a five-pronged *vajra*, and within its opening, visualize a blue drop the size of a white mustard seed upon a solar seat. Meditate on it until stable signs of touching and seeing appear. When stability arises, send forth the blue drop mentally into the lotus of your consort. Within the drop visualize the mandala—the celestial mansion and the deities dwelling there—with Akṣobhya as the principal deity. Visualize this Akṣobhya at the center of the mandala absorbed in union with his consort, and within their drop [27b] visualize once again the mandala—the celestial mansion and deities—with Akṣobhya as the principal deity. This is the essential point[274] of meditating on the subtle at the lower gate.

MANTRA RECITATION

There are two types of mantra recitation: outer and inner recitations. In the outer recitation recite *vajradhṛk* and so forth, and in the inner recitation recite the three syllables.[275]

How many times should you recite each mantra? In order to gain power for the self-entry into the mandala or in order to perform rituals such as initiations and consecrations for the sake of others, you should recite the mantras of the principal deity [Akṣobhya] and the mantra for the descent of wisdom[276] a hundred thousand times; recite as well the mantras of the deities surrounding the principal one and the garland mantra of Vighnāntaka[277] ten thousand times each. Likewise, when you perform a fire ritual for making up for omissions, you should recite these mantras ten thousand times.

The goal of this practice is to perceive all deities, yourself—visualized as the principal deity—and the surrounding deities as of a single continuum; and to perceive all the deities as display of bliss and emptiness. Then, to invoke mind's nondual-wisdom, visualize all the deities reciting the mantras in unison.

DISSOLUTION OF THE PRINCIPAL DEITIES INTO CLEAR LIGHT

> As the Father-Mother absorb in union, the Mother dissolves into the Father, the Father *samayasattva* dissolves into the *jñānasattva,* the *jñānasattva* into the *samādhisattva* [the syllable *hūṃ*], the vowel sign *ū*[278] of the *samādhisattva* into the *ha,*[279] the *ha* into its head,[280] its head into the crescent moon,[281] the crescent moon into the drop,[282] the drop into the *nāda,*[283] and the *nāda* dissolves into clear light.[284]

Visualize that as you as the principal deity are absorbed in union with your consort, the triple *sattvas* enter clear light one after the other; thereby wisdom and emptiness are united. This is the essential point[285] of the entry of the principal deity into clear light.

ARISING IN RESPONSE TO THE INVOCATION OF THE FOUR GODDESSES

> Unable to behold the principal deity, the four goddesses—who are in the nature of the four qualities beyond measure—are in anguish. Wishing to see him, they invoke him with melodious songs:
>
> O lord dwelling in the realm of sentient beings . . . take delight in me.[286]
>
> Thus invoked, I arise from the clear light in the body of the deity consisting of the triple *sattvas*, through the power of prior aspiration and compassion; all the deities of the mandala vividly perceive me.[287]

Then the four goddesses—who are in the nature of the four qualities beyond measure—praise by specifying the good qualities of the four *tathāgata* families, respectively, beginning with "O lord dwelling in the realm of sentient beings"[288] and so forth up to the arousing of the wisdom of great innate bliss by requesting, "Take delight in me." As a result of this request, the mind essence that is nondual wisdom arises in the form of the triple *sattvas*; [28a] thereby "all the deities of mandala vividly perceive me." This is the essential point[289] of invoking with a song the [principal deity who has] dissolved.

PRAISES

Praise by specifying the good qualities of the five *tathāgata* families, beginning with "Akṣobhyavajra."[290]

OFFERINGS

There are three kinds of offerings: outer, inner, and secret offerings.

Outer Offerings

[*Offer arghaṃ, pādyaṃ, puṣpe, dhūpe, āloke, gandhe, naivedye, śabda, rūpa, śabda, gandhe, rasa, sparśa.*[291]]

The presenter of the offerings is the yogi who has maintained divine identification with the principal deity and attained great bliss. The *recipients* of the offerings are the lama and the deities residing in the mandala of Akṣobhya. The offering *substances* are those held in the hands of the goddesses who have emanated from the yogi's heart. The mantra of the offerings is *oṃ sarva* [*tathāgata arghaṃ pūjā megha samudra spharaṇa samaya śriye āḥ hūṃ*] and so forth.[292]

As for [the visualization during] the recitation of this mantra: While reciting *oṃ* visualize the goddesses emanating from your heart and sending forth in the ten directions the water for welcoming[293] and the other offerings—vast as ocean-like clouds—for the lama and the deities of the mandala. Then, after reciting "Please accept, please accept as pledge"[294] while pronouncing *hūṃ*, visualize the goddesses withdrawing into the *hūṃ* in your heart.

Inner Offerings

Having been blessed as nectar, the inner offerings generate special untainted bliss for the lama and the deities of the mandala.[295]

Secret Offerings

As the principal deity and his consort are absorbed in union, all the deities surrounding them within the mandala are satisfied with great bliss.[296] [28b]

HOW THE STEPS OF THE MEDITATION ON THE SUPREME KING OF DEEDS ARE APPLIED TO THE FRUIT

The meditation on the subtle yoga corresponds to a buddha's "deed" of mind—abiding in perfect inner absorption.[297] The essential point[298] of reciting mantras corresponds to the deed of speech—turning the wheel of Dharma for the sake of the disciples. The essential point of the entry of the principal deity Father-Mother into clear light[299] corresponds to a buddha's *nirvāṇa* after his direct disciples in that buddha-field are exhausted. The essential point of arousing with a song [the principal deity] who has dissolved[300] corresponds to a buddha who, once his mind is stirred by the four qualities beyond measure, arises from clear light in a *rūpakāya,* in the buddha-field in which direct disciples of the buddha are found. The essential point of offering and praises[301] corresponds to a buddha's deed of becoming a recipient of offerings and accepting the offerings made by these disciples.

HOW THE STEPS OF THE MEDITATION ON THE SUPREME KING OF DEEDS ARE APPLIED TO THE COMPLETION STAGE

The meditation on the subtle yoga serves to ripen the mental continuum of the meditator on the completion stage during body isolation. The essential point of mantra recitation serves to ripen the mental continuum of the meditator on the completion stage during speech isolation. The essential point of the entry of the principal deity into clear light serves to ripen the mental continuum of the meditator on the completion stage during clear light [of mind isolation]. The essential point of arising when [the principal deity] who has dissolved is aroused with a song serves to ripen the mental continuum of the meditator on the completion stage during the arising from clear light in the illusory body. The essential points of making offering, reciting praises, and so forth are only ancillary activities for amassing the accumulations.

Here is concluded the explanation of the *samādhis* of the Supreme King of Mandalas and the Supreme King of Deeds in correspondence with the deeds of a fruitional buddha. [29a]

EXPLAINING THE FRAMEWORK OF THE SĀDHANA

There are five sections here:[302] (1) the framework of the forty-nine essential points,[303] (2) the framework of the four *vajras,* (3) the framework of the six yogas, (4) the framework of the three *samādhis,* and (5) the framework of the four limbs of familiarization and achievement.[304]

The Framework of the Forty-Nine Essential Points

[The Preliminaries]

(1) The place of meditation.[305]
(2) The essential point of great compassion begins with: "I visualize myself as Akṣobhyavajra."[306] [2a]
(3) Generating the principal deity of the protection wheel begins with: "I generate myself as Dveṣavajra."[307]
(4) Generating the fierce deities surrounding Dveṣavajra begins with: "Yamāntaka."[308]
(5) Driving the stakes begins with: "I look at Sumbharāja below."[309]
(6) The meditation on the *vajra* fence and tent begins with: "*Takki hūṃ jaḥ.*"[310]

[The Main Part]

(7) The meditation on the ground of wisdom begins with: "In the absence of being, there is no meditation," and so forth.[311]
(8) The generation of the *vajra* ground begins with: "From within the continuum of emptiness."[312]
(9) The generation of the celestial mansion in which the specially visualized deities reside begins with: "[Upon the navel of the crossed *vajra* appears] a white *bhrūṃ* syllable."[313]
(10) The meditation on the specially visualized deities residing in the celestial mansion begins with: "Upon these seats [instantly, the thirty-two deities . . .], at the center [I myself, blue Vajradhara, abide]."[314]
(11) Drawing the specially visualized deities into the body begins with: "Hook-like light rays emanating from the blue *hūṃ* at my heart, [draws the deities from] Vairocana [to Sumbharāja]."[315]
[(12*) Dissolution into clear light.][316]
(12) Arising [from emptiness-clear-light] through the visualization of the solar disk begins with: "Upon the central seat appears a *hūṃ* that becomes a solar disk."[317]
(13) Manifest awakening from the moon begins with: "All these mingle together."[318] [2b]
(14) Abiding in absorption on wisdom alone begins with: "Light rays

emanating [from the moon orb draw the entire] animate and inanimate realms."[319]

(15) Manifest awakening from the seed syllable begins with: "Upon the moon" and so forth "[like bubbles popping up] from water."[320]

(16) Manifest awakening from the emblem begins with: "Light rays emanating from these [syllables] invite the five *tathāgata* families."[321]

(17) Manifest awakening from the complete body begins with: "The *vajra* with the three syllables [transform]."[322]

(18) The transformation of the First Lord into [Vajrasattva's] *nirmāṇakāya* begins with: "[The Father-Mother *Tathāgatas*] from their natural abode."[323]

(19) The transformation of the body into the celestial mansion begins with: "The front, back, [right, and left sides of my] body."[324]

(20) The meditation on the five aggregates as the five *tathāgatas* begins with: "The area from the crown of my head to my hairline."[325]

(21) The meditation on the four physical elements as the four mothers begins with: "[*Laṃ*, the essence of the entirety of the body's earth element] at the navel."[326]

(22) The meditation on [the sense faculties], the eye, and so forth, as [the *bodhisattvas*] Kṣitigarbha and so forth begins with: "At my eyes."[327]

(23) The meditation on the five physical elements as the five *vajra* ladies begins with: "At the doors of my eyes."[328]

(24) The meditation on the limbs as the fierce deities begins with: "At my right arm."[329]

(25) Blessing the body begins with: "From the *oṃ* on the crown of my head."[330]

(26) Blessing the speech begins with: "From the *āḥ* at the center of my throat [or tongue]."[331]

(27) Blessing the mind begins with: "From the *hūṃ* [at the center] of my heart."[332]

(28) Blessing the body, speech, and mind together begins with: "I am [great Vajradhara, the indivisible triple *vajra* body, speech, and mind of all] *tathāgatas*."[333]

(29) The concentration on the *jñānasattva* begins with: "I appear as the *samayasattva* blue Vajradhara."[334]

(30) The concentration on the *samādhisattva* begins with: "On its [the *jñānasattva*'s] heart, a blue *vajra*."[335]

(31) Preparing the consort and so forth begins with: "A consort belonging to my own *tathāgata* family emanates from my heart."[336] [3a]

(32) The essential point of [passion and][337] offerings begins with: "I become Ratnasaṃbhava."[338]

[The Supreme King of Mandalas]

(33) Sending forth the male *tathāgatas* begins with: "Akṣobhya is drawn into my heart."[339]
(34) Sending forth the female *tathāgatas* begins with: "Locanā is drawn into my heart."[340]
(35) Sending forth the female *bodhisattvas* begins with: "Rūpavajrā is drawn into my heart."[341]
(36) Sending forth the male *bodhisattvas* begins with: "Maitreya is drawn into my heart."[342]
(37) Sending forth the fierce deities begins with: "Yamāntaka is drawn into my heart."[343]

[The Supreme King of Deeds]

(38) Meditation on the subtle emblem at the upper opening of the central channel.[344]
(39) Meditation on the subtle drop at the lower opening of the central channel.[345]
(40) Inner mental recitation.[346]
(41) Outer [voiced] recitation begins with: "[*Oṃ āḥ*] *vajradhṛk* [*hūṃ hūṃ*]."[347]
(42) The dissolution of the principal deity into clear light begins with: "As the Father-Mother absorb in union."[348]
(43) Arousing with a song the [principal deity] who has dissolved begins with: "[Unable to behold the principal deity, the four goddesses—who are in the nature of] the four qualities beyond measure."[349]
(44) The praises and offerings begin with: "O Akṣobhya Vajra."[350]
(45) The [final] dissolution of the mandala begins with: "[Hook-like light rays arising from] the blue seed syllable *hūṃ* [in my] heart]."[351]

[Concluding]

(46) The essential point of yoga of eating.[352]
(47) The essential point of body enhancement.[353]

(48) The essential point of attaining lesser *siddhis*.[354]
(49) The essential point of attaining middling *siddhis*.[355]

The Framework of the Four *Vajras*

The *Later Tantra* teaches: "The first is awakening from emptiness, the second is the gathered seed syllables, the third is completing the form, and the fourth is placing the syllables."[356]

(1) The "*vajra* of awakening from emptiness" is from the essential point of the place of meditation [no. 1] up to the essential point of manifest awakening from suchness [no. 12*].[357]

(2) The "*vajra* of the gathered seed syllables"[358] is from the essential point of arising by visualizing the solar mandala [no. 12] up to the essential point of manifest awakening from the emblem [no. 16]. [3b]

(3) The "*vajra* of completing the form" is from the essential point of manifest awakening from the complete body [no. 17] up to the essential point of generating the limbs of the body as the fierce deities [at the end of the meditation on the body mandala, no. 24].

(4) When you meditate according to the abridged *sādhana,* the "*vajra* of placing the syllables" begins with the blessing of the body [no. 25] and continues up to the essential point of offering [no. 32]; but when you meditate according to the extensive *sādhana,* it continues up to the essential point of the meditation on the subtle emblem at the upper gate [no. 38].

The Framework of the Six Yogas

The *Vajra Garland Tantra* teaches: "You should meditate on the *yoga, anuyoga, atiyoga,* and *mahāyoga* of the First Yoga. Then meditate on the five divisions of the supreme yoga of the Supreme King of Mandalas [nos. 33–37] and [4a] the twelve divisions of the yoga of the Supreme King of Deeds[359] [nos. 38–49]."[360]

(1) "Yoga"[361] is from the essential point of the place of meditation [no. 1] up to the essential point of abiding in absorption on wisdom alone [no. 14].

(2) *Anuyoga*[362] consists of three essential points: the manifest awakenings from the seed syllable [no. 15], the emblem [no. 16], and the complete body [no. 17].

(3) *Atiyoga*[363] is from the transformation of the *saṃbhogakāya* into the *nirmāṇakāya* [no. 18] up to the generation of the limbs of the body as the fierce deities [at the end of the body mandala, no. 24].

(4) *Mahāyoga*[364] begins with the blessing of the body [no. 25] and continues until the essential point of offerings [no. 32].

(5) The yoga of the Supreme King of Mandalas is from the essential point of offerings [no. 32] up to the sending forth of the fierce deities [no. 37].

(6) The yoga of the Supreme King of Deeds is from the essential point of meditating on the subtle object at the upper gate [no. 38] up to the [essential point of] attaining middling *siddhis* [no. 49].

The Framework of the Three *Samādhis*

(1) The *Samādhi* of the First Yoga begins with the essential point of the place of meditation [no. 1] and continues up to the essential point of offerings [no. 32].

(2) The *Samādhi* of the Supreme King of Mandalas begins with the essential point of offerings [no. 32] and continues up to [but not including] the meditation on the subtle [emblem] at the upper gate [no. 38].

(3) The *Samādhi* of the Supreme King of Deeds begins with the meditation on the subtle emblem at the upper gate [no. 38] and continues up to [the essential point of the final] dissolution of the mandala [no. 45].

The Framework of the Four Limbs of Familiarization and Achievement

The twelfth chapter of the *Guhyasamāja Tantra* teaches: "The four limbs are: uniting in the *samaya* of *familiarization*, arising in *approaching achievement*, *samaya* in order to [gain] *achievement*, and *great achievement*."[365]

(1) The limb of familiarization[366] begins with the essential point of the place [no. 1] and continues up to the essential point of manifest awakening from suchness [no. 12*]. Why is it called familiarization? The subjective wisdom *familiarizes* with and focuses constantly on the objective emptiness.

(2) The limb of approaching achievement[367] begins with the arising [from emptiness] by focusing on [the manifest awakenings] from the solar disk [no. 12] and continues up to the generation of the limbs of the body as the fierce deities [at the end of the body mandala, no. 24]. Why is it called approaching achievement? The object toward which one *approaches* is the wisdom body of *saṃbhogakāya;* and [that which approaches is] the mantra body of *saṃbhogakāya* that is about to *approach* and *achieve* it [the wisdom body of *saṃbhogakāya*].

(3) The limb of achievement[368] begins with the blessing of the body [no. 25]

and continues up to offerings and praises [no. 32]. Why is it called achievement? Because the body, speech, and mind of the practitioner and the three *vajras* of a buddha are *achieved as* [or become] indivisible.

(4) The limb of great achievement[369] begins with the offerings [no. 32] and continues up to the dissolution of the mandala [no. 45]. Why is it called great achievement? [4b] Since [the yogi] engages in [and achieves] great benefit for others.[370]

ADDENDUM

[29a] Another way to apply the four limbs of familiarization and achievement is as follows.

(1) The limb of familiarization refers to the entire meditation on the creation stage.

(2) The limb of approaching achievement is arousing the deity's heart by practicing the *caryā* of the meditator on the creation stage, taught in the tenth chapter of the *Guhyasamāja Tantra.*[371]

(3) The limb of achievement is the *caryā* of the meditator on the creation stage and the practice of *haṭhayoga* in order to [gain the blessing of] the deities.[372]

(4) The limb of great achievement is the practice for attaining the mundane *siddhis*, beginning with pacification, taught in the *Sādhana Incorporating the Scripture.*[373]

These are notes of the teachings of Jé Lama Tsongkhapa.

Through the efforts I make here,
may my death, intermediate state, and rebirth
transform into the *dharmakāya, saṃbhogakāya,* and *nirmāṇakāya,*
so that I will attain the body of the victorious one.
Bhavantu!

APPENDIX

In *Fulfilling the Bee's Hope*, Tsongkhapa explains the framework of the *sādhana* according to five different categories.[1] For the sake of easy navigation among them, the first and most detailed of them, the framework of the forty-nine essential points,[2] was taken as a point of reference for the last four of the five categories. This appendix explains the terse outline of the forty-nine essential points in some detail. This will also serve to clarify what the steps of the *sādhana* are according to the other listings.

THE FRAMEWORK OF THE FORTY-NINE ESSENTIAL POINTS

(1) The place of meditation is on a mountain abounding in pleasing flowers, fruit, and water, or an area of great isolation unfrequented by people.[3]

[Preliminaries]

(2) Generating the mind of great compassion consists of the meditation on establishing favorable conditions and amassing the accumulations, including the invitation of the merit field and the sevenfold worship.

(3) Generating the principal deity of the protection wheel consists of meditation on emptiness and visualization of the protection wheel with white Vajradhara and Vajradhātvīśvarī at its center as the triple *sattvas*, blessed by the three syllables *oṃ āḥ hūṃ*. Then Akṣobhya, surrounded by the ten fierce deities, is invited and

enters into Vajradhara, who thereby transforms into blue Dveṣavajra, while his consort Vajradhātvīśvarī transforms into blue Sparśavajrā.

(4) Generating the surrounding fierce deities involves meditation to draw the ten fierce deities into the heart of the yogi as the principal deity and then placing them over the spokes of the protection wheel.

(5) Driving the stakes begins with the yogi looking at Sumbharāja,[4] the fierce deity abiding in the nadir below. He emanates a second Sumbharāja, whom the yogi commands to fetch the ten guardians of the directions and to hand them over to the ten fierce deities. The fierce deities encase them in triangular pits, where the stakes are driven into their heads.

(6) Meditating on the *vajra* fence and tent is another way of protection through the visualization of concentric fences of iron *vajra,* water, fire, and wind all around, topped by a *vajra* canopy with a *vajra* ground below. Outside, there is a lattice of arrows radiating the blazing fire of wisdom in all directions.

[The Main Part]

(7) The meditation on the ground of wisdom is a meditation on emptiness as the ground for the evolution of the celestial mansion of the mandala.

(8) The generation of *vajra* ground consists of the instant reappearance of the *vajra* fence and canopy with the source of phenomena at its center, and the visualization of four mandalas of the physical elements that merge and transform into a crossed *vajra.*

(9) The generation of the celestial mansion in which the specially visualized deities reside begins with a white *bhrūṃ* syllable that transforms into the celestial mansion embellished with all its essential characteristics and the seats for the deities.

(10) The meditation on the specially visualized deities begins with the instant generation of the thirty-two deities and continues with the cultivation of the clarity of the visualization step by step.

(11) Drawing the specially visualized deities into the respective locations on the yogi's body from the head to the soles.

[(12*) The specially visualized deities along with the respective parts of the yogi's body dissolve into clear light.][5]

(12) Arising [from emptiness] by visualizing the solar disk from the syllable *hūṃ*.
(13) Manifest awakening from the moon is the meditation on the dissolution into a single moon orb of the lunar disk, the eight-petaled lotus, and the three syllables *oṃ āḥ hūṃ* stacked upon the lotus's navel.
(14) Abiding in absorption in wisdom alone consists of the meditation on the dissolution of the entire animate and inanimate realms into the moon orb followed by the cultivation of divine pride with the resolve: "The pure wind-and-mind arising as the extremely subtle wisdom body, that am I."
(15) Manifest awakening from the seed syllable is the visualization of the three seed syllables *oṃ āḥ hūṃ* arising from the moon, like bubbles popping up from water.
(16) Manifest awakening from the emblem is meditation on light rays emanating from the three seed syllables and inviting the deities of the five *tathāgata* families. This assemblage of deities then dissolves into the syllables, transforming them into the emblem of a white five-pronged *vajra* marked with *oṃ āḥ hūṃ*.
(17) Manifest awakening from the complete body is the transformation of the *vajra* into the yogi as the First Lord.
(18) The transformation of the First Lord into [Vajrasattva's] *nirmāṇakāya* takes place through the entry of Akṣobhya, formed from the *bodhicittas* of the Father-Mother *tathāgatas* into the First Lord.
(19) In the transformation of the body into the celestial mansion, specific parts of the body become respective parts of the celestial mansion.
(20) In the meditation on the five aggregates as the five *tathāgatas*, the entire body divided into five areas transforms respectively into the five *tathāgatas*.
(21) In the meditation on the four physical elements as the four mothers, the natures of the body's five physical elements transform respectively into the four female buddhas.
(22) In the meditation on the *bodhisattvas*, the five sense faculties are visualized as five of the *bodhisattvas* and the body, joints, and channels with sinews as the remaining three *bodhisattvas*.
(23) Meditation on the five sense objects as the five *vajra* ladies.
(24) Meditation on the ten limbs as the ten fierce deities.

(25) Blessing the body.
(26) Blessing the speech.
(27) Blessing the mind.
(28) Blessing the body, speech, and mind together.
(29) Concentration on the *jñānasattva.*
(30) Concentration on the *samādhisattva.*
(31) Preparing the consort and so forth includes the emanation of a wisdom consort from the yogi's heart; her dissolution into emptiness and arising as Sparśavajrā; placing the deities of the body mandala on her body; and blessing the secret places of both the yogi and the consort.
(32) The essential point[s] of [passion and] offerings[6] consist of becoming Ratnasaṃbhava and reciting the mantra of passion, then becoming Vajradhara and attaining bliss, and finally becoming Amoghasiddhi and reciting the mantra of offerings.

[The Supreme King of Mandalas]

The drop of *bodhicitta* emanated from the union with the consort splits. One part transforms into the celestial mansion and the other splits into thirty-two parts that become the deities residing in the mandala.

(33) Meditation on the five male *tathāgatas.*
(34) Meditation on the female *tathāgatas.*
(35) Meditation on the female *bodhisattvas* or *vajra* ladies.
(36) Meditation on the male *bodhisattvas.*
(37) Meditation on the fierce deities.

[The Supreme King of Deeds]

(38) Meditation on the subtle emblem at the upper opening of the central channel.
(39) Meditation on the subtle drop at the lower opening of the central channel.
(40) Inner mental recitation.
(41) Outer [voiced] recitation.
(42) The dissolution of the principal deity into clear light.
(43) Arousing with a song the principal deity who has dissolved.
(44) Praises and offerings.

(45) The final dissolution of the mandala.

[Concluding]

(46) The essential point of yoga of eating.
(47) The essential point of body enhancement.
(48) The essential point of attaining lesser *siddhis*.
(49) The essential point of attaining middling *siddhis*.

NOTES

Abbreviations

D. Sde dge (Derge) edition of the *Bka' 'gyur* and *Bstan 'gyur.*

P. Peking edition of the *Bka' 'gyur* and *Bstan 'gyur.*

Stog Stog Palace edition of the *Bka' 'gyur.*

Tōh. Tōhoku catalog of the Sde dge editions of the *Bka' 'gyur* and *Bstan 'gyur.*

Introduction

1. *Bandhu* as in Vasubandhu, a cognate of the term "bind" in English. The Tibetan for *prabandha* is *rgyun.*
2. Flood, *An Introduction,* 48.
3. *Rgyud phyi ma, Uttara Tantra,* regarded as one of the explanatory tantras of the *Guhyasamāja Tantra;* or else taken to be the eighteenth chapter of the *Guhyasamāja Tantra.* See Tōh. 443, D. 150a1–3; a Sanskrit edition in Matsunaga, *Guhyasamāja,* chap. 18, vv. 34–35.
4. Tib. *rgyun;* Skt. *prabandha.*
5. Tib. *rgyu, 'bras bu,* and *thabs;* Skt. *hetu, phala,* and *upāya.* These three aspects are also the nature, being "untakeable," and the basis, respectively. Tib. *rang bzhin, mi phrogs,* and *gzhi;* Skt. *prakṛti, asaṃhārya,* and *ādhāra.*
6. Nāropā, *Gsang ba thams cad kyi sgron ma'i rgya cher 'grel pa, Sarvaguhyapradīpaṭīkā,* Tōh. 1787, D. 210a5–b3. See also Tsong kha pa, *Sgron gsal mchan,* 2b4–3a1.
7. Tib. *rgyud.*
8. Tib. *rten cing 'brel bar 'byung ba;* Skt. *pratītyasamutpāda.*
9. Tib. *tha snyad 'dogs pa'i gzhi.*
10. Nāgabuddhi, Klu'i blo, *Rnam gzhag rim pa, Vyavastholi,* Tōh. 1809; Sanskrit and Tibetan editions in Tanaka, *Vyavastholi.*

11. See Tanaka, *Vyavastholi*, 58.
12. Tsong kha pa Blo bzang grags pa, *Rnam gzhag rim pa'i rnam bshad.*
13. Tib. *Dge lugs.*
14. Jinpa, *Tsongkhapa*, xv.
15. Tsong kha pa, *Sngags rim chen mo*, written in 1405.
16. Tib. *sku gsum;* Skt. *trikāya.*
17. Tib. *rigs 'dra'i rgyu.*
18. See also the section "Meditations in Correspondence with the Person—The Yogas of the Buddha's Three Bodies" in chap. 3.
19. Tib. *gzhi, lam,* and *'bras bu.*
20. Tib. *shin tu phra ba'i lus.*
21. Tib. *phung po lhag ma med pa'i mya ngan las 'das pa;* Skt. *nirupadhiśeṣanirvāṇa.*
22. Tib. *nyon mongs pa;* Skt. *kleśa.*
23. According to early Buddhist texts, the Buddha ceased to exist. His absence, though, was problematic for later Buddhist traditions that offered solutions for this. See Strong, *Buddhisms*, chap. 3.
24. Tib. *sems tsam;* Skt. *cittamātra.*
25. See Bentor and Dorjee, *The Ocean.*
26. See the section "The Material Basis for the Illusory Body" in chap. 3.
27. Tib. *de bzhin gshegs pa'i snying po;* Skt. *tathāgatagarbha.* See Buddha-Nature, https://buddhanature.tsadra.org/index.php/Key_Terms/tath%C4%81gata garbha.
28. See the section "Continuity according to Buddha Nature" in chap. 3.
29. Flood, *An Introduction*, 48.

1. The Cosmos and Cosmogony

1. Cabezón, "Three Buddhist Views," 35.
2. The Buddhist cosmogonies and cosmologies discussed in detail in this book are those described in Vasubandhu's *Abhidharmakośa* and those found in Mahāyāna Sūtras that are related to buddha-fields or "pure lands."
3. Tib. *sdug bsngal;* Skt. *duḥkha.*
4. *'Dul ba rnam par 'byed pa = Lung rnam 'byed, Vinayavibhaṅga,* Tōh. 3, D. *ca,* 48b1–51b5.
5. Vasubandhu, *Mdzod 'grel, Kośabhāṣya,* chap. 3, vv. 97cd–98ab, Tōh. 4090, D. *ku,* 162a4–63a2; a Sanskrit edition in Pradhan, *Abhidharmakośabhāṣyam,* 186–87; an English translation in Pruden, *Vasubandhu,* 487–88. See the *Mahāvastu,* 1, Senart, *Le Mahāvastu,* 338–48; an English translation in Jones, *The Mahāvastu,* 285–94.
6. Maudgalyāyana, *'Jig rten gzhag pa, Lokaprajñapti,* Tōh. 4086.
7. Asaṅga, *Sa'i dngos gzhi, Maulībhūmi,* part 1 of the *Rnal 'byor spyod pa'i sa, Yogācārabhūmi,* Tōh. 4035, D. 20b6–21a5; a Sanskrit edition in Bhattacharya, *The*

Yogācārabhūmi, 42.1–18; an English translation in Kajiyama, "Buddhist Cosmology," 196–97.

8. Vasubandhu, *Mdzod, Kośa,* chap. 3, v. 93ab, Tōh. 4089, D. 10b1; a Sanskrit edition in Pradhan, *Abhidharmakośabhāṣyam,* 180–81; an English translation in Pruden, *Vasubandhu,* 479.
9. Tsong kha pa, *Bung ba'i re skong,* 13b3–14b6. See also his *Rnam gzhag rim pa'i rnam bshad,* 20a6–21b2, commenting on Nāgabuddhi, *Rnam gzhag rim pa, Vyavastholi,* chap. 1, Tōh. 1809, D. 123a1–4 and 123b3–6; Sanskrit and Tibetan editions in Tanaka, *Vyavastholi,* 87–88, 91–92.
10. Tib. *'Dzam bu gling;* Skt. *Jambudvīpa* = Jambu-tree Continent or Jambu Island in the South.
11. Tib. *'od gsal;* Skt. *ābhāsvara.*
12. See Vasubandhu, *Mdzod 'grel, Kośabhāṣya,* chap. 3, vv. 97cd–98ab, Tōh. 4090, D. *ku,* 162a4–63a2; a Sanskrit edition in Pradhan, *Abhidharmakośabhāṣyam,* 186–87; an English translation in Pruden, *Vasubandhu,* 487–88; and the *'Dul ba rnam par 'byed pa, Vinayavibhaṅga,* Tōh. 3, D. *ca,* 48a1–51b5; an English translation in Jinpa, *Science and Philosophy,* 296–306. See also the *Aggañña Sutta* in the *Dīgha Nikāya;* English translations in Walshe, *Long Discourses,* 407–14, and Gethin, *Sayings of the Buddha,* 116–28.
13. Tsong kha pa, *Bung ba'i re skong,* 13b3–5. See also Tsong kha pa, *Rnam gzhag rim pa'i rnam bshad,* 20b3–21a3, commenting on Nāgabuddhi, *Rnam gzhag rim pa, Vyavastholi,* chap. 1, Tōh. 1809, D. 123a1–2; Sanskrit and Tibetan editions in Tanaka, *Vyavastholi,* 87–88.
14. Nāgabuddhi, *Rnam gzhag rim pa, Vyavastholi,* chap. 1, Tōh. 1809, D. 123a1; Sanskrit and Tibetan editions in Tanaka, *Vyavastholi,* 87.
15. See Vasubandhu, *Mdzod, Kośa,* chap. 3, v. 9b–c, Tōh. 4089, D. 7a5; a Sanskrit edition in Pradhan, *Abhidharmakośabhāṣyam,* 119; an English translation in Pruden, *Vasubandhu,* 381. See also Nāgabuddhi, *Rnam gzhag rim pa, Vyavastholi,* chap. 1, Tōh. 1809, D. 122a5; Sanskrit and Tibetan editions in Tanaka, *Vyavastholi,* 83–84.
16. *'Dul ba rnam par 'byed pa, Vinayavibhaṅga,* Tōh. 3, D. *ca,* 48a3–5; an English translation in Jinpa, *Science and Philosophy,* 303.
17. No gender exists yet.
18. Tsong kha pa, *Bung ba'i re skong,* 13b5–14a1.
19. *'Dul ba rnam par 'byed pa, Vinayavibhaṅga,* Tōh. 3, D. *ca,* 48a5–49b1; an English translation in Jinpa, *Science and Philosophy,* 303.
20. *Ṛg Veda,* 10.129; an English translation in Doniger O'Flaherty, *Textual Sources,* 13.
21. Tsong kha pa, *Bung ba'i re skong,* 14a1–2.
22. Tsong kha pa, *Bung ba'i re skong,* 14a2–3.
23. *'Dul ba rnam par 'byed pa, Vinayavibhaṅga,* Tōh. 3, D. *ca,* 49b3; an English translation in Jinpa, *Science and Philosophy,* 304.

24. See Strong, *Buddhisms,* 248.
25. Tib. *rten cing 'brel bar 'byung ba;* Skt. *pratītyasamutpāda.*
26. See Strong, *Buddhisms,* 257.
27. Tsong kha pa, *Bung ba'i re skong,* 14a3–5.
28. *'Dul ba rnam par 'byed pa, Vinayavibhaṅga,* Tōh. 3, D. *ca,* 49b5–50b5.
29. Skt. *śali.*
30. Tsong kha pa, *Bung ba'i re skong,* 14a5–6.
31. Tsong kha pa, *Bung ba'i re skong,* 14a6–b1.
32. Tsong kha pa, *Bung ba'i re skong,* 14b1.
33. *'Dul ba rnam par 'byed pa, Vinayavibhaṅga,* Tōh. 3, D. *ca,* 50b7–51a2; an English translation in Jinpa, *Science and Philosophy,* 305.
34. Tsong kha pa, *Bung ba'i re skong,* 14b1–2.
35. *'Dul ba rnam par 'byed pa, Vinayavibhaṅga,* Tōh. 3, D. *ca,* 51a2–b2; an English translation in Jinpa, *Science and Philosophy,* 305–6.
36. Vasubandhu, *Mdzod 'grel, Kośabhāṣya,* chap. 3, v. 98, Tōh. 4090, D. *ku,* 162a4–63a2; a Sanskrit edition in Pradhan, *Abhidharmakośabhāṣyam,* 187–88; an English translation in Pruden, *Vasubandhu,* 487–89.
37. Asaṅga, *Sa'i dngos gzhi, Maulībhūmi,* Tōh. 4035, D. 20b6–21a6; a Sanskrit edition in Bhattacharya, *The Yogācārabhūmi,* 42.1–20; an English translation in Kajiyama, "Buddhist Cosmology," 197–98.
38. Tsong kha pa, *Bung ba'i re skong,* 14b2–4.
39. Vasubandhu, *Mdzod 'grel, Kośabhāṣya,* chap. 3, vv. 97cd–98ab, Tōh. 4090, D. *ku,* 162a4–63a2; a Sanskrit edition in Pradhan, *Abhidharmakośabhāṣyam,* 186–87; an English translation in Pruden, *Vasubandhu,* 487–88. See also *Aggañña Sutta* in the *Dīgha Nikāya;* an English translation in Walshe, *Long Discourses,* 412, and Gethin, *Sayings of the Buddha,* 124.
40. Tsong kha pa, *Bung ba'i re skong,* 14b4.
41. Tib. *mang pos bkur ba'i rgyal po;* Skt. *rājamahāsaṃmata.*
42. This is the lineage of Buddha Śākyamuni. Tsong kha pa, *Bung ba'i re skong,* 14b5–6.
43. Wayman, "Buddhist Genesis," 130.
44. "The *Aggañña Sutta: On Knowledge of Beginnings,*" in *The Long Discourses of the Buddha, Dīgha Nikāya* III 80–98; English translations in Walshe, *Long Discourses,* 407–15, and Gethin, *Sayings of the Buddha,* 116–28. The Sanskrit accounts of the creation story do not include the frame story with its Buddhist-Brahmanic controversy. Still, the *Yogācārabhūmi* does mention the appearance of the four castes beginning with the rulers and warriors (*rgyal rigs, kṣatriya*). See Asaṅga, *Sa'i dngos gzhi, Maulībhūmi,* Tōh. 4035, D. 21a5; a Sanskrit edition in Bhattacharya, *The Yogācārabhūmi,* 42.16–17; an English translation in Kajiyama, "Buddhist Cosmology," 197.
45. The *Puruṣasūkta* in the *Ṛg veda* 10.90; an English translation in Doniger O'Flaherty, *Textual Sources,* 27–28.

46. Skt. *brāhmaṇa.*
47. Tib. *rgyal rigs;* Skt. *kṣatriya.*
48. Skt. *vaiśya.*
49. Skt. *śūdra.*
50. Gombrich, "Buddha's Book," 166.
51. See Collins, "Discourse on What Is Primary."
52. See Gethin, *Sayings of the Buddha,* 116–17.
53. Rhys Davids and Rhys Davids, *Dialogues of the Buddha.*
54. Gethin, "Cosmology and Meditation," 112–32; and Gethin, *Sayings of the Buddha,* 116–28.
55. *Brahmajāla Sutta* in the *Dīgha Nikāya* of the Pāli canon, and the *Tshangs pa'i dra ba'i mdo, Brahmajāla Sūtra,* Tōh. 352; an English translation in Bhikkhu Bodhi, *Discourse on the All-Embracing.*
56. *Dīgha Nikāya* i 17–18; an English translation in Bhikkhu Bodhi, *Discourse on the All-Embracing,* 66 (with minor changes).
57. *Bṛhadāraṇyaka Upaniṣad,* 4; an English translation in Olivelle, *Early Upanisads* 45–47. In this story as well, the world lacked real distinctions at the beginning.
58. Norman, "Theravāda Buddhism," 272.
59. *Brahmajāla Sutta* in the *Dīgha Nikāya* i 17, translated by Bhikkhu Bodhi, *Discourse on the All-Embracing,* 66 (with minor changes).
60. More specifically, this account is told as the fifth wrong view, which is part eternalism and part noneternalism. For an explanation of this view, see Anālayo, "Sixty-Two Views," 27–28.
61. For magnificent depictions of the cosmos in Himalayan Buddhism, see Huntington, *Creating the Universe.* See also Kloetzli, *Buddhist Cosmology;* and Sadakata, *Buddhist Cosmology.*
62. Tib. *bskal pa;* Skt. *kalpa.* Tsong kha pa, *Bung ba'i re skong,* 13b3.
63. Daśabalaśrīmitra (Stobs bcu dpal bshes gnyen), *'Dus byas dang 'dus ma byas rnam par nges pa, Saṃskṛtāsaṃskṛtaviniścaya,* chap. 8, Tōh. 3897, D. *ha,* 122b5–6.
64. According to Vasubandhu, there are eight *krośa* in a *yojana.* Thus, this is a massive enclosure. See his *Mdzod, Kośa,* chap. 3, v. 88a, Tōh. 4089, D. 10a5; a Sanskrit edition in Pradhan, *Abhidharmakośabhāṣyam,* 177; an English translation in Pruden, *Vasubandhu,* 474.
65. Tib. *gzugs khams;* Skt. *rūpadhātu.*
66. Tib. *khams gsum;* Skt. *traidhātuka.*
67. Tib. *gzugs med pa'i khams;* Skt. *ārūpyadhātu.*
68. See Gethin, "Cosmology and Meditation."
69. Tib. *snyoms par 'jug pa;* Skt. *samāpatti.*
70. Tib. *skye ba;* Skt. *upapatti.* Vasubandhu, *Mdzod 'grel, Kośabhāṣya,* chap. 8, v. 1, Tōh. 4090, D. *khu,* 65b2–3; a Sanskrit edition in Pradhan, *Abhidharmakośabhāṣyam,* 432; an English translation in Pruden, *Vasubandhu,* 1215. Vasubandhu explains *dhyāna* in the sense of birth or a place of rebirth in the third

chapter of his *Mdzod 'grel, Kośabhāṣya,* which is dedicated to the subject of the world; *dhyāna* as meditative absorption is explained in the eighth chapter of the same work, which is dedicated to the subject of absorptions.

71. See Vasubandhu, *Mdzod 'grel, Kośabhāṣya,* chap. 3, vv. 89d–93c, Tōh. 4090, D. *ku,* 155b3–57b5; a Sanskrit edition in Pradhan, *Abhidharmakośabhāṣyam,* 179–83; an English translation in Pruden, *Vasubandhu,* 475–78; Asaṅga, *Sa'i dngos gzhi, Maulībhūmi,* Tōh. 4035, D. 18a5–20b4; a Sanskrit edition in Bhattacharya, *The Yogācārabhūmi,* 36.19–41.17; an English translation in Kajiyama, "Buddhist Cosmology," 190–96. Nāgabuddhi, *Rnam gzhag rim pa, Vyavastholi,* chap. 1, Tōh. 1809, D. 121b5–22a3; Sanskrit and Tibetan editions in Tanaka, *Vyavastholi,* 81–83.
72. Tib. 'Dod lha; Skt. Kāmadeva. There are six gods in the upper spheres of the Desire Realm. They are listed in the section "The Destruction of the World and Its Inhabitants" in this chapter. Tsong kha pa, *Bung ba'i re skong,* 11b6–12a1.
73. Tsong kha pa, *Bung ba'i re skong,* 12a1–2.
74. Nāgabuddhi, *Rnam gzhag rim pa, Vyavastholi,* chap. 1, Tōh. 1809, D. 121b5–22a1; Sanskrit and Tibetan editions in Tanaka, *Vyavastholi,* 80–81.
75. These are the four higher heavens of the gods residing in the Desire Realm. For their names see the section "The Gods" in this chapter.
76. Tsong kha pa, *Rnam gzhag rim pa'i rnam bshad,* 10a1–2.
77. Tsong kha pa, *Bung ba'i re skong,* 12a2–4.
78. The water is held either by the power of the shared karma of beings or by the wind. See Vasubandhu, *Mdzod 'grel, Kośabhāṣya,* chap. 3, v. 46a–b, Tōh. 4090, D. *ku,* 144a7–b1; a Sanskrit edition in Pradhan, *Abhidharmakośabhāṣyam,* 158; an English translation in Pruden, *Vasubandhu,* 452; and for the second explanation alone, see Asaṅga, *Sa'i dngos gzhi, Maulībhūmi,* Tōh. 4035, D. 18b6; a Sanskrit edition in Bhattacharya, *The Yogācārabhūmi,* 37; an English translation in Kajiyama, "Buddhist Cosmology," 191.
79. Tsong kha pa, *Bung ba'i re skong,* 12a4.
80. Doniger, *Hindu Myths,* 22–23.
81. According to Vasubandhu, the wind cylinder is 1.6 million *yojanas* in height; the water is 800,000 *yojanas;* and the gold is 320,000 *yojanas* in height. The diameter of both the water and the gold cylinders is 1,203,450 *yojanas,* and its circumference is three times that. The diameter of the wind cylinder is immeasurable. See his *Mdzod 'grel, Kośabhāṣya,* chap. 3, vv. 45–48a, Tōh. 4090, D. *ku,* 144a4–b4; a Sanskrit edition in Pradhan, *Abhidharmakośabhāṣyam,* 157–58; an English translation in Pruden, *Vasubandhu,* 451–52.
82. This question is raised in Nāgabuddhi, *Rnam gzhag rim pa, Vyavastholi,* chap. 1, Tōh. 1809, D. 121b7–22a1; Sanskrit and Tibetan editions in Tanaka, *Vyavastholi,* 82. See also Tsong kha pa, *Rnam gzhag rim pa'i rnam bshad,* 10b4–6.
83. Tsong kha pa, *Bung ba'i re skong,* 12a4–5. Tsong kha pa relies here on Vasu-

bandhu, *Mdzod 'grel, Kośabhāṣya,* chap. 2, v. 22, which explains that the tiniest particles in the Desire Realm consist of eight components: earth, water, fire, wind, visible objects, scents, tastes, and tangibles. See his *Rnam gzhag rim pa'i rnam bshad,* 10b4–6.

84. Tsong kha pa, *Bung ba'i re skong,* 12a5–b1.
85. Tib. *ri rab* or *lhun po.*
86. Gnya' shing 'dzin, Yugandhara; Gshol mda' 'dzin, Īṣādhara; Seng ldeng can, Khadiraka; Blta na sdug, Sudarśana; Rta rna, Aśvakarṇa; Rnam 'dud, Vinitaka; and Mu khyud 'dzin ri, Nimindhara. See Vasubandhu, *Mdzod 'grel, Kośabhāṣya,* chap. 3, vv. 48b–49c, Tōh. 4090, D. *ku,* 144b4–5; a Sanskrit edition in Pradhan, *Abhidharmakośabhāṣyam,* 158–59; an English translation in Pruden, *Vasubandhu,* 452.
87. Tib. Lcags ri mu khyud, Lcags ri khor yug; Skt. Cakravāḍa.
88. These are cool, tasty, light, soft, clear, odorless, harmless to the throat if swallowed, and harmless to the stomach; see Vasubandhu, *Mdzod 'grel, Kośabhāṣya,* chap. 3, v. 51c, Tōh. 4090, *ku,* D. 145b1–2; a Sanskrit edition in Pradhan, *Abhidharmakośabhāṣyam,* 160; an English translation in Pruden, *Vasubandhu,* 454.
89. Tib. Mu khyud 'dzin; Skt. Nimindhara.
90. The height of the eight other mountains decreases by half, successively, the further the mountain is from Meru. See Vasubandhu, *Mdzod 'grel, Kośabhāṣya,* chap. 3, v. 51a, Tōh. 4090, D. *ku,* 145a6–b1; a Sanskrit edition in Pradhan, *Abhidharmakośabhāṣyam,* 160; an English translation in Pruden, *Vasubandhu,* 453–54.
91. While Vasubandhu (*Kośabhāṣya,* chap. 3, v. 50a) and Asaṅga (*Sa'i dngos gzhi, Maulībhūmi,* Tōh. 4035, D. 19a2 [Sanskrit edition in Bhattacharya, *The Yogācārabhūmi,* 38.7; English translation in Kajiyama, "Buddhist Cosmology," 192]) have crystal in the western direction (Tib. *shel;* Skt. *sphaṭika*), in the commentary on the *Kośa* by Mchims 'Jam pa'i dbyangs, it is a red crystal; see Coghlan, *Ornament of Abhidharma,* 438. According to Paṇchen Blo bzang chos kyi rgyal mtshan, the western direction of Meru is made of ruby (*Padmarāga*). See his *Bskyed rim dngos grub rgya mtsho'i snying po,* 33a1, and Bentor and Dorjee, *The Essence,* 107.
92. Vasubandhu, *Mdzod 'grel, Kośabhāṣya,* chap. 3, v. 50a, Tōh. 4090, D. *ku,* 144b6–45a1; a Sanskrit edition in Pradhan, *Abhidharmakośabhāṣyam,* 159; an English translation in Pruden, *Vasubandhu,* 452–53.
93. Tsong kha pa, *Rnam gzhag rim pa'i rnam bshad,* 11a1–2. Tsong kha pa is following here Vasubandhu: "The *kalpa* of creation lasts from the primordial wind until the formation of the hell dwellers." See his *Kośabhāṣya,* chap. 3, v. 90cd, Tōh. 4090, D. *ku,* 155b3–4; a Sanskrit edition in Pradhan, *Abhidharmakośabhāṣyam,* 179; an English translation in Pruden, *Vasubandhu,* 477–78.
94. See Kloetzli, *Buddhist Cosmology,* and Sadakata, *Buddhist Cosmology.*

95. See Vasubandhu, *Mdzod, Kośa,* chap. 3, v. 58ab, Tōh. 4089, D. 9a4; a Sanskrit edition in Pradhan, *Abhidharmakośabhāṣyam,* 163; an English translation in Pruden, *Vasubandhu,* 456.
96. Tib. *yi dwags;* Skt. *preta.*
97. See Vasubandhu, *Mdzod 'grel, Kośabhāṣya,* chap. 3, v. 59cd, Tōh. 4090, D. *ku,* 148a4–5; a Sanskrit edition in Pradhan, *Abhidharmakośabhāṣyam,* 165; an English translation in Pruden, *Vasubandhu,* 460.
98. Tib. *yi dwags;* Skt. *preta.*
99. Tib. *lha;* Skt. *deva.*
100. Tsong kha pa, *Lam gyi gtso bo rnam gsum gyi rtsa ba,* in *Bka' 'bum thor bu,* 230b5–31b5; a Tibetan edition and an English translation in Sonam, *Three Principal Aspects.*
101. Nāgārjuna, *Bshes pa'i spring yig, Suhṛllekha,* v. 99, Tōh. 4182, D. 45a; a Sanskrit edition in GRETIL; a Tibetan edition and an English translation in Padmakara Translation Group, *Nagarjuna's Letter,* 66–67, 137. Nāgārjuna describes in this work the suffering of all forms of *saṃsāric* living.
102. See Śāntideva, *Byang chub sems dpa'i spyod pa la 'jug pa, Bodhicaryāvatāra,* chap. 4, v. 20, Tōh. 3871; an English translation in Padmakara Translation Group, *Way of the Bodhisattva,* 57; and the *Sutta on Fools and Wise Men, Bālapaṇḍita Sutta* in the *Majjhima Nikāya,* 129, iii 169–70; an English translation in Ñāṇamoli and Bodhi, *The Middle Length,* 1020–21.
103. Tib. *sum cu gsum pa'i lha rnams;* Skt. *trayastriṃśā.* See Vasubandhu, *Mdzod, Kośa,* chap. 3, v. 65a, Tōh. 4089, D. 9a7; a Sanskrit edition in Pradhan, *Abhidharmakośabhāṣyam,* 167; an English translation in Pruden, *Vasubandhu,* 463.
104. Tib. *mnar med;* Skt. *avīci.*
105. Vasubandhu, *Mdzod 'grel, Kośabhāṣya,* chap. 3, v. 90ab, Tōh. 4090, D. *ku,* 155b4; a Sanskrit edition in Pradhan, *Abhidharmakośabhāṣyam,* 178; an English translation in Pruden, *Vasubandhu,* 475.
106. Vasubandhu, *Mdzod 'grel, Kośabhāṣya,* chap. 8, v. 38, Tōh. 4090, D. *khu,* 81a5–b1; a Sanskrit edition in Pradhan, *Abhidharmakośabhāṣyam,* 459; an English translation in Pruden, *Vasubandhu,* 1280.
107. See also Gethin, "Cosmology and Meditation," 197–98.
108. Tib. *chos nyid;* Skt. *dharmatā.* This force operates along with two other forces that can give rise to the *dhyānas* in the Realm of Subtle Materiality, the force of causality and the force of karma (Tib. *rgyu dang las kyi stobs;* Skt. *hetubala* and *karmabala*). The force of causality refers to repeated habituation.
109. Tib. *dge ba'i chos;* Skt. *kuśaladharma.*
110. Asaṅga, *Sa'i dngos gzhi, Maulībhūmi,* Tōh. 4035, D. 20b4–6; a Sanskrit edition in Bhattacharya, *The Yogācārabhūmi,* 41.17–42.2; an English translation in Kajiyama, "Buddhist Cosmology," 196.

111. *Visuddhimagga,* 13:33–35; an English translation in Ñāṇamoli, *Visuddhimagga,* 408–9, as Gethin, "Cosmology and Meditation," points out.
112. Vasubandhu, *Mdzod 'grel, Kośabhāṣya,* chap. 3, v. 90ab, Tōh. 4090, D. *ku,* 155b6–7; a Sanskrit edition in Pradhan, *Abhidharmakośabhāṣyam,* 178; an English translation in Pruden, *Vasubandhu,* 476.
113. Tsong kha pa, *Bung ba'i re skong,* 10a2.
114. Tsong kha pa, *Bung ba'i re skong,* 10a2–4.
115. Tib. *bsam gtan dang po.*
116. Tsong kha pa, *Bung ba'i re skong,* 10a4–6. See the section on "How the First People Appear in the World," above.
117. Vasubandhu, *Mdzod 'grel, Kośabhāṣya,* chap. 8, v. 38, Tōh. 4090, D. *khu,* 81a5–b1; a Sanskrit edition in Pradhan, *Abhidharmakośabhāṣyam,* 459; an English translation in Pruden, *Vasubandhu,* 1280.
118. Tib. *bdag nyid kyis slob dpon med par;* Skt. *svayam anācāryakaṃ.* See Vasubandhu, *Mdzod 'grel, Kośabhāṣya,* chap. 3, v. 90ab, Tōh. 4090, D. *ku,* 156a1; a Sanskrit edition in Pradhan, *Abhidharmakośabhāṣyam,* 178; an English translation in Pruden, *Vasubandhu,* 476. According to Mahāmaudgalyāyana, *'Jig rten gzhags pa, Lokaprajñapti,* Tōh. 4086, D. 52b4, *lung med par,* without a scriptural transmission.
119. Tib. Lus 'phags po.
120. Tib. Ba glang spyod.
121. Tib. Sgra mi snyan.
122. Tib. *rnam smin gyi sgrib pa;* Skt. *vipākāvaraṇa.* See Vasubandhu, *Mdzod 'grel, Kośabhāṣya,* chap. 4, before v. 96, Tōh. 4090, D. *ku,* 215a2; a Sanskrit edition in Pradhan, *Abhidharmakośabhāṣyam,* 158–59; an English translation in Pruden, *Vasubandhu,* 678–80.
123. Tsong kha pa, *Bung ba'i re skong,* 10a6–b2.
124. These six gods from lower to higher are: the Four Great Kings in the four directions (Rgyal chen [rigs] bzhi, Cāturmahārājakāyika); the gods of the Thirty-Three (Sum cu rtsa gsum, Trāyastriṃśa); the Gods Free from Conflict ('Thab bral, Yāma); the Joyful (Dga' ldan, Tuṣita); the Gods Delighting in Emanations ('Phrul dga', Nirmāṇarati); and the Masters over Others' Emanations (Gzhan 'phrul dbang byed, Paranirmitavaśavart). See also Vasubandhu, *Mdzod 'grel, Kośabhāṣya,* chap. 3, v. 1, Tōh. 4090, D. *ku,* 108b3–4; a Sanskrit edition in Pradhan, *Abhidharmakośabhāṣyam,* 111; an English translation in Pruden, *Vasubandhu,* 365. The Four Great Kings (in the first level) are Dhṛtarāṣṭra, Yul 'khor srung, in the east; Virūḍhaka, 'Phags skyes po, in the south; Virūpākṣa, Mig mi bzang, in the west; and Vaiśravaṇa, Rnam sras, in the north. They are listed in Tsong kha pa, *Bung ba'i re skong,* [10b].
125. Tsong kha pa, *Bung ba'i re skong,* 10b2–3.
126. Tsong kha pa, *Bung ba'i re skong,* 10b3–5.

127. Tsong kha pa, *Rnam gzhag rim pa'i rnam bshad,* 7b5–6.
128. See Asaṅga, *Sa'i dngos gzhi, Maulībhūmi,* Tōh. 4035, D. 17b1–6; a Sanskrit edition in Bhattacharya, *The Yogācārabhūmi,* 35.5–18; an English translation in Kajiyama, "Buddhist Cosmology," 188–89. In his *Bung ba'i re skong,* 10b5–11a3, Tsong kha pa describes the seven suns in detail following Asaṅga, *Sa'i dngos gzhi, Maulībhūmi,* Tōh. 4035.
129. Vasubandhu, *Mdzod, Kośa,* chap. 3, v. 100ab, Tōh. 4089, D. 10a5; a Sanskrit edition in Pradhan, *Abhidharmakośabhāṣyam,* 189; an English translation in Pruden, *Vasubandhu,* 490.
130. Asaṅga, *Sa'i dngos gzhi, Maulībhūmi,* Tōh. 4035, D. 18a2–3; a Sanskrit edition in Bhattacharya, *The Yogācārabhūmi,* 36.7–11; an English translation in Kajiyama, "Buddhist Cosmology," 190.
131. Vasubandhu, *Mdzod, Kośa,* chap. 3, v. 3a, Tōh. 4089, D. 7a2; a Sanskrit edition in Pradhan, *Abhidharmakośabhāṣyam,* 112; an English translation in Pruden, *Vasubandhu,* 366.
132. Vasubandhu, *Mdzod 'grel, Kośabhāṣya,* chap. 8, v. 2c, Tōh. 4090, D. *khu,* 66b2–3; a Sanskrit edition in Pradhan, *Abhidharmakośabhāṣyam,* 433–34; an English translation in Pruden, *Vasubandhu,* 1219.
133. Tib. *gzugs kyi phung po;* Skt. *rūpaskandha.*
134. *Mahāsaccaka Sutta.* For a study of this *Sutta* along with Sanskrit and Chinese parallel passages, see Anālayo, *Comparative Study,* 232–46.
135. As noted, "*dhyāna*" in Sanskrit is equivalent to "*jhāna*" in Pāli. In the following citation by Ñāṇamoli and Bodhi, the term "*jhāna*" is used.
136. *Majjhima Nikāya,* i 247; translated by Ñāṇamoli and Bodhi, *The Middle Length, Sutta* 36, 34–37, with minor adjustments.
137. *Laṭukikopama Sutta.* According to Anālayo (*Comparative Study,* 367), this *Sutta* is unique in attaching the four levels of the Immaterial Realm to the four *dhyānas.* Still the two sets of four absorptions do appear separately in various *Suttas* of the Pāli canon.
138. *Majjhima Nikāya,* i 455; translated by Ñāṇamoli and Bodhi, *The Middle Length, Sutta* 66, 26–29.
139. The meditation on infinite space surmounts the levels mentioned before it.
140. *Majjhima Nikāya,* i 455; translated by Ñāṇamoli and Bodhi, *The Middle Length, Sutta* 66, 30.
141. Tib. *nam mkha' mtha' yas, rnam shes mtha' yas, ci yang med pa,* and *'du shes med 'du shes med min;* Skt. *ākāśānantya, vijñānānantya, ākiñcanya,* and *naivasaṃjñānāsaṃjña.*
142. The meditation on the cessation of perception and feeling surmounts the meditation on neither-perception-nor-nonperception.
143. *Majjhima Nikāya,* i 456; translated by Ñāṇamoli and Bodhi, *The Middle Length, Sutta* 66, 34.
144. Tib. *'du shes dang tshor ba 'gog pa;* Skt. *saṃjñāvedayitanirodha.*

145. Vasubandhu, *Mdzod 'grel, Kośabhāṣya,* chap. 8, vv. 1–2, Tōh. 4090, D. *khu,* 65b2–66b5; a Sanskrit edition in Pradhan, *Abhidharmakośabhāṣyam,* 432–34; an English translation in Pruden, *Vasubandhu,* 1215–20.
146. The cessation of perception and feeling, however, appear in a different configuration. It follows the fourth *dhyāna* and the four absorptions of the Immaterial Realm as the eighth deliverance (Tib. *rnam par thar pa;* Skt. *vimokṣa*). The *Kośabhāṣya* explains that the cessation of perception and feeling is called deliverance because it turns away from perceptions and feelings (or rather from all conditional things) (Tib. *'du byed;* Skt. *saṃskṛta*). See Vasubandhu, *Mdzod 'grel, Kośabhāṣya,* chap. 8, v. 33c, Tōh. 4090, D. *khu,* 79b4–5; a Sanskrit edition in Pradhan, *Abhidharmakośabhāṣyam,* 455–56; an English translation in Pruden, *Vasubandhu,* 1273–74.
147. See Sasaki, "Concept of Remodelling."
148. Pāli *ucchedavāda.* See Bhikkhu Bodhi, *Connected Discourses,* 28–30.
149. This is evidenced by certain discussions in Pāli *Suttas* as cited in Sharf, "Is Nirvāṇa the Same?," 145–46. For example, in the *Discourse on the Simile of the Snake,* the Buddha explains that people who interpreted him as teaching annihilation or extermination misrepresent his words. Thus, the authors of this *Sutta* found it necessary to explain away the notion of extinction found in other Buddhist scriptures. See *Alagaddūpama Sutta,* in the *Majjhima Nikāya,* i 136 and 140, translated by Ñāṇamoli and Bodhi, *The Middle Length, Sutta* 22.20. Similarly in the *Yamaka Sutta* Sāriputta comforts a distressed monk by telling him that once he will destroy his taints and become arahant (arhat), it is his aggregates that will be destroyed and it is his suffering that will cease, but he himself will not perish. See *Saṃyutta Nikāya* 22.85.3, translated by Bhikkhu Bodhi, *Connected Discourses,* 931–33.
150. Nakamura, "Process of the Origination," 269–72, shows that in the *Pārāyana Vagga* the Buddha taught nothingness in order to put an end to clinging and desire. Later in the *Aṭṭhaka Vagga,* the Buddha taught neither-perception-nor-nonperception, as a means to avoid a nihilistic view that may arise from nothingness.
151. Skt. Ārāḍa Kālāma and Udraka Rāmaputra; Pāli, Āḷāra Kālāma and Uddaka Rāmaputta.
152. See, for example, *Ariyapariyesanā Sutta,* in the *Majjhima Nikāya,* i 163–68, translated by Ñāṇamoli and Bodhi, *The Middle Length, Sutta* 26.14–19. Other sources are discussed in Anālayo, *Comparative Study,* 174–78, including the *Madhyama Āgama,* Sanskrit fragments paralleling the *Mahāsaccaka Sutta, Divyāvadāna,* the *Lalitavistara,* the *Buddhacarita,* the *Mahāvastu,* the *Saṅghabhedavastu,* Dharmaguptaka *Vinaya,* and the Pāli commentary to the *Therīgāthā.* As Nakamura, "Process of the Origination," 275, points out, the two teachers Ārāḍa Kālāma and Udraka Rāmaputra are disparaged in the Pāli canon. For example, see *Saṃyutta Nikāya,* iv 83–84; an English translation in Bhikkhu

Bodhi, *Connected Discourses,* 1182–83; and *Dīgha Nikāya,* iii, 126–27; an English translation in Walshe, *Long Discourses,* 431–32.

153. Anālayo, "Buddha's Pre-awakening."
154. Tsong kha pa, *Bsam gzugs zin bris;* an English translation in Zahler, *Study and Practice,* 239–349.
155. Tib. *phar phyin;* Skt. *pāramitā.* See Zahler, *Study and Practice,* 291–93.
156. See Zahler, *Study and Practice,* 273.
157. Tsong kha pa, *Bung ba'i re skong,* 18b4 and 23a3.
158. Zahler, *Study and Practice,* 275.
159. Tib. *sa bcu;* Skt. *daśabhūmi.*
160. The path of accumulation (Tib. *tshogs lam;* Skt. *saṃbhāramārga*), the path of preparation (Tib. *sbyor lam;* Skt. *prayogamārga*), the path of seeing (Tib. *mthong lam;* Skt. *darśanamārga*), the path of meditation (Tib. *sgom lam;* Skt. *bhāvanāmārga*), and the path of no further practice (Tib. *mi slob lam;* Skt. *aśaikṣamārga*).
161. There were early spatial cosmologies such as the thousandfold world system, but these were not especially related to meditative states. See Gethin, "Cosmology and Meditation," 114.
162. These are Vipaśyin, Śikhin, Viśvabhuj, Krakucchanda, Kanakamuni, and Kāśyapa.
163. See Strong, *Buddhisms,* chaps. 3 and 8.
164. See the *Bahudhātuka Sutta:* "It cannot happen that two Accomplished Ones, Fully Enlightened Ones, could arise contemporaneously in one world-system—there is no such possibility." In the *Majjhima Nikāya,* iii 65; an English translation in Ñāṇamoli and Bodhi, *The Middle Length,* 929, *Sutta* 115.14. See likewise *Aṅguttara Nikāya;* an English translation in Bhikkhu Bodhi, *The Numerical Discourses,* 114. The commentary explains that this refers to the entire cycle from the point a buddha-to-be takes birth until his teachings completely disappeared. See Ñāṇamoli and Bodhi, *The Middle Length,* 1320–21, n. 1089.
165. Tib. *sangs rgyas zhing;* Skt. *buddhakṣetra.*
166. For Mahāyāna and Vajrayāna ways of meeting the buddhas, see Strong, *Buddhisms,* chap. 8.
167. The Larger and Shorter *Sukhāvatīvyūha Sūtras, Bde ba can gyi bkod pa.* See Gómez, *Land of Bliss.*
168. Gómez, *The Land of Bliss,* 73, vow 30.
169. See Strong, *Buddhisms,* chap. 8.
170. Gómez, *The Land of Bliss,* 71, vow 15.
171. Tib. Dga' ldan.
172. See the section above, "The Gods," in this chapter.
173. The first monastery Tsong kha pa founded is called Ganden (Dga' ldan), i.e., Tuṣita. On devotional practices related to Tsong kha pa, Maitreya, and Tuṣita as pure land in the Dge lugs school, see Apple, "Maitreya's Tuṣita Heaven."

174. Tib. *bde ba can.*
175. For more about buddha-fields and Sukhāvatī, see Gómez, *Land of Bliss,* and Strong, *Buddhisms,* chap. 8.3.
176. Orzech, "Note Concerning Contemplation."
177. See, for example, Kloppenborg and Poelmeyer, "Visualizations," 83; Lopez, *Elaborations on Emptiness,* 129; McMahan, *Empty Vision,* 149; and Sarbacker, *Samādhi,* 117–18.
178. Tsong kha pa, *Sngags rim chen mo,* chap. 12, 472–73; an English translation in Yarnall, *Tsong Khapa's Great Stages,* 158–59.
179. Tib. *nga rgyal;* Skt. *ahaṃkāra.*
180. Tib. *lus dran pa nye bar gzhag;* Skt. *kāyasmṛtyupasthāna.*
181. See, for example, *Blo gros mi zad pas bstan pa, Akṣayamatinirdeśa Sūtra,* Tōh. 175; a Tibetan edition in Braarvig, *Akṣayamatinirdeśa,* 1:126–28; an English translation in 2:481–89.
182. *Da ltar gyi sangs rgyas, Pratyutpanna,* Tōh. 133; see Harrison, *Samādhi of Direct Encounter,* viii.
183. Harrison, "Commemoration and Identification."
184. Harrison, *Samādhi of Direct Encounter,* 3B–3C, 32–33.
185. Harrison, "Commemoration and Identification," 226; see also Harrison, *Samādhi of Direct Encounter,* 8A, 69.
186. Tsong kha pa, *Rim lnga gsal sgron,* chap. 7, 261b1–5; an English translation in Kilty, *Lamp to Illuminate,* 427.
187. Tib. *khang pa [bu] brtsegs pa;* Skt. *kūṭāgāra.*
188. Gómez, "Bodhisattva as Wonder-Worker," and Gómez, "On Buddhist Wonders."
189. Strong, "Sudhana's Vision," 157.
190. See, for example, McMahan, "Transpositions of Metaphor," and *Empty Vision,* chaps. 4–5; and Osto, *Power, Wealth,* and "Proto-Tantric."
191. Tib. Sa skya pa. See Zhu chen, "Gsang ba 'dus pa," 2b6.
192. Tib. Dge lugs pa. See Tsong kha pa, *Gsang mngon,* 12b–13a.
193. See Tāranātha, *Gsang ba 'dus pa,* 102.
194. See *Sa bcu'i le'u* or *Sa bcu'i mdo, Daśabhūmika Sūtra* [included in Tōh. 44], chap. 10, passim, for example; Vaidya, *Daśabhūmikasūtra,* 61, lines 15–17; Honda, "Annotated Translation," 270.
195. The *Sgra sbyor bam po gnyis pa, Nighaṇṭu,* Tōh. 4347, Braarvig, Thesaurus Literaturae Buddhicae, that comments on a selection of terms found in the *Bye brag tu rtogs par byed pa, Mahāvyutpatti,* Tōh. 4346. See Verhagen, "The *Sgra-sbyor-bam-po-gñis-pa,*" 135; Lessing and Wayman, *Mkhas grub rje's Fundamentals,* 270, n. 1; and Wayman, "The *Maṇḍa* and the *-la,*" 23–30.
196. *Bye brag tu rtogs par byed pa, Mahāvyutpatti,* Tōh. 4346, in Braarvig, Thesaurus Literaturae Buddhicae.
197. Tib. *snying po, dbyings, dkyil;* Skt. *sāra.*

198. Tib. *len pa, 'dzin pa;* Skt. *ādana.*
199. Tib. *dkyil 'khor.*
200. Buddhaguhya, Sangs rgyas gsang ba, *Dkyil 'khor gyi chos mdor bsdus pa, Dharmamaṇḍala Sūtra,* Tōh. 3705, 2b1; an English translation in Lo Bue, "The *Dharmamaṇḍala-sūtra,*" 796.
201. Tsong kha pa, *Bung ba'i re skong,* 15a3.
202. Tib. *mi gnas pa'i mya ngan las 'das pa;* Skt. *apratiṣṭhanirvāṇa.*
203. Skt. *saṃsāra-nirvāṇābhyām avinivartanāt;* Tib. *'khor ba dang mya ngan las 'das pa gnyis las mi ldog pa.* Or else, they abide in neither *saṃsāra* nor *nirvāṇa.* Skt. *saṃsāra-nirvāṇāpratiṣṭhatā;* Tib. *'khor ba dang mya ngan las 'das pa la mi gnas pa.* See Vasubandhu, *Dbus dang mtha' rnam par 'byed pa'i 'grel pa, Madhyānta-vibhāgakārikābhāṣya,* chap. 5, v. 29, Tōh. 4027, D. 26b3–4.
204. Skt. *saṃsāra-nirvāṇa-vimukti.*
205. See the section "The *Samādhi* of Great Bliss" in chapter 3.

2. The Person

1. Tib. *mi rtag pa, bdag med,* and *sdug bsngal;* Skt. *anitya, anātman,* and *duḥkha.* The Great Vehicle points to emptiness as well.
2. Tib. *mi sdug pa bsgom pa;* Skt. *aśubhabhāvanā.*
3. Tib. *'od gsal;* Skt. *prabhāsvara.*
4. On various occasions, the fourteenth Dalai Lama relates that he practices this meditation every morning.
5. Tib. *phung po;* Skt. *skandha.*
6. Tib. *khams;* Skt. *dhātu.*
7. Tib. *dbang po;* Skt. *indriya.*
8. Tib. *yul;* Skt. *viṣaya.*
9. Tib. *[gzhi dus kyi] ye shes;* Skt. *jñāna.*
10. These are infinite space, infinite consciousness, nothingness, and neither-perception-nor-nonperception.
11. Tsong kha pa, *Bung ba'i re skong,* 15b4–5. This is based on Nāgabuddhi, *Rnam gzhag rim pa, Vyavastholi,* chap. 1, Tōh. 1809, D. 129b6; Sanskrit and Tibetan editions in Tanaka, *Vyavastholi,* 130–31; and Nāgārjuna, *Mdor byas, Piṇḍīkrama Sādhana,* Tōh. 1796, D. 3b1–2; a Sanskrit edition in de La Vallée Poussin, *Études et textes tantriques,* v. 39. See also Tsong kha pa, *Rnam gzhag rim pa'i rnam bshad,* 82b1–6.
12. See the section "How the First People Appear in the World" in chapter 1.
13. Dbyangs can dga' ba'i blo gros, *Gzhi sku gsum gyi rnam gzhag rab gsal sgron me,* 2a1–2; an English translation in Lati Rinbochay and Hopkins, *Death, Intermediate State,* 30.
14. Tib. *rtsa;* Skt. *nāḍi* or *nāḍī.*
15. Tib. *thig le;* Skt. *bindu.*

16. Tib. *mi shigs pa'i thig le.*
17. Tib. *srog 'dzin;* Skt. *prāṇa.*
18. Dbyangs can dga' ba'i blo gros, *Gzhi sku gsum gyi rnam gzhag rab gsal sgron me,* 2a2; an English translation in Lati Rinbochay and Hopkins, *Death, Intermediate State,* 30.
19. This explanation is found in Nāgabuddhi's *Rnam gzhag rim pa, Vyavastholi,* chap. 1, Tōh. 1809, D. 124b6–7; Sanskrit and Tibetan editions in Tanaka, *Vyavastholi,* 97.
20. Nāgārjuna, *Mdor byas, Piṇḍīkrama Sādhana,* Tōh. 1796, D. 3b1–4; a Sanskrit edition in de La Vallée Poussin, *Études et textes tantriques,* vv. 39–44ab.
21. Tsong kha pa, *Bung ba'i re skong,* 15b4–5.
22. Tsong kha pa, *Bung ba'i re skong,* 16a1–2.
23. Tsong kha pa, *Bung ba'i re skong,* 16a4–5.
24. Tsong kha pa, *Bung ba'i re skong,* 16b1–2.
25. Tib. *me long lta bu'i ye shes, mnyam pa nyid kyi ye shes, so sor rtog pa'i ye shes,* and *bya ba sgrub pa'i ye shes;* Skt. *ādarśajnāna samatājñāna, pratyavekṣaṇājñāna,* and *kṛtyānuṣṭhānajñāna.*
26. Tsong kha pa, *Rnam gzhag rim pa'i rnam bshad,* 80b1–4. Tsong kha pa follows here Āryadeva, *Spyod bsdus, Caryāmelāpakapradīpa,* chap. 2, Tōh. 1803, D. 65a7–b4; Sanskrit and Tibetan editions with an English translation in Wedemeyer, *Āryadeva's Lamp,* A: 13a–b.
27. Tsong kha pa follows here Nāgabuddhi, *Rnam gzhag rim pa, Vyavastholi,* chap. 4, Tōh. 1809, D. 130a2–b5; Sanskrit and Tibetan editions in Tanaka, *Vyavastholi,* 131–35; See also Tsong kha pa, *Rnam gzhag rim pa'i rnam bshad,* 82b1–6.
28. Tsong kha pa, *Bung ba'i re skong,* 15b5–16a1.
29. Tib. *smig rgyu 'dra ba, du ba lta bu, mkha' snang 'dra ba,* and *mar me ltar 'bar;* Skt. *marīcikākāra, dhūmrākāra, khadyotākāra,* and *dīpavajjvala.* Tsong kha pa, *Bung ba'i re skong,* 15b5–17b4. Here Tsong kha pa follows the *Rgyud phyi ma, Uttara Tantra,* Tōh. 443, D. 154b4; a Sanskrit edition in Matsunaga, *The Guhyasamāja,* chap. 18, vv. 150cd–151ab.
30. Note that they do appear in Lati Rinbochay and Jeffrey Hopkins, *Death, Intermediate State,* chart 6, apparently in following the attempt to create a greater systematization in later Dge lugs works, such as Blo bzang lhun grub Paṇḍita, *Rdo rje 'jigs byed chen po'i bskyed rdzogs kyi lam zab mo'i rim pa gnyis kyi rnam gzhag sku gsum nor bu'i bang mdzod las bskyed rim rnam gzhag,* 56a3; an English translation in Sharpa Tulku with Richard Guard, *Jewel Treasure House,* 101.
31. Tsong kha pa, *Bung ba'i re skong,* 16b5–17a2.
32. Note that in the *Concise Sādhana,* which Tsong kha pa follows in describing the first four cycles of dissolutions, there are only five cycles: In the fifth: "The intrinsic natures and appearances enter the aggregate of consciousness, and consciousness, too, enters into clear light. This is explained as 'accompanied by *nirvāṇa*', all-empty and *dharmakāya.*" See Nāgārjuna, *Mdor byas,*

Piṇḍīkrama Sādhana, Tōh. 1796, D. 3b3–4; a Sanskrit edition in de La Vallée Poussin, *Études et textes tantriques*, vv. 43–44.

33. In his commentary on this *Tantra*, *Ye rdor ṭīkā*, 23a4–6, Tsong kha pa explains that here the word "consciousness" (*rnam par shes pa*) refers to all three appearances together, while below it refers only to the third type of consciousness. The three appearances, [white] appearance, enhanced appearance, and approaching attainment, will be explained below.
34. Tib. *sems*, *yid*, and *rnam par shes pa*; Skt. *citta*, *manas*, and *vijñāna*.
35. Tib. *phung po lnga*, *skye mched drug*, and *yul lnga*; Skt. *pañca skandhāḥ*, *ṣaḍ āyatanāni*, and *pañca viṣayāḥ*.
36. The text of the tantra has *rang bzhin gyi snang ba*, meaning "natural appearance." Tsong kha pa, however, explains the term *rang bzhin gyi snang ba* as "intrinsic natures *and* appearances" (without any proposition but as a coordinative compound, Skt. *dvandva*). Intrinsic natures, he says, refer to the eighty inherent activities of the conceptual mind and appearances are trifold: white appearance, enhanced appearance, and approaching attainment. See Tsong kha pa, *Rnam gzhag rim pa'i rnam bshad*, 81a1–2; and *Mtha' gcod*, 101a4–b1.
37. *Ye shes rdo rje kun las btus pa*, *Vajrajñānasamuccaya Tantra*, Tōh. 447, D. 282b2–4.
38. Tib. *srid pa gsum po*; Skt. *bhavatraya*.
39. Tib. *sems*; Skt. *citta*.
40. Tib. *sems byung*; Skt. *caitasika*.
41. Tib. *ma rig pa*; Skt. *avidyā*.
42. Tib. *'od gsal*; Skt. *prabhāsvara*. Āryadeva, 'Phags pa lha, *Bdag byin gyis brlab pa'i rim pa rnam par dbye ba*, *Svādhiṣṭhānakramaprabheda*, vv. 18–21, Tōh. 1805, D. 112b5–7; Sanskrit and Tibetan editions in Pandey, *Bauddhalaghugranthasaṅgraha*, 173 and 183; an English translation in Wedemeyer, "Vajrayāna and Its Doubles," 386. Partly cited also in Tsong kha pa, *Rim lnga gsal sgron*, chap. 6, 213a2–3; an English translation in Kilty, *Lamp to Illuminate*, 355. These lines appear also in Abhayākaragupta, *Man ngag snye ma*, *Āmnāyamañjarī*, Tōh. 1198, D. 193a1–2.
43. Āryadeva, *Spyod bsdus*, *Caryāmelāpakapradīpa*, chap. 4, Tōh. 1803, D. 77a4–7; Sanskrit and Tibetan editions with an English translation in Wedemeyer, *Āryadeva's Lamp*, A: 29b–30a.
44. Tib. *snang ba*, *snang ba mched pa*, and *snang ba thob pa*; Skt. *āloka*, *ālokābhāsa*, and *ālokopalabdha*.
45. Tib. *stong pa*, *shin tu stong pa*, and *stong pa chen po*; Skt. *śūnya*, *atiśūnya*, and *mahāśūnya*.
46. Tib. *sems*, *sems las byung ba*, and *ma rig pa*; Skt. *citta*, *caitasika*, and *avidyā*.
47. Āryadeva, *Spyod bsdus*, *Caryāmelāpakapradīpa*, chap. 4, Tōh. 1803, D. 77b2–78a3; Sanskrit and Tibetan editions with an English translation in Wedemeyer, *Āryadeva's Lamp*, A: 30a–31a. The *Ye shes rdo rje kun las btus pa*, *Vajra-*

jñānasamuccaya Tantra (Tōh. 447, D. 282b6–7) also refers to states of mind that are sun-like and moon-like but does not elaborate.

48. *Ye shes rdo rje kun las btus pa, Vajrajñānasamuccaya Tantra,* Tōh. 447, D. 282b5.
49. *Ye shes rdo rje kun las btus pa, Vajrajñānasamuccaya Tantra,* Tōh. 447, D. 282a4–5. See also Āryadeva, *Spyod bsdus, Caryāmelāpakapradīpa,* chap. 4, Tōh. 1803, D. 78a2–3; Sanskrit and Tibetan editions with an English translation in Wedemeyer, *Āryadeva's Lamp,* A: 31a.
50. Tsong kha pa, *Bung ba'i re skong,* 16b5–17a2.
51. Tsong kha pa's commentary on the *Ye shes rdo rje kun las btus pa'i rgyud, Vajrajñānasamuccaya Tantra,* Tōh. 447, entitled *Ye rdor ṭīkā,* 16b1–2, and his *Rim lnga gsal sgron,* chap. 6, 213b2–4; an English translation in Kilty, *Lamp to Illuminate,* 356.
52. For this yogis must complete the entire tantric path with its two stages, the creation and completion stages.
53. Nāgārjuna, *Rim lnga, Pañcakrama,* chap. 2, vv. 30–32, Tōh. 1802, D. 49a5–7; Sanskrit and Tibetan editions in Mimaki and Tomabechi, *Pañcakrama,* 19–20; a Sanskrit edition and a French translation in Tomabechi, "Étude du *Pañcakrama,*" 131.
54. Tib. *rang bzhin rnam pa brgyad cu.* Āryadeva, *Spyod bsdus, Caryāmelāpakapradīpa,* Tōh. 1803, chap. 4, D. 78b3–4; Sanskrit and Tibetan editions with an English translation in Wedemeyer, *Āryadeva's Lamp,* A: 31b. Tsong kha pa has also *kun rtog brgyad cu rlung.* See his *Rim lnga gsal sgron,* chap. 6, 205b2; an English translation in Kilty, *Lamp to Illuminate,* 345.
55. *Ye shes rdo rje kun las btus pa, Vajrajñānasamuccaya Tantra,* Tōh. 447, D. 284a5 and 284b2.
56. Tib. *kun stong;* Skt. *sarvaśūnya.*
57. Tsong kha pa, *Rim lnga gsal sgron,* chap. 6, 205b1–4; an English translation in Kilty, *Lamp to Illuminate,* 345.
58. Pāli, *vivicca.*
59. See the section "The Meditative States of the Realm of Subtle Materiality and the Immaterial Realm" in chapter 1.
60. For the intermediate being, see Wayman, "The Intermediate-State"; Cuevas, "Predecessors and Prototypes"; Cuevas, *Hidden History,* 39–68; Blezer, *Kar gliṅ Źi khro;* and Kritzer, "Rūpa and the Antarābhava."
61. While the Tibetan tradition as a whole accepts the intermediate state, its existence was debated among Indian Buddhist schools. See Vasubandhu, *Mdzod 'grel, Kośabhāṣya,* chap. 3, vv. 10–12, Tōh. 4090, D. *ku,* 116a4–18a6; a Sanskrit edition in Pradhan, *Abhidharmakośabhāṣyam,* 120–23; an English translation in Pruden, *Vasubandhu,* 383–88.
62. See, for example, Gyurme Dorje, *Tibetan Book of the Dead,* and Thurman, *Tibetan Book of the Dead.*

63. Tib. *bar do thos grol.*
64. *Mngal gnas, Nandagarbhāvakrānti Nirdeśa,* Tōh. 57, D. 211a4–b2; an English translation in Kritzer, *Garbhāvakrāntisūtra.*
65. Vasubandhu, *Mdzod 'grel, Kośabhāṣya,* on chap. 3, vv. 10–17 and vv. 40c–41a, Tōh. 4090, D. *ku,* 116a4–22b5 and 140b3–5; a Sanskrit edition in Pradhan, *Abhidharmakośabhāṣyam,* 119–29 and 153; an English translation in Pruden, *Vasubandhu,* 383–99 and 441–42; Asaṅga's *Chos mngon pa kun las btus pa, Abhidharmasamuccaya,* Tōh. 4049, D. 78a3–b1; a Sanskrit edition in Pradhan, *Abhidharmasamuccaya,* 43; an English translation in Boin-Webb, *Abhidharmasamuccaya,* 93–94. As well as Asaṅga, *Sa'i dngos gzhi, Maulībhūmi,* Tōh. 4035, D. 10a1–b4; a Sanskrit edition in Bhattacharya, *The Yogācārabhūmi,* 18.21–20.14.
66. *Sdom 'byung, Saṃvarodaya Tantra,* Tōh. 373, D. 266a5–6; Sanskrit and Tibetan editions with an English translation in Tsuda, *The Saṃvarodaya Tantra,* chap. 2, 12cd–13.
67. Nāgabuddhi, *Rnam gzhag rim pa, Vyavastholi,* chap. 1, Tōh. 1809, D. 123a4–b1; Sanskrit and Tibetan editions in Tanaka, *Vyavastholi,* 89–90. See Tsong kha pa, *Rnam gzhag rim pa'i rnam bshad,* 23a1–b2. See also Dbyangs can dga' ba'i blo gros, *Gzhi sku gsum gyi rnam gzhag,* 6b8–10b5; an English translation in Lati Rinbochay and Hopkins, *Death, Intermediate State,* 49–57.
68. Tsong kha pa, *Bung ba'i re skong,* 18a4–5.
69. See also Tsong kha pa, *Rnam gzhag rim pa'i rnam bshad,* 29b6–30a3.
70. Tib. *nyer len, nye bar len pa.*
71. Tib. *lhan cig byed rkyen.*
72. See Mkhas grub rje, *Bskyed rim dngos grub rgya mtsho,* 99b3–5.
73. Tsong kha pa, *Bung ba'i re skong,* 11b6. See the section "The Creation of the Inanimate World" in chapter 1.
74. See Asaṅga, *Sa'i dngos gzhi, Maulībhūmi,* Tōh. 4035, D. 10a2–3; Bhattacharya, *The Yogācārabhūmi,* 19.1–2.
75. See Vasubandhu, *Mdzod 'grel, Kośabhāṣya,* chap. 3, v. 9bc, Tōh. 4090, D. *ku,* 115b3; a Sanskrit edition in Pradhan, *Abhidharmakośabhāṣyam,* 119; an English translation in Pruden, *Vasubandhu,* 381; and Nāgabuddhi, *Rnam gzhag rim pa, Vyavastholi,* chap. 1, Tōh. 1809, D. 122a5; Sanskrit and Tibetan editions in Tanaka, *Vyavastholi,* 83–84.
76. See the section "How the First People Appear in the World" in chapter 1.
77. Tsong kha pa, *Bung ba'i re skong,* 18a5–18b6.
78. Tsong kha pa, *Bung ba'i re skong,* 18a6–b1.
79. Vasubandhu, *Mdzod 'grel, Kośabhāṣya,* on chap. 3, vv. 40c–41a, Tōh. 4090, D. *ku,* 140b4–5; a Sanskrit edition in Pradhan, *Abhidharmakośabhāṣyam,* 130; an English translation in Pruden, *Vasubandhu,* 441–42. The explanation of the *Rnal 'byor spyod pa'i sa, Yogācārabhūmi* is akin to the name "birth seeker." See Asaṅga, *Sa'i dngos gzhi, Maulībhūmi,* Tōh. 4035, D. 10b2–4; a Sanskrit edition in Bhattacharya, *The Yogācārabhūmi,* 20.9–13.

80. Tib. *yid las byung ba;* Skt. *manomaya.*
81. Tib. *dri za;* Skt. *gandharva.*
82. Tib. *srid tshol;* Skt. *saṃbhavaiṣin.*
83. Tib. *mngon par 'grub pa;* Skt. *abhinirvṛtti.*
84. Asaṅga, *Sa'i dngos gzhi, Maulībhūmi,* Tōh. 4035, D. 10a7–b1; a Sanskrit edition in Bhattacharya, *The Yogācārabhūmi,* 20.4–6; an English translation in Wayman, "Intermediate-State," 261.
85. Tsong kha pa, *Bung ba'i re skong,* 18b1–2.
86. Vasubandhu, *Mdzod 'grel, Kośabhāṣya,* on chap. 3, v. 14d, Tōh. 4090, D. *ku,* 120b3; a Sanskrit edition in Pradhan, *Abhidharmakośabhāṣyam,* 126; an English translation in Pruden, *Vasubandhu,* 394. A related—but certainly not identical—notion is found in the *Bhaiṣajyaguru Sūtra;* see Schopen, "Help for the Sick," 244.
87. See Sasson and Law, *Imagining the Fetus;* Garrett, *Religion, Medicine;* Kritzer, *Garbhāvakrāntisūtra;* Jinpa, *Science and Philosophy,* 339–68; Langenberg, *Birth in Buddhism.*
88. Such as the *Carakasaṃhitā.* See Zysk, "Mythology and the Brahmanization."
89. See Garrett, *Religion, Medicine.*
90. *Mngal gnas, Nandagarbhāvakrānti Nirdeśa,* Tōh. 57, D. 211a2–4 and 211b5–12a5; and *Mngal 'jug, Āyuṣman Nandagarbhāvakrānti Nirdeśa,* Tōh. 58, D. 211b5–12a5; as appears in the *'Dul ba phran tshegs kyi gzhi, Vinayakṣudrakavastu,* Tōh. 6, D. vol. *tha,* 125a3–4 and 125b6–26a7; an English translation in Kritzer, *Garbhāvakrāntisūtra,* 39–44. See also Langenberg, *Birth in Buddhism;* Jinpa, *Science and Philosophy,* 349–50; and Anālayo, *Comparative Study,* 254.
91. Tsong kha pa, *Bung ba'i re skong,* 20a1–4. See also his *Rnam gzhag rim pa'i rnam bshad,* 33b6–34a6.
92. *Mngal gnas, Nandagarbhāvakrānti Nirdeśa,* Tōh. 57, D. 212a6–b1.
93. Vasubandhu, *Mdzod 'grel, Kośabhāṣya,* chap. 3, v. 15ab, Tōh. 4090, D. *ku,* 120b7–21a3; a Sanskrit edition in Pradhan, *Abhidharmakośabhāṣyam,* 126–27; an English translation in Pruden, *Vasubandhu,* 394–95.
94. Asaṅga, *Sa'i dngos gzhi, Maulībhūmi,* Tōh. 4035, D. 11b5–12a2; a Sanskrit edition in Bhattacharya, *The Yogācārabhūmi,* 23.5–12. See also Tsong kha pa, *Rnam gzhag rim pa'i rnam bshad,* 35a6–b2.
95. Tsong kha pa, *Bung ba'i re skong,* 20a5–6.
96. Tsong kha pa, *Bung ba'i re skong,* 20a6.
97. Asaṅga, *Sa'i dngos gzhi, Maulībhūmi,* Tōh. 4035, D. 12a5; a Sanskrit edition in Bhattacharya, *The Yogācārabhūmi,* 24.4–5; an English translation in Schmithausen, *Alayavijnāna,* 127.
98. Tib. *kun gzhi rnam par shes pa;* Skt. *ālayavijñāna.*
99. Tib. *sa bon thams cad pa;* Skt. *sarvabījaka.*
100. Tib. *yid kyi shes pa.* Tsong kha pa, *Rnam gzhag rim pa'i rnam bshad,* 35b3–5.
101. *Rgyud rdo rje phreng ba, Vajramālā Tantra,* Tōh. 445, chap. 17, D. 230a2–3; an

English translation in Kittay with Lozang Jamspal, *Vajra Rosary*, chap. 17, vv. 34–36.

102. *Sdom 'byung, Saṃvarodaya Tantra*, Tōh. 373, D. 266a6–7; Sanskrit and Tibetan editions with an English translation in Tsuda, *The Saṃvarodaya*, chap. 2, 14cd–16.
103. Nāgabuddhi, *Rnam gzhag rim pa, Vyavastholi*, chap. 1, Tōh. 1809, D. 123b4–24a1 Sanskrit and Tibetan editions in Tanaka, *Vyavastholi*, 93.
104. Amended based on Tsong kha pa's *Rnam gzhag rim pa'i rnam bshad*, 34b2–4.
105. Tsong kha pa, *Bung ba'i re skong*, 20a4–5.
106. *Sdom 'byung, Saṃvarodaya Tantra*, Tōh. 373, D. 266a6; Sanskrit and Tibetan editions with an English translation in Tsuda, *The Saṃvarodaya*, chap. 2, 14cd.
107. See Nāgabuddhi, *Rnam gzhag rim pa, Vyavastholi*, chap. 1, Tōh. 1809, D. 123b7–24a1 Sanskrit and Tibetan editions in Tanaka, *Vyavastholi*, 93.
108. Tib. *gtum mo.*
109. *Sdom 'byung, Saṃvarodaya Tantra*, Tōh. 373, D. 266a1; Sanskrit and Tibetan editions with an English translation in Tsuda, *The Saṃvarodaya*, chap. 2, 17ab; Asaṅga, *Sa'i dngos gzhi, Maulībhūmi*, Tōh. 4035, D. 12a3–5; a Sanskrit edition in Bhattacharya, *The Yogācārabhūmi*, 24.1–5; and Tsong kha pa's *Rnam gzhag rim pa'i rnam bshad*, 36a4–37a1.
110. Asaṅga, *Sa'i dngos gzhi, Maulībhūmi*, Tōh. 4035, D. 12b4–5; a Sanskrit edition in Bhattacharya, *The Yogācārabhūmi*, 24.18–25.1.
111. Tsong kha pa, *Rnam gzhag rim pa'i rnam bshad*, 37b5–6.
112. *'Dul ba phran tshegs kyi gzhi, Vinayakṣudrakavastu*, Tōh. 6, D. 127a4–5; *Mngal gnas, Nandagarbhāvakrānti Nirdeśa*, Tōh. 57, D. 212b4–6; and *Mngal 'jug, Āyuṣman Nandagarbhāvakrānti Nirdeśa*, Tōh. 58, D. 238b1. Note that these three accounts are not identical.
113. Mkhas grub rje, *Bskyed rim dngos grub rgya mtsho*, 115a3–5.
114. Tsong kha pa, *Bung ba'i re skong*, 20a6–b2.
115. Tsong kha pa, *Bung ba'i re skong*, 20b2–4. I have rearranged this paragraph.
116. *Mngal gnas, Nandagarbhāvakrānti Nirdeśa*, Tōh. 57, D. 225a7.
117. *'Dul ba phran tshegs kyi gzhi, Vinayakṣudrakavastu*, Tōh. 6, D. vol. *tha*, 142b6–7 and 146a3–4; an English translation in Kritzer, *Garbhāvakrāntisūtra*, 90–91, 95.
118. Vasubandhu, *Mdzod 'grel, Kośabhāṣya*, on chap. 3, v. 19, Tōh. 4090, D. *ku*, 123a5–6; a Sanskrit edition in Pradhan, *Abhidharmakośabhāṣyam*, 129–30; an English translation in Pruden, *Vasubandhu*, 400; Asaṅga, *Sa'i dngos gzhi, Maulībhūmi*, Tōh. 4035, D. 14a5; a Sanskrit edition in Bhattacharya, *The Yogācārabhūmi*, 28.1–2, that speaks of eight phases.
119. The names of these five phases may vary in the different Indian sources.
120. Tib. *mer mer po;* Skt. *kalala.*
121. Tib. *ltar ltar po* [or *ldar ldar po*]; Skt. *arbuda.*
122. Tib. *gor gor po;* Skt. *peśin.*

123. Tib. *mkhrang gyur* or *'khrang gyur;* Skt. *ghana.*
124. Tib. *rkang lag 'gyus pa;* Skt. *praśakha.*
125. The *Sdom 'byung, Saṃvarodaya Tantra,* Tōh. 373, D. 266a7–b1; Sanskrit and Tibetan editions with an English translation in Tsuda, *The Saṃvarodaya,* chap. 2, vv. 17cd–18.
126. Nāgabuddhi, *Rnam gzhag rim pa, Vyavastholi,* chap. 1, Tōh. 1809, D. 124a4–5; Sanskrit and Tibetan editions in Tanaka, *Vyavastholi,* 94.
127. Nāgabuddhi, *Rnam gzhag rim pa, Vyavastholi,* chap. 1, Tōh. 1809, D. 124a6–7; Sanskrit and Tibetan editions in Tanaka, *Vyavastholi,* 94–95.
128. Tsong kha pa, *Bung ba'i re skong,* 20b4–5.
129. *Sdom 'byung,* Tōh. 373, D. 266b2–3; Sanskrit and Tibetan editions with an English translation in Tsuda, *The Saṃvarodaya,* chap. 2, vv. 21–22. See also Nāgabuddhi, *Rnam gzhag rim pa, Vyavastholi,* chap. 1, Tōh. 1809, D. 124a7–b1; Sanskrit and Tibetan editions in Tanaka, *Vyavastholi,* 95.
130. Tsong kha pa, *Bung ba'i re skong,* 20b5–21a1.
131. Tsong kha pa, *Bung ba'i re skong,* 21a1–3.
132. Tsong kha pa, *Bung ba'i re skong,* 21a3–6.

3. A General Explanation of the *Sādhana*

1. Tib. *rgyun;* Skt. *prabandha.*
2. Nāgabuddhi, *Rnam gzhag rim pa, Vyavastholi,* Tōh. 1809; Sanskrit and Tibetan editions in Tanaka, *Vyavastholi.*
3. Tib. *sbyang gzhi.*
4. Tib *sbyong byed.*
5. Tib. *sbyangs pa'i 'bras bu.*
6. *Ye shes rdo rje kun las bsdus pa, Jñānavajrasamuccaya,* Tōh. 450, D. 20b1–2.
7. 'Gos Khug pa lhas btsas, *Gsang 'dus stong thun,* 7a2–14a4.
8. Tsong kha pa, *Mtha' gcod rin chen myu gu,* 38b9–39a1.
9. See the colophon at the end of the seventeenth chapter of the *Guhyasamāja Tantra;* see also Tsong kha pa, *Rim lnga gsal sgron,* chap. 2, 34a2–b2; an English translation in Kilty, *Lamp to Illuminate,* 75.
10. 'Gos Khug pa lhas btsas, *Gsang 'dus stong thun.*
11. Red mda' ba Gzhon nu blo gros, *Yid kyi mun sel,* 6b6–8b6.
12. See Roloff, *Red mda' ba.*
13. Tsong kha pa, *Rnam gzhag rim pa'i rnam bshad.*
14. Tsong kha pa, *Rnam gzhag rim pa'i rnam bshad,* 46a1–2.
15. In its narrow meaning, mantra (Tib. *sngags*) refers to the mantras recited during the practice, but at times the words tantra and mantra are synonymous. In specific instances, distinctions are drawn between the two terms, but for our purposes, the two words are interchangeable, and both will ap-

pear below. For a case where differentiation is made between these terms, see Mkhas grub rje, *Bskyed rim dngos grub rgya mtsho,* 142a; Bentor and Dorjee, *The Ocean.*

16. Tib. *gzhi'i chos sku, gzhi'i longs sku,* and *gzhi'i sprul sku.*
17. The three experiences are white appearance, enhanced appearance, and approaching attainment, described in the section "Death according to Vajrayāna" in chapter 2. As already noted, ordinary people are not aware of their occurrence.
18. The moment that the intermediate being enters the semen and blood of its parents and transforms into an embryo in the mother's womb, which is called conception in English, is called the moment of rebirth in our Buddhist texts. In accordance with the language of these texts, the term "taking birth" or "the intermediate being takes birth" will be used in this book to denote the moment of conception. This is in order to distinguish between conception and the moment the child emerges from the womb, which is called "birth" in English.
19. Tib. *rlung sems tsam las.*
20. Tsong kha pa, *Rnam gzhag rim pa'i rnam bshad,* 46b2–4.
21. The reverse order is "reversed" in relation to the forward order during death. See the section "Death according to Vajrayāna" in chapter 2.
22. This refers to Nāgabuddhi, *Rnam gzhag rim pa, Vyavastholi,* Tōh. 1809. Tsong kha pa, *Rnam gzhag rim pa'i rnam bshad,* 46b4–47a1.
23. Or divine pride: Tib. *nga rgyal;* Skt. *ahaṃkāra.*
24. Tsong kha pa, *Rnam gzhag rim pa'i rnam bshad,* 46b1–2.
25. Tsong kha pa, *Rnam gzhag rim pa'i rnam bshad,* 50a5–b1.
26. Tib. *'jig rten pa'i lam* and *'jig rten las 'das pa'i lam.*
27. *Lam rim chen mo,* 550; an English translation in Cutler, *The Great Treatise,* 3:91–92, where Tsong kha pa follows Asaṅga, *Rnal 'byor spyod pa'i sa las nyan thos kyi sa, Śrāvakabhūmi,* Tōh. 4036, D. 164a3–7.
28. Tib. *mi sdug pa bsgom pa;* Skt. *aśubhabhāvanā.*
29. Tib. *bdag tu 'dzin pa* or *bdag 'dzin.*
30. See the section "The Meditative States of the Realm of Subtle Materiality and the Immaterial Realm" in chapter 1.
31. Tsong kha pa, *Rnam gzhag rim pa'i rnam bshad,* 50b5.
32. Tsong kha pa, *Rnam gzhag rim pa'i rnam bshad,* 51b4–6.
33. Tib. *rigs 'dra'i rgyun.*
34. Mkhas grub rje, *Bskyed rim dngos grub rgya mtsho,* 81b3–5.
35. Our text skips the prose passage found in the *Tantra* here.
36. *Gsang ba 'dus pa,* chap. 17 [Tōh. 442], Stog 74b4–5; a Sanskrit edition in Matsunaga, *The Guhyasamāja,* vv. 50–51.
37. Tib. *rab tu bsgrags;* Skt. *prakīrtita.*
38. Mother Tantras, including the *Hevajra* and *Saṃvarodaya Tantras,* contain a whole chapter on the equivalence of bodily constituents and the deities of the

maṇḍala (in fact called purity: Tib. *rnam par dag pa;* Skt. *viśuddhi*). See the *Brtag gnyis, Hevajra Tantra,* part 1, chap. 9, Tōh. 417; and *Sdom 'byung, Saṃvarodaya Tantra,* chap. 4, Tōh. 373; Tsuda, *The Saṃvarodaya Tantra.*

39. Tsong kha pa, *Rnam gzhag rim pa'i rnam bshad,* 52a2–3.
40. Āryadeva, *Spyod bsdus, Caryāmelāpakapradīpa,* chap. 11, Tōh. 1803, D. 106a6–b1; a Tibetan edition and an English translation in Wedemeyer, *Āryadeva's Lamp,* 330, 656, no Sanskrit; reconstructed Sanskrit and Tibetan editions in Pandey, *Caryāmelāpakapradīpam,* 103 and 363; an English translation in Hopkins, *Tantric Techniques,* 235–36.
41. Āryadeva, *Spyod bsdus, Caryāmelāpakapradīpa,* chap. 11, Tōh. 1803, D. 106b3; a Tibetan edition and an English translation in Wedemeyer, *Āryadeva's Lamp,* 331, 656, no Sanskrit; reconstructed Sanskrit and Tibetan editions in Pandey, *Caryāmelāpakapradīpam,* 103 and 364.
42. See 'Gos Khug pa lhas btsas, *Gsang 'dus stong thun,* 14b6–15b5; Bu ston, *Mdor byas 'grel chen,* 1b4; Sa skya pa Grags pa rgyal mtshan's *Rgyud kyi mngon par rtogs pa rin po che'i ljon shing,* work 1, 68a2–4; Red mda' ba, *Yid kyi mun sel,* 6b4–5; and Ngor chen Kun dga' bzang po, *Zla zer,* work 55, 18b3–6.
43. Tsong kha pa, *Rnam gzhag rim pa'i rnam bshad,* 47a5–b4 and 49a2–6; see also his *Sngags rim chen mo,* chap. 11, 454; an English translation in Yarnall, *Tsong Khapa's Great Stages,* 125; and also Mkhas grub rje, *Rgyud sde spyi'i rnam gzhag;* a Tibetan edition and an English translation in Lessing and Wayman, *Mkhas grub rje's Fundamentals,* 330–33.
44. Tsong kha pa, *Sngags rim chen mo,* chap. 11, 454–55; an English translation in Yarnall, *Tsong Khapa's Great Stages,* 126–27.
45. For the illusory body, see the section "The Three Bodies of the Meditators on the Completion Stage" in this chapter.
46. Tsong kha pa, *Rnam gzhag rim pa'i rnam bshad,* 52a5–6.
47. Tsong kha pa, *Rnam gzhag rim pa'i rnam bshad,* 51b6.
48. *Rdo rje gcod pa, Vajracchedikā,* Tōh. 16, D. 121b5; a Sanskrit edition in Harrison and Watanabe, "*Vajracchedika,*" 104, folio 3, line 2; an English translation in Harrison, "*Vajracchedika,*" 142.
49. Tib. *sgo nga las skyes pa, mngal las skyes pa, drod gsher las skyes pa,* and *rdzus te skyes pa;* Skt. *aṇḍajā, jarāyujā, saṃsvedajā,* and *upapādukā.*
50. Nāgabuddhi, *Rnam gzhag rim pa, Vyavastholi,* chap. 1, Tōh. 1809, D. 122a5–b1; Sanskrit and Tibetan editions in Tanaka, *Vyavastholi,* 83–84.
51. *Sdom 'byung, Saṃvarodaya Tantra,* Tōh. 373, D. 265b6–7; Sanskrit and Tibetan editions with an English translation in Tsuda, *The Saṃvarodaya,* chap. 2, vv. 2–4; as well as its *Commentary* by Rin chen 'tsho, Ratnarakṣita, the *Padma can, Padminī,* Tōh. 1420, chap. 2, D. 11a2.
52. See Rin chen bzang po, *Rgyud sde spyi'i rnam par bzhag pa,* 19a2–3; Gser sdings pa, *Rim lnga don bzhi ma,* 164; Grags pa rgyal mtshan, *Rgyud kyi mngon rtogs,* work 1, 69a3–5; 'Ba' ra ba, *Bskyed rim zab don 'gal du skyon med,* 29b4–5;

Bu ston, *Mdor byas 'grel chen,* 24b3–25a1; Rong ston Shes bya kun rig, *Gsang 'dus rnam bshad,* 8b4–9a1, as well as his *Gsang sngags kyi spyi don slob dpon grags 'od kyi zhus lan,* 320.

53. Or Great Yoga Tantra, Tib. *rnal 'byor chen po'i rgyud.* The Unexcelled Mantra (Tib. *sngags bla med*) is the highest level among the four classes of tantras, to which the *Guhyasamāja Tantra* belongs.
54. Tib. *rin po che lta bu'i gang zag;* Skt. *ratnapudgala.*
55. Tib. *'gro ba lnga;* Skt. *pañca gatayaḥ.* See the section "The Beings of this World" in chapter 1.
56. Vasubandhu, *Mdzod 'grel, Kośabhāṣya,* on chap. 3, v. 4, Tōh. 4090, D. *ku,* 111a4–6; a Sanskrit edition in Pradhan, *Abhidharmakośabhāṣyam,* 114; an English translation in Pruden, *Vasubandhu,* 371.
57. Tsong kha pa, *Rnam gzhag rim pa'i rnam bshad,* 13b4–6.
58. This explains why the term "four modes of birth" is preferable when referring to all sentient beings in the world. Yet, *Formulating the Guhyasamāja Sādhana* does not simply mention the four modes of birth but, like the *Saṃvarodaya Tantra,* explains the meaning of each mode of birth and provides several examples for each of them.
59. Nāgabuddhi, *Rnam gzhag rim pa, Vyavastholi,* chap. 1, Tōh. 1809, D. 122b7–23a1; Sanskrit and Tibetan editions in Tanaka, *Vyavastholi,* 87.
60. Tib. *Thun mong ma yin pa'i gsang ba;* Skt. *Asādhāraṇaguhya.* We only know that a brief citation from a Sanskrit text by this title is reproduced in Lal, *Lupta bauddha vacana saṅgrahaḥ,* 3.
61. Rin chen 'tsho, Ratnarakṣita's commentary on the *Sdom 'byung, Saṃvarodaya Tantra,* Tōh. 373, entitled *Padma can, Padminī,* Tōh. 1420, chap. 2.
62. Tsong kha pa, *Rnam gzhag rim pa'i rnam bshad,* 19b3–5.
63. Tib. *'dod pa'i khams;* Skt. *kāmadhātu.*
64. Tib. *'og min;* Skt. *akaniṣṭha.*
65. Tsong kha pa, *Rnam gzhag rim pa'i rnam bshad,* 17a2–b1.
66. Tsong kha pa, *Bung ba'i re skong,* 23a1–3.
67. Candrakīrti, *Sgron gsal, Pradīpoddyotana,* chap. 1, Tōh. 1785, D. 3a7–b3; a Sanskrit edition in Chakravarti, *Pradīpoddyotana,* 4; an English translation in Campbell et al., *Esoteric Community,* 115–17. See also Tsong kha pa, *Bung ba'i re skong,* 23b2–3, and his *Rnam gzhag rim pa'i rnam bshad,* 19a1–2.
68. Tib. *utpala, pad dkar, padma, tsan dan,* and *rin po che;* Skt. *utpala, puṇḍarīka, padma, candana,* and *ratna.*
69. Tib. *tshogs bshad;* Skt. *satravyākhyāna.*
70. Tib. *slob bshad;* Skt. *śiṣyavyākhyāna.*
71. Tsong kha pa, *Bung ba'i re skong,* 23a3–5, and *Rnam gzhag rim pa'i rnam bshad,* 18a5–b6.
72. Tib. *yi dwags;* Skt. *preta.*

73. See the section "The Beings of This World" in chapter 1.
74. Lus 'phags, Pūrvavideha in the east; of Ba lang spyod, Aparagodānīya in the west; and Sgra mi snyan, Uttarakuru in the north.
75. Tib. *las kyi sa pa;* Skt. *karmabhūmi.* See Nāgabuddhi, *Rnam gzhag rim pa, Vyavastholi,* chap. 1, Tōh. 1809, D. 122b3–6; Sanskrit and Tibetan editions in Tanaka, *Vyavastholi,* 86; and the *Sdom 'byung, Saṃvarodaya Tantra,* Tōh. 373, D. 265a1–3; Sanskrit and Tibetan editions with an English translation in Tsuda, *The Saṃvarodaya,* chap. 2, vv. 5cd–9. See also Tsong kha pa, *Bung ba'i re skong,* 23a5–6; and his *Rnam gzhag rim pa'i rnam bshad,* 15a5–b2.
76. Nāgabuddhi, *Rnam gzhag rim pa, Vyavastholi,* chap. 1, Tōh. 1809, D. 122b1–6; Sanskrit and Tibetan editions in Tanaka, *Vyavastholi,* 85–87.
77. Tsong kha pa, *Rnam gzhag rim pa'i rnam bshad,* 19b2–3.
78. Tsong kha pa, *Bung ba'i re skong,* 23b1–3.
79. Tsong kha pa, *Bung ba'i re skong,* 23b3–6. See also Tsong kha pa, *Mtha' gcod,* 123a4–25b6, and *Rnam gzhag rim pa'i rnam bshad,* 19a3–6. See also Bentor, "Can Women," and "Women on the Way."
80. *Gsang ba 'dus pa,* chap. 13, [Tōh. 442], Stog 35a3; a Sanskrit edition in Matsunaga, *The Guhyasamāja,* v. 25.
81. Candrakīrti, *Sgron gsal, Pradīpoddyotana,* chap. 13, Tōh. 1785, D. 103b6–7; a Sanskrit edition in Chakravarti, *Pradīpoddyotana,* 127.
82. Tib. *sngags bla med;* the highest level among the four classes of tantras, to which the *Guhyasamāja Tantra* belongs.
83. The white appearance, the red enhanced appearance, and the black appearance of approaching attainment.
84. Tib. *bde ba chen po'i ting nge 'dzin;* Skt. *mahāsukhasamādhi. Ye shes rdo rje kun las btus pa, Vajrajñānasamuccaya Tantra,* Tōh. 447, D. 283b1–2. See also Tsong kha pa commentary on this tantra, *Ye rdor ṭīkā,* 34a6–35a1.
85. The Tibetan in both the *Ye shes rdo rje kun las btus pa, Vajrajñānasamuccaya Tantra,* and in Tsong kha pa, *Bung ba'i re skong,* is *rang bzhin snang ba.*
86. *Ye shes rdo rje kun las btus pa, Vajrajñānasamuccaya Tantra,* Tōh. 447, D. 283b3–4; Tsong kha pa, *Bung ba'i re skong,* 23b6–24a2.
87. Tsong kha pa, *Rim lnga gsal sgron;* an English translation in Kilty, *Lamp to Illuminate.*
88. Tib. *pha rol tu phyin pa'i theg pa.*
89. The Great Vehicle (the Mahāyāna) consists of two vehicles: Sūtra and Tantra or Pāramitā and Mantra Vehicles. The nontantric path of the Mahāyāna is the former the Sūtra or Pāramitā Vehicle.
90. The three Lower Tantras (Tib. *rgyud sde 'og ma gsum*) are ritual or action tantras (*bya rgyud, kriyā*), practice tantras (*spyod rgyud, caryā*), and yoga tantra (*rnal 'byor gyi rgyud*).
91. Tib. *gtum mo.*

92. Tsong kha pa, *Rim lnga gsal sgron*, chap. 2, 53a3–4; an English translation in Kilty, *Lamp to Illuminate*, 105. See also Tsong kha pa, *Rim lnga gsal sgron*, chap. 2, 54b5–6; an English translation in Kilty, *Lamp to Illuminate*, 107.
93. Tsong kha pa, *Rim lnga gsal sgron*, chap. 2, 67a3–4; an English translation in Kilty, *Lamp to Illuminate*, 124.
94. Tsong kha pa, *Rim lnga gsal sgron*, chap. 2, 55b2–3; an English translation in Kilty, *Lamp to Illuminate*, 108.
95. Tib. *mos pa yid byed;* Skt. *adhimuktimanaskāra.*
96. Tsong kha pa, *Rim lnga gsal sgron*, chap. 2, 55b6–56a1; English translations in Kilty, *Lamp to Illuminate*, 108–9, and Jinpa, *Science and Philosophy*, 270–71.
97. Tsong kha pa, *Rim lnga gsal sgron*, chap. 2, 56a1–3; English translations in Kilty, *Lamp to Illuminate*, 109, and Jinpa, *Science and Philosophy*, 271.
98. Tsong kha pa, *Rim lnga gsal sgron*, chap. 2, 56a3–4; an English translation in Kilty, *Lamp to Illuminate*, 109.
99. Tsong kha pa, *Sgron gsal mchan*, 54a1–3.
100. *Yang dag par sbyor ba, Saṃpuṭa Tantra*, Tōh. 381, D. 80a5; Sanskrit and Tibetan editions in Elder, "The *Saṃpuṭa Tantra*," 97, 148, and Skorupski, "The *Saṃpuṭatantra*," 236; English translations in Elder, "The *Saṃpuṭa Tantra*," 184, and Dharmachakra Translation Committee, *Emergence from Sampuṭa*, 84,000, chap. 1, v. 120.
101. Tsong kha pa, *Sgron gsal mchan*, 54a3.
102. *Gsang ba 'dus pa*, chap. 7, [Tōh. 442], Stog 17a5; a Sanskrit edition in Matsunaga, *The Guhyasamāja*, v. 7.
103. Nāgārjuna, *Mdo bsre, Sādhanasūtramelāpaka*, Tōh. 1797, D. 13b2–4; *Gsang ba 'dus pa, Guhyasamāja Tantra*, chap. 1, [Tōh. 442], Stog 3b3; a Sanskrit edition in Matsunaga, *The Guhyasamāja*, 4. The full name of this *samādhi* is "the method of great passion of all tathāgatas," *de bzhin gshegs pa thams cad kyi 'dod chags chen po'i tshul zhes bya ba'i ting nge 'dzin, sarva tathāgata mahā rāga vajraṃ [nayaṃ] nāma samādhi.*
104. Candrakīrti, *Sgron gsal, Pradīpoddyotana*, chap. 1, Tōh. 1785, D. 2a5–b1; a Sanskrit edition in Chakravarti, *Pradīpoddyotana*, 2; an English translation in Campbell et al., *Esoteric Community*, 110.
105. Candrakīrti, *Sgron gsal, Pradīpoddyotana*, chap. 1, Tōh. 1785, D. 2b1; a Sanskrit edition in Chakravarti, *Pradīpoddyotana*, 2; an English translation in Campbell et al., *The Esoteric Community*, 111.
106. Tsong kha pa, *Bung ba'i re skong*, 24a2–4.
107. The Realm of Subtle Materiality or Form Realm (*gzugs khams, rūpadhātu*) and the Immaterial Realm or Formless Realm (*gzugs med pa'i khams, ārūpyadhātu*).
108. Tib. *'dod khams;* Skt. *kāmadhātu.*
109. Tib. *'dod yon lnga* or *'dod pa'i yon tan lnga;* Skt. *pañcakāmaguṇa.*
110. Tsong kha pa, *Sgron gsal mchan*, 53b4–54a1.

111. See "With What Do the Subsequent Steps of the *Sādhana* Correspond?" in this chapter.
112. Tib. *sngon byung;* Skt. *bhūtapūrva.*
113. Tib. *rjes 'jug.*
114. Nāgabuddhi, *Rnam gzhag rim pa, Vyavastholi,* chap. 1, Tōh. 1809, D. 121a7–21b3; Sanskrit and Tibetan editions in Tanaka, *Vyavastholi,* 79–80.
115. The mandalas visualized here are the four mandalas of the physical elements—wind, fire, water, and earth. These are also called "mandalas," since in certain contexts all of them are round, but this is not the case here. See the section "Meditations that Correspond to the Evolution of the World" in chapter 4.
116. More on this term below.
117. Tib. *rnal 'byor, rjes su rnal 'byor, shin tu rnal 'byor,* and *rnal 'byor chen po.*
118. The verse recited here is: "In the absence of being, there is no meditation, and meditation cannot be meditated upon. Therefore a state of being that is nonbeing leaves no object for meditation." While reciting this verse, yogis meditate on emptiness, the ground of wisdom. See the section "Meditations that Correspond to the Destruction of the World" in chapter 4.
119. These are the specially visualized deities, Tib. *lhag mos kyi lha.* See the section "The Meditation on the Specially Visualized Deities" in chapter 4.
120. Nāgabuddhi, *Rnam gzhag rim pa, Vyavastholi,* chap. 1, Tōh. 1809, D. 121b4–5; Sanskrit and Tibetan editions in Tanaka, *Vyavastholi,* 80–81.
121. Tsong kha pa, *Rnam gzhag rim pa'i rnam bshad,* 50b1–2.
122. Tsong kha pa, *Bung ba'i re skong,* 11a4.
123. Nāgabuddhi, *Rnam gzhag rim pa, Vyavastholi,* chap. 1, Tōh. 1809, D. 123a2–125a1; Sanskrit and Tibetan editions in Tanaka, *Vyavastholi,* 87–98.
124. Tib. *nga rgyal;* Skt. *ahaṃkāra.*
125. Tib. *lha'i rnal 'byor.*
126. Tsong kha pa, *Sngags rim chen mo,* chap. 1, 21; an English translation in Hopkins, *Tantra in Tibet,* 116.
127. Tib. *rigs 'dra'i rgyu.*
128. Tsong kha pa, *Sngags rim chen mo,* chap. 1, 21–24; an English translation in Hopkins, *Tantra in Tibet,* 117–22.
129. See the section "Purification" in chapter 3.
130. Tib. *sbyin pa, tshul khrims, bzod pa, brtson 'grus, bsam gtan;* Skt. *dāna, śīla, kṣānti, vīrya, dhyāna.* The sixth *pāramitā* is wisdom (Tib. *shes rab;* Skt. *prajñā*).
131. Tsong kha pa maintains that having accumulated merit during many lives and attained the ārya level, practitioners of the Pāramitā Vehicle as well attain bodies that correspond to a buddha's body adorned with the major and minor marks. See his *Rim lnga gsal sgron,* chap. 2, 63a2–5; an English translation in Kilty, *Lamp to Illuminate,* 118.
132. The Teacher, the Buddha.

133. *Mkha' 'gro ma rdo rje gur, Ḍākinīvajrapañjara,* Tōh. 419, D. 31b1.
134. *Mkha' 'gro ma rdo rje gur, Ḍākinīvajrapañjara,* Tōh. 419, D. 31a6–b1.
135. Tib. *dkyil 'khor 'khor lo.*
136. Tib. *sangs rgyas nga rgyal.*
137. Tsong kha pa, *Sngags rim chen mo,* chap. 1, 22–23; an English translation in Hopkins, *Tantra in Tibet,* 117–20.
138. Tsong kha pa, *Sngags rim chen mo,* chap. 1, 24; an English translation in Hopkins, *Tantra in Tibet,* 122.
139. Tsong kha pa, *Sngags rim chen mo,* chap. 1, 25–26; an English translation in Hopkins, *Tantra in Tibet,* 123–24.
140. Tib. *lhan gcig byed pa'i rkyen.*
141. For this reason, the cooperative condition for the *rūpakāya* is found in the Pāramitā Vehicle, but the substantial cause is incomplete. See Tsong kha pa, *Rim lnga gsal sgron,* chap. 2, 65b1–2; an English translation in Kilty, *Lamp to Illuminate,* 121.
142. Tib. *dang po mgon po;* Skt. *ādinātha.*
143. Or divine pride: Tib. *nga rgyal;* Skt. *ahaṃkāra.*
144. Tsong kha pa, *Bung ba'i re skong,* 17b4–5.
145. See the section "Death according to Vajrayāna" in chapter 2.
146. Tsong kha pa, *Sgron gsal mchan,* 98b5–6.
147. Tsong kha pa has here "the specially visualized deities" (Tib. *lhag mos kyi lha*). This will be explained shortly.
148. Tsong kha pa, *Bung ba'i re skong,* 17b6–18a1.
149. While there are several clear lights that arise during the different steps of the completion stage, the most significant among them are the clear lights realized during the fourth and fifth steps of the five steps according to Nāgārjuna's *Five Stage.* Tib. *rim lnga;* Skt. *pañcakrama.*
150. Tsong kha pa, *Bung ba'i re skong,* 18a1–3.
151. Tib. *dang po mgon po;* Skt. *ādinātha.*
152. Tib. *mngon par byang chub pa,* or *mngon byang;* Skt. *abhisambodhi.* Tsong kha pa, *Bung ba'i re skong,* 19b4–5.
153. Tsong kha pa, *Bung ba'i re skong,* 19b2–4.
154. Tsong kha pa, *Bung ba'i re skong,* 22b2–3.
155. Tsong kha pa, *Sngags rim chen mo,* chap. 12, 462; an English translation in Yarnall, *Tsong Khapa's Great Stages,* 142.
156. Tsong kha pa, *Sngags rim chen mo,* chap. 12, 463–64; an English translation in Yarnall, *Tsong Khapa's Great Stages,* 143.
157. Tsong kha pa, *Bung ba'i re skong,* 22b4–23a1.
158. Tib. *mos pa yid byed;* Skt. *adhimuktimanaskāra.*
159. See Bentor and Dorjee, *The Ocean,* introductory essay.
160. Tsong kha pa, *Rim lnga gsal sgron,* chap. 2, 70b4; an English translation in Kilty, *Lamp to Illuminate,* 128.

161. Nāgārjuna, *Rim pa lnga pa, Pañcakrama,* Tōh. 1802; Mimaki and Tomabechi, *Pañcakrama;* and Tomabechi, "Étude du *Pañcakrama.*"
162. Speech isolation (*ngag dben, vāgviveka*), mind isolation (*sems dben, cittaviveka*), illusory body (*sgyu lus, māyādeha*), clear light (*'od gsal, prabhāsvara*), and union, (*zung 'jug, yuganaddha*).
163. Tib. *lus dben;* Skt. *kāyaviveka.*
164. Tsong kha pa, *Rnam gzhag rim pa'i rnam bshad,* 51b6–52a2.
165. At times speech isolation, which consists of mantra recitation and breathing exercises, is taken to correspond to breathing in the previous life.
166. Tsong kha pa, *Rnam gzhag rim pa'i rnam bshad,* 51b4–6. See also his *Bskyed rim zin bris,* 26a2–28a4.
167. Tsong kha pa, *Rim lnga gsal sgron,* chap. 2, 71a4–b5; an English translation in Kilty, *Lamp to Illuminate,* 129–30.
168. Āryadeva, *Spyod bsdus, Caryāmelāpakapradīpa,* chap. 6, Tōh. 1803, D. 85b2–4; Sanskrit and Tibetan editions with an English translation in Wedemeyer, *Āryadeva's Lamp,* B: 42a; an English translation in Kilty, *Lamp to Illuminate,* 130.
169. Tib. *bdag la byin gyis brlab pa'i rim;* Skt. *svādhiṣṭhānakrama.* See also Tsong kha pa, *Rim lnga gsal sgron,* chap. 2, 60b5–6; an English translation in Kilty, *Lamp to Illuminate,* 115.
170. Jñānapāda, *Zhal lung, Dvikrama,* Tōh. 1853, D. 15a5–b1; a Tibetan edition and an English translation in C. Dalton, "Enacting Perfection," vv. 351–57.
171. See Szántó, "Tantric Prakaraṇas," 756; and Dalton and Szántó, "Jñānapāda."
172. Jñānapāda, *Zhal lung, Dvikrama,* Tōh. 1853, D. 15b1; a Tibetan edition and an English translation in C. Dalton, "Enacting Perfection," v. 357c. First (in order to attain the *dharmakāya,* as Vaidyapāda's commentary explains), yogis endeavor in their meditation until their minds enter the realm (Tib. *dbying*) and they realize space-like clarity and supreme joy. Then (to attain the *saṃbhogakāya*), when they acquire the form of a five-year-old child that possesses supernatural powers, they experience an unparalleled perfect bliss. Finally, when they propel themselves to another rebirth, they truly realize the *nirmāṇakāya.* The phrase "the form of a five-year-old child endowed with supernatural powers" (Tib. *rdzu 'phrul shugs ldan pa, lo lnga lon pa'i byis pa'i gzugs*) recalls the explanation of the intermediate being as described by Vasubandhu: its size is that of a five- or six-year-old child (Tib. *byis pa lo lnga'am drug lon pa lta bu;* Skt. *pañcaṣaḍvarṣasya dāraka*) and it is endowed with supernatural powers (Tib. *las kyi rdzu 'phrul shugs dang ldan;* Skt. *karmarddhivegavān*). See Vasubandhu, *Mdzod, Kośa,* chap. 3, v. 14b, Tōh. 4089, D. 7b1; a Sanskrit edition in Pradhan, *Abhidharmakośabhāṣyam,* 125; an English translation in Pruden, *Vasubandhu,* 392; and Vasubandhu, *Mdzod 'grel, Kośabhāṣya,* chap. 3, v. 13ab, Tōh. 4090, D. *ku,* 119a3; Pradhan, *Abhidharmakośabhāṣyam,* 123–24; Pruden, *Vasubandhu,* 390.
173. Vaidyapāda, *Mdzes pa'i me tog, Sukusuma,* Tōh. 1866, D. 132b2–4.

174. This is in the form of a five-year-old child endowed with supernatural powers.
175. Tsong kha pa, *Rnam gzhag rim pa'i rnam bshad,* 47a1–48a2; and his *Rim lnga gsal sgron,* 72a4–6; an English translation in Kilty, *Lamp to Illuminate,* 130.
176. Tsong kha pa, *Rim lnga gsal sgron,* chap. 2, 63b2–4; an English translation in Kilty, *Lamp to Illuminate,* 120.
177. Āryadeva, *Spyod bsdus, Caryāmelāpakapradīpa,* chap. 6, Tōh. 1803, D. 84a5–b1; Sanskrit and Tibetan editions with an English translation in Wedemeyer, *Āryadeva's Lamp,* B: 40a; an English translation in Kilty, *Lamp to Illuminate,* 381.
178. The Tibetan text of the *Spyod bsdus* is *rang bzhin gyis snang ba,* and the Sanskrit is *prakṛtyābhāsa.* As mentioned in note 36 in chapter 2, the *Ye shes rdo rje kun las btus pa, Vajrajñānasamuccaya Tantra* (Tōh. 447, D. 282b2–4) has here *rang bzhin gyi snang ba,* and Tsong kha pa explains the meaning of this term as a coordinative compound meaning "intrinsic natures *and* appearances".
179. Tsong kha pa, *Rim lnga gsal sgron,* chap. 7, 230a1–2; an English translation in Kilty, *Lamp to Illuminate,* 382.
180. Tib. *tha snyad 'dogs pa'i gzhi.*
181. Tsong kha pa, *Rim lnga gsal sgron,* chap. 7, 230a2–3; an English translation in Kilty, *Lamp to Illuminate,* 381–82.
182. Tib. *mos pa yid byed;* Skt. *adhimuktimanaskāra.*
183. Tsong kha pa, *Rim lnga gsal sgron,* chap. 7, 229a3–30a4; an English translation in Kilty, *Lamp to Illuminate,* 381–82.
184. Āryadeva, *Spyod bsdus, Caryāmelāpakapradīpa,* chap. 6, Tōh. 1803, D. 84b4–5; Sanskrit and Tibetan editions with an English translation in Wedemeyer, *Āryadeva's Lamp,* B: 40b; an English translation in Kilty, *Lamp to Illuminate,* 393.
185. Tib. *sems 'ba' zhig tsam gyis;* Skt. *cittamātreṇa.* Note that earlier in this chapter, the edition of Āryadeva's text has Tib. *ye shes tsam gyis;* Skt. *jñānamātreṇa,* through wisdom alone. See his *Spyod bsdus, Caryāmelāpakapradīpa,* chap. 6, Tōh. 1803, D. 84b1; Sanskrit and Tibetan editions with an English translation in Wedemeyer, *Āryadeva's Lamp,* B: 40b; and an English translation in Kilty, *Lamp to Illuminate,* 381. In any case, the disciple mentions here mind or wisdom alone as the foundation for the illusory body. Tsong kha pa will have to interpret this as referring, in fact, to both body and mind.
186. Āryadeva, *Spyod bsdus, Caryāmelāpakapradīpa,* chap. 6, Tōh. 1803, D. 85a1–3; Sanskrit and Tibetan editions with an English translation in Wedemeyer, *Āryadeva's Lamp,* B: 41a; an English translation in Kilty, *Lamp to Illuminate,* 394–95. I have rearranged these lines.
187. Tsong kha pa, *Rim lnga gsal sgron,* chap. 2, 63b2–3; an English translation in Kilty, *Lamp to Illuminate,* 119.
188. In the system of five steps, body isolation is either included within speech isolation or regarded as a preparatory step. Therefore, the first of the five steps is speech isolation—with or without body isolation, the second step is mind

isolation and the third step is the illusory body. See the section above, "The Three Bodies of the Meditators on the Completion Stage," in this chapter.

189. Tib. *snang ba gsum;* Skt. *ālokatraya.*
190. Tib. *snang ba, snang ba mched pa,* and *snang ba thob pa;* Skt. *āloka, ālokābhāsa,* and *ālokopalabdha.*
191. Tsong kha pa, *Rim lnga gsal sgron,* chap. 2, 64a2–3; an English translation in Kilty, *Lamp to Illuminate,* 119.
192. Tib. *gnyug ma'i lus.*
193. Tsong kha pa, *Rim lnga gsal sgron,* chap. 7, 234a4–35a2; an English translation in Kilty, *Lamp to Illuminate,* 390–91.
194. Tib. *gnas skabs pa rags pa'i lus.*
195. Tib. *dbang shes.*
196. Tib. *yid kyi rnam shes.*
197. Tib. *srog 'dzin;* Skt. *prāṇa.*
198. For the ten winds, the five main winds and five ancillary winds, see, for example, Āryadeva, *Spyod bsdus, Caryāmelāpakapradīpa,* chap. 2, Tōh. 1803, D. 64b4; Sanskrit and Tibetan editions with an English translation in Wedemeyer, *Āryadeva's Lamp,* A: 12a; and Tsong kha pa, *Rnam gzhag rim pa'i rnam bshad,* 83b6–84a1. For the five main winds, see also Lati Rinbochay and Hopkins, *Death, Intermediate State,* 14.
199. For Tsong kha pa, seen from the Prāsaṅgika viewpoint, the innate body made of wind-and-mind is the basis for that person's designation; there is no innate body beyond this. See his *Rim lnga gsal sgron,* chap. 7, 234a4–5; an English translation in Kilty, *Lamp to Illuminate,* 390.
200. Tib. *sgrub gzhi.*
201. See Tsong kha pa, *Rim lnga gsal sgron,* chap. 7, 234b5–6 and 238b2; an English translation in Kilty, *Lamp to Illuminate,* 390 and 395.
202. Tsong kha pa, *Rim lnga gsal sgron,* chap. 7, 238b5–6; an English translation in Kilty, *Lamp to Illuminate,* 395.
203. Tib. *sgyu lus;* Skt. *māyādeha.*
204. Tib. *sgyu ma lta bu'i ting nge 'dzin;* Skt. *māyopamasamādhi.*
205. Tsong kha pa, *Lam rim chung ba,* 180b3–85a1; Hopkins, *Tsong-kha-pa's Final,* 75–85; Quarcoo, *Middle Length,* 271–78.
206. Tib. *rang bzhin;* Skt. *svabhāva.*
207. Nāgārjuna, *Rim pa lnga pa, Pañcakrama,* chap. 3, v. 20, Tōh. 1802, D. 52b5; Sanskrit and Tibetan editions in Mimaki and Tomabechi, *Pañcakrama,* 34; a Sanskrit edition and a French translation in Tomabechi, "Étude du *Pañcakrama,*" 158; an English translation in Kilty, *Lamp to Illuminate,* 391. The illusory body is illustrated by the twelve similes of illusion shared by the Pāramitā and Mantra Vehicles. Tsong kha pa explains the meaning of these similes with regard to the illusory body. See his *Rim lnga gsal sgron,* chap. 7, 241a3–b6; an English translation in Kilty, *Lamp to Illuminate,* 398–99.

208. Tsong kha pa, *Rim lnga gsal sgron,* chap. 7, 248a5–b1; an English translation in Kilty, *Lamp to Illuminate,* 408.
209. Tib. *don gyi 'od gsal.*
210. Tib. *stong bzhi;* or the three appearances. See the section "The Dissolutions of Consciousness" in chapter 2.
211. Tsong kha pa, *Rim lnga gsal sgron,* chap. 8, 278b1–3; an English translation in Kilty, *Lamp to Illuminate,* 455.
212. Tsong kha pa, *Rnam gzhag rim pa'i rnam bshad,* 19b6–20a4.
213. *Rgyud phyi ma, Uttara Tantra,* Tōh. 443, D. 150a1–3; a Sanskrit edition in Matsunaga, *The Guhyasamāja,* chap. 18, vv. 34–35 (see the introduction).
214. Tsong kha pa, *Sgron gsal mchan,* 2b4–3a1. Tsong kha pa follows here the second part of Nāropā's interpretation of these terms. See Nāropā's commentary on the *Rgyud phyi ma, Uttara Tantra,* entitled *Gsang ba thams cad kyi sgron ma'i rgya cher 'grel pa, Sarvaguhyapradīpaṭīkā,* Tōh. 1787, D. 210a5–b4.
215. Ratnākaraśānti explains that the cause is the beginningless and endless mind of awakening (*bodhicitta*), which is clear light by nature. When all the adventitious obscurations of this mind—which is clear light by nature—are exhausted, it becomes pure. See his *Sgyu 'phrul chen mo'i 'grel pa yon tan ldan pa, Guṇavatīśrīmahāmāyāṭīkā,* Tōh. 1623, D. 180b7–81a2; Sanskrit and Tibetan editions in Samdhong Rinpoche and Dvivedī, *Mahāmāyātantram,* 2 and 77–78. According to Ratnākaraśānti's commentary on the *Hevjara Tantra,* synonyms of "the cause" are terms used also for Buddha Nature, such as family or lineage (Tib. *rigs;* Skt. *gotra*) and genealogical line (Tib. *rus;* Skt. *kula*). See his *Dgyes pa'i rdo rje'i dka' 'grel mu tig phreng ba, Hevajrapañjikāmuktikāvalī,* Tōh. 1189, D. 225b2–5; a Sanskrit edition in Tripathi and Negi, *Hevajratantram,* 9.
216. According to Abhayākaragupta, the cause is nature or essence untainted by impurities of beginningless habitual tendencies, since only through a pure cause buddhahood can be attained. See his *Man ngag snye ma, Āmnāyamañjarī,* Tōh. 1198, D. 7b1–5. In his commentary, entitled *Abhayapāddhati,* he adds that this beginningless and endless causal tantra is the essence of the deity Heruka. See his *Sangs rgyas thod pa'i rgyud kyi rgyal po chen po'i rgya cher 'grel pa 'jigs pa med pa'i gzhung 'grel, Buddhakapālamahātantrarājaṭīkā-abhayapāddhati,* Tōh. 1654, 170b3; Sanskrit and Tibetan editions in Chog Dorje, *Abhayapaddhati,* 5–6 and 99.
217. Tib. *sems kyi chos nyid.*
218. Tsong kha pa, *Rim lnga gsal sgron,* chap. 7, 234a4–5; an English translation in Kilty, *Lamp to Illuminate,* 390.
219. Tib. *de bzhin gshegs pa snying po;* Skt. *tathāgatagarbha.*
220. Tib. *chos nyid;* Skt. *dharmatā.*
221. Tib. *de bzhin nyid;* Skt. *tathatā.*
222. Dwags po Bkra shis rnam rgyal, *Gsang sngags rdo rje theg pa'i spyi don mdor bsdus pa legs bshad nor bu'i 'od zer,* 35b4–36b1; an English translation in Roberts, *Mahāmudrā,* 439.

223. Kong sprul Yon tan rgya mtsho, *Shes bya kun khyab,* vol. 2, 613; an English translation in Guarisco and McLeod, *Systems of Buddhist Tantra,* 143–44.
224. Tsong kha pa, *Rim lnga gsal sgron,* chap. 8, 271b4–5; an English translation in Kilty, *Lamp to Illuminate,* 444.
225. Tib. *nyer len gyi rgyu.*
226. Tib. *rigs 'dra'i rgyu thun mong ma yin pa.* Tsong kha pa, *Rim lnga gsal sgron,* chap. 2, 65a6–b4; an English translation in Kilty, *Lamp to Illuminate,* 121–22. See also Tsong kha pa, *Sgron gsal mchan,* 4b1.
227. See the section above, "Meditations in Correspondence with the Person—The Yogas of the Buddha's Three Bodies," in this chapter.
228. In the opening verses of the *Sgron gsal, Pradīpoddyotana,* Candrakīrti refers to the two aspects that are united in the fifth step of the completion stage as the two truths. See Candrakīrti, *Sgron gsal, Pradīpoddyotana,* chap. 1, Tōh. 1785, D. 1b4–5; a Sanskrit edition in Chakravarti, *Pradīpoddyotana,* 1; an English translation in Campbell et al., *The Esoteric Community,* 109. In his annotations, the *Sgron gsal mchan,* Tsong kha pa explains that the conventional truth is the pure illusory body formed of mere-wind-and-mind, while the ultimate truth is the wisdom of the actual clear light. In the stage of union these two are united into a single taste. Moreover, the former is the body and the latter is the mind. Tib. *sku dang thugs.* See his *Sgron gsal mchan,* 4a1–3.
229. Tsong kha pa, *Sgron gsal mchan,* 11b4–6.
230. Tib. *rnal 'byor ma'i rgyud kyi skor.*
231. Tsong kha pa, *Rim lnga gsal sgron,* chap. 7, 232a5–6; an English translation in Kilty, *Lamp to Illuminate,* 385.
232. The clear-light-emptiness into which the specially visualized deities dissolve.
233. Nāgabuddhi, *Rnam gzhag rim pa, Vyavastholi,* chap. 1, Tōh. 1809, D. 123a1–4; Sanskrit and Tibetan editions in Tanaka, *Vyavastholi,* 87–89.
234. See the section "How the First People Appear in the World" in chapter 1.
235. 'Gos Khug pa lhas btsas, *Gsang 'dus stong thun,* 7b3–9a6; Red mda' ba, *Yid kyi mun sel,* 7a5–6.
236. *Tshad ma rnam 'grel,* Tōh. 4210, the chapter entitled *Tshad ma grub pa, Pramāṇasiddhi;* Sanskrit and Tibetan editions in Miyasaka, *Pramāṇavārttika,* vv. 278cd–279ab.
237. Tsong kha pa, *Rnam gzhag rim pa'i rnam bshad,* 45b5–6.
238. Tsong kha pa, *Bung ba'i re skong,* 24a4–24b1.
239. Tib. *lhag mos kyi lha.* These deities will be further discussed in the section "The Meditation on the Specially Visualized Deities" in chapter 4. Nāgabuddhi refers to them in his synopsis cited above as the deities of the mandala wheel, beginning with Akṣobhya, that are meditated upon with "special visualization."
240. See also Tsong kha pa, *Rnam gzhag rim pa'i rnam bshad,* 21b2–5.
241. Tsong kha pa, *Bung ba'i re skong,* 24b1–2.

242. Tsong kha pa, *Bung ba'i re skong,* 24b2–4. See also his *Rnam gzhag rim pa'i rnam bshad,* 48b1–4.
243. See the sections above, "Which Birth Can be Purified?" and "Why Do Our Texts Only Speak of Human Birth in Jambudvīpa and Not in the Other Continents?," in this chapter.
244. Tsong kha pa, *Bung ba'i re skong,* 24b4–5. See also Tsong kha pa, *Rnam gzhag rim pa'i rnam bshad,* 49a1–2.
245. Tsong kha pa, *Rnam gzhag rim pa'i rnam bshad,* 21b3–5.
246. Tsong kha pa, *Bung ba'i re skong,* 15a2–3. Tsong kha pa adds here: "The meditation on the deities appearing as males and females corresponds to the people of the first eon who gradually took the form of men and women."
247. See the sections above, "Which Birth can be Purified?" and "Why Do Our Texts Only Speak of Human Birth in Jambudvīpa and Not in the Other Continents?," in this chapter.
248. Nāgabuddhi, *Rnam gzhag rim pa, Vyavastholi,* chap. 1, Tōh. 1809, D. 122b1–6; Sanskrit and Tibetan editions in Tanaka, *Vyavastholi,* 86–87.
249. See the sections "Meditations in Correspondence with the Cosmos and the Person" and "Can the Meditation on the First Deities in the Mandala Purify the First People in the Eon?" in this chapter.
250. Tib. *sngon byung;* Skt. *bhūtapūrva.*
251. Tib. Dga' ldan.
252. Tsong kha pa, *Bung ba'i re skong,* 26b3–27a1. See also Candrakīrti, *Rdo rje sems dpa'i sgrub thabs, Vajrasattva Sādhana,* Tōh. 1814, D. 201b6–2a1; a Sanskrit edition in Luo and Tomabechi, *Candrakīrti's Vajrasattva,* 23.11–24.2 and 57.5–12; and Āryadeva, *Spyod bsdus, Caryāmelāpakapradīpa,* chap. 9, Tōh. 1803, D. 94b4–6; Sanskrit and Tibetan editions with an English translation in Wedemeyer, *Āryadeva's Lamp,* B: 54b–55a.
253. *Gsang ba 'dus pa,* chap. 1, [Tōh. 442], Stog 3b3; a Sanskrit edition in Matsunaga, *The Guhyasamāja,* 4. The name of the *samādhi* is Tib. *de bzhin gshegs pa thams cad kyi 'dod chags chen po'i tshul zhes bya ba'i ting nge 'dzin;* Skt. *sarvatathāgatamahārāgavajraṃ [nayaṃ] nāmasamādhi.* Candrakīrti, *Sgron gsal, Pradīpoddyotana,* chap. 1, Tōh. 1785, D. 12b7–13a1; a Sanskrit edition in Chakravarti, *Pradīpoddyotana,* 18; an English translation in Campbell et al., *The Esoteric Community,* 144. See also Tsong kha pa, *Sgron gsal mchan,* 53b3–54b2.
254. *Brtag gnyis, Hevajra Tantra,* Tōh. 418, D. 16a4–5; Sanskrit and Tibetan editions with an English translation in Snellgrove, *Hevajra Tantra,* II.ii.51.
255. These are body, speech, and mind.
256. Tsong kha pa, *Rnam gzhag rim pa rnam bshad,* 54a6–b3. But see also his *Sngags rim chen mo,* chap. 12, 509–10; an English translation in Yarnall, *Tsong Khapa's Great Stages,* 229.
257. 'Gos Khug pa lhas btsas, *Gsang 'dus stong thun,* 13b3–14a2.
258. Red mda' ba Gzhon nu blo gros, *Yid kyi mun sel,* 8a3–b1.

259. Bu ston Rin chen grub, *Mdor byas 'grel chen,* 51b7–52a5.
260. Tsong kha pa, *Mtha' gcod rin chen myu gu,* 39b5–6.
261. Khyung po lhas pa gzhon nu bsod nams.
262. Tsong kha pa, *Rnam gzhag rim pa rnam bshad,* 55b5–6.
263. Tsong kha pa, *Rnam gzhag rim pa rnam bshad,* 55b6–56a2.
264. Mkhas grub rje, *Bskyed rim dngos grub rgya mtsho,* 86a6–b4.
265. See the sections "The Supreme King of Mandalas" and "The Supreme King of Deeds" in chap. 4.

4. A Detailed Explanation of the *Sādhana*

1. Tsong kha pa, *Bung ba'i re skong,* 9b4–29a1.
2. In the translation below, the part on the framework of the *sādhana* appears at the end.
3. Tib. *ye shes kyi sa;* Skt. *jñānabhūmi.*
4. *Gsang ba 'dus pa,* chap. 2, [Tōh. 442], Stog 9a5–6; a Sanskrit edition in Matsunaga, *The Guhyasamāja,* v. 3. See Bentor, "The Convergence," and Bentor and Dorjee, *The Ocean.* During the usual meditation on emptiness, yogis recite a mantra of emptiness *oṃ śūnyatā jñāna vajra svabhāva ātmako 'haṃ* or *oṃ svabhāva śuddhāḥ sarvadharmāḥ svabhāva śuddho 'haṃ,* found in this tantra as well, at the beginning of the third chapter of *Gsang ba 'dus pa, Guhyasamāja Tantra,* [Tōh. 442], Stog 10b4–5; a Sanskrit edition in Matsunaga, *The Guhyasamāja,* 11.
5. Tsong kha pa, *Gsang mngon,* 28b4–6; a Tibetan edition and an English translation in Engle, *Guhyasamāja Practice,* 570–71, and his *Rnal 'byor dag rim,* 8b5–6.
6. Tsong kha pa, *Bung ba'i re skong,* 11a4. Tsong kha pa follows here Candrakīrti's interpretation of this verse in its literal and shared meanings. See Candrakīrti, *Sgron gsal, Pradīpoddyotana,* chap. 2, Tōh. 1785, D. 24a2–6; Chakravarti, *Pradīpoddyotana,* 31; an English translation in Campbell et al., *The Esoteric Community,* 175–76.
7. Nāgabuddhi, *Rnam gzhag rim pa, Vyavastholi,* chap. 1, Tōh. 1809, D. 121b4–5; Sanskrit and Tibetan editions in Tanaka, *Vyavastholi,* 80–81.
8. Tib. *khams gsum pa;* Skt. *traidhātuka.* As we have seen the *Ārūpyadhātu,* the Immaterial Realm is not a place and is not destroyed.
9. Tsong kha pa, *Bung ba'i re skong,* 11a4–6.
10. Tib. *snod med.*
11. Tib. *nges ngo na.*
12. Tib. *snod mi snang ba.*
13. Tib. *snang ngo na.*
14. Tib. *kun rdzob bden pa;* Skt. *saṃvṛtisatya,* from among the two truths (Tib. *bden pa gnyis;* Skt. *satyadvaya*); the other being the ultimate truth (Tib. *don dam bden pa;* Skt. *paramārthasatya*).

15. Tib. *bde ba chen po* or *bde chen.*
16. Tsong kha pa, *Bung ba'i re skong,* 11a6–b1.
17. Tib. *rnam thar sgo;* Skt. *vimokṣamukha* (emptiness, signlessness, and wishlessness).
18. Tsong kha pa, *Bung ba'i re skong,* 11a4.
19. Tsong kha pa, *Bung ba'i re skong,* 11b1–5. In the first part of this list Tsong kha pa follows Dīpaṅkaraśrījñāna's commentary on *Cakrasaṃvara Sādhana* by Lūyipa (*Bcom ldan 'das mngon par rtogs pa, Bhagavadabhisamaya,* Tōh. 1427), as well as Rin chen bzang po's commentary on Dīpaṅkaraśrījñāna. See Dīpaṅkaraśrījñāna, Mar me mdzad ye shes, *Mngon par rtogs pa rnam par 'byed pa, Abhisamayavibhaṅga,* Tōh. 1490, D. 189b1–2; and Rin chen bzang po, *Mngon par rtogs pa'i dka' ba'i gnas bshad pa,* 4a6–7, edited by Kano and Kawasaki, "A Critical Edition," 16.
20. Tsong kha pa, *Bung ba'i re skong,* 4b2–8a3.
21. Tib. *tha mal gyi snang zhen rtog pa.* See the end of the section "Three Bodies of the Meditators on the Creation Stage" in chapter 3.
22. Tib. *snang la rang bzhin med pa sgyu ma lta bu.* See also the discussion of the illusion-like *samādhi* in the section "The Illusory Body" in chapter 3.
23. Tsong kha pa, *Sngags rim chen mo,* chap. 12, 493; an English translation in Yarnall, *Tsong Khapa's Great Stages,* 195.
24. Tib. *bden 'dzin.*
25. Mkhas grub rje, *Bskyed rim dngos grub rgya mtsho,* 37a3–5.
26. See Tsong kha pa, *Lam rim chen mo,* the chapters on serenity and insight; an English translation in Cutler, *Great Treatise,* passim, on sprouts or seedlings and the absence of intrinsic existence.
27. Tsong kha pa, *Bung ba'i re skong,* 8a3–9b4.
28. Candrakīrti, *Rdo rje sems dpa'i sgrub thabs, Vajrasattva Sādhana,* Tōh. 1814, D. 197b5; a Sanskrit edition in Luo and Tomabechi, *Candrakīrti's Vajrasattva,* 9.8 and 41.12.
29. See Tsong kha pa, *Sngags rim chen mo,* chap. 12, 500; an English translation in Yarnall, *Tsong Khapa's Great Stages,* 208.
30. See the section "How Does This Meditation Correspond to the Ground, Path and Fruit?" below in this chapter.
31. See Tsong kha pa, *Gsang mngon,* 28b6–31a4; Engle, *Guhyasamāja Practice,* 570–77.
32. Tib. *chos 'byung;* Skt. *dharmodaya.*
33. Tsong kha pa, *Gsang mngon,* 29a1–2; Engle, *Guhyasamāja Practice,* 570–71.
34. See Abhayākaragupta, *Dkyil chog rdo rje phreng ba, Vajrāvalī Maṇḍalavidhi,* Tōh. 3140, D. 38a5; Sanskrit and Tibetan editions in Mori, *Vajrāvalī,* §13.2.2, 236–37.
35. The female sexual organ.
36. Tsong kha pa, *Bung ba'i re skong,* 12b5–6.

37. *Gsang ba 'dus pa,* chap. 1, [Tōh. 442], Stog 1b3–2a2; a Sanskrit edition in Matsunaga, *The Guhyasamāja,* 4.
38. Tsong kha pa, *Gsang mngon,* 29a2–b1; Engle, *Guhyasamāja Practice,* 570–73.
39. This is so in the macrocosm, according to Vasubandhu, who describes the world resting on three cylinders of wind, water, and earth, one on top of the other. See his *Mdzod 'grel, Kośabhāṣya,* chap. 3, vv. 45–48a, Tōh. 4090, D. *ku,* 144a4–b4; a Sanskrit edition in Pradhan, *Abhidharmakośabhāṣyam,* 157–58; an English translation in Pruden, *Vasubandhu,* 451–52. See also the following paragraph. In Tsong kha pa's *Sādhana,* however, the water mandala is round, the wind "mandala" is bow-shaped, the fire "mandala" is a triangle, and the earth "mandala" is square. See Tsong kha pa, *Gsang mngon,* 29a2–b1; Engle, *Guhyasamāja Practice,* 570–73.
40. Nāgabuddhi, *Rnam gzhag rim pa, Vyavastholi,* chap. 1, Tōh. 1809, D. 121b5–22a1; Sanskrit and Tibetan editions in Tanaka, *Vyavastholi,* 80–81; Tsong kha pa, *Bung ba'i re skong,* 12b2.
41. Tsong kha pa, *Bung ba'i re skong,* 12b2–3.
42. Tib. *gzhi la.*
43. Tib. Spyan ma, Māmakī, Gos dkar mo, and Sgrol ma. Tsong kha pa, *Gsang mngon,* 29b1; Engle, *Guhyasamāja Practice,* 572–73.
44. According to Nāgārjuna's *sādhana,* yogis should meditate on the four physical elements in the aspects of solidity, fluidity, warmth, and motility, respectively. See his *Mdor byas, Piṇḍīkrama Sādhana,* Tōh. 1796, 4a6; L. 61.
45. Tib. *ngo bor.*
46. Tib. *mnyam gnas;* Skt. *samāna.*
47. Tib. *gyen rgyu;* Skt. *udāna.*
48. Tib. *srog 'dzin;* Skt. *prāṇa.*
49. Tib. *thur sel;* Skt. *apāna.* Tsong kha pa, *Bung ba'i re skong,* 13a1–2.
50. Tib. *khyab byed;* Skt. *vyāna.*
51. For the five main winds, see *Rgyud rdo rje phreng ba, Vajramālā Tantra,* Tōh. 445, chap. 68, D. 276b1–2; an English translation in Kittay with Lozang Jamspal, *Vajra Rosary,* chap. 68, vv. 52–54.
52. Tib. *rtsa dbu ma;* Skt. *avadhūtī.*
53. Tib. *mi shigs pa'i thig le.*
54. Tib. *thig le;* Skt. *bindu.*
55. See, Tsong kha pa, *Rim lnga gsal sgron,* chap. 2, 67a3–4; an English translation in Kilty, *Lamp to Illuminate,* 124.
56. Tib. *nang gi rkyen.*
57. Tib. *phyi'i rkyen.*
58. Tib. Spyan ma, Māmakī, Gos dkar mo, and Sgrol ma.
59. Tib. Padma can, Dung can ma, Glang po can ma, and Ri dwags can ma. In the completion stage Locanā, Māmakī, Pāṇḍarā, and Tārā become Padminī, Śaṅkhinī, Hastinī, and Citriṇī, who belong, respectively, to the same tathāgata

families. These goddesses are described in Jñānapāda, *Zhal lung, Dvikrama,* Tōh. 1853, D. *di,* 4a3–5a5; a Tibetan edition and an English translation in C. Dalton, "Enacting Perfection," vv. 50–82.

60. Tsong kha pa, *Bung ba'i re skong,* 13a2–4.
61. Tsong kha pa, *Gsang mngon,* 29b1–2; Engle, *Guhyasamāja Practice,* 572–73.
62. This is the first of the five steps during the completion stage according to Nagārjuna's *Rim lnga, Pañcakrama,* Tōh. 1802; Mimaki and Tomabechi, *Pañcakrama;* Tomabechi, "Étude du *Pañcakrama.*"
63. Tsong kha pa, *Bung ba'i re skong,* 13a2–5.
64. Tsong kha pa *Gsang mngon,* 29b2–31a4; Engle, *Guhyasamāja Practice,* 572–77.
65. Tsong kha pa, *Bung ba'i re skong,* 12b3–4.
66. Mkhas grub rje, *Bskyed rim dngos grub rgya mtsho,* 50a1–2.
67. See the section "Can the Meditation on the First Deities in the Mandala Purify the First People in the Eon?" in chapter 3.
68. Tib. *lhag mos kyi lha.*
69. In fact, the origin of their name is in the instruction to meditate on them through "special visualization" or "special aspiration," as we have seen in the synopsis of the *sādhana* in *Formulating the Guhyasamāja Sādhana,* cited above. Similar instructions are found also in the two basic *sādhanas* of the Guhyasamāja by Nāgārjuna, *Mdor byas, Piṇḍīkrama Sādhana,* Tōh. 1796, D. 3a7; a Sanskrit edition in de La Vallée Poussin, *Études et textes tantriques,* v. 36ab; and Nāgārjuna, *Mdo bsre, Sādhanasūtramelāpaka,* Tōh. 1797, D. 12a3.
70. Tib. Reg bya rdo rje ma; Skt. Sparśavajrā.
71. According to Nāgabuddhi, the principal deity of the specially visualized deities is Akṣobhya (as cited in the section "The Meditation according to the *Sādhana*" in chapter 3). See Nāgabuddhi, *Rnam gzhag rim pa, Vyavastholi,* chap. 1, Tōh. 1809, D. 121b2; Sanskrit and Tibetan editions in Tanaka, *Vyavastholi,* 79. In the basic *sādhana,* the *Concise Sādhana,* the principal deity of the specially visualized deities is Vajrasattva. See Nāgārjuna, *Mdor byas, Piṇḍīkrama,* Tōh. 1796, D. 3a4; a Sanskrit edition in de La Vallée Poussin, *Études et textes tantriques,* v. 30d. On the other hand, in the second *sādhana* by Nāgārjuna and in Candrakīrti's *sādhana,* the principal deity is Vajradhara. See Nāgārjuna, *Mdo bsre, Sādhanasūtramelāpaka,* Tōh. 1797, D. 12a3; and Candrakīrti, *Rdo rje sems dpa'i sgrub thabs, Vajrasattva Sādhana,* Tōh. 1814, D. 198a4; a Sanskrit edition in Luo and Tomabechi, *Candrakīrti's Vajrasattva,* 11.6 and 43.13. On debates about the identity of the principal deity of the specially visualized deities, see also Tsong kha pa, *Rnam gzhag rim pa'i rnam bshad,* 5a4–6a6.
72. These are Tib. Gzugs rdo rje ma, Sgra rdo rje ma, Dri rdo rje ma, and Ro rdo rje ma; Skt. Rūpavajrā, Śabdavajrā, Gandhavajrā, and Rasavajrā.
73. Maitreya and Kṣitigarbha in the east, Vajrapāṇi and Khagarbha in the south, Lokeśvara and Mañjuśrī in the west, and Sarvāvaraṇavikṣambhin and Samantabhadra in the north.

74. Tsong kha pa, *Bung ba'i re skong,* 15a3–4.
75. See the section "Can the Meditation on the First Deities in the Mandala Purify the First People in the Eon?" in chapter 3.
76. Tib. *sngon byung;* Skt. *bhūtapūrva.* This refers to the events in the first chapter of the *Gsang ba 'dus pa, Guhyasamāja Tantra.* See the end of the section "The *Samādhi* of Great Bliss" in chapter 3.
77. Tsong kha pa, *Bung ba'i re skong,* 15a5–6.
78. See the section "Methods of Purifications" in chapter 3.
79. See the section "Placing the Deities on the Body" in this chapter.
80. Tsong kha pa, *Bung ba'i re skong,* 15a3–4.
81. Tib. *phung po;* Skt. *skandha.*
82. Tib. *khams;* Skt. *dhātu.*
83. Tib. *dbang po;* Skt. *indriya.*
84. Tib. *yul;* Skt. *viṣaya.*
85. Tib. *[gzhi dus kyi] ye shes;* Skt. *jñāna.*
86. The scriptural authority here is the *Vajra Garland Tantra,* cited by Nāgārjuna in his basic *Sādhana.* See *Rdo rje phreng ba, Vajramālā Tantra,* Tōh. 445, chap. 68, D. 275a7–b6; an English translation in Kittay with Lozang Jamspal, *Vajra Rosary,* chap. 68, vv. 28–36. Nāgārjuna's verses are similar but not identical. See his *Mdor byas, Piṇḍīkrama Sādhana,* Tōh. 1796, D. 3b1–5; a Sanskrit edition in de La Vallée Poussin, *Études et textes tantriques,* vv. 38cd–45.
87. Tib. Rnam snang, Spyan ma, Sa'i snying po, Gzugs rdo rje ma, Byams pa, Gshin rje gshed, and Mi g.yo.
88. Tsong kha pa, *Bung ba'i re skong,* 17a2–3.
89. Tsong kha pa, *Bung ba'i re skong,* 17a3–4.
90. Tsong kha pa, *Gsang mngon,* 38b5–39a2; Engle, *Guhyasamāja Practice,* 588–89.
91. Or Ṭarkvirāja.
92. In the fourth cycle two faculties and two sense objects dissolve. The faculties are those of the tongue and the body, and the sense objects are tastes and tangible objects.
93. Tsong kha pa, *Bung ba'i re skong,* 17a4. For these three experiences or three appearances, see the section "The Dissolutions of Consciousness" in chapter 2.
94. Tib. *stong pa, shin tu stong pa,* and *stong pa chen po;* Skt. *śūnya, atiśūnya,* and *mahāśūnya.*
95. Tsong kha pa, *Bung ba'i re skong,* 17b3–4.
96. See the section "Death according to Vajrayāna" in chapter 2.
97. Mkhas grub rje, *Bskyed rim dngos grub rgya mtsho,* 94b3–6.
98. See the description of the deities who reside in the mandala in the section "The Meditation on the Specially Visualized Deities" in this chapter.
99. Mkhas grub rje, *Bskyed rim dngos grub rgya mtsho,* 95a3–6. On different views of Dge lugs scholars about this meditation, see Bentor, "Interpreting the Body *Maṇḍala.*"

100. Tsong kha pa, *Bung ba'i re skong,* 17a4–5. See also his *Gsang mngon,* 39a2–4; Engle, *Guhyasamāja Practice,* 588–89.
101. Tsong kha pa, *Bung ba'i re skong,* 17b4.
102. Tsong kha pa, *Slob tshul,* 14a6.
103. Mkhas grub rje, *Bskyed rim dngos grub rgya mtsho,* 94b6–95a2. Similar descriptions are found regarding the two meditative absorptions of the completion stage; see Nāgārjuna, *Rim lnga, Pañcakrama,* chap. 4, vv. 25–28, Tōh. 1802, D. 55a1–2; Sanskrit and Tibetan editions in Mimaki and Tomabechi, *Pañcakrama,* 45–46; a Sanskrit edition and a French translation in Tomabechi, "Étude du *Pañcakrama,*" 171. Āryadeva, *Spyod bsdus, Caryāmelāpakapradīpa,* chap. 7, Tōh. 1803, D. 88b4–5; Sanskrit and Tibetan editions with an English translation in Wedemeyer, *Āryadeva's Lamp,* B: 46b.
104. Tsong kha pa, *Bung ba'i re skong,* 17b4–5.
105. See Tsong kha pa, *Sgron gsal mchan,* 98b5–6.
106. Tsong kha pa, *Bung ba'i re skong,* 17b5–18a1.
107. Tib. *de bzhin nyid las byang chub pa.*
108. Tib. *mngon par byang chub pa,* or *mngon byang;* Skt. *abhisambodhi.* For the other four manifest awakenings, see the section "Meditations that Correspond to the Intermediate State" below in this chapter.
109. Tib. *dang po mgon po;* Skt. *ādinātha.*
110. Tib. *de nyid zhe dgu.* See Tsong kha pa, *Bung ba'i re skong,* 1b4–3a5.
111. For some reason this point is missing in our text, but it appears in Tsong kha pa, *Rnal 'byor dag rim,* 13b3, as the twelfth essential point.
112. Tsong kha pa, *Bung ba'i re skong,* 17b6–18a1.
113. Tsong kha pa, *Bung ba'i re skong,* 18a1–3.
114. On the relations between the five and six steps of the completion stage, see the section "The Three Bodies of the Meditators on the Completion Stage" in chapter 3.
115. Tib. *zhugs gnas thim gsum.*
116. See also Tsong kha pa, *Rnam gzhag rim pa'i rnam bshad,* 29a6–30b4.
117. Tib. *dang po mgon po;* Skt. *ādinātha.*
118. These three stages are included in the essential point of arising by visualizing the solar disk and so forth (Tib. *nyi ma la sogs pa la dmigs pa ldang ba'i de nyid*). This is one of the forty-nine essential points (Tib. *de nyid zhe dgu*) that constitute the entire *sādhana.* See Tsong kha pa, *Bung ba'i re skong,* 1b4–3a5, and his *Rnal 'byor dag rim,* 13b3–14a5, but note that the listings in these two works are not identical.
119. This the essential point of the concentration on the moon (Tib. *zla ba la dmigs pa'i de nyid*) or awakening from the moon (Tib. *zla ba las byang chub ba'i de nyid*).
120. This the essential point of abiding in absorption on wisdom alone (Tib. *ye shes tsam la snyoms par zhugs pa'i de nyid*).

121. The Tibetan here is *zla ba'i dkyil 'khor,* just as in the case of the word translated above as "lunar disk." However, since these two lunar circles have different roles here, I translate the first as "lunar disk" and the second as "moon orb."
122. Bentor, "Tsong-kha-pa's *Guhyasamāja Sādhana,*" and Bentor and Dorjee, *The Ocean.*
123. This the essential point of awakening from the emblem (Tib. *phyag mtshan las byang chub ba'i de nyid*).
124. This the essential point of awakening from the complete body (Tib. *sku rdzogs pa las byang chub ba'i de nyid*).
125. Tsong kha pa, *Bung ba'i re skong,* 18a1–5.
126. Tsong kha pa, *Bung ba'i re skong,* 18a5–b2. The five manifest awakenings (Tib. *mngon par byang chub pa,* or *mngon byang;* Skt. *abhisambodhi*) comprise the meditation on emptiness and on the First Lord. The manifest awakening from suchness (Tib. *de bzhin nyid las byang chub pa*), which consists of meditation on suchness or emptiness, took place in the previous step of the meditation, the dissolution of the specially visualized deities into clear light. The visualization of the First Lord from emptiness comprises the remaining four. On the five manifest awakenings, see, for example, English, *Vajrayoginī,* 149–54.
127. Tsong kha pa, *Bung ba'i re skong,* 19b2–4.
128. Tsong kha pa, *Bung ba'i re skong,* 19b4–5.
129. Namely, body, speech, and mind isolations.
130. Tsong kha pa, *Bung ba'i re skong,* 19b5–6.
131. On the term "taking birth," see the section "Rebirth" in chapter 2.
132. Tsong kha pa, *Bung ba'i re skong,* 21a6.
133. Tsong kha pa, *Gsang mngon,* 40a1–6; Engle, *Guhyasamāja Practice,* 590–91.
134. Nāgabuddhi, *Rnam gzhag rim pa, Vyavastholi,* chap. 1, Tōh. 1809, D. 124a2; Sanskrit and Tibetan editions in Tanaka, *Vyavastholi,* 93.
135. Tib. *de bzhin gshegs pa thams cad zil gyis gnon pa rdo rje zhes bya ba'i ting nge 'dzin;* Skt. *sarvatathāgatābhibhavanavajra samādhi.*
136. *Gsang ba 'dus pa,* chap. 1, [Tōh. 442], Stog, 4a6–7 [the rest is missing]; a Sanskrit edition in Matsunaga, *The Guhyasamāja,* 5.
137. Tsong kha pa, *Sgron gsal mchan,* 63b2–6, commenting on the hidden level of interpretation (Tib. *sbas pa,* Skt. *garbhī*) of this *samādhi* in Candrakīrti, *Sgron gsal, Pradīpoddyotana,* chap. 1, Tōh. 1785, D. 15a2–5; a Sanskrit edition in Chakravarti, *Pradīpoddyotana,* 20; an English translation in Campbell et al., *The Esoteric Community,* 177. Tsong kha pa furnishes here also the literal level of interpretation (Tib. *yig don,* Skt. *akṣarārtha*).
138. Tsong kha pa, *Rnam gzhag rim pa'i rnam bshad,* 42b6–43a3. See also the *Sdom 'byung, Saṃvarodaya Tantra,* Tōh. 373, chap. 2; Sanskrit and Tibetan editions with an English translation in Tsuda, *The Saṃvarodaya,* chap. 2, vv. 14cd–16; referred to in Nāgabuddhi, *Rnam gzhag rim pa, Vyavastholi,* chap. 1, Tōh. 1809, D. 124a2; Sanskrit and Tibetan editions in Tanaka, *Vyavastholi,* 93.

139. See the section "Rebirth" in chapter 2. These sources include the *Sdom 'byung, Saṃvarodaya Tantra,* Tōh. 373; Sanskrit and Tibetan editions with an English translation in Tsuda, *The Saṃvarodaya;* and Nāgabuddhi, *Rnam gzhag rim pa, Vyavastholi,* chap. 1, Tōh. 1809; Sanskrit and Tibetan editions in Tanaka, *Vyavastholi.*
140. Tsong kha pa, *Rnam gzhag rim pa'i rnam bshad,* 53b4–6. See Bentor, "Tsong-kha-pa's *Guhyasamāja Sādhana,*" 183; and Bentor and Dorjee, *The Ocean,* introductory essay.
141. Tsong kha pa, *Bung ba'i re skong,* 21b1–3.
142. Tsong kha pa, *Gsang mngon,* 40a6–41a2; Engle, *Guhyasamāja Practice,* 592–93.
143. Tib. *rigs 'dra.*
144. Tsong kha pa, *Bung ba'i re skong,* 21b3–5.
145. Tsong kha pa, *'Dod 'jo,* 121a2–6, and 122b4–6.
146. See Tsong kha pa, *Gsang mngon,* 29b2–31a4; Engle, *Guhyasamāja Practice,* 572–75.
147. For more about this, see Bentor, "Interpreting the Body *Maṇḍala.*"
148. Tsong kha pa, *Slob tshul,* 16b1–3.
149. Mkhas grub rje, *Bskyed rim dngos grub rgya mtsho,* 130b4–6.
150. Tsong kha pa, *Bung ba'i re skong,* 21b5–6.
151. These are the two arms, the mouth, the *vajra,* the two shoulders, the two knees, the head, and the soles.
152. Tsong kha pa, *Bung ba'i re skong,* 21b6–22a1.
153. See Bentor, "Interpreting the Body *Maṇḍala.*"
154. Tsong kha pa, *Bung ba'i re skong,* 21b4–5 and 22a1.
155. Tsong kha pa elaborates on the specific attainments that ensue from the meditation on the different classes of deities on the body in his *Bung ba'i re skong,* 22a1–3.
156. See Paṇ chen Blo bzang chos kyi rgyal mtshan, *Bskyed rim dngos grub rgya mtsho'i snying po,* 58a3–4, 58b5, and 59a5–6; Bentor and Dorjee, *The Essence,* 171–75.
157. Paṇ chen Blo bzang chos kyi rgyal mtshan, *Bskyed rim dngos grub rgya mtsho'i snying po,* 54a3–4; Bentor and Dorjee, *The Essence,* 162–63.
158. Tib. *yul, tshul, ngo bo,* and *rnam pa.*
159. The three *tathāgatas*, Vairocana, Amitābha, and Akṣobhya, with their consorts, the goddesses or female *tathāgatas*, Locanā, Pāṇḍarā, and Māmakī.
160. *Oṃ sarva tathāgata kāya vajra svabhāva ātmako 'haṃ, oṃ sarva tathāgata vāk vajra svabhāva ātmako 'haṃ,* and *oṃ sarva tathāgata citta vajra svabhāva ātmako 'haṃ.*
161. Tsong kha pa, *Bung ba'i re skong,* 22a3–b1.
162. Tib. *dam tshig sems dpa', ye shes sems dpa',* and *ting nge 'dzin sems dpa'.*
163. Abhayākaragupta, *Man ngag snye ma, Āmnāyamañjarī,* Tōh. 1198, D. 122a4–

5; Tsong kha pa, *Sngags rim chen mo,* chap. 12, 516; an English translation in Yarnall, *Tsong Khapa's Great Stages,* 240; and Tsong kha pa, *Slob tshul,* 20a1–3.

164. Tsong kha pa, *Bung ba'i re skong,* 22b1–2.
165. Mkhas grub rje, *Bskyed rim dngos grub rgya mtsho,* 116a5–6.
166. Bentor and Dorjee, *The Ocean,* introductory essay.
167. Tsong kha pa, *Bung ba'i re skong,* 22b2–4.
168. Tib. *dkyil 'khor rgyal mchog;* Skt. *maṇḍalarājāgrī.*
169. Tsong kha pa, *Bung ba'i re skong,* 24b5–6.
170. Tsong kha pa, *Rim lnga gsal sgron,* chap. 2, 55b5–56a3; English translations in Kilty, *Lamp to Illuminate,* 108–9; and Jinpa, *Science and Philosophy,* 270–71.
171. Tsong kha pa, *Bung ba'i re skong,* 25b1–3.
172. See the section "Can Women in Jambudvīpa Reach Awakening in Their Present Lives?" in chapter 3.
173. See the section "The Name 'Illusory Body'" in chapter 3.
174. Tib. *las kyi phyag rgya,* or *dngos kyi rig ma;* Skt. *karmamudrā.*
175. Tib. *ye shes kyi phyag rgya;* Skt. *jñānamudrā.*
176. Tsong kha pa, *Bung ba'i re skong,* 24b6.
177. The path common to the Mantra and Pāramitā Vehicles or to Sūtra and Tantra.
178. Tib. *'Dod pa'i bstan bcos.*
179. Tsong kha pa, *Bung ba'i re skong,* 24b6–25a2.
180. See also Tsong kha pa, *Rim lnga gsal sgron,* chap. 2, 67b6–68a1; English translations in Kilty, *Lamp to Illuminate,* 125; and Jinpa, *Science and Philosophy,* 273–74.
181. Tsong kha pa, *Gsang mngon,* 50a2–3; Engle, *Guhyasamāja Practice,* 612–13.
182. See the next paragraph for her identity.
183. Tsong kha pa, *Bung ba'i re skong,* 25a2–3.
184. Tsong kha pa, *Bung ba'i re skong,* 25a3.
185. According to the *Sādhana,* from emptiness yogis visualize the syllable *khaṃ,* which turns into a *vajra* marked with *khaṃ,* and the *vajra* transformed into Sparśavajrā, Vajra Lady of Tangibles. See Tsong kha pa, *Gsang mngon,* 50a3–4; Engle, *Guhyasamāja Practice,* 612–13.
186. Tib. Reg bya rdo rje ma; Skt. Sparśavajrā.
187. Generally speaking, Sparśavajrā, Vajra Lady of Tangibles, is the consort of Akṣobhya in the Guhyasamāja mandala. On certain occasions, however, such as blessing the mind, Māmakī is Akṣobhya's consort. In this passage, she can be either one, but in Tsong kha pa's *Sādhana* she is Sparśavajrā. See Tsong kha pa, *Gsang mngon,* 50a4; Engle, *Guhyasamāja Practice,* 612–13, and his *Rnal 'byor dag rim,* 19b2.
188. The number of deities placed on the consort's body is twenty-nine and not thirty-two as for the yogi, because only five *bodhisattvas* are placed on her body: the four *bodhisattvas* Kṣitigarbha, Vajrapāṇi, Khagarbha, and Lokeśvara that are placed on her four sense faculties, the eye, ear, nose, and tongue,

respectively, as well as Sarvāvaraṇavikṣambhin, who is placed on her *bhaga.* The three *bodhisattvas* Mañjuśrī, Samantabhadra, and Maitreya placed on the yogi's mental faculty, joints, and channels with sinews are not placed on the body of the consort. See Tsong kha pa, *Gsang mngon,* 50b1–51b5; Engle, *Guhyasamāja Practice,* 612–15. The association of Samantabhadra with the joints and Maitreya with the channels and sinews is not obvious.

189. See the section "Placing the Deities on the Body" above in this chapter.
190. Tsong kha pa, *Bung ba'i re skong,* 25a4.
191. Tsong kha pa, *Gsang mngon,* 51b5–52a2; Engle, *Guhyasamāja Practice,* 614–17.
192. Tsong kha pa, *Bung ba'i re skong,* 25a5–6.
193. See Tsong kha pa, *Rim lnga gsal sgron,* chap. 4, 117a1–3; an English translation in Kilty, *Lamp to Illuminate,* 202–3.
194. Tib. *mchog tu dga' ba;* Skt. *paramānanda.*
195. Tsong kha pa, *Bung ba'i re skong,* 25a6–b1.
196. Tsong kha pa, *Gsang mngon,* 52a4–6; Engle, *Guhyasamāja Practice,* 616–17.
197. Tsong kha pa, *Bung ba'i re skong,* 4a1–2.
198. *Gsang ba 'dus pa,* chap. 6, [Tōh. 442], Stog 14b5–15a5; a Sanskrit edition in Matsunaga, *The Guhyasamāja,* 17.
199. See Tsong kha pa, *Sgron gsal mchan,* 173b1–3.
200. As we have seen in the section "The *Samādhi* of Great Bliss" in chapter 3, while there is no distinction between the objective emptiness meditated upon in the Pāramitā and Mantra Vehicles, the subjective mind of great bliss that meditates on emptiness is superior.
201. Tib. *dang po sbyor ba['i ting nge 'dzin];* Skt. *ādiyoga[samādhi].*
202. Tib. *dkyil 'khor rgyal mchog [gi ting nge 'dzin];* Skt. *maṇḍalarājāgrī[samādhi].*
203. Tib. *las kyi rgyal mchog [gi ting nge 'dzin];* Skt. *karmarājāgrī[samādhi].*
204. Tsong kha pa, *Bung ba'i re skong,* 4a1–2. Also see the section "The Yoga with a Consort" above in this chapter.
205. Tsong kha pa, *Bung ba'i re skong,* 25b3–4.
206. Tsong kha pa, *Gsang mngon,* 52a5–b2; Engle, *Guhyasamāja Practice,* 616–17.
207. See the section "The Yoga with a Consort" above in this chapter.
208. Tsong kha pa, *Bung ba'i re skong,* 25b5.
209. Tib. *cho ga gsum.*
210. Tib. *sgo bdun.*
211. Tib. *phyag rgya bzhi.*
212. Tsong kha pa, *Bung ba'i re skong,* 25b6–26a1.
213. See the section "Meditations that Correspond to the Intermediate State" above in this chapter.
214. For instance, the emblems of the five tathāgatas: Akṣobhya, Vairocana, Ratnasaṃbhava, Amitābha, and Amoghasiddhi are a *vajra,* wheel, jewel, lotus, and crossed *vajra,* respectively.
215. Tsong kha pa, *Bung ba'i re skong,* 25b6–26a1.

216. Tsong kha pa, *Gsang mngon*, 52b2–67b3; Engle, *Guhyasamāja Practice*, 616–47.
217. Tib. *bskyed pa'i sgo.*
218. Tib. *ye shes sems dpa'*; Eng. wisdom being.
219. See Tsong kha pa, *Gsang mngon*, 59b3–60a3; Engle, *Guhyasamāja Practice*, 630–31.
220. Tib. Reg bya rdo rje ma; Skt. Sparśavajrā.
221. Therefore, there only thirty-one seats for the thirty-two deities of the mandala.
222. See also the section "The Meditation on the Specially Visualized Deities" in this chapter.
223. Tib. *phyag rgya;* Skt. *mudrā.*
224. Tib. *chos kyi phyag rgya, dam tshig gi phyag rgya, phyag rgya chen po,* and *las kyi phyag rgya;* Skt. *dharmamudrā, samayamudrā, mahāmudrā,* and *karmamudrā.*
225. See J. Dalton, "On the Significance," 331.
226. Tsong kha pa, *Bung ba'i re skong*, 26a4–6. See also the *Rnam gzhag rim pa*, chap. 3, D. 127b2–4; Sanskrit and Tibetan editions in Tanaka, *Vyavastholi*, 113–14; and Tsong kha pa's commentary on this, *Rnam gzhag rim pa'i rnam bshad*, 66a1–67a2.
227. Tsong kha pa, *Bung ba'i re skong*, 26a6–b3. See also Nāgabuddhi, *Rnam gzhag rim pa*, chap. 3, D. 127b4–28a4; Sanskrit and Tibetan editions in Tanaka, *Vyavastholi*, 114–18, and Tsong kha pa's commentary on this, *Rnam gzhag rim pa'i rnam bshad*, 67a2–71b1.
228. Tsong kha pa, *Bung ba'i re skong*, 27a1–2.
229. Tib. *nang du yang dag 'jog pa;* Skt. *pratisaṃlayana.* See Tsong kha pa, *Bung ba'i re skong*, 27a2–3.
230. Tsong kha pa's *Rnal 'byor dag rim*, 23a1–3.
231. Tsong kha pa, *Bung ba'i re skong*, 28b1.
232. See Mkhas grub rje, *Bskyed rim dngos grub rgya mtsho*, 159b5–6.
233. Tsong kha pa, *Sngags rim chen mo*, chap. 12, 480; an English translation in Yarnall, *Tsong Khapa's Great Stages*, 170.
234. Tib. *zhi gnas;* Skt. *śamatha.*
235. Mkhas grub rje, *Bskyed rim dngos grub rgya mtsho*, 160a4.
236. Tsong kha pa, *Bung ba'i re skong*, 27a3–5.
237. Tsong kha pa, *Sngags rim chen mo*, chap. 12, 480; an English translation in Yarnall, *Tsong Khapa's Great Stages*, 170.
238. Tib. *lhag mthong;* Skt. *vipaśyanā.*
239. Tib. *zhi lhag zung du 'brel ba'i ting nge 'dzin.*
240. See the section "Additional Buddhist Antecedents of Tantric Visualizations" in chapter 1.
241. Tsong kha pa, *Bung ba'i re skong*, 28b1–2.
242. Tsong kha pa, *Bung ba'i re skong*, 27b1–2.
243. Tib. *de kho na nyid kyi snying po.* See Tsong kha pa, *Rnal 'byor dag rim*, 24b2.

In his *Sādhana,* Tsong kha pa describes a more elaborate practice of mental recitation: when breath is exhaled along with mantra recitation, the deities of the mandala emanate and act for the sake of sentient beings; and when breath is inhaled along with mantra recitation, the deities gather back. See his *Gsang mngon,* 67b3–5; Engle, *Guhyasamāja Practice,* 646–47. But this practice is not mentioned in Tsong kha pa's *Bung ba'i re skong.*

244. Tib. *snying po.* See Tsong kha pa, *Rnal 'byor dag rim,* 24b6.
245. Tsong kha pa, *Bung ba'i re skong,* 27b4–5.
246. Tsong kha pa, *Gsang mngon,* 68a6–b2; Engle, *Guhyasamāja Practice,* 648–49.
247. Tib. Reg bya rdo rje ma; Skt. Sparśavajrā.
248. The ུ at the bottom of the *hūṃ* ཧཱུྃ.
249. The ཧ་.
250. The horizontal line at the top of the syllable ཧ་.
251. The crescent moon above the syllable ཧ་.
252. The small circle, *bindu* or *anusvāra,* the *ṃ,* above the crescent moon.
253. The squiggle or "flame" on top of the drop or the small circle.
254. Tsong kha pa, *Bung ba'i re skong,* 28b2.
255. Tsong kha pa, *Bung ba'i re skong,* 28b4–6.
256. Tsong kha pa, *Gsang mngon,* 68b2–3; Engle, *Guhyasamāja Practice,* 650–51.
257. Tib. *tshad med pa bzhi;* Skt. *catvāryapramāṇāni.*
258. Tsong kha pa, *Gsang mngon,* 69a6–b1; Engle, *Guhyasamāja Practice,* 650–51.
259. *Gsang ba 'dus pa,* chap. 17, [Tōh. 442], Stog 79b7–80b2; a Sanskrit edition in Matsunaga, *The Guhyasamāja,* vv. 72–75.
260. Tsong kha pa, *Bung ba'i re skong,* 27b6–28a1.
261. Tsong kha pa, *Bung ba'i re skong,* 28b2–3.
262. Tsong kha pa, *Bung ba'i re skong,* 28b3–4.
263. Tsong kha pa, *Bung ba'i re skong,* 28a1–2.
264. *Gsang ba 'dus pa,* chap. 17, [Tōh. 442], Stog 68b5–69a2; a Sanskrit edition in Matsunaga, *The Guhyasamāja,* vv. 1–5; Nāgārjuna, *Mdor byas, Piṇḍīkrama Sādhana,* Tōh. 1796, D. 10a4–7; a Sanskrit edition in de La Vallée Poussin, *Études et textes tantriques,* vv. 211–15; Tsong kha pa, *Gsang mngon,* 69b1–6; Engle, *Guhyasamāja Practice,* 652–53.
265. Tsong kha pa, *Bung ba'i re skong,* 28a2–3.
266. Tib. *mchod yon;* Skt. *arga.*
267. Tsong kha pa, *Bung ba'i re skong,* 28a4–5.
268. Tsong kha pa, *Bung ba'i re skong,* 28a5–6.
269. Tsong kha pa, *Bung ba'i re skong,* 28a6–b1.
270. Tsong kha pa, *Gsang mngon,* 72b5–73a1; Engle, *Guhyasamāja Practice,* 660–61.
271. Tsong kha pa, *Gsang mngon,* 73a1–74a1; Engle, *Guhyasamāja Practice,* 660–63.

Fulfilling the Bee's Hope

1. The full title of *Fulfilling the Bee's Hope* in Tibetan: *Dpal gsang ba 'dus pa'i bskyed rim blo gsal bung ba'i re skong gnad don gsal ba,* shortened here to *Bung ba'i re skong.* "Hope" in the title refers to "nectar," while "bee" to "disciple." The principal Tibetan version of this work (to which correspond the bracketed page numbers and the notes on variant readings) is the old *Bkra shis lhun po* redaction from the library of Klu 'khyil monastery of Ladakh, printed by Ngawang Gelek Demo in 1977. This is the work that appears in the bibliography. In addition, two other versions were consulted. First, the Zhol version of the *Bung ba'i re skong,* in Tsong kha pa's *Collected Works,* vol. 7, 695–748, published by the Mongolian Lama Guru Deva in New Delhi, India (1978–79). And second, the Kumbum (Sku 'bum) version found in Tsong kha pa's *Collected Works,* vol. 7, 751–809, published in *Sku 'bum byams pa gling,* n.d.
2. The full title of Tsong kha pa's *Guhyasamāja Sādhana* in Tibetan: *Gsang ba 'dus pa'i bla brgyud gsol 'debs dang bdag bskyed ngag 'don bkra shis lhun po rgyud pa grwa tshang gi 'don rgyud rje thams cad mkhyen pas zhus dag mdzad pa,* is shortened here to *Gsang mngon.*
3. For an excellent English translation of the entire *Guhyasamāja Sādhana* by Tsong kha pa, see Engle, *Guhyasamāja Practice,* 515–93. The Tibetan text appears on the opposite pages in Engle's translation.
4. Tib. Mi bskyod rdo rje.
5. Tsong kha pa's *Sādhana, Gsang mngon,* 18a5–b2; Engle, *Guhyasamāja Practice,* 548–49.
6. Tsong kha pa, *Gsang mngon,* 18b2–4; Engle, *Guhyasamāja Practice,* 548–51.
7. Tib. *'og min;* Skt. *akaniṣṭha.*
8. The numbers in brackets refer to the pagination of the *Bung ba' re skong* in the old Bkra shis lhun po redaction, the version that appears in the bibliography.
9. See above for the list of the offerings.
10. *Rgyud rdo rje phreng ba, Vajramālā Tantra,* Tōh. 445, chap. 54, D. 257b1; a translation in Kittay with Lozang Jamspal, *Vajra Rosary,* chap. 54, v. 83.
11. Tib. *dam tshig.* This term has multiple meanings, including "pledge" and "joining together"; see J. Dalton, "Bridging Yoga and Mahāyoga."
12. While making the outer offerings, yogis should meditate that while they exist merely as nominal imputations, they are endowed with three special qualities: their essence is wisdom of indivisible bliss and emptiness; they appear in individual forms of offering substances such as flowers; and function to generate untainted bliss in the experiential domain of each of the six senses of the recipients.
13. Tsong kha pa, *Gsang mngon,* 18b4–19a4; Engle, *Guhyasamāja Practice,* 550–53. These verses are found in the *Rgyud phyi ma, Uttara Tantra,* Tōh. 443, D. 157a3–6; a Sanskrit edition in Matsunaga, *The Guhyasamāja,* chap. 18, vv. 205–7.

14. In his explanation Tsong kha pa glosses the verses recited while making prostrations. These glossed lines are marked here in italics.
15. Tib. *Byang chub kyi sems rdo rje;* Eng. "Vajra Mind for Enlightenment," the main *tathāgata* in the first chapter of the *Guhyasamāja Tantra.*
16. Tib. Rnam par snang mdzad, Mi bskyod pa, Rin chen 'byung ldan, 'Od dpag med, and Don yod grub pa.
17. Tib. Gzugs rdo rje ma, Sgra rdo rje ma, Dri rdo rje ma, Ro rdo rje ma, and Reg bya rdo rje ma; Skt. Rūpavajrā, Śabdavajrā, Gandhavajrā, Rasavajrā, and Sparśavajrā.
18. Tib. Kun bzang or Kun tu bzang po.
19. Tib. Sa'i snying po, Phyag na rdo rje or Phyag rdor, Nam mkha'i snying po or Nam snying, 'Jig rten dbang phyug, Sgrib pa thams cad rnam sel or Sgrib sel, and Byams pa.
20. Tib. Spyan ma, Māmakī, Gos dkar mo, and Sgrol ma.
21. Tib. 'Jam dpal.
22. Tib. Gshin rje gshed.
23. Tib. Shes rab mthar byed.
24. Tib. Rta mgrin.
25. Tib. Bgegs mthar byed.
26. The following are the six remaining fierce deities of the Guhyasamāja mandala: Tib. 'Dod pa'i rgyal po, Dbyug sngon can, Stobs po che, Mi g.yo ba, Gnod mdzes, and Gtsug tor 'khor lo sgyur ba.
27. Tsong kha pa, *Gsang mngon,* 19a4–5; Engle, *Guhyasamāja Practice,* 552–53. This and the following verses are found in Ye shes zhabs, Jñānapāda, *Kun bzang sgrub thabs, Samantabhadra Sādhana,* Tōh. 1855, D. 29a6–b3; Sanskrit and Tibetan editions in Tanaka, *Indo-Chibetto,* 181–86.
28. Tsong kha pa explains the verse recited for confession through the following key points that are marked with small caps: nature (*ngo bo*), time (*dus*), spheres of addressees (*yul*), and method (*tshul*). Mkhas grub rje adds here the place (*gnas*), which is the river of existence. See his *Bskyed rim dngos grub rgya mtsho,* 20b.
29. The power of support, the power of applying the antidote, the power of repentance, and the power of refraining forever from wrongdoing.
30. The person who makes the confession, the lamas and the deities residing in the mandala before whom the confession is made, and the nonvirtuous deeds that are confessed.
31. Tsong kha pa, *Gsang mngon,* 19a5–b2; Engle, *Guhyasamāja Practice,* 552–53.
32. Tsong kha pa, *Gsang mngon,* 19b2–3; Engle, *Guhyasamāja Practice,* 552–53. A straightforward translation could be: "I seek refuge in the Sugatas who dwell in my mind." However, the translation here follows the explanation of Tsong kha pa, who tends to avoid connotations of mind-only in the context of the Ārya school of the Guhyasamāja.

33. Tsong kha pa, *Gsang mngon*, 19b3–4; Engle, *Guhyasamāja Practice*, 552–53.
34. The fourth among the four truths of the noble ones.
35. The third among the four truths of the noble ones.
36. Tsong kha pa, *Gsang mngon*, 19b4–20a1; Engle, *Guhyasamāja Practice*, 552–53.
37. Tsong kha pa, *Gsang mngon*, 20a1–2; Engle, *Guhyasamāja Practice*, 554–55.
38. Tsong kha pa, *Gsang mngon*, 20a2–4; Engle, *Guhyasamāja Practice*, 554–55.
39. Tsong kha pa, *Gsang mngon*, 20a4–b1; Engle, *Guhyasamāja Practice*, 554–55. These vows are not shared with the general Mahāyāna Vehicle but are unique to the Mantra Vehicle. The verses recited while making the vows are found in a number of Indian tantras and treatises including the *Rdo rje rtse mo, Vajraśekhara Tantra* (chap. 2, Tōh. 480, D. 184a1–6); the *Ngan song, Sarvadurgatipariśodhana*, Tōh. 483 (Skorupski, *The Sarvadurgatipariśodhana*, 146); the *Yang dag par sbyor ba'i rgyud, Sampuṭa Tantra*, chap. 3.4, Tōh. 381 (Dharmachakra Translation Committee, *Emergence from Sampuṭa*); the *Rdo rje mkha' 'gro rgyud, Vajraḍāka Tantra* (chap. 12, Tōh. 370, D. 34b1–6, Sugiki, "Perfect Realization," 16–17); and Abhayākaragupta's *Dkyil chog rdo rje phreng ba, Vajrāvalī*, Tōh. 3140; Sanskrit and Tibetan editions in Mori, *Vajrāvalī*, §20.6. Tsong kha pa dedicated a whole treatise to this subject, *Dngos grub kyi snye ma*, especially 11b–22a; an English translation in Sparham, *Tantric Ethics*, 45–62.
40. Tsong kha pa, *Gsang mngon*, 20b2–4; Engle, *Guhyasamāja Practice*, 554–55. While these vows are classified according to the five *tathāgatas* families, they are in fact common to all five.
41. Tsong kha pa, *Gsang mngon*, 20b4–5; Engle, *Guhyasamāja Practice*, 554–55.
42. Tsong kha pa, *Gsang mngon*, 20b5–21a1; Engle, *Guhyasamāja Practice*, 554–57.
43. Tsong kha pa, *Gsang mngon*, 21a1–2; Engle, *Guhyasamāja Practice*, 556–57.
44. All the vows classified under the first four tathāgata families.
45. Tsong kha pa, *Gsang mngon*, 21a2–3; Engle, *Guhyasamāja Practice*, 556–57.
46. Tsong kha pa, *Gsang mngon*, 21a3–5; Engle, *Guhyasamāja Practice*, 556–57.
47. Amassing the accumulations or accumulation of merit is the topic of the present section, that ends at this point.
48. Tsong kha pa, *Gsang mngon*, 21b1–2; Engle, *Guhyasamāja Practice*, 558–59.
49. The essence of all phenomena as empty of intrinsic nature is the door to liberation of emptiness. The cause of all phenomena refers to the absence of any real cause that produces them, which is the door to liberation of signlessness. The fruit of all phenomena denotes that the wished-for results are empty of intrinsic nature and this is called the door to liberation of wishlessness.
50. Tsong kha pa, *Gsang mngon*, 21b2–5; Engle, *Guhyasamāja Practice*, 558–59. "At the center the yogis should visualize a wheel with ten spokes that is yellow all around, with ten fierce deities issuing from ten embodiments of wisdom, one above each spoke. They envision the wheel as a blocking *vajra*, perfect and most splendid, that radiates a multitude of *vajra* flames. While the wheel is spinning, [the deities] do not seem to be in motion." *Rgyud phyi ma, Ut-*

tara Tantra, Tōh. 443, D. 151b7–52a1; a Sanskrit edition in Matsunaga, *The Guhyasamāja,* chap. 18, vv. 81–82.

51. Tsong kha pa, *Gsang mngon,* 21b5–27a3; Engle, *Guhyasamāja Practice,* 558–67.
52. Nāgārjuna cites here the *Guhyasamāja Tantra,* chap. 15, v. 35bcd, and then concludes: "Therefore you should visualize yourself as great Vajradhara white in color." See his *Mdo bsre, Sādhanasūtramelāpaka,* Tōh. 1797, D. 11a7–b1.
53. In his commentary on the *Guhyasamāja Sādhana,* Abhayākaragupta instructs the yogis to meditate on themselves as white Vajrasattvas with three faces and six arms. See his *Rim pa lnga pa'i dgongs 'grel zla ba'i 'od zer, Pañcakramamatiṭīkācandraprabhā,* Tōh. 1831, D. 183a7.
54. Thub pa dpal, *Rim pa lnga'i don mdor bshad pa, Pañcakramārthaṭippaṇi,* Tōh. 1813, D. 152a4–5; a Sanskrit edition in Jiang and Tomabechi, *The Pañcakramaṭippanī,* 10. Note, however, that according to Muniśrībhadra, Vajradhara has only one face and two arms.
55. Tib. Rdo rje dbyings kyi dbang phyug ma; Eng. She Who Rules the Vajra Realm.
56. Tib. *sems dpa' gsum brtsegs.* These are: Tib. *dam tshig sems dpa', ye shes sems dpa',* and *ting nge 'dzin sems dpa';* Skt. *samayasattva, jñānasattva,* and *samādhisattva.*
57. The *Rgyud phyi ma* teaches: "Meditate on the Vajra Holder (*rdo rje can, vajrin*), the personification (*skyes bu, puruṣa*) of the *vidyā,* endowed with the four resources. Meditate on him as trifold, through the divisions into body, speech, and mind." See *Rgyud phyi ma, Uttara Tantra,* Tōh. 443, D. 151b6–7; a Sanskrit edition in Matsunaga, *The Guhyasamāja,* chap. 18, v. 80. These lines are interpreted also to mean that Vajradhara should be visualized as triple *sattvas.* See Mkhas grub rje, *Bskyed rim dngos grub rgya mtsho,* 25b4–6.
58. Nāgārjuna's *Mdo bsre, Sādhanasūtramelāpaka,* Tōh. 1797, D. 11b1–2, cites here the *Gsang ba 'dus pa, Guhyasamāja Tantra,* chap. 13, [Tōh. 442], Stog 35a3; a Sanskrit edition in Matsunaga, *The Guhyasamāja,* v. 27, and then concludes: "Therefore the ten fierce kings arise from long syllables *hūṃs.*" In commenting on this verse, Candrakīrti explains that the fierce deities arise from the syllable *hūṃ.* See Candrakīrti, *Sgron gsal, Pradīpoddyotana,* chap. 13, Tōh. 1785, D. 104a3; a Sanskrit edition in Chakravarti, *Pradīpoddyotana,* 127.
59. Tib. *Zhe sdang rdo rje;* Eng. Hatred Vajra.
60. The *Guhyasamāja Tantra* has: "[Yogis] meditatively absorbed in lustrous Vajrasattva emanating sparkling and radiant light should visualize the image that consists of the triple *vajra* body." See *Gsang ba 'dus pa,* chap. 14, [Tōh. 442], Stog 49b4–5; a Sanskrit edition in Matsunaga, *The Guhyasamāja,* v. 61. According to Candrakīrti, the yogis meditate on themselves at the center of red mandala of light. He then glosses *rdo rje sku ni gsum gyi mthar* (*trivajrakāyaprayantaṃ*) with *sku gsum gyi bdag nyid can* (*tryātmakaṃ*). See Candrakīrti, *Sgron gsal, Pradīpoddyotana,* chap. 14, Tōh. 1785, D. 133a7; a Sanskrit edition in Chakravarti, *Pradīpoddyotana,* 158.

61. Tib. Reg bya rdo rje ma; Skt. Sparśavajrā.
62. As we have seen above, all the fierce deities arise from long *hūṃs*. In his *Sādhana,* Tsong kha pa delineates the meditation on the fierce deities: The yogi and his consort as the principal deities are absorbed in union. Light rays emanating from the *samādhisattva* at the yogi's heart invite Akṣobhya surrounded by the ten fierce deities. Entering the yogi's mouth, they travel through his *vajra* path and emerge at the lotus of the Mother as eleven melted drops and then become eleven long *hūṃ* syllables, which transform into Akṣobhya and the ten fierce deities. Tsong kha pa, *Gsang mngon,* 22b5–23a1; Engle, *Guhyasamāja Practice,* 560–61.
63. According to Nāgārjuna's *Concise Sādhana:* [The yogis] should emanate the ten fierce deities from *hūṃs* that rest upon suns. They are terrifying with their dazzling lights radiating and their left legs stretched forth. See Nāgārjuna, *Mdor byas, Piṇḍikrama Sādhana,* Tōh. 1796, D. 2a2–3; a Sanskrit edition in de La Vallée Poussin, *Études et textes tantriques,* v. 8.
64. Candrakīrti explains that the fierce deities are generated while the yogis recite long *hūṃ* syllables. See his *Rdo rje sems dpa'i sgrub thabs, Vajrasattva Sādhana,* Tōh. 1814, D. 197a1; a Sanskrit edition in Luo and Tomabechi, *Candrakīrti's Vajrasattva,* 6.5 and 38.14. In a previous note we have seen that likewise in his *Sgron gsal, Pradīpoddyotana,* Candrakīrti explains that the fierce deities arise from the syllable *hūṃ*.
65. This mantra is found in the *Gsang ba 'dus pa, Guhyasamāja Tantra,* chap. 14, [Tōh. 442], Stog 48a3–4; a Sanskrit edition in Matsunaga, *The Guhyasamāja,* 65.
66. Tsong kha pa, *Gsang mngon,* 26a6 and 27b2; Engle, *Guhyasamāja Practice,* 564–67.
67. The *m,* in Sanskrit *anusvāra,* is written as a dot or drop above the syllable to indicate a nasal sound.
68. See Candrakīrti, *Sgron gsal, Pradīpoddyotana,* Tōh. 1785, chap. 14, D. 128a4–6; a Sanskrit edition in Chakravarti, *Pradīpoddyotana,* 153.
69. While our text has *gang na bgegs rnams so,* on the basis of the *Sgron gsal* and Paṇ chen Blo bzang chos kyi rgyal mtshan, *Bskyed rim dngos grub rgya mtsho'i snying po,* 25a6, this line could be read as *gang na bgegs rnams 'bros pa.*
70. Nag po dam tshig rdo rje, *Rim pa lnga'i dka' 'grel, Pañcakramapañjikā,* Tōh. 1841, D. 158b1–7. D. has *bgegs kyi bdag po* for *bgegs rnams kyi gtso bo* and *khron pa'i nang du chud par byas pa'o* for *'brub khung gi rnam pa can rnams su bcug par gyur* in our text.
71. Tsong kha pa, *Gsang mngon,* 27b6–28a1; Engle, *Guhyasamāja Practice,* 568–69. This mantra is found in the *Gsang ba 'dus pa, Guhyasamāja Tantra,* chap. 14, [Tōh. 442], Stog 49b1–2; a Sanskrit edition in Matsunaga, *The Guhyasamāja,* 69. See also Nāgārjuna, *Mdor byas, Piṇḍikrama Sādhana,* Tōh. 1796, D. 2b2; a Sanskrit edition in de La Vallée Poussin, *Études et textes tantriques,* following verse 13; and Candrakīrti, *Rdo rje sems dpa'i sgrub thabs, Vajrasattva Sādhana,*

Tōh. 1814, D. 197a6–7; a Sanskrit edition in Luo and Tomabechi, *Candrakīrti's Vajrasattva,* 7.9–11 and 39.18–40.3.

72. Following Candrakīrti, *Sgron gsal, Pradīpoddyotana,* chap. 14, Tōh. 1785, D. 132b7; a Sanskrit edition in Chakravarti, *Pradīpoddyotana,* 158, which has *kīlaya kīlaya niścalī kuru,* and therefore adds *mi 'gul bar gyis shig pa.* Our text has *mi g.yo bar gyis shig pa.*
73. Candrakīrti, *Sgron gsal, Pradīpoddyotana,* chap. 14, Tōh. 1785, D. 132b7–33a1, explains *bya ba la bod pa.*
74. Reading *vajrakīla* for *vajrakīlaya.*
75. Vajradhara is the yogi as the deity. See Mkhas grub rje, *Bskyed rim dngos grub rgya mtsho,* 29b3.
76. Reading *kīlaya* for *vajrakīlaya,* since *vajra* is mistakenly repeated twice here.
77. See Candrakīrti, *Sgron gsal, Pradīpoddyotana,* chap. 14, Tōh. 1785, D. 132b6–133a2; a Sanskrit edition in Chakravarti, *Pradīpoddyotana,* 158. See also Tsong kha pa's *Slob tshul,* 7b6–8a4, and *Bskyed rim zin bris,* 13b4–6.
78. Tsong kha pa, *Gsang mngon,* 28a5–b1; Engle, *Guhyasamāja Practice,* 568–69. Tsong kha pa's *Sādhana* describes a *vajra* tent upon the iron fence with a canopy above and a *vajra* ground below surrounded by a lattice of arrows radiating blazing fire of wisdom in all the cardinal and intermediate directions.
79. For the scriptural authorities for these dimension, see Tsong kha pa, *'Dod 'jo,* 41b5–42a2.
80. Tib. *'og min;* Skt. *akaniṣṭha.*
81. See Abhayākaragupta, *Dkyil chog rdo rje phreng ba, Vajrāvalī Maṇḍalavidhi,* Tōh. 3140, D. 38a6–7; Sanskrit and Tibetan editions in Mori, *Vajrāvalī,* §13.2.2, 236–37.
82. See *Kambala, Lwa ba pa, *Bde mchog gi sgrub thabs, Cakrasaṃvara Sādhana Ratnacūḍāmaṇi,* Tōh. 1443, D. 246b5. For the wind mandala, the abode of Brahmā, and the golden earth, see chapter 1.
83. See Kṛṣṇācārya, Spyod pa nag po pa, *Bcom ldan 'das bde mchog 'khor lo'i dkyil 'khor gyi cho ga, Bhagavaccakrasamvara Maṇḍalavidhi,* Tōh. 1446, D. 281b2.
84. See *Kampala, Lwa ba pa, *Bde mchog gi sgrub thabs,* Tōh. 1443, 246a4.
85. Tsong kha pa, *Gsang mngon,* 28ab2–3; Engle, *Guhyasamāja Practice,* 570–71.
86. The ground (Tib. *gzhi*) refers to ordinary *saṃsāric* processes, such as the periodic evolution and destruction of the world as well as death, birth, and intermediate state of beings in the world.
87. Tib. *mnar med;* Skt. *avīci.*
88. Tib. *yi dwags;* Skt. *preta.*
89. See Vasubandhu, *Mdzod, Kośa,* chap. 3, v. 90ab, Tōh. 4089, D. 10a6–7; and his autocommentary, *Mdzod 'grel, Kośabhāṣya,* Tōh. 4090, D. *ku,* 155b3–56b4; a Sanskrit edition in Pradhan, *Abhidharmakośabhāṣyam;* 178, an English translation in Pruden, *Vasubandhu,* 475–77.
90. When the three lower realms of the world are emptied.

91. Tib. *bsam gtan dang po.*
92. That is to say, without a teacher; see Vasubandhu, *Mdzod 'grel, Kośabhāṣya,* on chap. 3, v. 90ab, Tōh. 4090, D. *ku,* 156a1; a Sanskrit edition in Pradhan, *Abhidharmakośabhāṣyam,* 178; an English translation in Pruden, *Vasubandhu,* 475–77; and Vasubandhu, *Mdzod 'grel, Kośabhāṣya,* chap. 8, v. 38cd, Tōh. 4090, D. *khu* 81a5–b1; a Sanskrit edition in Pradhan, *Abhidharmakośabhāṣyam,* 459; an English translation in Pruden, *Vasubandhu,* 1280.
93. Tib. 'Dzam bu gling. The Jambu-tree Continent or Jambu Island in the South.
94. Tib. Lus 'phags po.
95. Tib. Ba glang spyod.
96. Tib. Sgra mi snyan.
97. Tib. *rnam smin gyi sgrib pa;* Skt. *vipākāvaraṇa;* see Vasubandhu, *Mdzod 'grel, Kośabhāṣya,* chap. 4, before v. 96, Tōh. 4090, D. *ku,* 215a2; a Sanskrit edition in Pradhan, *Abhidharmakośabhāṣyam,* 158–59; an English translation in Pruden, *Vasubandhu,* 678–80.
98. Tib. Rgyal chen (rigs) bzhi; Skt. Cāturmahārājakāyika.
99. Tib. Sum cu rtsa gsum; Skt. Trāyastriṃśa.
100. Tib. 'Thab bral; Skt. Yāma.
101. Tib. Dga' ldan; Skt. Tuṣita.
102. Tib. 'Phrul dga'; Skt. Nirmāṇarati.
103. Tib. Gzhan 'phrul dbang byed; Skt. Paranirmitavaśavartin.
104. Reading *bde* for *ba de* in our text, as in Vasubandhu, *Mdzod 'grel, Kośabhāṣya,* chap. 3, v. 90ab, Tōh. 4090, D. *ku,* 156a1.
105. This description partly follows the *Sa'i dngos gzhi, Maulībhūmi,* part 1 of the *Rnal 'byor spyod pa'i sa, Yogācārabhūmi,* Tōh. 4035, D. 17b1–6; a Sanskrit edition in Bhattacharya, *The Yogācārabhūmi,* 35.5–18; an English translation in Kajiyama, "Buddhist Cosmology," 188–89. See also *Aṅguttara Nikāya* 7.66 (2), *Seven Suns;* an English translation in Bhikkhu Bodhi, *The Numerical Discourses,* 1071–73.
106. Tib. Mtsho ma dros pa.
107. Tib. Lcags ri mu khyud, Lcags ri khor yug; Skt. Cakravāḍa, the mountain range made of iron that defines the outer limit of the world.
108. Tsong kha pa, *Gsang mngon,* 28b4–6; Engle, *Guhyasamāja Practice,* 570–71.
109. This verse is found in the *Gsang ba 'dus pa, Guhyasamāja Tantra,* chap. 2, [Tōh. 442], Stog 9a5–6; a Sanskrit edition in Matsunaga, *The Guhyasamāja,* v. 3; and is quoted in Nāgārjuna's *Mdor byas, Piṇḍīkrama Sādhana,* Tōh. 1796, D. 2b4; a Sanskrit edition in de La Vallée Poussin, *Études et textes tantriques,* v. 17.
110. See Nāgārjuna, *Mdor byas, Piṇḍīkrama Sādhana,* Tōh. 1796, D. 2b3–5; a Sanskrit edition in de La Vallée Poussin, *Études et textes tantriques,* 16cd–18; and Candrakīrti, *Sgron gsal, Pradīpoddyotana,* chap. 2, Tōh. 1785, D. 24a2–6; a Sanskrit edition in Chakravarti, *Pradīpoddyotana,* 31; an English translation in Campbell et al., *The Esoteric Community,* 175–76, which interprets the verse

of the *Guhyasamāja Tantra* in literal and shared meanings. See *Gsang ba 'dus pa,* chap. 2, [Tōh. 442], Stog 9a5–6; a Sanskrit edition in Matsunaga, *The Guhyasamāja,* v. 3.

111. Nāgabuddhi, *Rnam gzhag rim pa, Vyavastholi,* chap. 1, Tōh. 1809, D. 121b4–5; Sanskrit and Tibetan editions in Tanaka, *Vyavastholi,* 80–81.
112. Tib. *nges ngo.*
113. Tib. *ye shes kyi sa.*
114. Tib. *snang ngo.*
115. Note that after citing the verse beginning with, "In the absence of being," Nāgārjuna says: "Uttering this verse, meditate on the nature of the animate and inanimate worlds as empty and bless them through this yoga as the ground of wisdom." See his *Mdor byas, Piṇḍīkrama Sādhana,* Tōh. 1796, D. 2b4–5; a Sanskrit edition in de La Vallée Poussin, *Études et textes tantriques,* v. 18.
116. As we have seen in a note to the *Preliminaries,* the essence, cause, and fruit of phenomena are respectively the three doors to liberation.
117. See Mar me mdzad ye shes, Dīpaṅkaraśrījñāna, *Mngon par rtogs pa rnam par 'byed pa, Abhisamayavibhaṅga,* Tōh. 1490, D. 189b1–2; Rin chen bzang po, *Mngon par rtogs pa'i dka' ba'i gnas bshad pa,* 4a6–7; a Sanskrit edition in Kano, "Newly Available," 16; See also Tsong kha pa, *'Dod 'jo,* 52a2–5.
118. See Vasubandhu, *Mdzod 'grel, Kośabhāṣya,* Tōh. 4090, chap. 3, vv. 90cd and 45–52, D. *ku,* 156b4–57a1 and 144a5–45b6; a Sanskrit edition in Pradhan, *Abhidharmakośabhāṣyam,* 179 and 157–61; an English translation in Pruden, *Vasubandhu,* 477–78 and 451–54; see also the *Rnal 'byor spyod pa'i sa, Yogācārabhūmi,* part 1, *Sa'i dngos gzhi, Maulībhūmi,* Tōh. 4035, D. 18a6–20b4; a Sanskrit edition in Bhattacharya, *The Yogācārabhūmi,* 36.19–41.16; an English translation in Kajiyama, "Buddhist Cosmology," 190–96; Jinpa, *Science and Philosophy,* 299–300.
119. "Masters over Others' Emanations" (Tib. Gzhan 'phrul dbang byed; Skt. Paranirmitavaśavartin). Here are included the gods Delighting in Emanations (Tib. 'Phrul dga'; Skt. Nirmāṇarati) and the gods in the Joyful Realm (Tib. Dga' ldan; Skt. Tuṣita); "Free from Conflict" (Tib. 'Thab bral; Skt. Yāma).
120. While the celestial mansion rests on the four mandalas of wind, fire, water, and earth, according to the system of the *Abhidharmakośa* followed here, the physical world rests on circles of wind, water, and gold alone, and therefore the physical world—the ground—has no equivalent for the fire mandala. The present statement is meant to account for this. This question is discussed in Nāgabuddhi, *Rnam gzhag rim pa, Vyavastholi,* chap. 1, Tōh. 1809, D. 121b7–22a1; Sanskrit and Tibetan editions in Tanaka, *Vyavastholi,* 82; Tsong kha pa, *Rnam gzhag rim pa'i rnam bshad,* 10b4–6; Mkhas grub rje, *Bskyed rim dngos grub rgya mtsho,* 49a3–6.
121. Tib. Lcags ri mu khyud, Lcags ri khor yug; Skt. Cakravāḍa, the mountain range made of iron that defines the outer limit of the world.

122. Tsong kha pa, *Gsang mngon*, 28b6–29b2; Engle, *Guhyasamāja Practice*, 570–73.
123. Here is described the entire celestial mansion of the mandala with the seats of the deities.
124. Tsong kha pa, *Gsang mngon*, 29b2–31a4; Engle, *Guhyasamāja Practice*, 572–77.
125. Nāgārjuna, *Mdor byas, Piṇḍīkrama Sādhana*, Tōh. 1796, D. 2b5–3a2; a Sanskrit edition in de La Vallée Poussin, *Études et textes tantriques*, vv. 19–26.
126. Nāgabuddhi, *Rnam gzhag rim pa, Vyavastholi*, chap. 1, Tōh. 1809, D. 121b5–22a4; Sanskrit and Tibetan editions in Tanaka, *Vyavastholi*, 81–82.
127. Tib. *mos spyod;* Skt. *adhimukticaryā*, the first two of the five paths, which are the paths of accumulation and preparation.
128. See Abhayākaragupta, *Dkyil chog rdo rje phreng ba, Vajrāvalī Maṇḍalavidhi*, Tōh. 3140, D. 38a5; Sanskrit and Tibetan editions in Mori, *Vajrāvalī*, §13.2.2, 236–37.
129. The female sexual organ.
130. *Rgyud phyi ma, Uttaratantra*, Tōh. 443, D. 149a3; a Sanskrit edition in Matsunaga, *The Guhyasamāja*, chap. 18, 113, v. 15c.
131. *Rgyud phyi ma, Uttaratantra*, Tōh. 443, D. 151b7; a Sanskrit edition in Matsunaga, *The Guhyasamāja*, chap. 18, 119, v. 80cd.
132. For the five main winds, see *Rgyud rdo rje phreng ba, Vajramālā Tantra*, chap. 68, Tōh. 445, D. 276b1; an English translation in Kittay with Lozang Jamspal, *Vajra Rosary*, chap. 68, vv. 52–54.
133. Tib. *mnyam gnas;* Skt. *samāna*.
134. Tib. *gyen rgyu;* Skt. *udāna*.
135. Tib. *srog 'dzin;* Skt. *prāṇa*.
136. Tib. *thur sel;* Skt. *apāna*.
137. Tib. Spyan ma, Māmakī, Gos dkar mo, and Sgrol ma.
138. Tib. Padma can, Dung can ma, Glang po can ma, and Ri dwags can ma.
139. See, Tsong kha pa, *Rim lnga gsal sgron*, chap. 7, 225b2–4; an English translation in Kilty, *Lamp to Illuminate*, 372.
140. Tib. *bsam gtan*. See Tsong kha pa, *Rnam gzhag rim pa'i rnam bshad* (20a6–21b2), and Mkhas grub rje, *Bskyed rim dngos grub rgya mtsho* (70b6–72b1), which in turn follow Vasubandhu, *Mdzod 'grel, Kośabhāṣya*, chap. 3, vv. 97cd–98ab, Tōh. 4090, D. *ku*, 162a4–63a2; a Sanskrit edition Pradhan, *Abhidharmakośabhāṣyam*, 186–87; an English translation in Pruden, *Vasubandhu*, 487–88; see as well the *'Dul ba rnam par 'byed pa, Vinayavibhaṅga*, Tōh. 3, D. *ca*, 48b1–51b5. See also the *Rnal 'byor spyod pa'i sa, Yogācārabhūmi*, Tōh. 4035, D. 20b4–21a5; a Sanskrit edition in Bhattacharya, *The Yogācārabhūmi*, 41.17–42.18; an English translation in Kajiyama, "Buddhist Cosmology," 196–97. See also the commentary of Rgyal ba Dge 'dun grub on the *Mdzod, Kośa, Dam pa'i chos mngon pa'i mdzod kyi rnam par bshad pa thar lam gsal byed*, 115b6–16a5 and 118a6–19b1; English translations in Patt, "Elucidating," 687 and 694–97; and Jinpa, *Science and Philosophy*, 302–6. See also the *Aggañña Sutta* in the

Dīgha Nikāya, 27; an English translation in Walshe, *Long Discourses,* 407–14; Kong sprul, *Shes bya kun khyab,* 1, 202–4; an English translation in the International Translation Committee, *Myriad Worlds,* 132–34; and Wayman, "Buddhist Genesis."

141. Tib. *'dod lha;* Skt. *kāmadeva.*
142. These are: (1) The Masters over Others' Emanations (Tib. Gzhan 'phrul dbang byed; Skt. Paranirmitavaśavartin); (2) The Delighting in Emanations (Tib. 'Phrul dga'; Skt. Nirmāṇarati); (3) The Joyful (Tib. Dga' ldan; Skt. Tuṣita); (4) The Free from Conflict (Tib. 'Thab bral; Skt. Yāma); (5) The Heaven of the Gods of the Thirty-Three (Tib. Sum cu rtsa gsum; Skt. Trāyastriṃśa); (6) The Four Great Kings (Tib. Rgyal chen rigs bzhi; Skt. Cāturmahārājakāyika).
143. Tib. Sgra mi snyan; Skt. Uttarakuru.
144. These include the people of the four continents, the hungry ghosts, the animals, the eight cold hells, the eight hot hells, and the designated and peripheral hells.
145. Tib. *mnar med;* Skt. *avīci.*
146. See Vasubandhu, *Mdzod 'grel, Kośabhāṣya,* chap. 3, vv. 89d–93c, Tōh. 4090, D. *ku,* 155b3–57b5; a Sanskrit edition in Pradhan, *Abhidharmakośabhāṣyam,* 179–83; an English translation in Pruden, *Vasubandhu,* 475–79.
147. This is based on Nāgabuddhi, *Rnam gzhag rim pa, Vyavastholi,* chap. 1, Tōh. 1809, D. 123a1–2; Sanskrit and Tibetan editions in Tanaka, *Vyavastholi,* 87–88, see also Tsong kha pa, *Rnam gzhag rim pa'i rnam bshad,* 20b3–21a3; Vasubandhu, *Mdzod 'grel, Kośabhāṣya,* chap. 3, vv. 97cd–98ab, Tōh. 4090, D. *ku,* 162a4–63a2; a Sanskrit edition in Pradhan, *Abhidharmakośabhāṣyam,* 186–87; an English translation in Pruden, *Vasubandhu,* 487–88; and the *'Dul ba rnam par 'byed pa, Vinayavibhaṅga,* Tōh. 3, *ca,* D. 48b1–51b5; see also the *Aggañña Sutta* in the *Dīgha Nikāya;* English translations in Walshe, *Long Discourses,* 407–14, and Jinpa, *Science and Philosophy,* 296–306.
148. No gender exists yet.
149. Skt. *śali.*
150. Tib. *mang pos bkur ba'i rgyal po;* Skt. *rājamahāsaṃmata.*
151. This is the lineage of Buddha Śākyamuni.
152. Tib. Reg bya rdo rje ma; Skt. Sparśavajrā.
153. Tsong kha pa, *Gsang mngon,* 31a4–37b3; Engle, *Guhyasamāja Practice,* 576–87.
154. Nāgārjuna, *Mdor byas, Piṇḍīkrama Sādhana,* Tōh. 1796, D. 3a2–7; a Sanskrit edition in de La Vallée Poussin, *Études et textes tantriques,* vv. 27–36ab.
155. Nāgabuddhi, *Rnam gzhag rim pa, Vyavastholi,* chap. 1, Tōh. 1809, D. 123a1–4; Sanskrit and Tibetan editions in Tanaka, *Vyavastholi,* 87–88.
156. Tsong kha pa, *Gsang mngon,* 37b3–6; Engle, *Guhyasamāja Practice,* 586–87.
157. Tsong kha pa, *Gsang mngon,* 37b6–38b4; Engle, *Guhyasamāja Practice,* 586–89.
158. Tib. Gnod mdzes rgyal po.

159. Tib. *sngon byung;* Skt. *bhūtapūrva.* This refers to the events in the first chapter of the *Gsang ba 'dus pa, Guhyasamāja Tantra.*
160. According to Nāgabuddhi, *Rnam gzhag rim pa, Vyavastholi,* chap. 1, Tōh. 1809, D. 124b6–7 (Sanskrit and Tibetan editions in Tanaka, *Vyavastholi,* 97), the six constituents are the bones, marrow, and semen obtained from the father, and the skin, flesh, and blood obtained from the mother. Or else these are earth, water, fire, air-wind, channels, and drops.
161. See Tsong kha pa, *Rnam gzhag rim pa'i rnam bshad,* 80a5–86a5, commenting on Nāgabuddhi, *Rnam gzhag rim pa, Vyavastholi,* chap. 4, Tōh. 1809, D. 129b5–30b6; Sanskrit and Tibetan editions in Tanaka, *Vyavastholi,* 129–37.
162. The "ground time" refers to ordinary existence. According to Āryadeva, the mirror-like wisdom is the instantaneous perception of entire objects, similar to the way reflected images appear in a mirror. See his *Spyod bsdus, Caryāmelāpakapradīpa,* chap. 2, Tōh. 1803, D. 65a7–b1; Sanskrit and Tibetan editions with an English translation in Wedemeyer, *Āryadeva's Lamp,* A: 13a.
163. According to Āryadeva, the wisdom of equanimity is the understanding of beings with no legs, with two legs, with four legs, and with many legs as being of the same type. See his *Spyod bsdus, Caryāmelāpakapradīpa,* chap. 2, Tōh. 1803, D. 65b1–2; Sanskrit and Tibetan editions with an English translation in Wedemeyer, *Āryadeva's Lamp,* A: 13a.
164. See Nāgabuddhi, *Rnam gzhag rim pa, Vyavastholi,* chap. 4, Tōh. 1809, D. 130a4–30b1; Sanskrit and Tibetan editions in Tanaka, *Vyavastholi,* 132–33.
165. According to Tsong kha pa, *Rnam gzhag rim pa'i rnam bshad,* 60b5, the wisdom of discernment refers to the discernment of the parts of phenomena.
166. See Nāgabuddhi, *Rnam gzhag rim pa, Vyavastholi,* chap. 4, Tōh. 1809, D. 130b1–3; Sanskrit and Tibetan editions in Tanaka, *Vyavastholi,* 133–34.
167. According to Āryadeva, the nature of the wisdom of purposive acts is bringing to completion the activities of the body, speech, and mind done for the sake of both oneself and others. See his *Spyod bsdus, Caryāmelāpakapradīpa,* chap. 2, Tōh. 1803, D. 65b3; Sanskrit and Tibetan editions with an English translation in Wedemeyer, *Āryadeva's Lamp,* A: 13b.
168. See Nāgabuddhi, *Rnam gzhag rim pa, Vyavastholi,* chap. 4, Tōh. 1809, D. 130b3–4; Sanskrit and Tibetan editions in Tanaka, *Vyavastholi,* 134.
169. For the ten winds, the five main winds and five ancillary winds, see, for example, Āryadeva, *Spyod bsdus, Caryāmelāpakapradīpa,* chap. 2, Tōh. 1803, D. 64b4; Sanskrit and Tibetan editions with an English translation in Wedemeyer, *Āryadeva's Lamp,* A: 12a; and Tsong kha pa, *Rnam gzhag rim pa'i rnam bshad,* 83b6–84a1.
170. These are sweet, sour, pungent, salty, bitter, and astringent.
171. Tib. *snang ba;* Skt. *āloka.*
172. Tib. *mched* or *snang ba mched pa;* Skt. *ālokābhāsa.*

173. Tib. *thob* or *snang ba thob pa;* Skt. *ālokopalabdha.*
174. Tib. Rnam snang, Spyan ma, Sa'i snying po, Gzugs rdo rje ma, Byams pa, Gshin rje gshed and Mi g.yo.
175. Tsong kha pa, *Gsang mngon,* 38b5–39a2; Engle, *Guhyasamāja Practice,* 588–89.
176. Tib. Rin 'byung, Māmakī, Phyag rdor, Sgra rdo rje ma, and also the two wrathful ones, Shes rab mthar byed and 'Dod rgyal. See Tsong kha pa, *Gsang mngon,* 38b5–6; Engle, *Guhyasamāja Practice,* 588–89.
177. Tib. 'Od dpag med, Gos dkar mo, Nam mkha'i snying po, Dri rdo rje ma, Rta mgrin, and Dbyug sngon can. See Tsong kha pa, *Gsang mngon,* 38b6–39a1; Engle, *Guhyasamāja Practice,* 588–89.
178. Tib. Don grub, Sgrol ma, 'Jig rten dbang phyug, Ro rdo rje ma, Sgrib sel, Reg bya rdo rje ma, Kun bzang, Bgegs mthar byed, and Stobs po che. See Tsong kha pa, *Gsang mngon,* 39a1–2; Engle, *Guhyasamāja Practice,* 588–89.
179. Tib. Gtsug tor 'khor los bsgyur ba, Gnod mdzes rgyal po, and 'Jam dpal.
180. Reading *gtogs* for *rtogs* in our text.
181. The Sanskrit in two of the basic Indian *Sādhanas* add Maitreya here. See Nāgārjuna, *Mdor byas, Piṇḍīkrama Sādhana,* Tōh. 1796, D. 3b1–2; a Sanskrit edition in de La Vallée Poussin, *Études et textes tantriques,* 39; and Nāgabuddhi, *Rnam gzhag rim pa, Vyavastholi,* chap. 4, Tōh. 1809, D. 129b6; Sanskrit and Tibetan editions in Tanaka, *Vyavastholi,* 130.
182. The Tibetan in both Nāgārjuna, *Mdor byas, Piṇḍīkrama Sādhana,* and in Tsong kha pa, *Bung ba'i re skong,* is *rang bzhin gyis ni snang ba.* The Sanskrit in the *Piṇḍīkrama Sādhana* is *prakṛtyābhāsa.*
183. Reading *bcas* for *gces* in our text, as in the *Mdor byas* and the *Rnam gzhag rim pa.* The Sanskrit in both texts is *saṃyuktaṃ.*
184. The *Rgyud rdo rje phreng ba, Vajramālā Tantra,* Tōh. 445; an English translation in Kittay with Lozang Jamspal, *Vajra Rosary.* Our text follows the readings in Nāgārjuna, *Mdor byas, Piṇḍīkrama Sādhana,* Tōh. 1796, D. 3b1–4; a Sanskrit edition in de La Vallée Poussin, *Études et textes tantriques,* vv. 39–44ab; and in Nāgabuddhi, *Rnam gzhag rim pa, Vyavastholi,* chap. 4, Tōh. 1809, D. 129b6–30a2; Sanskrit and Tibetan editions in Tanaka, *Vyavastholi,* 129–31.
185. See Vasubandhu, *Mdzod 'grel, Kośabhāṣya,* chap. 3, v. 14, Tōh. 4090, D. *ku,* 119b5–20a5; a Sanskrit edition in Pradhan, *Abhidharmakośabhāṣyam,* 124–25; an English translation in Pruden, *Vasubandhu,* 392–93.
186. See Vasubandhu, *Mdzod, Kośa,* chap. 3, vv. 40c–41a, Tōh. 4089, D. 8b1; a Sanskrit edition in Pradhan, *Abhidharmakośabhāṣyam,* 130; an English translation in Pruden, *Vasubandhu,* 441–42; and *Rnal 'byor spyod pa'i sa, Yogācārabhūmi,* Tōh. 4035, D. 102–4, a Sanskrit edition in Bhattacharya, *The Yogācārabhūmi,* 20.9–13.
187. See Vasubandhu, *Mdzod 'grel, Kośabhāṣya,* chap. 3, v. 13ab, Tōh. 4090, D. *ku,* 119a3; a Sanskrit edition in Pradhan, *Abhidharmakośabhāṣyam,* 124; an English translation in Pruden, *Vasubandhu,* 390.

188. See the *Yogācārabhūmi, Rnal 'byor spyod pa'i sa,* Tōh. 4035, D. 10a7–b1; a Sanskrit edition in Bhattacharya, *The Yogācārabhūmi,* 20.4–6; an English translation in Wayman, "The Intermediate-State," 261.
189. See also Tsong kha pa, *Rnam gzhag rim pa'i rnam bshad,* 22b4–23b2.
190. The *Sa'i dngos gzhi, Maulībhūmi,* the first part of the *Rnal 'byor spyod pa'i sa,* Tōh. 4035, D. 10a3–4; a Sanskrit edition in Bhattacharya, *The Yogācārabhūmi,* 19.3–5; see also the *Chos mngon pa kun las btus pa, Abhidharmasamuccaya,* Tōh. 4049, D. 78a3–4; a Sanskrit edition in Pradhan, *Abhidharmasamuccaya,* 44; an English translation in Boin-Webb, *Abhidharmasamuccaya,* 93.
191. According to the *Mngal gnas, Nandagarbhāvakrānti Nirdeśa,* Tōh. 57 (see the next note), the color of an intermediate being destined for the animals resembles smoke, while that of an intermediate being destined for the hungry ghosts resembles water.
192. *Mngal gnas, Nandagarbhāvakrānti Nirdeśa,* Tōh. 57, D. 211a4; see also *'Dul ba phran tshegs kyi gzhi, Vinayakṣudrakavastu,* Tōh. 6, D. vol. 10, 125a5–6. For the different versions of the *Sūtras on Entering the Womb* (the *Mngal gnas,* Tōh. 57, and the *Mngal 'jug,* Tōh. 58), see Kritzer, *Garbhāvakrāntisūtra.*
193. See also the *Rnal 'byor spyod pa'i sa, Yogācārabhūmi,* Tōh. 4035, D. 10b4; Sanskrit edition in Bhattacharya, *The Yogācārabhūmi,* 20.14; and Vasubandhu, *Mdzod 'grel, Kośabhāṣya,* chap. 3, v. 13cd, Tōh. 4090, D. *ku,* 119b5; a Sanskrit edition in Pradhan, *Abhidharmakośabhāṣyam,* 124; an English translation in Pruden, *Vasubandhu,* 391.
194. See Vasubandhu, *Mdzod, Kośa,* chap. 3, v. 14a, Tōh. 4089, D. 7b1; a Sanskrit edition in Pradhan, *Abhidharmakośabhāṣyam,* 124–25; an English translation in Pruden, *Vasubandhu,* 392; and the *Yogācārabhūmi, Rnal 'byor spyod pa'i sa,* Tōh. 4035, D. 10a6–7; a Sanskrit edition in Bhattacharya, *The Yogācārabhūmi,* 19.9–20.1.
195. The *Sa'i dngos gzhi,* in the *Rnal 'byor spyod pa'i sa, Yogācārabhūmi,* Tōh. 4035, D. 10a6–7; a Sanskrit edition in Bhattacharya, *The Yogācārabhūmi,* 20.2–3.
196. Vasubandhu, *Mdzod, Kośa,* chap. 3, v. 14d, Tōh. 4089, D. 7b1; a Sanskrit edition in Pradhan, *Abhidharmakośabhāṣyam,* 125; an English translation in Pruden, *Vasubandhu,* 392.
197. *Chos mngon pa kun las btus pa, Abhidharmasamuccaya,* Tōh. 4049, 78a5; a Sanskrit edition in Pradhan *Abhidharmakośabhāṣyam,* 43; an English translation in Boin-Webb, *Abhidharmasamuccaya,* 93.
198. Tsong kha pa, *Gsang mngon,* 39a4–40a1; Engle, *Guhyasamāja Practice,* 588–91.
199. Nāgārjuna, *Mdor byas, Piṇḍīkrama Sādhana,* Tōh. 1796, D. 3b5–4a1; a Sanskrit edition in de La Vallée Poussin, *Études et textes tantriques,* vv. 46–52.
200. Nāgabuddhi, *Rnam gzhag rim pa, Vyavastholi,* chap. 1, Tōh. 1809, D. 123a4–b1; Sanskrit and Tibetan editions in Tanaka, *Vyavastholi,* 89–90.
201. Tib. *thob* or *snang ba thob pa;* Skt. *ālokopalabdha.*
202. Tib. *mched* or *snang ba mched pa;* Skt. *ālokābhāsa.*

203. Tib. *snang ba;* Skt. *āloka.*
204. These are the three syllables out of which the lunar disk, solar disk, and lotus are visualized.
205. These are the three winds that serve as the mounts of the three types of consciousness in the reverse order.
206. These are the three syllables placed one on top of the other after the lunar disk, solar disk, and lotus have been visualized.
207. The two sets of winds here refer to the two winds, engendering wind and coexisting wind, which each of the three types of consciousness has.
208. The white five-pronged *vajra* arises from the complete transformation of the three seed syllables.
209. These light rays emanating from the seed syllables invite the five *tathāgata* families together with a circle of numerous deities and then dissolve them back into the syllables.
210. Reading *rdzogs rim pa'i* for *rdzogs rim gis* in our text as above [18a].
211. These are body, speech, and mind isolations.
212. See the *'Dul ba phran tshegs kyi gzhi, Vinayakṣudrakavastu,* Tōh. 6, D. 125a3–4; *Mngal gnas, Nandagarbhāvakrānti Nirdeśa,* Tōh. 57, D. 211a2–4. English translations of this and the following passages from these scriptures in Kritzer, *Garbhāvakrāntisūtra,* 39–108.
213. See the *'Dul ba phran tshegs kyi gzhi, Vinayakṣudrakavastu,* Tōh. 6, D. 125b6–26a7; and *Mngal gnas, Nandagarbhāvakrānti Nirdeśa,* Tōh. 57, D. 211b5–12a6.
214. Amended on the basis of Tsong kha pa's *Rnam gzhag rim pa'i rnam bshad,* 34b2.
215. Variations are found among the Indian sources in their lists of these stages. Our text has here: *mer mer po, ltar ltar po, gor gor po, 'khrang gyur,* and *rkang lag 'gyus pa.* See also Vasubandhu, *Mdzod 'grel, Kośabhāṣya,* Tōh. 4090, following verse 199c; *Mngal gnas, Nandagarbhāvakrānti Nirdeśa,* Tōh. 57, D. 225a7; *Mngal 'jug, Āyuṣman Nandagarbhāvakrānti Nirdeśa,* Tōh. 58, D. 239b5–40a7; the *'Dul ba phran tshegs kyi gzhi, Vinayakṣudrakavastu,* Tōh. 6, D. *tha,* 142b6–7 and 146a3–4; Asaṅga, *Sa'i dngos gzhi, Maulībhūmi,* Tōh. 4035, 53b1–2; a Sanskrit edition in Bhattacharya, *The Yogācārabhūmi,* 104.3–5; and Nāgabuddhi, *Rnam gzhag rim pa, Vyavastholi,* chap. 1, Tōh. 1809, D. 124a4–5; Sanskrit and Tibetan editions in Tanaka, *Vyavastholi,* 94. The Sanskrit terms in the latter text are *kalala, arbuda, peśin, ghana,* and *praśakha.*
216. Nāgabuddhi, *Rnam gzhag rim pa, Vyavastholi,* chap. 1, Tōh. 1809, D. 124a6–7; Sanskrit and Tibetan editions in Tanaka, *Vyavastholi,* 94–95. See also the *Sdom 'byung, Saṃvarodaya Tantra,* Tōh. 373; Sanskrit and Tibetan editions with an English translation in Tsuda, *The Saṃvarodaya,* chap. 2, vv. 17ab–20.
217. *Sdom 'byung, Saṃvarodaya Tantra,* Tōh. 373; Sanskrit and Tibetan editions with an English translation in Tsuda, *The Saṃvarodaya,* chap. 2, v. 22. See also

Nāgabuddhi, *Rnam gzhag rim pa, Vyavastholi,* chap. 1, Tōh. 1809, D. 124a7–b1; Sanskrit and Tibetan editions in Tanaka, *Vyavastholi,* 95.

218. As well as the abdomen, throat, nose, teeth, lips, and the crown of the head.
219. Our text has *yan lag* as does the *'Dul ba phran tshegs kyi gzhi, Vinayakṣudraka-vastu,* Tōh. 6, 136b3, while the *Sūtra* has *yan lag sdud pa,* "assembling the limbs." See *Mngal gnas, Nandagarbhāvakrānti Nirdeśa,* Tōh. 57, D. 219b4; see also Kritzer, *Garbhāvakrāntisūtra,* 72, n. 386.
220. Tib. *kha thur du lta ba;* Skt. *avāṅmukha.*
221. Tsong kha pa, *Gsang mngon,* 40a1–6; Engle, *Guhyasamāja Practice,* 590–91.
222. Tsong kha pa, *Gsang mngon,* 49b6–50a2; Engle, *Guhyasamāja Practice,* 612–13.
223. Nāgārjuna, *Mdor byas, Piṇḍīkrama Sādhana,* Tōh. 1796, D. 4a1–5b2; a Sanskrit edition in de La Vallée Poussin, *Études et textes tantriques,* vv. 53–92.
224. Nāgabuddhi, *Rnam gzhag rim pa, Vyavastholi,* chap. 1, Tōh. 1809, D. 123b6–24b7; Sanskrit and Tibetan editions in Tanaka, *Vyavastholi,* 92–97.
225. Tsong kha pa, *Gsang mngon,* 40a1–2; Engle, *Guhyasamāja Practice,* 590–91.
226. Tsong kha pa, *Gsang mngon,* 40a2–50a2; Engle, *Guhyasamāja Practice,* 590–613.
227. Tsong kha pa, *Gsang mngon,* 40a6–41a2; Engle, *Guhyasamāja Practice,* 592–93.
228. Tib. *rigs 'dra.*
229. Tsong kha pa, *Gsang mngon,* 41a2–47a2; Engle, *Guhyasamāja Practice,* 592–605.
230. Tib. Sgrib pa thams cad rnam sel or Sgrib sel.
231. Tsong kha pa, *Gsang mngon,* 47a2–b5; Engle, *Guhyasamāja Practice,* 604–7.
232. Tsong kha pa, *Gsang mngon,* 49b1–2; Engle, *Guhyasamāja Practice,* 610–11.
233. "May the holder of a buddha body, endowed with glory, on whom I meditate as indivisible from the three *vajras,* bless me now with *vajra* body. May the buddhas who reside in the ten directions, upon whom I meditate as indivisible from the three *vajras,* bless me now with *vajra* body." See *Gsang ba 'dus pa, Guhyasamāja Tantra,* chap. 12, [Tōh. 442], Stog 33a4–6; a Sanskrit edition in Matsunaga, *The Guhyasamāja,* vv. 70–71.
234. The three *tathāgatas* Vairocana, Amitābha, and Akṣobhya with their consorts, the goddesses Locanā, Pāṇḍarā, and Māmakī.
235. *Oṃ sarva tathāgata kāya vajra svabhāva ātmako 'haṃ, oṃ sarva tathāgata vāk vajra svabhāva ātmako 'haṃ,* and *oṃ sarva tathāgata citta vajra svabhāva ātmako 'haṃ.*
236. Tsong kha pa, *Gsang mngon,* 49b2–6; Engle, *Guhyasamāja Practice,* 610–11.
237. Tsong kha pa, *Gsang mngon,* 49b6–50a2; Engle, *Guhyasamāja Practice,* 610–11.
238. Tib. *mos pa yid byed;* Skt. *adhimuktimanaskāra.*
239. This is explained in Nāgabuddhi, *Rnam gzhag rim pa, Vyavastholi,* chap. 1, Tōh. 1809, D. 122b3–6; Sanskrit and Tibetan editions in Tanaka, *Vyavastholi,*

86–87; and in the *Sdom 'byung, Saṃvarodaya Tantra,* Tōh. 373, D. 266a1–2; Sanskrit and Tibetan editions with an English translation in Tsuda, *The Saṃvarodaya,* chap. 2, vv. 5cd–7.

240. Nāgabuddhi, *Rnam gzhag rim pa, Vyavastholi,* chap. 1; Tōh. 1809, D. 122b7–23a1; Sanskrit and Tibetan editions in Tanaka, *Vyavastholi,* 87.

241. See Candrakīrti, *Sgron gsal, Pradīpoddyotana,* chap. 1, Tōh. 1785, D. 3a7–b3; a Sanskrit edition in Chakravarti, *Pradīpoddyotana,* 4; an English translation in Campbell et al., *The Esoteric Community,* 115–17. Tib. *utpala, pad dkar, padma,* and *tsan dan;* Skt. *utpala, puṇḍarīka, padma,* and *candana.*

242. *Gsang ba 'dus pa, Guhyasamāja Tantra,* chap. 13, [Tōh. 442], Stog 35a3; a Sanskrit edition in Matsunaga, *The Guhyasamāja,* v. 25.

243. Candrakīrti, *Sgron gsal, Pradīpoddyotana,* chap. 13, Tōh. 1785, D. 103b6–7; a Sanskrit edition in Chakravarti, *Pradīpoddyotana,* 127.

244. The white appearance, the red enhanced appearance, and the black appearance of approaching attainment.

245. *Ye shes rdo rje kun las btus pa, Vajrajñānasamuccaya Tantra,* Tōh. 447, D. 283b1–2. See also Tsong kha pa's commentary, *Ye rdor ṭīkā,* 34a6–35a1.

246. *Ye shes rdo rje kun las btus pa, Vajrajñānasamuccaya Tantra,* Tōh. 447, D. 283b3–4.

247. *Gsang ba 'dus pa, Guhyasamāja Tantra,* chap. 7, [Tōh. 442], Stog 17a5; a Sanskrit edition in Matsunaga, *The Guhyasamāja,* v. 7.

248. Nāgārjuna, *Mdo bsre, Sādhanasūtramelāpaka,* Tōh. 1797, D. 13b2–4. *Gsang ba 'dus pa, Guhyasamāja Tantra,* chap. 1, [Tōh. 442], Stog 3b3; a Sanskrit edition in Matsunaga, *The Guhyasamāja,* 4. The full name of this *samādhi* is "the method of great passion of all *tathāgatas,*" *de bzhin gshegs pa thams cad kyi 'dod chags chen po'i tshul zhes bya ba'i ting nge 'dzin, sarvatathāgata mahārāga vajraṃ* [*nayaṃ*] *samādhi.* D. and some of the Sanskrit manuscripts have "the *vajra* of great passion of all *tathāgatas.*"

249. Candrakīrti, *Sgron gsal, Pradīpoddyotana,* chap. 1, Tōh. 1785, D. 2a5–b1; a Sanskrit edition in Chakravarti, *Pradīpoddyotana,* 2; an English translation in Campbell et al., *The Esoteric Community,* 110.

250. Candrakīrti, *Sgron gsal, Pradīpoddyotana,* chap. 1, Tōh. 1785, D. 2b1; Chakravarti, *Pradīpoddyotana,* 2; an English translation in Campbell et al., *The Esoteric Community,* 111.

251. Tib. Reg bya rdo rje ma; Skt. Sparśavajrā.

252. Tsong kha pa, *Gsang mngon,* 50a2–52a4; Engle, *Guhyasamāja Practice,* 612–17.

253. The path common to the Mantra and Pāramitā Vehicles or to Sūtra and Tantra.

254. Tib. *'Dod pa'i bstan bcos.*

255. These are the nine female deities in the mandala of the Guhyasamāja: the four female buddhas, Locanā, Pāṇḍarā, Māmakī, and Tārā, as well as the five *vajra* ladies, Rūpavajrā, Śabdhavajrā, Gandhavajrā, Rasavajrā, and Sparśavajrā.

256. Tib. Reg bya rdo rje ma; Skt. Sparśavajrā.

257. Tsong kha pa, *Gsang mngon,* 51b5–52a2; Engle, *Guhyasamāja Practice,* 614–17.

258. Tib. Rin 'byung.
259. Tsong kha pa, *Gsang mngon,* 52a3; Engle, *Guhyasamāja Practice,* 616–17.
260. Tsong kha pa, *Gsang mngon,* 52a5–59b3; Engle, *Guhyasamāja Practice,* 616–29.
261. Tsong kha pa, *Gsang mngon,* 52a5; Engle, *Guhyasamāja Practice,* 616–17.
262. The third chapter of this treatise is devoted to the emanated mandala.
263. Tsong kha pa, *Gsang mngon,* 59b3–67b3; Engle, *Guhyasamāja Practice,* 630–47.
264. The source of this query, Nāgabuddhi, *Rnam gzhag rim pa, Vyavastholi* (chap. 3, Tōh. 1809, D. 127b4; Sanskrit and Tibetan editions in Tanaka, *Vyavastholi,* 114), has here "the *Tattvasaṃgraha* (see the following note) and so forth and the *Ubhaya Tantras.*" In his commentary on this Indian work, the *Rnam gzhag rim pa'i rnam bshad,* 67a2–3, Tsong kha pa explains that the term "*Tattvasaṃgraha* and so forth" refers to Yoga Tantras such as the explanatory tantra *Rdo rje rtse mo, Vajraśekhara Tantra,* Tōh. 480, and *Dpal mchog dang po'i rtog pa'i rgyal po, Śrīparamādya-kalparāja,* Tōh. 487, while *Ubhaya Tantra* refers to *Vairocanābhisambodhi,* and so forth. On the term *Ubhaya Tantra* in relation to *Vairocanābhisambodhi,* see J. Dalton, "A Crisis of Doxography," 123.
265. *Tattvasaṃgraha* or *Sarvatathāgatatattvasaṃgraha,* Tib. *Bsdus pa,* i.e., *De kho na nyid bsdus pa,* is a main Yoga Tantra, Tōh. 479. For a Sanskrit edition, see Lokesh Chandra, *Sarvatathāgatatattvasaṅgraha;* and for a partial English translation from Chinese, see Giebel, *Two Esoteric Sutras.*
266. Our text has here *spyod pa'i rgyud rnam snang mngon byang bzhi.*
267. Skt. *Mahāvairocanābhisambodhi;* Tib. *Rnam snang mngon byang,* nowadays regarded as a main Caryā Tantra, Tōh. 494. An English translation in Hodge, *The Mahā-Vairocana.*
268. Tib. *sngon byung.* These are deeds of a buddha performed for instructing his disciples during his "exemplary life."
269. Tib. Dga' ldan.
270. These are the deeds the Teacher performed at the opening of the *Gsang ba 'dus pa, Guhyasamāja Tantra,* chap. 1, [Tōh. 442], Stog 3b3; a Sanskrit edition in Matsunaga, *The Guhyasamāja,* 4.
271. This is the upper nose; below, the yogis will meditate on the lower nose as well.
272. Reading *gnyis dang gsum la sogs pa* for *de bzhi dang gnyis nas,* as in Tsong kha pa, *Rnal 'byor dag rim,* 23a5.
273. This meditation on the subtle emblem and the following one on the subtle drop are not found in Tsong kha pa's *Gsang mngon,* but here he explains them in detail. See also his *Rnal 'byor dag rim,* 23a3–b4.
274. Tib. *de nyid.* Tsong kha pa's *Sādhana* is divided into forty-nine essential points, and this is the thirty-ninth among them. See "Framework of the Forty-nine Essential Points," below.
275. Tsong kha pa, *Gsang mngon,* 67b3–68a6; Engle, *Guhyasamāja Practice,* 646–49.
276. *Oṃ āḥ vajradhṛk hūṃ hūṃ hūṃ ha āḥ jhaiḥ.*

277. *Namaḥ samantakāyavākcittavajrāṇām. namo vajrakrodhāya mahādaṃṣṭrotkaṭabhairavāya asimusalaparaśupāśagṛhītahastāya oṃ amṛtakuṇḍali kha kha khāhi khāhi tiṣṭha tṣṭha bandha bandha hana hana daha daha garja garja visphoṭaya visphoṭaya sarvavighnavināyakān mahāgaṇapatijīvitāntakarāya svāhā.* See *Gsang ba 'dus pa, Guhyasamāja Tantra,* chap. 14, following v. 11, [Tōh. 442], Stog 44b1–3; a Sanskrit edition in Matsunaga, *The Guhyasamāja,* 62.
278. The ཱུ at the bottom of the *hūṃ* ཧཱུྃ.
279. The ཧ་.
280. The horizontal line at the top of the syllable ཧ་.
281. The crescent moon above the syllable ཧ་.
282. The small circle, *bindu* or *anusvāra,* the *ṃ,* above the crescent moon.
283. The squiggle or "flame" on top of the drop or the small circle.
284. Tsong kha pa, *Gsang mngon,* 68a6–68b2; Engle, *Guhyasamāja Practice,* 648–49.
285. This is the forty-second essential point (*de nyid*). See "Framework of the Forty-nine Essential Points," below.
286. *Gsang ba 'dus pa, Guhyasamāja Tantra,* chap. 17, vv. 72–75, [Tōh. 442], Stog 79b7–80b2; a Sanskrit edition in Matsunaga, *The Guhyasamāja,* vv. 72–75; quoted in Nāgārjuna, *Mdor byas, Piṇḍīkrama Sādhana,* Tōh. 1796, D. 9b7–10a4; a Sanskrit edition in de La Vallée Poussin, *Études et textes tantriques,* vv. 206–9.
287. Tsong kha pa, *Gsang mngon,* 68a6–68b1; Engle, *Guhyasamāja Practice,* 648–49.
288. Note that the Sanskrit is different here.
289. This is the forty-third essential point (*de nyid*). See "Framework of the Forty-Nine Essential Points," below.
290. Tsong kha pa, *Gsang mngon,* 68b1–6; Engle, *Guhyasamāja Practice,* 652–53. See *Gsang ba 'dus pa, Guhyasamāja Tantra,* chap. 17, [Tōh. 442] Stog 68b5–69a2; a Sanskrit edition in Matsunaga, *The Guhyasamāja,* vv. 1–5; quoted in Nāgārjuna's *Mdor byas, Piṇḍīkrama Sādhana,* Tōh. 1796, D. 10a4–7; a Sanskrit edition in de La Vallée Poussin, *Études et textes tantriques,* vv. 211–15.
291. These are: water for welcoming, water for washing the feet, flowers, incense, lights, scents, food, sounds, forms, sounds, scents, tastes, and tangible objects.
292. Tsong kha pa, *Gsang mngon,* 68b6–70a2; Engle, *Guhyasamāja Practice,* 652–55.
293. Tib. *mchod yon;* Skt. *argam.*
294. Tib. *dam tshig bzhin du bzhes shig bzhes shig;* Skt. *samayaśriye.*
295. Tsong kha pa, *Gsang mngon,* 70a2–72b1; Engle, *Guhyasamāja Practice,* 654–61.
296. Tsong kha pa, *Gsang mngon,* 72b1–5; Engle, *Guhyasamāja Practice,* 660–61.
297. Tib. *nang du yang dag 'jog pa;* Skt. *pratisaṃlayana.*
298. These are the fortieth and the forty-first essential points (*de nyid*). See "Framework of the Forty-nine Essential Points," below.
299. This is the forty-second essential point (*de nyid*).
300. This is the forty-third essential point (*de nyid*).
301. This is the forty-fourth essential point (*de nyid*).

302. As mentioned at the beginning of the translation, in Tsong kha pa's text the explanation of the framework of the *Sādhana* appears in the first section, but in this English translation, this explanation has been placed at the end. Note that the listing of the forty-nine essential points here is not identical to the famous delineations in Tsong kha pa's *Rnal 'byor dag rim*. See the appendix for a more detailed description of these forty-nine steps. The scriptural authority for this is found in the *Rgyud rdo rje phreng ba, Vajramālā Tantra,* chap. 35, Tōh 445, 245a6–7. See below.
303. Tib. *de nyid.*
304. Tib. *bsnyen sgrub.*
305. See Tsong kha pa's *Rnal 'byor dag rim,* 2a5–b1.
306. See Tsong kha pa, *Gsang mngon,* 18a5; Engle, *Guhyasamāja Practice,* 548–49.
307. Tib. Zhe sdang rdo rje; Eng. Vajra Hatred. The actual meditation on the protection wheel begins in Tsong kha pa, *Gsang mngon,* 21b1; Engle, *Guhyasamāja Practice,* 556–57. The transformation into Zhe sdang rdo rje, Dveṣavajra, is found in Tsong kha pa, *Gsang mngon,* 23a6; Engle, *Guhyasamāja Practice,* 560–61.
308. Tib. Gshin rje bshed. See Tsong kha pa, *Gsang mngon,* 24a5; Engle, *Guhyasamāja Practice,* 562–63.
309. Tib. Gnod mdzes. See Tsong kha pa, *Gsang mngon,* 27a3; Engle, *Guhyasamāja Practice,* 566–67.
310. Tsong kha pa, *Gsang mngon,* 28a5; Engle, *Guhyasamāja Practice,* 568–69.
311. See Tsong kha pa, *Gsang mngon,* 28b4; Engle, *Guhyasamāja Practice,* 570–71.
312. See Tsong kha pa, *Gsang mngon,* 28b6; Engle, *Guhyasamāja Practice,* 570–71.
313. See Tsong kha pa, *Gsang mngon,* 29b2; Engle, *Guhyasamāja Practice,* 572–73.
314. See Tsong kha pa, *Gsang mngon,* 31a4; Engle, *Guhyasamāja Practice,* 576–77.
315. See Tsong kha pa, *Gsang mngon,* 37b6; Engle, *Guhyasamāja Practice,* 576–77.
316. This point is not found in our text here. Still, it is an important step of the *Sādhana* that has been explained above. In Tsong kha pa's *Rnal 'byor dag rim,* 13b3, it is the twelfth essential point. See Tsong kha pa, *Gsang mngon,* 37b4; Engle, *Guhyasamāja Practice,* 588–89.
317. See Tsong kha pa, *Gsang mngon,* 39a4; Engle, *Guhyasamāja Practice,* 588–89.
318. See Tsong kha pa, *Gsang mngon,* 39a6; Engle, *Guhyasamāja Practice,* 588–89.
319. See Tsong kha pa, *Gsang mngon,* 39b1; Engle, *Guhyasamāja Practice,* 588–91.
320. See Tsong kha pa, *Gsang mngon,* 39b2; Engle, *Guhyasamāja Practice,* 590–91.
321. See Tsong kha pa, *Gsang mngon,* 39b3; Engle, *Guhyasamāja Practice,* 590–91.
322. See Tsong kha pa, *Gsang mngon,* 39b5; Engle, *Guhyasamāja Practice,* 590–91.
323. See Tsong kha pa, *Gsang mngon,* 40a1; Engle, *Guhyasamāja Practice,* 590–91.
324. See Tsong kha pa, *Gsang mngon,* 40a6; Engle, *Guhyasamāja Practice,* 592–93.
325. See Tsong kha pa, *Gsang mngon,* 41a2; Engle, *Guhyasamāja Practice,* 592–93.
326. See Tsong kha pa, *Gsang mngon,* 42a2; Engle, *Guhyasamāja Practice,* 594–95.
327. See Tsong kha pa, *Gsang mngon,* 43a4; Engle, *Guhyasamāja Practice,* 596–97.
328. See Tsong kha pa, *Gsang mngon,* 43a6; Engle, *Guhyasamāja Practice,* 596–97.

329. See Tsong kha pa, *Gsang mngon,* 45a4; Engle, *Guhyasamāja Practice,* 600–601.
330. See Tsong kha pa, *Gsang mngon,* 47a2; Engle, *Guhyasamāja Practice,* 604–5.
331. See Tsong kha pa, *Gsang mngon,* 47b5; Engle, *Guhyasamāja Practice,* 606–7.
332. See Tsong kha pa, *Gsang mngon,* 48b3; Engle, *Guhyasamāja Practice,* 608–9.
333. See Tsong kha pa, *Gsang mngon,* 49b1; Engle, *Guhyasamāja Practice,* 610–11.
334. See Tsong kha pa, *Gsang mngon,* 49b2; Engle, *Guhyasamāja Practice,* 610–11.
335. See Tsong kha pa, *Gsang mngon,* 49b4; Engle, *Guhyasamāja Practice,* 610–11.
336. See Tsong kha pa, *Gsang mngon,* 50a2; Engle, *Guhyasamāja Practice,* 612–13.
337. In Tsong kha pa, *Rnal 'byor dag rim,* 20a3 and 20a6, passion and offerings are two separate essential points. For passion, see Tsong kha pa, *Gsang mngon,* 52a3; Engle, *Guhyasamāja Practice,* 616–17.
338. See Tsong kha pa, *Gsang mngon,* 52a4; Engle, *Guhyasamāja Practice,* 616–17.
339. See Tsong kha pa, *Gsang mngon,* 59b3; Engle, *Guhyasamāja Practice,* 630–31.
340. See Tsong kha pa, *Gsang mngon,* 61b3; Engle, *Guhyasamāja Practice,* 634–35.
341. See Tsong kha pa, *Gsang mngon,* 62b2; Engle, *Guhyasamāja Practice,* 636–37.
342. See Tsong kha pa, *Gsang mngon,* 63b2; Engle, *Guhyasamāja Practice,* 638–39.
343. See Tsong kha pa, *Gsang mngon,* 65a5; Engle, *Guhyasamāja Practice,* 642–43.
344. The meditation on the subtle emblem is not described in *Gsang mngon,* but see *Rnal 'byor dag rim,* 23a3–b1.
345. The meditation on the subtle drop is not described in *Gsang mngon,* but see *Rnal 'byor dag rim,* 23b1–4.
346. See Tsong kha pa, *Gsang mngon,* 67b3; Engle, *Guhyasamāja Practice,* 646–47.
347. See Tsong kha pa, *Gsang mngon,* 67b5; Engle, *Guhyasamāja Practice,* 646–47.
348. See Tsong kha pa, *Gsang mngon,* 68a6; Engle, *Guhyasamāja Practice,* 648–49.
349. See Tsong kha pa, *Gsang mngon,* 68b2; Engle, *Guhyasamāja Practice,* 650–51.
350. See Tsong kha pa, *Gsang mngon,* 69b1; Engle, *Guhyasamāja Practice,* 652–53.
351. See Tsong kha pa, *Gsang mngon,* 73a1; Engle, *Guhyasamāja Practice,* 660–61.
352. The meditation on the yoga of eating is not described in *Gsang mngon,* but see *Rnal 'byor dag rim,* 30a5–b5.
353. The meditation on body enhancement is not described in *Gsang mngon,* but see *Rnal 'byor dag rim,* 31b1–3.
354. The attainment of lesser *siddhis* is not described in *Gsang mngon,* but see *Rnal 'byor dag rim,* 31b3–5.
355. The attainment of middling *siddhis* is not described in *Gsang mngon,* but see *Rnal 'byor dag rim,* 31b5.
356. *Rgyud phyi ma, Uttara Tantra,* Tōh. 443, D. 154a4–5; a Sanskrit edition in Matsunaga, *Guhyasamāja Tantra,* chap. 18, v. 138. This line is cited also in Candrakīrti, *Sgron gsal, Pradīpoddyotana,* chap. 12, Tōh. 1785, D. 98b1–2; a Sanskrit edition in Chakravarti, *Pradīpoddyotana,* 120; an English translation in Campbell et al., *The Esoteric Community,* 395. In our text this citation appears at the end of this paragraph. See also Tsong kha pa, *Sgron gsal mchan,* vol. 7, 285a5–b4.

357. For #12* see above, "The Framework of the Forty-nine Essential Points."
358. This term refers to the mingling of the seed syllables, the lotus, and the lunar and solar disks during the manifest awakening from the moon.
359. Tib. *las kyi rgyal po rnal 'byor mchog.*
360. This is an abbreviated form of verses from the *Rdo rje phreng ba'i rgyud, Vajramālā Tantra,* chap. 35, Tōh. 445, D. 272a1–2; an English translation in Kittay with Lozang Jamspal, *Vajra Rosary,* chap. 35, vv. 5–6. In the following verse the tantra adds that the creation stage is comprised of forty-nine divisions [of essential points].
361. Tib. *rnal 'byor.*
362. Tib. *rjes su rnal 'byor;* Eng. subsequent yoga.
363. Tib. *shin tu rnal 'byor;* Eng. higher yoga.
364. Tib. *rnal 'byor chen po;* Eng. great yoga.
365. *Gsang ba 'dus pa,* chap. 12, [Tōh. 442], Stog 32b4–6; a Sanskrit edition in Matsunaga, *The Guhyasamāja,* vv. 60–63. See also the commentary on this in Candrakīrti, *Sgron gsal, Pradīpoddyotana,* chap. 12, Tōh. 1785, D. 94a5–95a7; a Sanskrit edition in Chakravarti, *Pradīpoddyotana,* 114–15; an English translation in Campbell et al., *The Esoteric Community,* 384. In our text this citation appears at the end of this paragraph.
366. Tib. *bsnyen pa;* Skt. *sevā.*
367. Tib. *nye sgrub;* Skt. *upasādhana.*
368. Tib. *sgrub pa;* Skt. *sādhana.*
369. Tib. *sgrub chen;* Skt. *mahāsādhana.*
370. In our text, the *Bung ba'i re skong,* 4b2, Tsong kha pa adds here: "Having explained the framework of the *Sādhana,* I shall continue the explanation of the *Sādhana* beginning with the field for the accumulation of merit and then proceed to the practice of the main part of the *Sādhana.*" Although the subject matter continues, the previous paragraph appears at the beginning of our text (ending in folio 4b), while the next one ("Addendum") is found at the end (folio 29a). As noted above, the explanation of the framework that appears at the beginning of Tsong kha pa's work is placed at the end in this translation. One reason for doing this is the continuity of discussion.
371. *Gsang ba 'dus pa,* chap. 10, [Tōh. 442], Stog 24a7–b5; a Sanskrit edition in Matsunaga, *The Guhyasamāja,* vv. 10–16.
372. See *Rgyud phyi ma, Uttara Tantra,* Tōh. 443, D. 155a2–4; a Sanskrit edition in Matsunaga, *The Guhyasamāja,* chap. 18, vv. 160–64ab. Tsong kha pa explains this in his *Mtha' gcod,* 104b5–5b6.
373. Reading *Mdo bsre,* as in the Zhol woodblocks, for *Mdo sde* in the Tashilhunpo woodblocks. See Nāgārjuna's *Mdo bsre, Sādhanasūtramelāpaka,* Tōh. 1797, D. 15a1–2, which refers to chap. 10, v. 18, of the *Guhyasamāja Tantra.*

Appendix

1. Tsong kha pa, *Bung ba'i re skong,* 1b3–4b2.
2. Tib. *de nyid zhe dgu.* See Tsong kha pa, *Bung ba'i re skong,* 1b4–3a5. Note that the listing of the forty-nine essential points in Tsong kha pa's *Bung ba'i re skong* is not identical to the famous delineations in his *Rnal 'byor dag rim.*
3. See Tsong kha pa, *Rnal 'byor dag rim,* 2a5–b1.
4. Tib. Gnod mdzes.
5. This point is not found in our text. Nonetheless, it is an important step of the *Sādhana* that is discussed in the section "The Actual Dissolution into Clear Light" in chap. 4. In Tsong kha pa, *Rnal 'byor dag rim,* it is the twelfth essential point.
6. In Tsong kha pa, *Rnal 'byor dag rim,* 20a3 and 20a6, passion and offerings are two separate essential points.

BIBLIOGRAPHY

Canonical Tibetan Texts

Bka' 'gyur

Blo gros mi zad pas bstan pa, Akṣayamatinirdeśa. Tōh. 175, D. *mdo sde, ma,* 79a1–174b7. Tibetan edition and English translation in Braarvig, *Akṣayamatinirdeśa.*

Da ltar gyi sangs rgyas = *Da ltar gyi sangs rgyas mngon sum du bzhugs pa'i ting nge 'dzin, Pratyutpanna* = *Pratyutpannabuddhasaṃmukhāvasthitasamādhi.* Tōh. 133, D. *mdo sde, na,* 1b1–70b2. Tibetan edition in Harrison, *Tibetan Text;* English translation in Harrison, *Samādhi of Direct Encounter.*

De kho na nyid bsdus pa = *De bzhin gshegs pa thams cad kyi de kho na nyid bsdus pa, Sarvatathāgatatattvasaṃgraha.* Tōh. 479, *rgyud, nya,* 1b1–142a7. Sanskrit edition in Lokesh Chandra, *Sarvatathāgatatattvasaṅgraha;* partial English translation from Chinese in Giebel, *Two Esoteric Sutras.*

Dpal mchog dang po'i rtog pa'i rgyal po, Śrīparamādyakalparāja. Tōh. 487, D. *rgyud, ta,* 150b1–73a1.

'Dul ba phran tshegs kyi gzhi, Vinayakṣudrakavastu. Tōh. 6, D. *'dul ba, tha,* 1b1–310a7 and *da,* 1b1–333a7.

'Dul ba rnam par 'byed pa or *Lung rnam 'byed, Vinayavibhaṅga.* Tōh. 3, D. *'dul ba, ca,* 21a1–292a7, continued in vols. *cha, ja,* and *nya.*

Gsang 'dus = *Gsang ba 'dus pa* = *De bzhin gshegs pa thams cad kyi sku gsung thugs kyi gsang chen gsang ba 'dus pa, Guhyasamāja Tantra* = *Sarvatathāgatakāyavākcitta-rahasyaguhyasamāja.* Stog, *rgyud, ca,* 1b1–82a5. Sanskrit edition in Matsunaga, *The Guhyasamāja;* partial English translation (chaps. 1–12) in Campbell et al., *The Esoteric Community.* I do not make references to the version in the Derge, Tōh. 442, which is a different translation.

Guhyasamāja Tantra. See *Gsang 'dus.*

Hevajra Tantra. See *Kye'i rdo rje rgyud* and *Kye'i rdo rje mkha' 'gro ma dra ba'i sdom pa.*

Kye'i rdo rje mkha' 'gro ma dra ba'i sdom pa'i rgyud kyi rgyal po, Hevajra Tantra II. Tōh. 418, D. *rgyud, nga,* 13b5–30a3. Sanskrit and Tibetan editions with an English translation in Snellgrove, *Hevajra Tantra.*

Kye'i rdo rje rgyud, Hevajra Tantra I, Kye'i rdo rje rgyud kyi rgyal po. Tōh. 417, D. *rgyud, nga,* 1b1–13b5. Sanskrit and Tibetan editions with an English translation in Snellgrove. *Hevajra Tantra.*

Mkha' 'gro ma rdo rje gur rgyud, Vajrapañjara Tantra = Ḍākinīvajrapañjara Tantra. Tōh. 419, D. *rgyud, nga,* 30a4–65b7.

Mngal gnas = Dga' bo la mngal na gnas pa bstan pa theg pa chen po'i mdo, Nandagarbhāvakrānti Nirdeśa. Tōh. 57, D. *dkon brtsegs, ga,* 205b1–36b7. Tibetan edition and English translation in Kritzer, *Garbhāvakrāntisūtra.*

Mngal 'jug =Tshe dang ldan pa dga' bo la mngal du 'jug pa bstan pa theg pa chen po'i mdo, Āyuṣman Nandagarbhāvakrānti Nirdeśa. Tōh. 58, D. *dkon brtsegs, ga,* 237a1–48a7. Tibetan edition and English translation in Kritzer, *Garbhāvakrāntisūtra.*

Ngan song = Ngan song thams cad yongs su sbyong ba gzi brjid, Sarvadurgatipariśodhana. Tōh. 483, D. *rgyud, ta,* 58b1–96a3 (version A); Tōh. 485, *rgyud, ta,* 96b1–146a7 (version B). Sanskrit and Tibetan editions with English translations in Skorupski, *The Sarvadurgatipariśodhana.*

Rdo rje gcod pa, Vajracchedikā. Tōh. 16, D. *shes rab sna tshogs, ka,* 121a1–132b7. Sanskrit edition and English translation in Harrison and Watanabe, "*Vajracchedikā,*" and Harrison, "*Vajracchedikā.*"

Rdo rje mkha' 'gro rgyud, Vajraḍāka Tantra. Tōh. 370, *rgyud, kha,* 1b1–125a7.

Rdo rje rtse mo, Vajraśekhara Tantra. Tōh. 480, D. *rgyud, nya,* 142b1–274a5.

Rgyud phyi ma, Uttara Tantra. Tōh. 443, D. *rgyud, ca,* 148a6–57b7. Sanskrit edition in Matsunaga, *The Guhyasamāja.*

Rgyud rdo rje phreng ba, Vajramālā Tantra. Tōh. 445, D. *rgyud, ca,* 208a1–77b3. English translation in Kittay with Lozang Jamspal, *The Vajra Rosary.*

Rnam snang mngon byang = Rnam par snang mdzad chen po mngon par rdzogs par byang chub pa, Mahāvairocanābhisambodhi. Tōh. 494, *rgyud, tha,* 151b2–260a7. English translation in Hodge, *The Mahā-Vairocana.*

Sa bcu'i le'u or *Sa bcu'i mdo, Daśabhūmika Sūtra.* Tōh. 44, D. *phal chen, kha,* 166a6–283a7. Sanskrit edition in Vaidya, *Daśabhūmikasūtra;* English translation in Honda, "Annotated Translation."

Saṃpuṭa Tantra. See *Yang dag par sbyor ba'i rgyud.*

Saṃvarodaya Tantra. See *Sdom 'byung.*

Sdom 'byung = Bde mchog 'byung ba'i rgyud, Saṃvarodaya Tantra. Tōh. 373, D. *rgyud, kha,* 265a1–311a6. Partial Sanskrit and Tibetan editions with English translation in Tsuda, *The Saṃvarodaya.*

Tshangs pa'i dra ba'i mdo, Brahmajāla Sūtra. Tōh. 352, D. *mdo sde, aḥ,* 70b2–86a2.

Yang dag par sbyor ba'i rgyud = Kha sbyor, Saṃpuṭa Tantra. Tōh. 381, D. *rgyud, ga,* 73b1–158b7. Partial Sanskrit editions in Elder, "The *Saṃpuṭa Tantra,*" and Skorupski, "The *Saṃpuṭatantra*"; a partial English translation in Elder, "The *Saṃpuṭa Tantra*"; and a complete English translation in Dharmachakra Translation Committee, 84,000.

Ye shes rdo rje kun las bsdus pa, Jñānavajrasamuccaya. Tōh. 450, D. *rgyud, cha,* 1b1–35b7.

Ye shes rdo rje kun las btus pa'i rgyud, Vajrajñānasamuccaya Tantra. Tōh. 447, D. *rgyud, ca,* 282a1–86a6.

Bstan 'gyur

Arranged alphabetically according to authors' Sanskrit names.

Abhayākaragupta ('Jigs med 'byung gnas sbas pa). *Dkyil chog rdo rje phreng ba = Dkyil 'khor gyi cho ga rdo rje phreng ba, Vajrāvalī Maṇḍalavidhi.* Tōh. 3140, D. *rgyud 'grel, phu,* 1b1–94b4. Sanskrit and Tibetan editions in Mori, *Vajrāvalī.*

———. *Man snye* or *Man ngag snye ma = Yang dag par sbyor ba'i rgyud kyi rgyal po'i rgya cher 'grel pa man ngag gi snye ma, Āmnāyamañjarī = Sampuṭatantrarāja-ṭīkāmnāyamañjarī.* Tōh. 1198, D. *rgyud 'grel, cha,* 1b1–316a7.

———. *Rim pa lnga pa'i dgongs 'grel zla ba'i 'od zer, Pañcakramamatiṭīkā Candraprabhā.* Tōh. 1831, *rgyud 'grel, ci,* 180b3–203a4.

———. *Sangs rgyas thod pa'i rgyud kyi rgyal po chen po'i rgya cher 'grel pa 'jigs pa med pa'i gzhung 'grel, Buddhakapālamahātantrarājaṭīkā-abhayapaddhati.* Tōh. 1654, *rgyud 'grel, ra,* 166b1–225b3. Sanskrit and Tibetan editions in Chog Dorje, *Abhayapaddhati.*

Āryadeva ('Phags pa lha). *Bdag byin gyis brlab pa'i rim pa rnam par dbye ba, Svādhiṣṭhānakramaprabheda.* Tōh. 1805, D. *rgyud 'grel, ngi,* 112a3–14b1. Sanskrit and Tibetan editions in Pandey, *Bauddhalaghugranthasaṅgraha,* 169–94; English translation in Wedemeyer, "Vajrayāna and Its Doubles," 383–91.

———. *Spyod bsdus = Spyod pa bsdus pa'i sgron ma, Caryāmelāpakapradīpa = Sūtakamelāpaka.* Tōh. 1803, D. *rgyud 'grel, ngi,* 57a2–106b7. Sanskrit and Tibetan editions with English translation in Wedemeyer, *Āryadeva's Lamp.*

Asaṅga (Thogs me). *Chos mngon pa kun las btus pa, Abhidharmasamuccaya.* Tōh. 4049, D. *sems tsam, ri,* 44b1–120a7. Sanskrit edition in Pradhan, *Abhidharmasamuccaya;* French translation in Walpola, *Le Compendium;* English translation (from the French) in Boin-Webb, *Abhidharmasamuccaya.*

———. *Rnal 'byor spyod pa'i sa las nyan thos kyi sa, Śrāvakabhūmi.* Tōh. 4036, D. *sems tsam, dzi,* 1b1–195a7. Sanskrit edition in Shukla, *Śrāvakabhūmi.*

———. *Sa'i dngos gzhi, Maulībhūmi.* Tōh. 4035, D. *sems tsam, tshi,* 1b1–283a7. Sanskrit edition in Bhattacharya, *The Yogācārabhūmi.* This is the first part of the *Rnal 'byor spyod pa'i sa, Yogācārabhūmi.*

Buddhaguhya (Sangs rgyas gsang ba). *Dkyil 'khor gyi chos mdor bsdus pa, Dharmamaṇḍalasūtra.* Tōh. 3705, D. *rgyud 'grel, tsu,* 1b1–5b4. English translation in Lo Bue, "The *Dharmamaṇḍala-sūtra.*"

Candrakīrti (Zla ba grags pa). *Rdo rje sems dpa'i sgrub thabs, Vajrasattva Sādhana.* Tōh. 1814, D. *rgyud 'grel, ngi,* 195b6–204b6. Sanskrit and Tibetan editions in Luo and Tomabechi, *Candrakīrti's Vajrasattva.*

———. *Sgron gsal* = *Sgron ma gsal bar byed pa'i rgya cher bshad pa, Pradīpoddyotanaṭīkā.* Tōh. 1785, D. *rgyud 'grel, ha,* 1b1–201b2. Sanskrit edition in Chakravarti, *Guhyasamājatantra-pradīpoddyotana;* partial English translation (chaps. 1–12) in Campbell et al., *The Esoteric Community.*

Daśabalaśrīmitra (Stobs bcu dpal bshes gnyen). *'Dus byas dang 'dus ma byas rnam par nges pa, Saṃskṛtāsaṃskṛtaviniścaya.* Tōh. 3897, D. *dbu ma, ha,* 109a1–317a7.

Dharmakīrti (Chos kyi grags pa). *Tshad ma rnam 'grel gyi tshig le'ur byas pa, Pramāṇavārttikakārikā.* Tōh. 4210, D. *tshad ma, ce,* 94b1–151a7. Sanskrit and Tibetan editions in Miyasaka, *Pramāṇavārttika.*

Dīpaṅkaraśrījñāna (Mar me mdzad ye shes). *Mngon par rtogs pa rnam par 'byed pa, Abhisamayavibhaṅga.* Tōh. 1490, D. *rgyud 'grel, zha,* 186a1–202b3.

Jñānapāda or Buddhaśrījñāna (Sangs rgyas dpal ye shes). *Kun bzang sgrub thabs* = *Kun tu bzang po'i sgrub pa'i thabs, Samantabhadra Sādhana.* Tōh. 1855, D. *rgyud 'grel, di,* 28b6–36a5. Partial Sanskrit editions in Tanaka, *Indo-Chibetto,* and Kano, "Newly Available."

———. *Zhal lung* = *Rim pa gnyis pa'i de kho na nyid bsgom pa'i zhal lung, Dvikrama* = *Dvikramatattvabhāvanā.* Tōh. 1853, D. *rgyud 'grel, di,* 1b1–17b2.

*Kambala (Lwa ba pa). *Bde mchog gi sgrub thabs gtsug nor* = *Bcom ldan 'das 'khor lo bde mchog gi sgrub thabs rin po che gtsug gi nor bu, Cakrasaṃvara Sādhana Ratnacūḍāmaṇi.* Tōh. 1443, *rgyud 'grel, wa,* 243b6–51a7.

Kṛṣṇācārya (Spyod pa nag po pa). *Bcom ldan 'das bde mchog 'khor lo'i dkyil 'khor gyi cho ga, Bhagavacchrīcakrasamvara Maṇḍalavidhi.* Tōh. 1446, *rgyud 'grel, wa,* 276b7–92b7.

*Kṛṣṇasamayavajra (Nag po dam tshig rdo rje). *Rim pa lnga'i dka' 'grel, Pañcakramapañjikā.* Tōh. 1841, *rgyud 'grel, chi,* 157b1–87a7. Sanskrit edition in Tomabechi, in progress.

Lūyīpāda (Lū'i pa). *Bcom ldan 'das mngon par rtogs pa, Bhagavadabhisamaya.* Tōh. 1427, D. *rgyud 'grel, wa,* 186b3–93a1. Sanskrit edition in Sakurai, "A Critical Study."

Mahāmatideva (Lha'i rigs blo gros chen po). *Mkha' 'gro ma rdo rje dra ba'i dka' 'grel de kho na nyid rgyas pa, Ḍākinīvajrajālatattvapauṣṭika/ viśadā/ pañjikā.* Tōh. 1196, D. *rgyud 'grel, ca,* 54a7–94b1.

Mahāmaudgalyāyana (Maudgal gyi bu chen po). *'Jig rten gzhag pa, Lokaprajñapti.* Tōh. 4086, D. *mngon pa, ai,* 1b1–93a7.

Muniśrībhadra (Thub pa dpal bzang po). *Rim pa lnga'i don mdor bshad pa* = *Rim pa lnga'i don mdor bshad pa rnal 'byor pa'i yid kyi 'phrog, Pañcakramārthaṭippaṇi* = *Pañcakramārthayogimanoharāṭippaṇī.* Tōh. 1813, *rgyud 'grel, ngi,* 148b4–95b6. Sanskrit edition in Jiang and Tomabechi *The Pañcakramaṭippanī.*

Nāgabuddhi (Klu'i blo). *Rnam gzhag rim pa* = *'Dus pa'i sgrub pa'i thabs rnam par gzhag pa'i rim pa, Vyavastholi* = *Samājasādhanavyavastholi.* Tōh. 1809, D. *rgyud 'grel, ngi,* 121a6–31a5. Sanskrit and Tibetan editions in Tanaka, *Vyavastholi.*

Nāgārjuna (Klu sgrub). *Bshes pa'i spring yig, Suhṛllekha.* Tōh. 4182, D. *spring yig, nge,*

40b4–46b3. Sanskrit edition in GRETIL (= Göttingen Register of Electronic Texts in Indian Languages, https://gretil.sub.uni-goettingen.de/gretil.html); Tibetan edition and English translation in Padmakara Translation Group, *Nagarjuna's Letter.*

———. *Mdo bsre = Rnal 'byor chen po'i rgyud gsang ba 'dus pa'i bskyed pa'i rim pa bsgom pa'i thabs mdo dang bsres pa, Sūtra-meśravaka* [*melāpaka*] = *Guhyasamājamahāyogatantrautpādakrama Sādhana Sūtra-meśravaka* [*melāpaka*]. Tōh. 1797, D. *rgyud 'grel, ngi,* 11a2–15b1; Ōtani 2662, P. *gi,* 12a7–17a7.

———. *Mdor byas = Sgrub pa'i thabs mdor byas pa, Piṇḍīkrama Sādhana* or *Piṇḍīkṛta Sādhana.* Tōh. 1796, D. *rgyud 'grel, ngi,* 1b1–11a2; Ōtani 2661 and 4788. Sanskrit edition in de La Vallée Poussin, *Études et textes tantriques.*

———. *Rim lnga = Rim pa lnga pa, Pañcakrama.* Tōh. 1802, D. *rgyud 'grel, ngi,* 45a5–57a1. Sanskrit and Tibetan editions in Mimaki and Tomabechi, *Pañcakrama;* Sanskrit edition and French translation in Tomabechi, "Étude du *Pañcakrama.*"

Nāropā. *Rim pa lnga bsdus pa gsal ba, Pañcakramasaṅgrahaprakāśa.* Tōh. 2333, D. *rgyud 'grel, zhi,* 276a7–78a7.

Ratnākaraśānti (Rin chen 'byung gnas zhi ba or Śāntipa). *Dgyes pa'i rdo rje'i dka' 'grel mu tig phreng ba, Hevajrapañjikāmuktikāvalī.* Tōh. 1189, *rgyud 'grel, ga,* 221a1–97a7. Sanskrit edition in Tripathi and Negi, *Hevajratantram.*

———. *Sgyu 'phrul chen mo'i 'grel pa yon tan ldan pa, Guṇavatīśrīmahāmāyāṭīkā.* Tōh. 1623, *rgyud 'grel, ya,* 180b1–201a3. Sanskrit and Tibetan editions in Samdhong Rinpoche and Dvivedī, *Mahāmāyātantram.*

Ratnarakṣita (Rin chen 'tsho). *Padma can = Sdom pa 'byung ba'i dka' 'grel padma can, Padminī = Samvarodayapadminīpañjikā.* Tōh. 1420, D. *rgyud 'grel, wa,* 1b1–101b3.

Śāntideva (Zhi ba'i lha). *Byang chub sems dpa'i spyod pa la 'jug pa, Bodhisattvacaryāvatāra.* Tōh. 3871, D. *dbu ma, la,* 1b1–40a7. Sanskrit edition online at Thesaurus Literaturae Buddhicae, https://www2.hf.uio.no/polyglotta/index.php?page=library&bid=2; English translation in Padmakara Translation Group, *The Way of the Bodhisattva.*

Vaidyapāda or Vitapāda (Sman zhabs), *Mdzes pa'i me tog = Mdzes pa'i me tog ces bya ba rim pa gnyis pa'i de kho na nyid bsgom pa zhal gyi lung gi 'grel pa, Sukusuma = Sukusumanāmadvikramatattvabhāvanāmukhāgamavṛtti.* Tōh. 1866, D. *rgyud 'grel, di,* 87a3–139b3.

Vasubandhu (Dbyig gnyen). *Dbus dang mtha' rnam par 'byed pa'i 'grel pa, Madhyāntavibhaṅgaṭīkā.* Tōh. 4027, D. *sems tsam, bi,* 1b1—27a7. Sanskrit edition at GRETIL.

———. *Mdzod = Chos mngon pa'i mdzod kyi tshig le'ur byas pa, Abhidharmakośakārikā.* Tōh. 4089, D. *mngon pa, ku,* 1b1–25a7. Sanskrit edition in Pradhan, *Abhidharmakośabhāṣyam;* French translation in de La Vallée Poussin, *L'Abhidharmakośa;* English translation (from the French) in Pruden, *Vasubandhu.*

———. *Mdzod 'grel = Chos mngon pa'i mdzod kyi bshad pa, Kośabhāṣya = Abhidharmakośabhāṣya.* Tōh. 4090, D. *mngon pa, ku,* 26b1–258a7, continued in *khu,* 1b1–

95a7. For a Sanskrit edition as well as French and English translations, see the previous entry.

*Yaśobhadra (Snyan grags bzang po). *Gsang ba thams cad kyi sgron ma'i rgya cher 'grel pa, Sarvaguhyapradīpaṭīkā.* Tōh. 1787, *rgyud 'grel, ha,* 203b5–34a7. [Cited in Tibetan sources as a work by Nāropā.]

Glossaries

Bye brag tu rtogs par byed pa, Mahāvyutpatti. Tōh. 4346, D. *sna tshogs, co,* 1b1–131a4. Sanskrit and Tibetan editions online at Thesaurus Literaturae Buddhicae.

Sgra sbyor bam po gnyis pa, Nighaṇṭu. Tōh. 4347, D. *sna tshogs, co,* 131b1–60a7 Sanskrit and Tibetan editions at Thesaurus Literaturae Buddhicae, https://www2.hf.uio.no/polyglotta/index.php?page=library&bid=2.

Tibetan Works

A khu ching Shes rab rgya mtsho (1803–75). "'Dus pa 'phags lugs lha so gnyis pa'i lam rim pa dang po'i khrid dmigs kyi brjed byang mi bskyod mgon po'i zhal lung." In his *Collected Works,* vol. 2, 102 folios, 5–208. New Delhi: Ngawang Sopa, 1973 [based on New Zhol blocks].

Blo bzang lhun grub Paṇḍita (1781–1859). *Rdo rje 'jigs byed chen po'i bskyed rdzogs kyi lam zab mo'i rim pa gnyis kyi rnam gzhag sku gsum nor bu'i bang mdzod las bskyed rim rnam gzhag,* 397 folios. *Sman rtsis shes rig spen dzod,* vol. 32. S. W. Tashigangpa: Leh, 1973. English translation in Sharpa Tulku with Guard, *Jewel Treasure.*

Bu ston Rin chen grub (1290–1364). *Mdor byas 'grel chen = Gsang ba 'dus pa'i sgrub thabs mdor byas kyi rgya cher bshad pa bskyed rim gsal byed, ta.* 98 folios. In his *Collected Works.* New Delhi: International Academy of Indian Culture, 1967.

'Ba' ra ba Rgyal mtshan dpal bzang po (1310–91). *Bskyed rim zab don 'gal du skyon med.* In *Rtsib ri spar ma, tsha,* 68 folios. Darjeeling: Kargyud Sungrab Nyamso, 1985.

Dbyangs can dga' ba'i blo gros Ā kyā yongs 'dzin (1740–1827). *Gzhi sku gsum gyi rnam gzhag rab gsal sgron me.* In *Dpe cha dpar gsar 'debs pa dge.* 16 folios. Mossorie: Shri Dalam, 1963. English translation in Lati Rinbochay and Hopkins, *Death, Intermediate State.*

Dwags po Bkra shis rnam rgyal (1512–87). *Gsang sngags rdo rje theg pa'i spyi don mdor bsdus pa legs bshad nor bu'i 'od zer.* Delhi: Drikung Kagyu Publications, 2004. English translation in Roberts, *Mahāmudrā,* 401–620.

'Gos Khug pa lhas btsas (11th century). *Gsang 'dus stong thun.* 270 folios, 1–539. New Delhi: Trayang, 1973.

Grags pa rgyal mtshan (1147–1216). *Rgyud kyi mngon par rtogs pa rin po che'i ljon shing.* In *Collected Works of the Sa skya,* vol. 3, work 1, 139 folios. Tokyo: Toyo Bunko, 1968.

Gser sdings pa Gzhon nu 'od (12th–13th century). *Rim lnga don bzhi ma.* In *Rngog slob brgyud dang bcas pa'i gsung 'bum,* vol. 252, 154–85. Beijing: Krung go'i bod rig pa dpe skrun khang, 2011.

Kong sprul Yon tan rgya mtsho or 'Jam dbyangs Kong sprul blo 'gros mtha' yas (1813–1900). *Shes bya kun khyab.* 3 vols. Beijing: Mi rigs dpe skrun khang, 1982. English translation as the ten-volume *Treasury of Knowledge Series,* by Kalu Rinpoché Translation Group = International Translation Committee Founded by the V. V. Kalu Rinpoché, and several individual translators. Snow Lion/Shambhala/Tsadra Foundation, 1995–2012.

Mkhas grub rje Dge legs dpal bzang po (1385–1438). *Bskyed rim dngos grub rgya mtsho = Rgyud thams cad kyi rgyal po dpal gsang ba 'dus pa'i bskyed rim dngos grub rgya mtsho, ja.* 190 folios. English translation in Bentor and Dorjee, *The Ocean.*

Ngor chen Kun dga' bzang po (1382–1456). *Zla zer = Kyai rdo rje'i sgrub thabs kyi rgya cher bshad pa bskyed rim gnad kyi zla zer.* Work 55, vol. 9, 209 folios. *Collected Works of the Sa skya.* Tokyo: Toyo Bunko, 1968.

Paṇ chen Blo bzang chos kyi rgyal mtshan (1570–1662). *Bskyed rim dngos grub rgya mtsho'i snying po = Rgyud thams cad kyi rgyal po gsang ba 'dus pa'i bskyed rim gyi rnam bshad dngos grub kyi rgya mtsho'i snying po.* In his *Collected Works, kha,* 77 folios. New Delhi: Gurudeva, 1973. An English translation in Bentor and Dorjee, *The Essence.*

Red mda' ba Gzhon nu blo gros (1348–1412). *Yid kyi mun sel = Gsang ba 'dus pa'i 'grel pa sgron ma gsal ba dang bcas pa'i bshad sbyar yid kyi mun sel.* In his *Collected Works, ga,* work 1, 380 folios. Kathmandu: Sa skya rgyal yongs gsung rab slob gnyer khang, 2009.

Rin chen bzang po (958–1055). *Mngon par rtogs pa'i dka' ba'i gnas bshad pa.* In *Bka' gdams gsung 'bum phyogs bsgrigs,* vol. 1, work 5, 13 folios. Khreng tu'u: Si khron dpe skrun tshogs pa / Si khron mi rigs dpe skrun khang, 2006. Tibetan edition in Kano and Kawasaki, "A Critical Edition."

———. *Rgyud sde spyi'i rnam par bzhag pa 'thad ldan lung gi rgyan gyis spras pa.* In *Sngon byon sa skya pa'i mkhas pa rnams kyi rgyud 'grel skor, ka,* 39 folios. Kathmandu: Sa skya rgyal yongs gsung rab slob gnyer khang, 2007.

Rong ston Shes bya kun rig (1367–1449). *Gsang 'dus rnam bshad = Gsang ba 'dus pa'i rnam bshad byin rlabs kyi bdud rtsi rnam par rol pa'i gter.* In his *Collected Works, kha,* 414 folios. Jyekundo (Skye dgu mdo): Gangs ljongs rig rgyan gsung rab par khang, 2004.

———. *Gsang sngags kyi spyi don slob dpon grags 'od kyi zhus lan.* In his *Collected Works,* 1:319–23. Chengdu, China: Si khron dpe skrun tshogs pa, 2008.

Tāranātha (1575–1634?). "Gsang ba 'dus pa 'jam pa'i rdo rje'i mngon par rtogs pa ye shes snang byed." In his *Collected Works* [Dpe bsdur ma], vol. 9, work 3, 75–104. Pe cin: Krung go'i bod rig pa dpe skrun khang, 2008.

Tsong kha pa Blo bzang grags pa (1357–1419). Works listed below are found in his *Collected Works,* 27 vols. New Delhi: Ngawang Gelek Demo, 1975–79. Reproduced from an example of the old Bkra shis lhun po redaction from the library of Klu 'khyil monastery of Ladakh.

———. *Bskyed rim zin bris* = *Gsang 'dus bskyed rim gyi zin bris, ca.* 40 folios, vol. 9, work 2.

———. *Bung ba'i re skong* = *Gsang ba 'dus pa'i bskyed rim blo gsal bung ba'i re skong gnad don gsal ba, ja.* 29 folios, vol. 10, work 14.

———. *Dngos grub snye ma* = *Gsang sngags kyi tshul khrims kyi rnam bshad dngos grub kyi snye ma, ka.* 75 folios, vol. 1, work 11. English translation in Sparham, *Tantric Ethics.*

———. *'Dod 'jo* = *Bcom ldan 'das 'khor lo bde mchog gi mngon par rtogs pa'i rgya cher bshad pa 'dod pa 'jo ba, ta.* 195 folios, vol. 14, work 3.

———. *Gsang mngon* = *The Sādhana* = *Gsang ba 'dus pa'i bla brgyud gsol 'debs dang bdag bskyed ngag 'don bkra shis lhun po rgyud pa grwa tshang gi 'don rgyud rje thams cad mkhyen pas zhus dag mdzad pa.* N.p., n.d., 82 folios, 17–180. My notes refer to this publication. Published also in *The Collected Ritual Texts of the Rnam rgyal grwa tshang Phan bde legs bshad gling.* Dharamsala, India: Namgyel Dratsang 1977. English translation in Engle, *Guhyasamāja Practice.*

———. *Lam gyi gtso bo rnam gsum gyi rtsa ba, kha.* 3 folios, vol. 2, work 67. In *Bka' 'bum thor bu,* 230b5–31b5. English translation in Sonam, *Three Principal Aspects.*

———. *Lam rim chen mo* = *Byang chub lam rim che ba, pa.* 491 folios, vols. 19 and 20. English translation in Cutler, *The Great Treatise.* My notes refer to the edition published in Xining, China: Mtsho sngon mi rigs dpe skrun khang, 1997.

———. *Mtha' gcod* = *Rgyud kyi rgyal po gsang ba 'dus pa'i rgya cher bshad pa sgron ma gsal ba'i dka' ba'i gnas kyi mtha' gcod rin chen myu gu, ca.* 143 folios, vol. 8, work 2.

———. *Rim lnga gsal sgron* = *Rgyud kyi rgyal po gsang ba 'dus pa'i man ngag rim pa lnga rab tu gsal ba'i sgron me, ja.* 344 folios, vol. 11. English translation in Kilty, *Lamp to Illuminate.*

———. *Rnal 'byor dag rim* = *Gsang ba 'dus pa'i sgrub thabs rnal 'byor dag pa'i rim pa, ja.* 32 folios, vol. 10, work 12.

———. *Rnam gzhag rim pa'i rnam bshad* = *Rnam gzhag rim pa'i rnam bshad gsang ba 'dus pa'i gnad kyi don gsal ba, [Don gsal], ca.* 90 folios, vol. 9, work 4.

———. *Sgron gsal mchan* = *Rgyud thams cad kyi rgyal po gsang ba 'dus pa'i rgya cher bshad pa sgron me gsal ba'i tshig don ji bzhin 'byed pa'i mchan gyi yang 'grel, nga.* 521 folios, vols. 6 and 7.

———. *Slob tshul* = *Rdo rje 'chang gi go 'phang brnyes par byed pa'i lam la slob pa'i tshul, nya.* 22 folios, vol. 13, work 1.

———. *Sngags rim chen mo* = *Rgyal ba khyab bdag rdo rje 'chang chen po'i lam gyi rim pa gsang ba kun gyi gnad rnam par phye ba, ga.* 512 folios, vols. 4 and 5. My notes

refer to the edition published in Xining, China: Mtsho sngon mi rigs dpe skrun khang, 1995.
———. *Ye rdor ṭīkā = Gsang ba 'dus pa'i bshad pa'i rgyud ye shes rdo rje kun las btus pa'i ṭīkā, ca.* 69 folios, vol. 8, work 4.
Zhu chen Tshul khrims rin chen (1697–1774). "Gsang ba 'dus pa spyan ras gzigs dbang phyug gi dkyil 'khor du slob ma smon par byed pa'i cho ga skal ldan shing rta." In his *Collected Works,* vol. 4, 44 folios, pp. 41–127. Kathmandu: Sachen International, 2005.

Modern Works

Anālayo, Bhikkhu. "The Buddha's Pre-Awakening Practices and Their Mindful Transformation." *Mindfulness* 12 (2021): 1892–98.
———. *A Comparative Study of the Majjhima-nikāya.* Taipei: Dharma Drum Publishing, 2011.
———. "The Sixty-Two Views—A Comparative Study." *Fuyan Buddhist Studies* 5 (2010): 23–42.
Apple, James B. "Maitreya's Tuṣita Heaven as a Pure Land in Gelukpa Forms of Tibetan Buddhism." In *Pure Lands in Asian Texts and Contexts: An Anthology,* edited by Georgios T. Halkias and Richard K. Payne, 188–222. Honolulu: University of Hawai'i Press, 2019.
Bentor, Yael. "Can Women Attain Enlightenment through Vajrayāna Practices?" In *Karmic Passages: Israeli Scholarship on India,* edited by David Shulman and Shalva Weil, 123–37. New Delhi: Oxford University Press, 2008.
———. "The Convergence of Theoretical and Practical Concerns in a Single Verse of the *Guhyasamāja Tantra.*" In *Tibetan Rituals,* edited by José Cabezón, 89–102. Oxford University Press, New York, 2009.
———. "Interpreting the Body *Maṇḍala:* Tsongkhapa versus Later Gelug Scholars." *Revue d'Etudes Tibétaines* 31 (2015): 63–74. Reprinted in *Trails of the Tibetan Tradition: Papers for Elliot Sperling,* edited by Roberto Vitali, 63–74. Dharamsala: Amnye Machen Institute, 2015.
———. "Tsong-kha-pa's *Guhyasamāja Sādhana* and the Ārya Tradition." In *Śāsanadhara: Papers in Honor of Robert A. F. Thurman on the Occasion of his 70th Birthday,* edited by Christian K. Wedemeyer, John D. Dunne, and Thomas F. Yarnall, 165–92. New York: American Institute of Buddhist Studies at Columbia University, 2015.
———. "Women on the Way to Enlightenment." In *From Bhakti to Bon: Festschrift for Per Kvaerne,* edited by Charles Ramble and Hanna Havnevik, 89–96. Oslo: Novus forlag. Institute for Comparative Research in Human Culture, 2015.
Bentor, Yael, and Penpa Dorjee, transl. *The Essence of the Ocean of Attainments.* By Paṇchen Losang Chökyi Gyaltsen. Boston: Wisdom Publications, 2019.
———transl. *The Ocean of Attainments: The Creation Stage of the Guhyasamāja Tantra*

According to Khedrup Jé, edited and introduced by Yael Bentor. Boston: Wisdom Publications, forthcoming 2024.

Bhattacharya, Vidhushekhara. *The Yogācārabhūmi of Ācārya Asaṅga.* Calcutta: University of Calcutta, 1957.

Blezer, Henk. *Kar gliṅ Źi khro: A Tantric Buddhist Concept.* Leiden: Research School CNWS, 1997.

Bodhi, Bhikkhu. *The Connected Discourses of the Buddha: A New Translation of the Saṃyutta Nikāya.* Boston: Wisdom Publications, 2000.

———. *The Discourse on the All-Embracing Net of Views: The Brahmajāla Sutta and Its Commentaries.* Kandy: Buddhist Publication Society, 1978.

———. *The Numerical Discourses of the Buddha: A Translation of the Aṅguttara Nikāya.* Boston: Wisdom Publications, 2012.

Boin-Webb, Sara, transl. (from French). *Abhidharmasamuccaya: The Compendium of the Higher Teaching (Philosophy) by Asaṅga.* Fremont, CA: Asian Humanities Press, 2001.

Braarvig, Jens. *Akṣayamatinirdeśa Sūtra.* Oslo: Solum Forlag.

———. *Mahāvyutpatti with sGra sbyor bam po gnyis pa.* Online at Thesaurus Literaturae Buddhicae, https://www2.hf.uio.no/polyglotta/index.php?page=volume&vid=263.

Cabezón, José Ignacio. "Three Buddhist Views of the Doctrines of Creation and Creator." In *Buddhism, Christianity and the Question of Creation,* ed. Schmidt-Leukel, 33–45. Aldershot, UK: Ashgate Publishing, 2006.

Campbell, John R., Robert A. F. Thurman, et al. *The Esoteric Community Tantra with the Illuminating Lamp.* Vol. 1, chaps. 1–12. Somerville, MA: Wisdom Publications, 2020.

Chakravarti, Chintaharan. *Guhyasamājatantra-pradīpoddyotana-ṭīkāṣaṭkoṭīvyākhyā.* Patna, India: Kashi Prasad Jayaswal Research Institute, 1984.

Chog Dorje. *Abhayapaddhati of Abhayākaragupta: Commentary on the Buddhakapālamahātantra.* Sarnath, India: Central Institute of Higher Tibetan Studies, 2009.

Coghlan, Ian James, transl. *Ornament of Abhidharma: A Commentary on Vasubandhu's Abhidharmakośa.* By Chim Jampalyang. Somerville, MA: Wisdom Publications, 2019.

Collins, Steven. "The Discourse on What Is Primary (*Aggañña Sutta*)." *Journal of Indian Philosophy* 21 (1993): 301–93.

Cuevas, Bryan J. *The Hidden History of the Tibetan Book of the Dead.* Oxford: University Press, 2003.

———. "Predecessors and Prototypes: Towards a Conceptual History of the Buddhist Antarābhava." *Numen* 43 (1996): 263–302.

Cutler, Joshua W. C., ed. *The Great Treatise on the Stages of the Path to Enlightenment, Lam-rim-chen-mo.* 3 vols. Ithaca, NY: Snow Lion Publications, 2000–2004.

Dalton, Catherine. "Enacting Perfection: Buddhajñānapāda's Vision of a Tantric Buddhist World." PhD diss., University of California, Berkeley, 2019.

Dalton, Catherine, and Péter-Dániel Szántó. "Jñānapāda." In *Brill's Encyclopedia of Buddhism,* edited by. Jonathan A. Silk, 2 (2019): 264–68. Leiden: Brill.

Dalton, Jacob. "Bridging Yoga and Mahāyoga—Samaya in Early Tantric Buddhism." In *Buddhism in Central Asia II: Practices and Rituals, Visual and Material Transfer,* edited by Yukiyo Kasai and Henrik H. Sørensen, 270–87. Leiden: Brill, 2022.

———. "A Crisis of Doxography: How Tibetans Organized Tantra during the 8th–12th Centuries." *Journal of the International Association of Buddhist Studies* 28, no. 1 (2005): 115–81.

———. "On the Significance of the *Ārya-tattvasaṃgraha-sādhanopāyikā* and Its Commentary." In *Chinese and Tibetan Esoteric Buddhism,* edited by Yael Bentor and Meir Shahar, 321–37. Leiden: Brill, 2017.

Dharmachakra Translation Committee and 84,000: Translating the Words of the Buddha. *Emergence from Sampuṭa.* Tōh. 381, D., vol. 79, *rgyud 'bum, ga,* 73b1–158b7. https://read.84000.co/translation/toh381.html#:~:text=The%20tantra%20Emergence%20from%20Sampu%E1%B9%ADa%20is%20an%20all-inclusive,Tibetan%20classification%2C%20the%20Father%20and%20the%20Mother%20tantras.

Doniger, Wendy. *Hindu Myths: A Sourcebook Translated from the Sanskrit.* London: Penguin, 1975.

Doniger O'Flaherty, Wendy. *Textual Sources for the Study of Hinduism.* Manchester University Press 1988.

Elder, George Robert. "The *Saṃpuṭa Tantra:* Edition and Translation, Chapters I–IV." PhD diss., Columbia University, New York, 1978.

Engle, Artemus B., transl. *Guhyasamāja Practice in the Ārya Nāgārjuna System.* Vol. 1: *The Generation Stage.* By Lobsang Jampa, Gyumé Khensur, and Tsongkhapa. Boulder, CO: Snow Lion Publications, 2019.

English, Elizabeth. *Vajrayoginī: Her Visualizations, Rituals and Forms.* Boston: Wisdom Publications, 2002.

Flood, Gavin. *An Introduction to Hinduism.* Cambridge: Cambridge University Press, 1996.

Garrett, Frances. *Religion, Medicine, and the Human Embryo in Tibet.* Abingdon, Oxon, [England]: Routledge, 2008.

Gethin, Rupert. "Cosmology and Meditation: From the *Aggañña Sutta* to the Mahāyāna." *History of Religions* 36 (1997): 183–219.

———. *Sayings of the Buddha: A Selection of Suttas from the Pali Nikāyas.* Oxford: Oxford University Press, 2008.

Giebel, Rolf W. *Two Esoteric Sutras: The Adamantine Pinnacle Sutra and the Susiddhikara Sutra.* Berkeley, CA: Numata Center for Buddhist Translation and Research, 2001.

Gombrich, Richard. "The Buddha's Book of Genesis?" *Indo-Iranian Journal* 35, nos. 2/3 (1992): 159–78.

Gómez, Luis O. "The Bodhisattva as Wonder-Worker." In *Prajñāpāramitā and Related Systems,* edited by Lewis Lancaster, 221–61. Berkeley, CA: Berkeley Buddhist Studies Series, 1977.

——. *The Land of Bliss: The Paradise of the Buddha of Measureless Light.* Honolulu: University of Hawai'i Press, 1996.

——. "On Buddhist Wonders and Wonder-Working." *Journal of the International Association of Buddhist Studies* 33, nos. 1/2 (2010 [2011]): 513–54.

Guarisco, Elio, and Ingrid McLeod, transl. *Systems of Buddhist Tantra.* In *The Treasury of Knowledge.* By Jamgön Kongtrul, book 6, part 4. Ithaca, NY: Snow Lion Publications, 2005.

Gyurme Dorje, transl. *The Tibetan Book of the Dead.* By Karma Glingpa. New York: Viking, 2006.

Harrison, Paul M. "Commemoration and Identification in Buddhānusmṛti." In *In the Mirror of Memory,* edited by Janet Gyatso, 215–38. Albany: State University of New York Press, 1992.

——. *The Samādhi of Direct Encounter with the Buddhas of the Present.* Tokyo: International Institute of Buddhist Studies, 1990.

——. *Tibetan Text of the Pratyutpanna-Buddha-Saṃmukhāvasthita-Samādhi-Sūtra.* Tokyo: Reiyukai Library, 1978.

——. "*Vajracchedikā Prajnāpāramitā*: A New English Translation of the Sanskrit Text, Based on Two Manuscripts from Greater Gandhara." In *Buddhist Manuscripts,* vol. 3, edited by Jens Braarvig, 133–59. Oslo: Hermes Publishing, 2006.

Harrison, Paul M., and Shōgo Watanabe. "*Vajracchedikā Prajnāpāramitā.*" In *Buddhist Manuscripts,* edited by Jens Braarvig, 3:89–132. Oslo: Hermes Publishing, 2006.

Hodge, Stephen. *The Mahā-Vairocana-Abhisambodhi Tantra with Buddhaguhya's Commentary.* London: Curzon, 2003.

Honda, Megumu. "Annotated Translation of the Daśabhūmika-Sūtra." Revised by Johannes Rahder. In *Studies in South, East, and Central Asia* (presented as a memorial volume to the late Prof. Raghu Vira), edited by Denis Sinor, 115–276. New Delhi: International Academy of Indian Culture, 1968.

Hopkins, Jeffrey. *Tantra in Tibet: The Great Exposition of Secret Mantra.* Vol. 1. London: George Allen and Unwin, 1980 [1977].

——. *Tantric Techniques.* Ithaca, NY: Snow Lion Publications, 2008.

——. *Tsong-kha-pa's Final Exposition of Wisdom.* Ithaca, NY: Snow Lion Publications, 2008.

Huntington, Eric. *Creating the Universe: Depictions of the Cosmos in Himalayan Buddhism.* Seattle: University of Washington Press, 2018.

International Translation Committee Founded by the V. V. Kalu Rinpoché. *Myr-*

iad Worlds: Buddhist Cosmology in Abhidharma, Kālacakra and Dzog-chen. By Jamgön Kongtrul Lodrö Tayé. Ithaca, NY: Snow Lion Publications, 1995.

Jiang, Zhongxin, and Tōru Tomabechi. *The Pañcakramaṭippanī of Muniśrībhadra: Introduction and Romanized Sanskrit Text.* Bern: Peter Lang, 1996.

Jinpa, Thupten, ed. *Science and Philosophy in the Indian Buddhist Classics: The Physical World.* Vol. 1, translated by Ian J. Coghlan. Somerville, MA: Wisdom Publications, 2017.

———. *Tsongkhapa: A Buddha in the Land of Snows.* Boulder: Shambhala Publications, 2019.

Jones, J. J., transl. *The Mahāvastu.* Vol. 1. London: Luzac, 1949.

Kajiyama, Yūichi. "Buddhist Cosmology as Presented in the *Yogācārabhūmi.*" In *Wisdom, Compassion, and the Search for Understanding,* edited by Jonathan A. Silk, 183–99. Honolulu: University of Hawai'i Press, 2000.

Kano, Kazuo. "Newly Available Sanskrit Materials of Jñānapāda's *Samantabhadrasādhana.*" *Mikkyōgakukenkū* 46 (2014): 61–73.

Kano, Kazuo, and Kazuhiro Kawasaki. "A Critical Edition of Rin chen bzang po's *Cakrasaṃvarābhisamaya* Commentary." *Kōyasandaigaku ronsō* 49 (2014): 1–36.

Kilty, Gavin. *A Lamp to Illuminate the Five Stages: Teachings on Guhyasamāja Tantra.* By Tsongkhapa. Boston: Wisdom Publications, 2013.

Kittay, David R., with Lozang Jamspal. *The Vajra Rosary Tantra with Commentary by Alaṁkakalasha.* Somerville, MA: Wisdom Publications, 2020.

Kloetzli, Randolph W. *Buddhist Cosmology: Science and Theology in the Images of Motion and Light,* Delhi: Motilal Banarsidass Publishers, 1983.

Kloppenborg, Ria, and Ronald Poelmeyer. "Visualizations in Buddhist Meditation." In *Effigies Dei: Essays on the History of Religions,* edited by Dirk van der Plas, 83–95. Leiden: E. J. Brill, 1987.

Kritzer, Robert. *Garbhāvakrāntisūtra: The Sūtra on Entry into the Womb.* Tokyo: International Institute for Buddhist Studies, 2014.

———. "Rūpa and the Antarābhava." *Journal of Indian Philosophy* 28, no. 3 (2000): 235–72.

Lal, Banarsi. *Lupta-bauddha-vacana-saṅgrahaḥ (Part 2).* Sarnath, India: Central Institute of Higher Tibetan Studies, 2001.

Langenberg, Amy Paris. *Birth in Buddhism: The Suffering Fetus and Female Freedom.* New York: Routledge, 2017.

Lati Rinbochay and Jeffrey Hopkins. *Death, Intermediate State and Rebirth in Tibetan Buddhism.* Ithaca, NY: Snow Lion Publications, 1979.

Lessing, Ferdinand D., and Alex Wayman. *Mkhas grub rje's Fundamentals of the Buddhist Tantras.* The Hague: Mouton, 1968.

Lo Bue, Erberto. "The *Dharmamaṇḍala-sūtra* by Buddhaguhya." In *Orientalia Iosephi Tucci Memoriae Dicata,* edited by Gherardo Gnoli and L. Lanciotti, 2:787–818. Rome: Istituto Italiano per il Medio ed Estremo Oriente, 1987.

Lokesh Chandra. *Sarvatathāgatatattvasaṅgraha: Sanskrit Text.* New Delhi: Motilal Banarsidass, 1987.

Lopez, Donald S., Jr. *Elaborations on Emptiness: Uses of the Heart Sūtra.* Princeton, NJ: Princeton University Press, 1996.

Luo Hong, and Tōru Tomabechi. *Candrakīrti's Vajrasattva-niṣpādana-sūtra (Vajrasattva-sādhana) Sanskrit and Tibetan Texts.* Beijing: China Tibetology Publishing House and Vienna: Austrian Academy of Sciences Press, 2009.

Matsunaga, Yukei. *The Guhyasamāja Tantra: A New Critical Edition.* Osaka: Toho shuppan, 1978.

McMahan, David L. *Empty Vision: Metaphor and Visionary Imagery in Mahāyāna Buddhism.* New York: Routledge Curzon, 2002.

———. "Transpositions of Metaphor and Imagery in the *Gaṇḍavyūha* and Tantric Buddhist Practice." *Pacific World: Journal of the Institute of Buddhist Studies* 3, no. 6 (2004): 181–94.

Mimaki, Katsumi, and Tōru Tomabechi. *Pañcakrama: Sanskrit and Tibetan Texts Critically Edited with Verse Index and Facsimile Edition of the Sanskrit Manuscripts.* Tokyo: Centre for East Asian Cultural Studies for UNESCO, 1994.

Miyasaka, Yūsho. "*Pramāṇavārttika-kārikā* (Sanskrit and Tibetan)." *Acta Indologica* 2 (1971–72): 1–206.

Mori, Masahide. *Vajrāvalī of Abhayākaragupta.* Tring, UK: Institute of Buddhist Studies, 2009.

Nakamura, Hajime. "A Process of the Origination of Buddhist Meditations in Connection with the Life of the Buddha." In *Studies in Pali and Buddhism: A Memorial Volume in Honor of Bhikkhu Jagdish Kashyap,* edited by A. K. Narain, 269–77. Delhi: B. R. Publications, 1979.

Ñāṇamoli, Bhikkhu. *Visuddhimagga: The Path of Purification.* Colombo, Sri Lanka: Buddhist Publication Society, 1975/2010.

Ñāṇamoli, Bhikkhu, and Bhikkhu Bodhi, transl. *The Middle Length Discourses of the Buddha: Translation of the Majjhima Nikāya.* Boston: Wisdom Publications, 1995.

Norman, K. R. "Theravāda Buddhism and Brahmanical Hinduism." In his *Collected Papers,* edited by K. R. Norman, vol. 4, 271–80. Oxford: Pāli Text Society, 1991/1993.

Olivelle, Patrick, ed. and transl. *The Early Upanisads: Annotated Text and Translation.* Oxford: Oxford University Press, 1998.

Orzech, Charles D. "A Note Concerning Contemplation of the Marks of the Buddha." In *Methods in Buddhist Studies—Essays in Honor of Richard K. Payne,* edited by Scott A. Mitchell and Natalie Fisk Quli, 86–92. London: Bloomsbury Academic, 2019.

Osto, Douglas. *Power, Wealth, and Women in Indian Mahayana Buddhism: The Gaṇḍavyūha-sūtra.* New York: Routledge, 2008.

———. "'Proto-Tantric' Elements in *The Gaṇḍavyūha-sūtra.*" *Journal of Religious History* 33, no. 2 (2009): 165–77.

Padmakara Translation Group. *Nagarjuna's Letter to a Friend.* Ithaca: Snow Lion Publications, 2005.

———. *The Way of the Bodhisattva.* English translation of the *Bodhicaryāvatāra.* Boston: Shambhala Publications, 2003.

Pandey, Janardan. *Bauddhalaghugranthasaṅgraha: A Collection of Minor Buddhist Texts.* Sarnath, India: Central Institute of Higher Tibetan Studies, 1997.

———. *Caryāmelāpakapradīpam of Ācārya Āryadeva.* Sarnath, India: Central Institute of Higher Tibetan Studies, 2000.

Patt, David. "Elucidating the Path to Liberation: A Study of the Commentary on the Abhidharmakośa by the First Dalai Lama." PhD diss., University of Wisconsin, Madison, 1993.

de La Vallée Poussin, Louis. *Études et textes tantriques: Pañcakrama.* Ghent, Belgium: Ghent University, 1896.

———. *L'Abhidharmakośa de Vasubandhu.* Brussells: Institut Belge des Hautes Études Chinoises, 1971 [1926].

Pradhan, Pralhad. *Abhidharmakośabhāṣyam of Vasubandhu.* Patna, India: K. P. Jayaswal Research Institute, 1975.

———. *Abhidharmasamuccaya of Asanga.* Santiniketan, India: Santiniketan Press, 1950.

Pruden, Leo M. Vasubandhu. *Abhidharmakośabhāṣyam.* 4 vols. Translated into English from French. Berkeley: Asian Humanities Press, 1988–90.

Quarcoo, Philip. *Middle Length Lam-Rim by Lama Tsongkhapa.* Portland: FPMT, 2008. Reprinted 2021 by Wisdom Publications, Somerville, MA.

Rhys Davids, T. W., and C. A. F. *Dialogues of the Buddha.* 3 vols. London: Pali Text Society, 1899–1921.

Roberts, Peter A. *Mahāmudrā and Related Instructions: Core Teachings of the Kagyu Schools.* Boston: Wisdom Publications and the Institute of Tibetan Classics 2011.

Roloff, Carola. *Red mda' ba: Buddhist Yogi-Scholar of the Fourteenth Century.* Wiesbaden, Germany: Ludwig Reichert Verlag, 2009.

Sadakata, Akira. *Buddhist Cosmology: Philosophy and Origins.* Tokyo: Kōsei Publishing, 1997.

Sakurai, Munenobu. "A Critical Study on Lūyīpāda's *Cakrasaṃvarābhisamaya.*" *Journal of Chisan Studies* 47 (1998): 1–32.

Samdhong Rinpoche and Vrajavallabh Dvivedī. *Mahāmāyātantram with Guṇavatī by Ratnākaraśānti.* Sarnath, India: Central Institute of Higher Tibetan Studies, 1992.

Sarbacker, Stuart Ray. *Samādhi: The Numinous and Cessative in Indo-Tibetan Yoga.* New York: SUNY Press, 2005.

Sasaki, Shizuka. "The Concept of Remodelling the World." In *Setting Out on the*

Great Way: Essays on Early Mahayana Buddhism, edited by Paul Harrison, 141–76. Sheffield, UK: Equinox Publishing, 2018.

Sasson, Vanessa R., and Jane Marie Law, eds. *Imagining the Fetus: The Unborn in Myth, Religion, and Culture.* Oxford: Oxford University Press, 2009.

Schmithausen, Lambert. 1987. *Alayavijnāna: On the Origin and Early Development of a Central Concept of Yogācāra Philosophy.* 2 vols. Tokyo: International Institute for Buddhist Studies.

Senart, É. *Le Mahāvastu: Texte sanscrit.* Paris: l'Imprimerie nationale, 1882–97.

Sharf, Robert. "Is Nirvāṇa the Same as Insentience? Chinese Struggles with an Indian Buddhist Ideal." In *India in the Chinese Imagination,* edited by John Kieschnick and Meir Shahar, 141–70. Philadelphia: University of Pennsylvania Press, 2014.

Sharpa Tulku with Richard Guard. *Jewel Treasure House of the Three Bodies and Staircase that Leads to the Three Bodies.* Yamāntaka Cycle Texts, vol. 2, parts 1 and 2. New Delhi: Tibet House, 2002.

Schmidt-Leukel, Perry, ed. *Buddhism, Christianity, and the Question of Creation: Karmic or Divine?* Aldershot, UK: Ashgate Publishing, 2006.

Schopen, Gregory. "Help for the Sick, the Dying, and the Misbegotten: A Sanskrit Version of the Sūtra of Bhaiṣajyaguru." In *Buddhism and Medicine: An Anthology of Premodern Sources,* edited by C. Pierce Salguero, 235–51. New York: Columbia University Press, 2017.

Shukla, Karunesha, ed. *Śrāvakabhūmi of Ācārya Asaṅga.* Patna, India: K. P. Jayaswal Research Institute 1973.

Skorupski, Tadeusz. "The *Saṃpuṭatantra:* Sanskrit and Tibetan Versions of Chapter One." In *The Buddhist Forum IV,* edited by Tadeuz Skorupski, 191–244. London: School of Oriental and African Studies, 1996.

———. *The Sarvadurgatipariśodhana Tantra: Elimination of All Evil Destinies.* Delhi: Motilal Banarsidass, 1983.

Snellgrove, David L. *Hevajra Tantra: A Critical Study.* London: Oxford University Press, 1959.

Sonam, Ruth. *The Three Principal Aspects of the Path.* Ithaca, NY: Snow Lion Publications, 1999.

Sparham, Gareth. *Tantric Ethics: An Explanation of the Precepts for Buddhist Vajrayāna Practice.* By Tsongkhapa. Boston: Wisdom Publications, 2005.

Strong, John S. *Buddhisms: An Introduction.* London: Oneworld Publications, 2015.

———. "Sudhana's Vision of the Cosmos." In *The Experience of Buddhism: Sources and Interpretations,* edited by John S. Strong, 157–58. Belmont, CA: Wadsworth Publishing, 1995.

Sugiki, Tsunehiko. "Perfect Realization (*Sādhana*) of Vajraḍāka and His Four Magical Females—Critical Editions of the Sanskrit *Vajraḍākamahātantra* Chapters 12 and 13." *Waseda Daigaku Kōtō Kenkyūjo Kiyō (WIAS Research Bulletin),* 9 (2017): 5–31.

Szántó, Péter-Dániel. "Tantric Prakaraṇas," In *Brill's Encyclopedia of Buddhism*, edited by Jonathan A. Silk, 1:755–61. Leiden: Brill, 2015.

Tanaka, Kimiaki. *Indo-Chibetto mandara no kenkyū [Studies in the Indo-Tibetan Maṇḍala]*. In Japanese with English chapter summaries. Kyoto: Hōzōkan, 1996.

———. *Vyavastholi = SamājasādhanaVyavastholi of Nāgabodhi/Nāgabuddhi: Introduction and Romanized Sanskrit and Tibetan Texts*. Tokyo: Watanabe Publishing, 2016.

Thurman, Robert A. F., transl. *The Tibetan Book of the Dead: Liberation through Understanding in the Between*. By Karma Glingpa. New York: Bantam Books, 1994.

Tomabechi, Tōru. "Étude du *Pañcakrama*: Introduction et traduction annotée." PhD diss., University of Lausanne, Switzerland, 2006.

Tripathi, Ramshankar, and Thakur Sain Negi. *Hevajratantram with Muktikāvalīpañjikā of Mahāpaṇḍitācārya Ratnākaraśānti*. Sarnath, India: Central Institute of Higher Tibetan Studies, 2001.

Tsuda, Shinichi. *The Saṃvarodaya-Tantra: Selected Chapters*. Tokyo: Hokuseido Press, 1974.

Vaidya, P. L. *Daśabhūmikasūtra*. Darbhanga, India: Mithila Institute, 1967.

Verhagen, Pieter. "The *Sgra-sbyor-bam-po-gñis-pa* on the *Maṇḍala*: 'Seeing the Essence.'" *Studies in Central and East Asian Religions*, nos. 5/6 (1992–93): 134–38.

Walpola, Rahula. *Le Compendium de la Super-Doctrine (Philosophie) Abhidharmasamuccaya d'Asaṅga*. Paris: École française d'Extrême-Orient, 1971.

Walshe, Maurice, transl. *The Long Discourses of the Buddha: A Translation of the Dīgha Nikāya*. Boston: Wisdom Publications, 1987.

Wayman, Alex. "Buddhist Genesis and the Tantric Tradition." *Oriens Extremus* 9 (1962): 127–31.

———. "The Intermediate-State Dispute in Buddhism." In *Buddhist Studies in Honour of I. B. Horner*, edited by L. Cousins et al., 251–67. Dordrecht, The Netherlands: D. Reidel Publishing, 1974. Reprinted in Wayman, *Buddhist Insight*, 251–67. Delhi: Motilal Banarsidass Publishers, 1983.

———. "The *Maṇḍa* and the *-la* of the Term *Maṇḍala*." In *Tantric Buddhism: Centennial Tribute to Dr. Benoytosh Bhattacharyya*, edited by N. N. Bhattacharyya, 23–30. New Delhi: Manohar, 1999.

Wedemeyer, Christian Konrad. *Āryadeva's Lamp that Integrates the Practices, Caryāmelāpakapradīpa: The Gradual Path of Vajrayāna Buddhism according to the Esoteric Community Noble Tradition*. New York: American Institute of Buddhist Studies at Columbia University, 2007.

———. "Vajrayāna and Its Doubles: A Critical Historiography, Exposition, and Translation of the Tantric Works of Āryadeva." PhD diss., Columbia University, New York, 1999.

Yarnall, Thomas F. *Tsong Khapa's Great Stages of Mantra: The Creation Stage: A Study and Annotated Translation of Chapters 11–12 of the Sngags rim chen mo*. New York: American Institute of Buddhist Studies at Columbia University, 2013.

Zahler, Leah. *Study and Practice of Meditation: Tibetan Interpretations of the Concentrations and Formless Absorptions.* Ithaca, NY: Snow Lion Publications, 2009.

Zysk, Kenneth Gregory. "Mythology and the Brahmanization of Indian Medicine: Transforming Heterodoxy into Orthodoxy." In *Categorisation and Interpretation: Indological and Comparative: A Volume Dedicated to the Memory of Gösta Liebert,* edited by Folke Josephson, 125–45. Göteborg, Sweden: Göteborg University, 1999.

INDEX

Pages numbers in italics refer to illustrations.

Abhayākaragupta, 150, 232n216, 250n53
Abhidharmakośa (Vasubandhu): *bardo* in, 55; on beings of this world, 26–27; on cultivation of properties, 16; on cylinder of water, 24; on *dhyānas*, 22–23, 51; on infinite space, 34; meditative absorptions, 29, 30
absences, 155
absorptions. *See* meditative absorptions
Acala, 109
achievement, 193–94
actual-clear-light, 89
affinities, 64–65
afflictive emotions, 13, 14, 17, 38, 56
aggregate of consciousness, 47–48
Akṣobhya, 106–7, 119, 123, 124, 136, 138, 147, 181, 185, 195
Amitābha, 38, 123, 124, 148
Amoghasiddhi, 124, 148–49
annihilationism, 35, 211n149
Annotations to the Illuminating Lamp (Tsongkhapa), 72, 88, 119
anuyoga, 73
approaching attainment, 49–51, 53–54, 57, 84, *117, 118*, 165, 166, 170, 172, 225n83
Āryadeva: *Compendium of Practices*, 48–49, 80–82, 84; on equanimity, 257n163; on purposive acts, 257n167; on tantric practice, 4
Ārya Nāgārjuna. *See* Nāgārjuna
Ārya tradition, 91, 106–7
Asaṅga, 169
atiyoga, 73
Aṭṭhaka Vagga, 211n150
awakening, 7
awareness, 48

Bahudhātuka Sutta, 212n164
bandhu, as term, 1, 74, 201n1. *See also* connections
bardo, 52, 55
basis of designation, 83
Bee's Hope. See *Fulfilling the Bee's Hope*
beginningless time, 8
beings: birth of, 68–69; types of, 26–27. *See also* first human beings
bhaga, 103, 158
bhrūṃ, 73, 131
biblical creation stories, 7, 8
birth of human beings, 68–69. *See also* first human beings
birth purification, 66–68
blessings, 124–25, 175–76, 198
bliss, 70–72, 89, 126–27
bodhicitta, 70–71, 120, 126, 130, 178, 198

Bodhisattva Maitreya, 39
bodhisattvas, 38, 41, 76, 107, 111, 132, 158, 197
Bodhisattva Samantabhadra, 39
body isolation, 81, 230n188
body mandala, 121–22, 174
Brahmā, 19–21
Brahmajāla Sutta, 35
Brahmanic gods, 28
Buddha, 145, 202n23, 211n149
buddha-fields, 36–38, 41, 202n2. *See also* cosmogony
Buddhaghosa, 29
Buddhaguhya, 40
Buddha Nature theory, 88–90
buddhānusmṛti, 38–40
Buddhist creation stories. *See* creation stories
Butön Rinchen Drup, 97

Cabezón, José, 7
Cakrasaṃvara Tantra, 184, 236n19
Candrakīrti, 69–70, 150, 233n228
Caryā Tantras, 183
castes, 204n44
causality, 8, 13
cause, the, 3
celestial mansion, 105–6, 121–22, 153, 157, 174, 182, 254n120
circular representation. *See* mandalas
clear light, 81, 89, 110–12, 114, 136–37, 159
Clear Light. *See* Realm of Clear Light
clear-light-emptiness, 77–78, 86, 89, 92, 113, 136, 233n232. *See also* emptiness
coarse bodies, 44–45, 53, 56–57
Compendium of Abhidharma (Asaṅga), 169
Compendium of Practices (Āryadeva), 48–49, 80–82, 84
Compendium of Truth, 183
Compendium of Vajra Wisdom Tantra, 49, 51, 178–79
completion stage: purifications by, 65–66; three bodies of meditators on, 80–83; Tsongkhapa on, 108
Concise Sādhana (Nāgārjuna), 45, 155, 157–58, 162, 169, 173, 215n32, 238n71, 251n63
confessions, 142, 144, 248n28, 248n30
connections, 1, 74, 201n1
consciousness, 47–52, 216n33
consort, 180–81, 198
continuity: Buddha Nature theory on, 88–90; of a person, 2; pure illusory bodies and, 86–87; as term, 1, 74, 201n1; Tsongkhapa on, 4, 74. *See also* tantras
corresponding object, 156–57, 171–73
cosmic levels, 22
cosmogony, 44, 202n2. See also *Abhidharmakośa;* buddha-fields; creation stories
cosmological maps, 5, 34–37
cosmology, 22–23. *See also* creation stories
cosmos and the person, meditations on, 73–75
creation stage: purifications by, 65–66; as season, 9; three bodies of meditators on, 77–80
creation stories, 7–9, 14–17, 23–26, 204n44. *See also* cosmogony; cosmology; Origin of Things

Dakpo Tashi Namgyal, 88
Dalai Lama, 214n4
darkness, 11
Daśabhūmika Sūtra, 40, 135
death: meditations on, 42–43, 108, 109–10; Vajrayāna on, 43–44. *See also* intermediate state; rebirth
decaying corpses, 43
dedication, 144–45
Deeds of the Fruitional Buddha, 181
deities: on the body, 122–23, 243n188; four seals on, 183; seven steps on, 183; specially visualized, 91–92, 106–8, 114,

159–67, 196; three faces on, 183–84; of yoga, 75, 76–77, 128
Desire Realm, 22, 27–28, 30, 31, 37, 41, 72, 154, 178, 206n72
desires, 11, 70–72
destruction of the world, 8, 9, 21, 28–32, 99–103
dharma, 3, 145
dharmadhātu, 48
dharmakāya, 3, 38, 52, 75–78, 92, 108, 113–15, 167
Dharmakīrti, 91
dhyānas, 22, 23, 32–34, 35, 44, 47, 51, 153, 205n70
Discourse on Brahmā's Net, 19–21
Discourse on the Origin of Things, 18–19
Discourse on the Simile of the Quail, 33, 34, 51, 52
Discourse on the Simile of the Snake, 211n149
dissolutions, 139; into clear light, 109, 110–12, 136–37; of consciousness, 47–52; four cycles of, 44–47, 239n92
driving the stakes, 151
Dveṣavajra, 150

earthly desires, 11
earth mandala, 24, 25, 65, 103, 104, 109, 123, 144, 157, 227n115, 237n39
eight hot hells, 159, 256n144
elements, physical, 24–25, 44–45
elements of nature, 44–45
emanation body, 3. See also *nirmāṇakāya*
emptiness: bliss and, 89; mantra recitations on, 78; meditations on, 73, 74, 75–76, 100–101, 103, 112–13, 149, 227n118; phenomena of, 249n49; of the physical world, 154; yoga on, 126. *See also* clear-light-emptiness
empty states (four), 51–52
enhanced appearance, 49
eons, 21, 25–26, 44, 90–95
evolution of the world, 103–6
existence, as season, 9
existential suffering, 13
Explanation of Formulating the Guhyasamāja Sādhana (Tsongkhapa), 2, 40, 60, 61, 64, 81, 119, 178

"fall" from Buddhist "paradise," 11
familiarization, 193
fences, 151–52, 196
fetus development, 57–58
fire mandala, 24–25, 103, 104, 144, 227n115, 237n39. *See also* mandalas of the physical elements
first human beings, 9–12, 20, 29, 30, 90–92. *See also* beings; birth of human beings
First Lord, 77, 78–79, 90, 113, 114–15, 119–21, 125, 167–77
First Yoga, 130, 152
five phases of development, 57
Five Stages (Nāgārjuna), 81, 82, 86, 228n149
Flood, Gavin, 1
Formless Realm. *See* Immaterial (or Formless) Realm
Form Realm, 22
Formulating the Guhyasamāja Sādhana (Nāgabuddhi): connections in, 2, 3, 4; on first beings adornment, 10; on four elements, 24–25; on inanimate world, 23–24; on intermediate beings, 56; on *sādhana,* 73–74, 90; on three bodies of a buddha, 75, 91–92; Tsongkhapa on, 2, 40, 60, 61, 64, 81, 94–95, 99–100, 119, 178
forty-nine essential points, 189–92, 195–99, 263n274, 264n289, 264nn298–300, 265n301
foul, meditation on the, 42–43
four cycles of dissolution, 44–47, 239n92
four elements, 24–25
four fences, 151–52
four goddesses, 105, 137, 186
four limbs of familiarization and achievement, 193–94

four modes of birth, 224n58
Four Noble's Truths, 7, 13
four seals, 183
Freud, Sigmund, 55–56
fruit, the, 3, 89–90, 93, *118*, 187–88
Fulfilling the Bee's Hope (Tsongkhapa): on blessings, 124–25; on clear light, 77–78; on completion stage, 108; on desires, 11, 70–72; on *dhyānas*, 35; on dissolutions, 44–48, 49, 109; on eons, 21; framework of the forty-nine essential points, 195–99; full title of, 247n1; on gender balance, 69–70; on inanimate world, 23; on intermediate state, 52–53, 54–55, 57; on the preliminaries to the *Sādhana*, 141–52; on rebirth, 55–56; on *saṃbhogakāya*, 78–79, 116–17; on three bodies of the meditator, 91–94, 123; on triple *sattvas*, 125. See also *Guhyasamāja Sādhana* (Tsongkhapa); Tsongkhapa Lozang Drakpa
fundamental notions of Buddhist philosophy, 13

Gaṇḍavyūha Sūtra, 39, 40, 135
gathered seed syllables, 192, 267n358
Geluk (or Gelukpa) school of Tibetan Buddhism, 2, 35, 40, 122, 125
gender, 10, 15, 69
generating the mind-for-enlightenment, 146–47
Genesis, book of, 7, 12
Gethin, Rupert, 19
Godānīya, 31
goddesses, 105, 137, 186
gods, 26–28, 209n124
Gö Khukpa Lhetsé, 90, 97
Gombrich, Richard Francis, 18–19
great bliss, 70–72, 89, 126–27, 178–80
Greater Discourse to Saccaka, 32, 34, 52
Great Treatise on the Stages of the Mantric Path (Tsongkhapa), 2, 75, 79–80, 102
Great Vehicle. *See* Mahāyāna (the Great Vehicle)
ground, 101, 104, *113*, *117*, *120*, 155
ground, the, 3
Guhyasamāja cycle, 1, 82, 87, 90
Guhyasamāja mandala, 91–92, 106, 126, 262n255
Guhyasamāja Sādhana (Tsongkhapa): addendum to, 194; explaining the framework of, 188–94; explaining the text of, 152–88; on the fruit and the ground, 93; on mandala of world realms, 40; preliminary explanations to the, 141–52; on the source of phenomena, 103. See also *Fulfilling the Bee's Hope*; *sādhana*
Guhyasamāja Tantra, 48, 69–72, 96, 99, 103, 108, 120, 178
gyü, as term, 1. *See also* tantras

Harrison, Paul, 39
Hell of Ceaseless Torment, 28–31, 153, 159
hells, 28–31, 153, 159, 256n144
Hevajra Tantra, 96, 222n38
How to Practice on the Path of Achieving the Stage of Vajradhara (Tsongkhapa), 112
hūṃ, 125, 129, 136, 142–43, 151, 162, 187, 250n58, 251nn62–64, 264n278. See also *oṃ āḥ hūṃ*
human beings. *See* birth of human beings; first human beings

ignorance, 50
Illuminating Lamp, 69–70, 96, 119, 179
illusion-like *samādhi*, as term, 86
illusory body, 81, 83–87, 231n207
Immaterial (or Formless) Realm, 22, *22*, 32–34, 35, 44, 47, 178
impermanence, 2, 42
inanimate world creation, 23–26
infinite consciousness, 214n10
infinite space, 34, 210n139, 214n10

innate body, 85
interdependent arising, 2, 7, 9, 13
intermediate beings, 168–69, 222n18, 259n191
intermediate state, 52–55, 108, 115–18, 217n61. *See also* death; rebirth

Jambudvīpa, 10, 19, 23, 31, 33, 41, 68–70, 92–95, 163, 177–78
jhānas. See *dhyānas*
Jñānapāda, 82
jñānasattva, 125, 136
Jonangpa, 40
Judeo-Christian tradition, 7, 12

kalpa, 207n93
Kāmaśāstra, 127
karma: Amoghasiddhi's vow and, 148–49; of beings, 11–12, 20, 25, 26; during creation and destruction of the world, 9, 29; as fundamental notion, 13
kāyas, 83
Kedrup Jé, 97–98, 105–6, 111, 122–23, 125
khaṃ, 243n185
Khyungpo Lhépa Zhönu Sönam, 97
Kongtrul Yönten Gyatso, 88
Kośabhāṣya (Vasubandhu), 206n70, 211n146
Kṣitigarbha, 109, 111

la, as term, 40
Lamp to Illuminate the Five Stages (Tsongkhapa), 70, 81
Land of Bliss, 37, 38
Later Tantra, 158
Laṭukikopama Sutta, 210n137
Letter to a Friend (Nāgārjuna), 28
life-cycle events. *See* death; intermediate state; rebirth
Locanā, 65, 104, 109, 123–24
Lower Tantras, 71, 75, 225n90
lucid clarity, 50
lunar disk, 115, *117, 118,* 169, 170, 175, 197, 241n121, 260n204, 267n358. *See also* solar disk

macrocosm, 1–2, 237n39
Mahāyāna (the Great Vehicle), 3, 35–36, 41, 49, 225n89, 249n39
Mahāyāna Sūtras, 37, 40, 41, 202n2
mahāyoga, 73
Maitreya, 109
Māmakī, 65, 104, 105, 123, 128, 181
maṇḍa, as term, 40
mandalas, 40, 227n115; creation stage, 95–96; of Guhyasamāja, 91–92, 106, 126, 262n255; meditations on, 121–22, 156–59
mandalas of the physical elements, 24–25, 227n115, 237n39; earth, 24, 25, 65, 103, 104, 109, 123, 144, 157; fire, 24–25, 103, 144; water, 24, 103, 104, 144; wind, 25, 73, 103, 104, 144, 152, 156–59
mantra recitation, 73, 74, 135–36, 185–86, 229n165, 246n243
mantras, defined, 221n15
Mantra Vehicle, 75, 86, 95, 127–28, 137, 178
meditations, 197; on death, 42–43, 109–10; on emptiness, 100–101, 112–13, 149, 227n118; on evolution of the world, 103–6; on the intermediate state, 115–18; on the mandala, 156–59; on rebirth, 119–21; states of, 22, 22–23, 32–34; on subtle objects, 134–35; that correspond to the person, 106–7; on three bodies of the buddha, 108–9, 180; on the wheel of specially visualized deities, 159–61
meditative absorptions, 22–23, 29, 30, 34–36, 206n70, 240n103
merit field, 142, 195, 227n131
Meru, 25, 154, 207n90
method, the, 3

microcosm, 1–2
Middle Length Discourses, 32–33
mind-for-enlightenment, 146
mindfulness meditations, 42
mind isolation, 81
Mind Only theory, 3, 115–16
Monastic Guidelines: on creation story, 10–11, 14; on intermediate beings, 12, 56; on sexual desire, 15
monotheism, 7, 8
Mother Tantras, 222n38
multiplicity, 8–9

Nāgabuddhi, 2. See also *Formulating the Guhyasamāja Sādhana*
Nāgārjuna, 28, 50–51, 81, 82, 86, 150, 254n115. See also *Concise Sādhana; Five Stages; Letter to a Friend*
Nāropā, 1, 3
neither-perception-nor-nonperception, 22, 34–35, 47, 210, 211n150, 214n10
Nikāya Suttas, 35
nirmāṇakāya, 3, 52, 75, 77, 78, 79–83, 92–95, 119–22, 126, 171–73
nirvāṇa, 3, 13, 17, 43
nonexistence, as season, 9
Norman, K. R., 20
nothingness, 214n10

Ocean of Attainments (Kedrup Jé), 111
offerings, 138–39, 142–43, 187, 194, 247n12
oṃ, 150–51
oṃ āḥ hūṃ, 115, 131, 136, 150, 176, 182, 195, 197. See also *hūṃ*
Oral Instruction of Mañjuśrī (Jñānapāda), 82
Origin of Things, 17–19. *See also* creation stories
Orzech, Charles, 38

Pāṇḍarā, 65, 104, 105, 123
Pāramitā Vehicle, 71, 75, 76, 86, 89
Pārāyana Vagga, 211n150
parents and intermediate beings, 55–57, 222n18
parinirvāṇa, 37
path, the, 3
Path of Purification (Buddhaghosa), 29
perception, 210n142, 211n146
Perfect Awakening of Vairocana, 183–84
physical world: emptying, 154; evolution of, 156–57; meditations on, 237n44
pledging reliance on the path, 146
prabandha, as term, 1, 74, 201n1. *See also* continuity
praises, 138–39, 187
Pramāṇavārttika (Dharmakīrti), 91
Prāsaṅgika Madhyamaka, 4, 83, 87, 100
Presentation on the World (*Mahāmaudgalyāyana*), 9
prostrations, 143–44
protecting deities, 150–51
pure lands, 36–38
purifications, 59–68, 72, 81, 93, 120, 171

Ratnākaraśānti, 88, 232n215
Ratnasaṃbhava, 124, 128–29, 148, 181, 198
Realm of Clear Light, 9–10, 19, 20, 29, 43, 54
Realm of Subtle Materiality, 22, 23, 24, 27, 30–34, 47, 178
rebirth, 55–58; of first human beings, 9–11, 92–93; meditations on, 108, 119–21; purifying, 60, 176–77; types of, 95. *See also* death; intermediate state
recreation of the world, 29
refuge, 145–46
rejoicing, 144–45
Rendawa Shönu Lodrö, 90, 97
resources, body of, 3. See also *saṃbhogakāya*
Ṛg Veda, 11
Rgyud phyi ma, Uttara Tantra. See *Subsequent Tantra, The*
rice, 14, 16
rūpakāya, 52, 53, 76, 78, 89, 188

Rūpavajrā, 109, 111

sādhana: on correspondence with the cosmos and the person, 73–74; on destruction of the world, 99–103; meditations on, 41; Nāgabuddhi on, 73–74, 90; purification, 59–64; steps of the, 95–98; as term, 1. See also *Guhyasamāja Sādhana*
Śākya dynasty, 16
Śākyamuni, 16, 17–18, 36, 43
Sakyapa, 40
salu rice, 15–16, 161
Samādhi of Direct Encounter with the Buddhas of the Present, 39, 152
samādhisattva, 125
samayasattva, 125, 136
saṃbhogakāya, 3, 52, 75, 78–79, 81–82, 89, 90, 92–95, 115, 167–71
Saṃpuṭa Tantra, 71
saṃsāra, 12, 17, 21, 26, 42
Saṃvarodaya Tantra, 56, 222n38
Sarvāvaraṇavikṣambhin, 175
śāstras, 52
sattvas, 125–26, 137, 150, 176
seclusion, 51
selflessness, 2
sentient beings, 48
sevenfold worship, 142, 195
seven steps, 183
Short Treatise on the Stage of the Path (Tsongkhapa), 86
Simile of the Quail. See *Discourse on the Simile of the Quail*
"Sixty-Two Kinds of Wrong Views, The" (*Discourse on Brahmā's Net*), 19
solar disk, 115–18, 142, 169, 170, 189, 193, 197, 240n118, 260n204, 260n206, 267n358. *See also* lunar disk
solar seat, 132, 134, 150, 152, 157, 183, 185
spatial cosmological map, 5, 34–37
special affinities, 64–65
specially visualized deities, 91–92, 106–8, 114, 159–67, 196
speech isolation, 81
Stages of Self-Blessing (Āryadeva), 48
Subsequent Tantra, The, 1, 3, 88, 201n3
subtle bodies, 44–45, 53, 134–35
subtle drop, 185
subtle objects, 134–35
suchness, 88
Sudhana, 39
suffering, 55, 208n101
Sukhāvatīvyūha Sūtras, 38
sumbha, 151
Sumbharāja, 150–51, 196
Supreme King of Deeds, 130–31, 133–34, 136, 139, 181–82, 188
Supreme King of Mandalas, 129, 130, 131–33, 136, 181–82, 184, 188, 198
Supreme Kings, 129–34
Sūtra on Entering the Womb, 55, 56

tantras: *Fulfilling the Bee's Hope* and, 52–53; on intermediate state, 53–54; as term, 1; visualizations, 38–40. *See also* continuity
Tārā, 65, 104, 105
tathāgatas, 38, 96, 119, 123, 124, 126, 132, 158, 173, 198, 244n214
temporality, 8
thousandfold world system, 212n161
three bodies of a buddha, 3, 75–83, 91–92, 106, 159–61, 180
three faces, 183–84
three lower realms, 27–28, 30, 68, 149, 178, 252n90
three rituals, 182–83
Thupten Jinpa, 2
"Tibetan Book of the Dead," 52–53, 55
Treasury of Knowledge (Kongtrul), 88
triple *sattvas,* 125, 150, 176
Tsongkhapa Lozang Drakpa, 2; *Annotations to the Illuminating Lamp,* 72, 88, 119; on correspondence with the cosmos, 74–75; on destruction of the world, 99–100; on *dharmakāya,* 112–13; on emptiness, 100–101; on

Tsongkhapa Lozang Drakpa (*continued*) eons, 25–26; *Explanation of Formulating the Guhyasamāja Sādhana,* 81; on first human beings, 30; on *Formulating the Guhyasamāja Sādhana,* 94–95; *The Great Treatise on the Stages of the Mantric Path,* 2, 75, 79–80, 102; *How to Practice on the Path of Achieving the Stage of Vajradhara,* 112; Jé Lama Tsongkhapa, 194; *Lamp to Illuminate the Five Stages,* 70, 81; on Mind Only theory, 3–4; on Prāsaṅgika Madhyamaka, 4; on purifications, 81; on Realm of Clear Light, 10; *Short Treatise on the Stage of the Path,* 86. See also *Fulfilling the Bee's Hope*
tummo, 70
Tuṣita, 37
twenty-five coarse elements, 44

Ubhaya Tantras, 183–84
Unexcelled Mantra, 69–72, 75, 93
Unexcelled Tantras, 184
union, 81, 89–90, 130
uniqueness, 8

Vairocana (deity), 96, 109, 111, 122–23, 124
Vairocana palace, 39–40, 123, 124, 135
Vairocana's Vow, 147
Vajra Canopy Tantra, 76–77
Vajradhara, 73, 126, 129, 181, 252n75
Vajradhātvīśvarī, 150, 196
vajradhṛk, 135
vajra fence, 196
Vajra Garland Explanatory Tantra, 56, 166–67
vajra ground, 157
vajrakāya, 38
Vajra Lady of Tangibles, 106, 128, 136, 150, 181, 243n187
vajra mind, 56, 172
Vajra Queen, 103
vajras, 73, 103, 111, 116, 125, 130, 147, 150, 151–52, 192, 260n208
Vajrasattva, 119–20, 122, 171–73, 250n60
Vajrasattva Sādhana, 103
Vajra Vehicle. *See* Vajrayāna
Vajrayāna, 36, 41, 43–44, 49
Vasubandhu, 22–23, 29–30, 201n1, 205n70. See also *Abhidharmakośa; Kośabhāṣya*
Vighnāntaka, 185–86
Vimalakīrtinirdeśa, 135
vows, 146–49

water mandala, 24, 103, 104, 144, 227n115, 237n39
Wayman, Alex, 17
white appearance, 49–51, 53–54, 57, 84, 110, *117*
wind-and-mind, 3, 84, 90, 170, 197, 231n199
wind cylinder, 206n81
wind mandala, 25, 73, 103, 104, 144, 152, 156–59, 227n115, 237n39
winds, 260n205, 260n207
wisdom of discernment, 46

Yamaka Sutta, 211n149
Yamāntaka, 109
Yangchen Gawé Lodrö, 44, 45
Yogācārabhūmi, 9, 15, 29, 32, 54–56, 204n44
yogas, 73–74, 75–77, 125–30, 192–93

Zahler, Leah, 35

TRADITIONS AND TRANSFORMATIONS IN TIBETAN BUDDHISM

This series investigates the stability of Tibetan religious culture from its historical beginnings in the sixth century through the modern era as well as how the religious tradition has changed in reaction to historical realities, technological transformation, and social unrest. To facilitate an interdisciplinary approach, the series publishes projects on four interconnected themes: ritual traditions and textual transformations, Tibet in its historical milieu, Tibet and the modern world, and Tibetan Buddhism in diaspora.

Longing to Awaken: Buddhist Devotion in Tibetan Poetry and Song
Holly Gayley and Dominique Townsend, editors

Singer of the Land of Snows: Tibet as a Buddhist Imagined Community
Rachel H. Pang

Buddha in the Marketplace: The Commodification of Buddhist Objects in Tibet
Alex John Catanese

www.ingramcontent.com/pod-product-compliance
Lightning Source LLC
Chambersburg PA
CBHW030821230426
43667CB00008B/1313
9780813951058